Praise for *The Serv*

"I have been sharpening my wits on Kenne[...] [...] for over half a century, and this latest book is as intellectually stimulating as his classic assault on liberalism all those years ago. For anyone who believes, as I do, that the contemporary political culture is profoundly sick, this is an original diagnosis of where it has gone wrong, and how it can be put to right. What is more, in spite of the seriousness of the subject, the writing is as clear as a bell. Don't miss it."

—Sir Peregrine Worsthorne

"This is a work of meticulous logic and vast erudition. It provides an invaluable resource for anyone who has wondered why European elites embarked upon their disastrous cultural revolution in pursuit of an abstract internationalist idealism, destroying in the process their intellectual and cultural heritage."

—David Martin Jones, Associate Professor, Political Science and International Studies, University of Queensland, Brisbane, Australia

"Can democracy survive in a nation of slaves? Aristotle thought not. But what if the slaves don't recognize their servile condition? Kenneth Minogue explores the many ways in which the citizens of the modern West have thoughtlessly exchanged independence of mind and body for government promises of security and harmony. The result is a topsy-turvy democracy where the rulers hold the people to account for their incorrect behavior and attitudes. Will the rulers one day throw the rascally people out? This is an insightful and unsettling book—and it would also be a frightening one if it were not so consistently entertaining."

—John O'Sullivan, *Radio Free Europe*

"Minogue is one of the most illustrious representatives of what survives of the European classical liberal tradition . . . In *The Servile Mind*, Minogue makes clear where he stands."

—Paul Gottfried, *The American Conservative*

"*The Liberal Mind, Alien Powers*, and *The Servile Mind* compose a chronological critique that has kept fully abreast of the rapid progress of political illusion and unreality in the West during the author's lifetime."

—Chilton Williamson, Jr., *Chronicles*

"It would be remiss on my part not to use this opportunity to assert that this splendid book confirms the status of Professor Minogue as a most distinguished observer and analyst of our moment in history."
—Claudio Veliz, *Quadrant*

"Historically and theoretically rich analysis."
—Diana Schaub, *National Review*

"Minogue's argument is unfailingly intelligent . . . Forceful, persuasive, and illuminating. . . . "
—Mark Blitz, *The Weekly Standard*

"A remarkable sequel . . . An elegant essayist of the old school, Prof. Minogue advances his argument by small steps that can end abruptly in crisp revelation."
—Neil Reynolds, *The Globe and Mail*

"*The Servile Mind* is a bold and wide-ranging study of the ills of contemporary politics and society in the West. The argument is elaborated in fairly abstract terms, but the abstractions are always aimed at making sense of the concrete irritations and idiocies of modern life."
—Noel Malcolm, *Standpoint*

"Minogue writes squarely in the tradition of Tocqueville and Bryce in seeing what is new about democracy as well as placing it within the broader current of Western intellectual life . . . *The Servile Mind* is a crucial book for the task of understanding and reconstructing the proper bases for a free society."
—Gerald J. Russello, *City Journal*

"This book is an update, including rethinking and reformulations, that absorbs the experience and legacy of the late '60s. Readers of the earlier work [*The Liberal Mind*] would not have been as surprised as most people were by that event, but they will now find its author somewhat less libertarian and more conservative. In *The Servile Mind* his targets are not cited by name, but they do not need to be. His expounding of the diverse items in the servile mind does more justice to them, and runs deeper, than do the statements of their exponents-the intellectual elite behind a new kind of democratic politics. Minogue has written a polemic without harsh words, striking blows without wounding feelings."
—Harvey C. Mansfield, The Claremont Institute

THE SERVILE MIND

HOW DEMOCRACY ERODES THE MORAL LIFE

Kenneth Minogue

Encounter Books New York • London

First American edition published in 2010 by Encounter Books,
an activity of Encounter for Culture and Education, Inc.,
a nonprofit, tax exempt corporation.
Encounter Books website address: www.encounterbooks.com

Manufactured in the United States and printed on
acid-free paper. The paper used in this publication meets
the minimum requirements of ANSI/NISO Z39.48–1992
(R 1997) (*Permanence of Paper*).

First paperback edition published in 2012.
Paperback edition ISBN: 978-1-59403-636-1

The Library of Congress has catalogued the hardcover edition as follows:

Minogue, Kenneth R., 1930–
The servile mind: how democracy erodes the moral life/
by Kenneth Minogue.
p. cm.—(Encounter broadsides)
Includes bibliographical references and index.
ISBN-13: 978-1-59403-381-0 (hardback: alk. paper)
ISBN-10: 1-59403-381-1 (hardback: alk. paper)
1. Democracy—Moral and ethical aspects. 2. Political ethics.
3. Social ethics. I. Title.
JC423.M6234 2010
172—dc22
2009039512

CONTENTS

PREFACE:
HOW FREE CAN A JUST
STATE BE?

The Servile Mind was concerned above all to explore the character of illusion in politics—or at least in contemporary democracy. All human projects are guided by what we think is desirable. Given that what we desire seldom ever yields the satisfactions we dream of, illusion can never be far behind. All political projects, like political careers, thus end in failure. They raise more hopes than they can possibly satisfy. Wisdom therefore demands a constant alertness to the fragility of the hopes that often enslave us. And in introducing the paperback edition of *The Servile Mind* I can do no better than point to one specific conflict in our culture that dooms virtually all our projects to disappointment. That conflict emerges from our basic ambivalence towards the modern world.

The essential point is that Europeans have, uniquely, created a civilization based on the practice of freedom. Commercial freedom, for example, has made us the richest and most inventive culture in history. Our industrial success certainly results from freedom, but in fact freedom extends far beyond commerce and invades every sphere of our lives. It has generated astonishing knowledge about what human beings are, and of their destiny in time and space. On this point, we immediately think of science, but that is to ignore archaeology, anthropology, critical history and many other specialised worlds of inquiry. Our freedom has created forms of art, music and letters of kinds never seen before. It has also evolved something quite distinct which I shall identify as the moral life. And our political forms have been imitated the world over, with varying success. Cultures whose peoples have very different inclinations find themselves having to learn such unfamiliar practices as elections and political parties. For today there is no way for any society or culture to have standing in the modern world other than by being the thing called a "state", and thus embracing "modernity."

All such achievements have emerged from the working out in Europe of our passion for freedom, a practice that can be seen emerging in the later Middle Ages with the appearance of a quite specific new type of human personality: namely, the individualist. As individualists, people become in some degree detached from rank or status because they indulge and explore their subjectivity. They often have individual projects of their own. Confident in their intellectual and moral independence, individualists find it essential to live in a society in which others have the same character. Living in a free society involves a dislike of servility, and that is why the modern world finds slavery intolerable, and led our ancestors, by contrast with other cultures, to abolish that institution. With the growth of the individualist, freedom became the mark of a distinct social, moral and political form of life, and it crystallised during the sixteenth century in the sovereign state. It is notable that free European states long successfully resisted attempts to mould them into one empire, culture or confessional unity. The resulting variety of national cultures may have been highly quarrelsome, but the cultures also stimulated each other as elements of a shared world.

As time went on, these free societies became increasingly different from earlier forms of civilization. What were their fruits? One might briefly mention wealth, tolerance, technology and all of these as sustaining a specific kind of civility in social relations. The technological achievement could not be ignored by other states, if only because it soon transformed military life. But one might also mention styles of art, music and literature not seen before. The art of the Italian Renaissance, the scepticism of Montaigne, the creation of character types in Shakespeare and much else were aspects of this new world that would lead on to the novels that explored whole new varieties of human subjectivity.

There is, however, a second, very different view of modern European experience, one advanced from within the West itself. It is focused not on the achievements but on the imperfections of the modern world. On this view, modernity is called "capitalism." Modern Western powers are presented as behaving in the world a bit like a clever and bullying child in a school playground, throwing its weight around and causing misery in all directions. European political power was imperialistic, and arguably the wealth of the West resulted partly from plundering the "East" and the "South". It has been argued that our consumerist attitude to wealth was destroying the environment in which all of us in the human and animal world must live. Above all, by the criterion of equality, free societies constitute a dramatic failure. Instead of creating just societies in which human needs were broadly satisfied for everybody, they were marked by immense differences in the wealth and resources available to some, and "denied" to others. This contrast between rich and poor in modern states is even more dramatically true of the world at large. Millions are on the edge of starvation. Could the practices of free societies perhaps be responsible for this terrible condition? And in one sense, indeed, our freedom obviously is involved, since the sudden vast increase in the size of populations in non-Western countries, the precondition of the "bottom billion", has resulted, ironically, from the benefits of Western medical techniques.

Here then we have a dramatic clash of judgements. On the one hand, modernity is a brilliant prosperity-enhancing, life-preserving, freedom-enhancing civilisation. On the other hand, capitalism is an out of control machine that, in spite of remarkable creative capacities, has corrupted some and brought misery to others. The rejection of capitalism was formulated, of course, by Marxists but a vague and unfocused antipathy to the modern world goes far beyond any kind of socialist theory. And this rejection of modernity as "capitalism" has to be vague and unfocused because it is essentially utopian. The only alternative to "capitalism" is to be found in dreams, in ideals. But human life does not assimilate easily to ideals.

Our problem, then, is to discover what conceptual understanding of the world lies at the heart of this conflict, this remarkable disappointment with our own modern world which has such notable accomplishments to its credit. But one or two features of the conflict can at once be noted. One of them is that the rejection of modernity as capitalist comes not from critics outside Western culture but from within the West itself. Other cultures never worried about inequality; they took it for granted. It might follow from this that the critics would respond by emigrating to other cultures, but in fact the opposite is the case. It is not only that the critics of capitalism stick very firmly indeed to their Western comforts, but that millions of people from all other parts of the world cannot migrate fast enough into our vile capitalist world. There is thus a remarkable difference between critical theory on the one hand and, on the other, the actions of people whose actual lives and happiness depend on the decisions they make.

In trying to understand the basic conflict that generates our ambivalence, we might consider that it is precisely freedom itself that causes the imperfections of capitalism. For there is no doubt that one of the things people do most enthusiastically with the freedom they enjoy is compete with one another. This may not lead to attractive results. Competition sometimes means that some win and some lose. One must say "sometimes" because absurdities can arise when the idea of competition is imposed on situations where it does not belong. The average plumber, for example, is not competing with the average entrepreneur. They are simply engaged in different activities. Social critics, however, interpret everybody as engaged in the single task of making money, in which case wealth amounts to winning and poverty (or even modest prosperity) might be taken as failure that illustrates the injustice of competition. The complex term "competition" has thus been corruptly used. But leaving muddles of this kind aside, those who actually do engage in competition may face the prospect of failure. A powerful opinion has recently surfaced (especially in teaching circles) that losing in some competition is bad for the self-esteem of the young and vulnerable, and therefore the ideal institutional arrangement is to avoid any activity that might seem competitive. Schools sometimes ban competitive games on just this principle. The same attempt to mitigate imagined unhappiness operates in the "politically correct" project of protecting supposedly vulnerable people from "hate speech." Collective respect here turns into a kind of right, and must be enforced by society.

Similar considerations arise in the demand that the economy should be made, as a matter of policy, to <u>reflect</u> society, one example being the demand for something called "gender justice." Free societies have been found defective in that women hold fewer managerial positions than men, and their average earnings are less. The policy assumes—and proposes to enforce upon employers—the judgement that men and women are equal units of economic production. No doubt they are less suitable for military combat and furniture removalism, but they are assumed to be no less talented than men in better paid managerial roles, which is what basically concerns the lobbyist for gender justice. Some women of course are very able indeed, some not, but the proposal is to abandon the test of ability in free societies in favour of a test of "social reflectiveness" that is supposedly more just. The criterion that is here, and widely, invoked against freedom is thus justice. And it is precisely the conflict between these criteria of social value that lies at the heart of the conflict we have been discussing.

The term "justice" supplies the clue as to what is basically at stake in the conflict between current opinions about our modern world. For, as we shall see, in other cultures than that of the West, justice is the normative principle that structures society, and it is sustained partly from custom and partly from religion. Custom and religion are also influential in European states, but here a distinct form of reasoning about normative issues has emerged. Max

Weber's "Protestant ethic" is one celebrated exploration of this development, which descends distantly from the Socratic concern with the good life as rational and independent of both custom and the gods. Secularists appealto this aspect of our lives in claiming that religion is not a sanction necessary for goodness and decency in our lives.

The modern European world may be free, then, but is it also just? Justice, as John Rawls and others have emphasised, is as basic to society as truth is to explanation, and a whole philosophical speciality has grown up to elaborate the details of how a just society would, in abstract terms, be constituted. The cash value of justice, as it is widely understood in European countries, is equality. One of the more insistent judgements of imperfection in our societies takes the form of sensitivity to a multitude of "gaps" in modern life—the gap between rich and poor, in longevity of different classes, of the taste to enjoy high culture and so on, even down (it has been argued) to the resources with which to take foreign holidays. Each gap is one further instance of injustice in the variable condition of difference classes of people in Western states. Freedom, as creating these gaps, must therefore be recognised as in some degree creating its own nemesis.

Here then seems to be the basic conflict that explains the remarkable variations in how the world today thinks about the modernity which it has nevertheless been embracing with such enthusiasm. A free world turns out to be in some respects an unjust world. Our Western states have a kind of justice, of course, in the form of the rule of law that supplies a certain predictability within which the enterprising individualist can live, but freedom allows for a variety of outcomes that many judge to doom many people to unfulfilled lives. This contrast is a puzzle that has been haunting European societies since the thing called the "Enlightenment" in the eighteenth century, but it certainly does not haunt the rest of the world as those cultures play "catchup." Yet much hangs upon this conflict. We cannot but remember the communist states of the twentieth century in which the domination of a comprehensive form of social justice entranced so many with its promises, and turned out to be despotic, corrupt and murderous.

But we can press the question even further than this. For I have suggested that European states are unique in having created cultures based upon freedom. And their uniqueness derives from the fact that every other civilization in the world has started from the opposite direction. Those cultures have created states in which the basic value was, indeed, justice.

For the point about the Hindu caste system, the Muslim Sharia, those living under the Mandate of Heaven and other variants of what are often called "traditional societies" is that they instantiate a specific form of life that was long regarded not merely as just, but as the only really just way for any human being to live. The same is true of tribal societies. Justice here accords each necessary social role a defined status as contributing to the good of the whole community. This is not the limited civility of the Western rule of law. It is, rather, a comprehensive value that notionally covers all human possibility. Justice of this all-embracing kind satisfies the deep human need to know where one stands and what one's condition requires. Such systems are validated both by custom and by the kinds of belief we normally call "religious." In these hierarchical systems, a ruler has distinct and almost unlimited powers, and other roles feature when exercising appropriate power as warriors, peasants, husbands, wives, elder brothers or sisters, priests and all the other functions the particular society recognises. From inside these systems, each is believed to be the perfect exemplar of justice. From the outside, of course, very different judgements will be made.

Needless to say, the reality of these ideal systems of comprehensive justice diverges dramatically from the ideal. For one thing, they are all despotically governed, because, there is no rule of law in the technical sense recognised in Western societies. No independent judges limit the will of the ruler. Further, although the "rights" and "duties" of each social status are closely specified, there is inevitably an indeterminate area in which the higher status may tyrannise over the lower. Indeed, this fact is vital to the success of these societies: it provides a decision procedure in cases of dispute that might lead to what such systems most fear: namely, disharmony. In disputes, the higher status decides.

And it is because these societies lack the kind of law and moral agency that Europeans have developed that they are systematically corrupt—rather than episodically corrupt, as Europeans are. The most reliable way to get what one wants is by pleasing superiors. It therefore makes an immense difference to life whether one's superiors (at all levels) are "enlightened" or not. What I have called "servility" is thus, in this social structure, not a vice but the only sensible way of engaging with others.

What in such societies becomes of freedom and independence? Some independence of judgement will happen, because independence (at least in the form of wilfulness) is no less basic to human life than accommodation and servility. But freedom in this kind of justice can be nothing other than a licence to indulge impulses likely to subvert the just or communal way of doing things. For this reason, Western ideas of freedom have almost universally been mistrusted in such societies.

Freedom, as we have seen, involves competition in which some do better than others. In traditional societies, however, such competition cannot in principle happen between the social roles of the system because each status has its own exclusive and distinct sphere. In practice, no doubt, competition finds many outlets even in such a world, but the dominant self-understanding of such societies is that they constitute, in principle, perfectly cooperative communities. To establish just such a perfect community was of course the explicit aim of Communist and other ideological revolutions in the twentieth century, and this project still seems to be the dominant understanding of justice in our time. In this ideal of social justice, each individual would be focussed not on his or her own enterprises but upon the good of the community itself. To make our societies just would therefore require that individualists should cease to be individualists and become, as it were, "comrades" working together for the perfection of the community itself. It is striking, for example, how far this principle can be taken. The Soviet Union in its early days abolished even private charity because, like everything else, it was the responsibility of the community as a whole. Correspondingly paradoxical is the fact that it has been the supposedly selfish capitalist societies of the West that have been immensely altruistic and creative in their charitable endeavours to help the vulnerable all over the world.

The whole relation between freedom and justice is evidently a complex of paradoxes. How might one build a just community whose essence would be that competition gives way to cooperation? Such was in large part the aim of those who created welfare states after 1945, and one crisp version of the thinking involved was given by Tony Blair: "I want people to care for society because society cares for them." This remark posits a relationship of gratitude linking the people to the government that redistributes wealth in order to benefit them. But are welfare recipients grateful for what they get? No doubt it varies, but the main response seems to be little more than an alertness to the politics of vulnerability and the hope of raised levels of benefit. Capitalist individualism is often criticised as consumerist, but there is also a consumerism of welfare, and it is a good deal more atomising socially than the luxurious consumerism of commercial societies. Such welfarism is notably destructive of family cohesion.

It is one aspect of this problem that rulers have in the past, for a variety of reasons including the hope of increasing justice, changed the character of politics, yet failed to silence the discontent of which politics is basically constituted. Parliamentary supremacy, democratic extensions of the franchise, votes for women, increasing doses of welfare have all been grand scheme designed to please voters and advance justice, yet time and time again, they fail to achieve general satisfaction among the people they rule. A cynic might well conclude at this point that discontent is our default position in modern Western societies. Without grievances to respond to, and struggles to engage in, many of us would find life rather flat. Perhaps it is injustice rather than justice that is the hidden secret of our world? It certainly generates notable types of satisfaction.

The conflict between freedom and justice lies at the heart of our politics, and like everything political, it is a conflict that cannot be isolated from the many dimensions of political concern. A well-known tension pits supposedly just policies on the one hand against the actual inclinations of people on the other.

Only profound changes in human nature can make possible many versions of justice. The individualist must, as we have seen, give way to the comrade. He or she must find satisfaction not in personal enterprises but in membership of a real community. Politics, however, is never engaged merely with the attainment of one goal, or even one type of goal. To be concerned with the ideal necessarily raises the problem of power, of lifestyle fashions, of competing interests, of the light that will be shed on a problem by considering its causes, and much else. Besides, not even the ideal, in politics or in anything else, is a single seamless object of universal admiration. It is precisely the normative focus only upon the ideal that means it has little of direct interest to say about political reality.

Freedom conflicts with justice not only because they are different values, but because they value different *kinds* of situation. Freedom values a process that leaves individuals unhindered in pursuing their own enterprises within the law, and must therefore lead to unpredictable results in each generation, whereas justice is concerned with what idealists take to be the only desirable outcome. The process of freedom fails to produce the just outcome. But what would constitute the desirability of any such outcome? Does human happiness in fact depend on the way society is constituted? For the fact is that the absoluteness of ideals is illusory in the sense that there is no valid way of choosing between entire social systems. Happy and fulfilled lives can, it seems, be lived in any society while some will achieve misery in utopia. All that one can do in recommending one form of life rather than another is to point to abstract aspects of what is desired. We European moderns prefer tolerant to intolerant, but others demand the universal dominance of what they take to be the one right set of beliefs and practices. Our judgements may not be relative, but they are certainly contextual.

And our context is the clash between values. It is hardly new. In 1861 it was influentially formulated by Sir Henry Maine as the evolution from status to contract, and some of the issues involved appear in contemporary politics as the conflict between the state and the free market as arenas in which preferable results emerge. But at base, the issue is whether freedom and justice are compatible.

We do know that freedom is compatible with the kind of justice—civility and the rule of law—that has long been established in European states. And the point here is that this kind of justice—what Michael Oakeshott described as "adverbial qualifications" on action—merely requires subscription to a set of rules.[*] This is society understood as an association of independent individuals, and it is not concerned with outcomes. Today, however, many construe a modern society as an association of vulnerable people trying to create a community based on cooperation rather than competition. Vulnerable people need protection, and protection is the business not of markets but of states. The moral criterion is the supposed benefits that accrue to vulnerable people. People being helped, however, is merely one side of the situation in which those helpers exercise power. And as we have seen, there is no obvious limit to the nature and number of things that will, in a theory of relative rather than absolute poverty, be demanded on behalf of the vulnerable. The essence of welfare benefits is that they are unconditional, because making them conditional is likely to reactivate the disabilities that constituted their vulnerability in the first place.

Spreading vulnerability, and the resulting growth of entitlement in the name of justice, is threatening to bankrupt Western economies. Here is one of those practical dimensions of politics that must qualify even such a bewitching ideal. But the basic point is that freedom, not justice, is the secret of Western dynamism. Can the current enthusiasm for "social justice" really be distinguished from those reactionary systems of comprehensive "justice" that dominated traditional societies? If not, the future of our freedom—and our uniqueness—is distinctly bleak.

---

[*]   Michael Oakeshott, On Human Conduct, Clarendon Press, Oxford, 1975, p. 113.

INTRODUCTION

I am of two minds about democracy, and so is everybody else. We all agree that it is the sovereign remedy for corruption, tyranny, war, and poverty in the Third World. We would certainly tolerate no different system in our own states. Yet most people are disenchanted with the way it works.

One reason is that our rulers now manage so much of our lives that they cannot help but do it badly. They have overreached themselves. Blunder follows blunder, and we come to regard them with the same derision as those who interview them on radio and television. We love it that our rulers are—up to a point—our agents. They must account to us for what they do. And we certainly don't live in fear, because democracy involves the rule of law. Internationally, democracies are by and large a peaceful lot. They don't like war, and they try to behave like "global citizens." There is much to cherish.

Yet it is hard to understand what is actually happening in our public life under the surface of public discussion. Informational overload makes it difficult for anyone but enthusiasts to distinguish the important from the trivial. The sheer abundance of politics— of democracy, one might say—obscures as much as it illuminates. How do we make sense of these confusions? The first clarifying step must be to recognize that "democracy" in the abstract misleads us. Living in a democracy—and it is living experience that must be our theme—becomes a different thing in each generation. Something that benefits us in one generation may no longer be a benefit in the next. Experiencing twenty-first-century democracy is radically different from what our ancestors cherished in 1901. Rising levels of prosperity, for example, change many responses. For, as Plato noted, constitutions are made out of human beings: when the people change, the system cannot remain the same.

My concern with democracy is highly specific. It begins in observing the remarkable fact that while democracy means a government accountable to the electorate, our rulers now make *us* accountable to *them*. Most Western governments hate me smoking, or eating the wrong kind of food, or riding to hounds, or drinking too much, and these are merely the surface disapprovals, the ones that provoke legislation or public campaigns. We borrow too much money for our personal pleasures, and many of us are very bad parents. Ministers of state have been known to instruct us in elementary matters, such as reading stories to our children. Again, many of us have unsound views about people of other races, cultures, or religions, and the distribution of our friends does not always correspond, as governments think that it ought, to the cultural diversity of our society. We must face up to the grim fact that the rulers we elect are losing patience with us.

No philosopher can contemplate this interesting situation without beginning to reflect on what it can mean. The gap between political realities and their public relations is so great that the term "paradox" tends to crop up from sentence to sentence. Our rulers are theoretically "our" representatives, but they are busy turning us into the instruments of the projects *they* keep dreaming up. The business of governments, one might think, is to supply the framework of law within which we may pursue happiness on our own account. Instead, we are constantly being summoned to reform ourselves. Debt, intemperance, and incompetence in rearing our children are no doubt regrettable, but they are vices, and if left to generate their own consequences, vices soon lead to the pain that corrects. Life is a better teacher of virtue than politicians, and most sensible governments in the past left moral faults alone. Instead, democratic citizenship in the twenty-first century means receiving a stream of improving "messages" from authority. Some may forgive these intrusions because they are so well intentioned. Who would defend prejudice, debt, or excessive drinking? The point, however, is that our rulers have no business telling us how to live. They are tiresome enough in their exercise of authority. They are intolerable when they mount the pulpit. We should never doubt that nationalizing the moral life is the first step toward totalitarianism.

We might perhaps be more tolerant of rulers turning preachers if they were moral giants. But what citizen looks at the government today thinking how wise and virtuous it is? Public respect for politicians has long been declining, even as the population at large has been seduced into responding to each new problem by demanding that the government should act. That we should be constantly demanding that an institution we rather despise should solve large problems argues a notable lack of logic in the demos. The statesmen of times past have been replaced by a set of barely competent social workers eager to help "ordinary people" solve daily problems in their lives. This strange aspiration is a very large change in public life. The electorates of earlier times would have responded with derision to politicians seeking power in order to solve our problems. Today, the demos votes for them.

Our rulers, then, increasingly deliberate on our behalf, and decide for us what is the right thing to do. Socrates argued that the most important activity of a human being was reflecting on how one ought to live. Most people, of course, are not philosophers, but they cannot avoid encountering moral issues. The evident problem with democracy today is that the state is pre-empting—or "crowding out," as the economists say—our moral judgments. Rulers are adding moral judgments to the expanding schedule of powers they exercise. Nor does the state deal merely with principles. It is actually telling its subjects to do very specific things. Yet decisions about how we live are what we mean by "freedom," and freedom is incompatible with a moralizing state. That is why I am provoked to ask the question: can the moral life survive democracy?

By "the moral life," I simply mean that dimension of our inner experience in which we deliberate about our obligations to parents, children, employers, strangers, charities, sporting associations, and other elements of our world. We may not always devote much conscious thought to these matters, but such involvements make up the substance of our lives and also constitute the conditions of our happiness. In deliberating, and acting on what we have decided, we discover who we are and we reveal ourselves to the world. This kind of self-management emerges from the inner life, and is the stream of thoughts and decisions that make us human. The modern West is distinguished by the practice of individuals exhibiting just such moral autonomy. To the extent that this element of our humanity has been appropriated by authority we are diminished, and our civilization loses the special character that has made it the dynamic animator of so much hope and happiness in modern times.

It is this element of dehumanization that I am calling "the servile mind." The charge of servility or slavishness is a serious one. It emerges from the classical Greek view that slaves lacked the capacity for self-movement, and had to be animated by the superior class of masters. Aristotle thought that some people were "natural slaves"; in our democratic world, by contrast, we recognize at least some element of the "master" in everyone. Indeed, in our entirely justified hatred of slavery, we sometimes think that the passion for freedom is a constitutive drive of all human beings. Such a judgment can hardly survive the most elementary inspection of history. Both traditional societies and totalitarian states in the twentieth century suggested that many people are, in most circumstances, happy to sink themselves in some collective enterprise that guides their lives and guarantees them security. It is the emergence of freedom rather than the extent of servility that needs explanation.

By invoking the idea of servility, I am incidentally paying homage to Hilaire Belloc, whose curious book *The Servile State* is approaching its centenary. Belloc's book is eccentric in a number of ways, one being his identification of capitalism as driving modern British culture toward servility. He derives freedom not from the Greeks but from the Christian transformation of Europe during the Middle Ages, and the social structure he takes for granted in this book echoes the socialist and capitalist disputes of his time. But within an argument that was eccentric in some ways even in his own time, there lurks an understanding of the contemporary drift toward servility as a new moral condition. His key idea is the tendency of legislation to reward the acceptance of a servile status by offering the promise of future security. The proletariat was being bribed, and bribability is one important element of servility. One of Belloc's basic examples is the minimum wage, and the structure that concerns him is the developing stratification of the country into capitalists and a proletariat offered benefits for fitting into a system that takes away the freedom of those who dispose of their labor and their resources to decide things for themselves.

Servility is not an easy idea with which to operate, and it should be clear that the world we live in, like any world, cannot be fully captured in ideal structures. All human life is characterized by conflicting ideas and signals, but our time would seem to be a rather nightmarish cacophony of such influences. Somehow we manage to deal with it, or most of us do, without succumbing to fake complaints such as "stress." But it is important here to specify what servility is and how it fits into our understanding of social and moral situations. It is dependence of mind, as exhibited in allowing the beliefs or the passions of others to determine one's own beliefs and passions. It does not necessarily exclude a bit of situational caution. The assistant to Lord Copper in Evelyn Waugh's *Scoop*, who responded to whatever idiotic remark his press baron employer might make with the words "up to a point, Lord Copper," was not necessarily being servile—merely wary about keeping his job in a tricky environment. One problem with servility is that its opposite might seem to be a swaggering parade of one's own independence, but that is likely itself to be a cover

for a servile spirit. A concern not to be misunderstood by others—
something no one can avoid—often leads people to affect bravado
about commitments they cannot seriously sustain. Such problems
of understanding mean that we find ourselves in an area where
casuistries and hypocrisies are hard to avoid.

The real opposite of servility is individuality, as it has long
been understood in European thought. But the very word "individuality" is often confused with egoistic self-interest and the pursuit
of mere passion. One needs to tread with delicacy in using any of
the common words in this area. In our time, the structural rigidi-
ties that have emerged from the basic ideas of social justice and
of vulnerability in contemporary society constitute a new world of
servility that no one in Belloc's time could have imagined. But his
recognition of the general structure of what was happening then
remains acute even today: "Society is recognised as no longer consisting of free men bargaining freely for their labour or any other
commodity in their possession, but of two contrasting statuses,
owners and non-owners."[1] Today, the contrast is between the many
versions of protected victims and the protecting government, but
the structure in its rigidity is in large just what Belloc described
in small. But within our new world, servility as it emerges in the
spirit in which we conduct our lives is much more difficult to
specify. It can only result from a tricky inference made about individuals on the basis of speech or conduct.

The structural conditions of the servile mind as it expresses
itself in conduct are much less elusive than the personal. They
consist clearly in the welfare dependency that has been widely
recognized, and which even governments themselves today find
intolerable. But they are also evident in the legal and regulatory
structures designed to protect one or other abstract category in
the community from being harassed, offended, damaged in self-
esteem, or made to suffer many other things officially construed
as oppressive. They are to be found in the structures that protect
people from victimhood, which are simultaneously an education
in how to be a victim. And one of the collateral corruptions of this
situation is that the control must often be exercised not against
those who commit whatever offense is in question, but against

those who might conveniently be made accountable. An employer, for example, may become accountable for sexual harassment committed by an employee because he has not provided what is known as a "safe environment" for women. This is clearly a transposition of the idea of "deep pocket" found in much contemporary litigation. Again, Belloc was ahead of us. In a hypothetical example, concerning an employee who has accidentally injured another, for which the employer "A" is responsible, he writes: ". . . it is clear that 'A' has peculiar duties not because he is a citizen, but because he is something more: *an employer*; and 'B' and 'D' have special claims on 'A,' not because they are citizens, but because they are something less: *viz., employees.*"[2] More generally, the duty not to offend the vulnerable classes today in speech has been codified as the amorphous thing called "political correctness," and such codification makes the codifiers our masters whom we must obey not because it is the law, but because they are our masters. Such is a servile relationship. Codification of this kind removes the situational freedom with which citizens in what is recognizably a civil relationship ought to be free to respond to each other.

Here then we have a large-scale erosion of the free societies created in modern times, societies that were certainly risky but also creative. In responding to the blizzard of regulation to which we are subjected, we are sometimes lulled into thinking that all human beings seek freedom by nature, and that our liberal ways are merely an expression of this natural human passion that has at last been liberated from oppressors. No glance at history, and especially at the history of the last century, would sustain such an idea. Even where the real oppressions of communism have been overthrown, there remain many who yearn for the security that is lost when freedom comes. No doubt there is one kind of freedom that everybody does desire—the freedom to do what one wants without interference. But this is merely the slave's dream of escape from a master; it is quite distinct from the freedom on which the greatness of European societies has been constructed. Freedom as a moral condition is only possible when combined with responsibility. To be free in this sense is, of course, to live in terms of the rule of law, but more importantly it is to be guided by one's own sense of virtues and commitments. In a free society, it is not only individuals but also professions and associations that regulate themselves within the law. To respond to moral sentiments in one form or another is inseparable from being human, but the modern West has generated a self-managing form of moral agency that is the basis of its freedom. It is a moral agency that takes the form not of agreement with others on some right way of living, but of an entrenched civil respect for the independence and autonomy of others.

And if it should seem that invoking servility as characterizing some of the conduct of modern Europeans is excessively dramatic, let me observe that we do actually have a vocabulary that recognizes slavishness in the everyday life of our societies. It emerges, for example, when we call someone a toady, creep, wimp, careerist, or some other such denigration. Indeed, our vocabulary reveals a variety of ways in which we recognize tendencies that are quite precisely servile. Any failure to perform a public duty unless some private benefit is given, for example, is an exercise in corruption, and such corruption is indicative of the moral life characteristic of the slave. Again, our common moral disapproval of "greed" characterizes those who go beyond the capitalist drive for the best deal, in order to gain something to which they are not entitled. This judgment implicitly invokes the charge of being enslaved to passions. But of course, servility has much more evident characteristics. Let us bring them out by a contrast.

The European societies that became democracies in the course of the last two centuries understood themselves as associations of self-moving individuals. Rich and poor alike made their own arrangements within a civil society containing a large and increasing range of associations—social, charitable, religious, mutually supportive, unionized, and so on. These associations expressed that capacity for spontaneous institutional creativity that so impressed visitors to Europe, and especially to Anglophone countries. The crucial mark of independence was the ability to generate the resources needed for life without dependence on governmental subsidy, and it constituted "respectability." It may have been easier for the rich to achieve respectability, but moral character was the crucial point. Servile forms of flattery could be and always can be found at all levels of society. The respectable poor, however, were characterized by a proud sense of their independence. Such an attitude emerged from medieval times in England, and was based on a sense of personal dignity within whatever "rank" one might have, a sense developed by the common law. English society as a set of independent individuals had emerged slowly during the eighteenth and nineteenth centuries with the move from agriculture to the cities, and out of the relics of a semi-feudal dependence. Whole new classes of people became absorbed into the existing political traditions of Europe.

The large change from the late nineteenth and early twentieth century is thus that our very conception of society itself has changed. It is no longer an association of independent self-moving individuals, but rather an association of vulnerable people whose needs and sufferings must be remedied by the power of the state. The idea of "vulnerability" has become such a cannibal that it now covers not only the victims of misfortune or delinquency but even the delinquents themselves. It is not only the victims of knife crime, for example, who have turned out to be "vulnerable" but also those who do the killing. The implication of this remarkable semantic development is that "society itself" has failed in its duty to instill decency and integrity in these people. Here we have the most direct possible challenge to the basic idea of moral agency.

Moral agency is undermined as governments take over the tasks individuals used to do for themselves. Removing problems from the lives of people certainly enhances their convenience, but such helpfulness is generally presented in grander terms as expressing social justice, or compassion. We should never, however, confuse justice with convenience. In the long run, convenience has costs, even if only in the form of a steady decline of our own resourcefulness. The convenience of supermarkets that never close diminishes the necessity, indeed often the capacity, to plan household arrangements. Technological advances in warfare make us more formidable, but often diminish the need for courage. Mobile phones are useful in making arrangements, but they weaken respect for punctuality, once touted as the virtue of kings. Medical help free at the point of need may be a great benefit, but it erodes any urgency we may feel to exercise the virtue of thrift, which once taught us to save for a rainy day. Prudence, wisdom, and our solidarity with friends and family become less necessary. It thus becomes our habit and our interest—and our habit *because* it is our interest—to do what the government requires. After all, who are we to stand out against democracy? The state can supply these benefits only, of course, by taking more and more of our money in taxation, and the result is that over a considerable range of incomes, the individual is increasingly able to devote his or her money—whatever may be left of it—to the satisfaction of impulses rather than to the management of autonomy. Part of the slide into servility is also to be seen in the trivialization of much modern life.

Considerations of this sort are what lead me to assimilate the condition of modern Europeans in some degree to that of the slaves of the ancient world. We must today as citizens accommodate ourselves to increasing regulation and dependence on authority, even to the point of falling in with the correct opinions. The moral world of the classical individualist emerged from the coherence of self-chosen commitments. His basic duty was to his own conception of himself. Contemporary moral life, by contrast, is marked by compliance with externally imposed rules, a structure of personal responses to the world that the sociologist David Riesman once called "other directed." Such obedience cannot be forthcoming unless the state can access vastly more information about each of us, even down to where we are physically situated at this or that time. We now live in a "surveillance society."

Changes in social and moral life are difficult to recognize because we retain old admirations long after we have lost the disciplines that sustained them. We still admire freedom and the virtues associated with it—courage, pride, self-reliance, and such like, even though other admirations may be invoked to cover this or that betrayal of our independence. The world we have allowed to emerge out of the rather austere restrictiveness of earlier times is remarkably pleasant and permissive most of the time for most people. We strongly feel that some of its features—democracy, liberty, tolerance, rights, and so on—are a pattern that ought to be adopted throughout the world. Besides, we are now immensely wealthier than those in earlier generations. It is only partly because of our wealth that we are a magnet for immigrants from every part of the world. Seen from the vantage point of traditional societies in other parts of the world, we seem to be admirably free. Attending to these features of our current condition will no doubt make it seem unlikely that we are sliding into what I am calling "the servile mind."

Contemporary society has certainly liberated us from many of the austerities and conventions of earlier times. It has allowed impulsiveness to flourish, and we enjoy "negative freedom" over a whole range of actions previously restricted. The other side of this admirable condition of things is, however, the rise in crime, drug use, anti-social behavior, and the breakdown of family life. As democratic, the modern world is very responsive to what we want, and what we want is not always good for us.

"Democracy" today covers a vast range of changes expected to improve the lives of all. In arguing that democracy erodes the moral life, I am not suggesting that it *causes* the servility I am diagnosing. What causes what in social life is so complicated that we can hardly be sure of any particular connection; we only ever grasp parts of it. Technology and economic enterprise, the secularization of life, changing opinions, new moral tastes—many such things are implicated in these changes. But democracy is central because sooner or later it will be used to explain, justify, and make coherent the way things are going, at least to the extent that we approve of the way they are going.

This justificatory role can be seen in the fact that very few activities are immune from proposals that they ought to be democratized. Household democracy is men and women equally sharing the burdens of running the household. Educational democracy consists in switching resources to the pupils currently less capable of getting good results. No remnants of hereditary constitutions are safe from this homogenizing steamroller: the House of Lords is in the process of becoming something like a democratized federal chamber. Democratization is the most dramatic of all the corruptions of modernity in which the inherited practice of balance is to be replaced by a single ideal believed to solve all problems. The moral life can no more be isolated from this drive than anything else. It too must be democratized.

Such a grand desirability as democracy at its most ambitious clearly needs to be examined. Notionally, it stands for the will of the people and for universal equalization as the content of that will. This is a combination of two logically distinct considerations. The democratic project itself is the belief that the benefits of a civilized Western life ought to be, more or less unconditionally, available to everybody, not excluding at its limit the entire population of the planet. The democratic ground of this project is that the demos actually wills this project. The conjunction of the project and its notional grounding creates a moral imperative thought to override the moral deliberations of individuals.

The Servile Mind thus presents an argument exploring this evolution of moral sensibilities in Western life since 1900. "Western" life here refers to the cultures of Europe, North America, Australia, and much else. I sometimes use "European" as a synonym because that is where this culture evolved. Elements of such a life will now be found everywhere, because few peoples have not in some degree been influenced by our practices. There are, of course, many different national versions of modern European life, but they do not greatly affect my argument. At the heart of Western life as we inherited it within living memory are self-conscious individuals guiding their destinies according to whatever moral sentiments they entertain. Such moral sentiments are certainly variable, but they are not mere matters of taste.

My argument is that this moral idiom is being challenged by another, in which individuals find their identifying essence in supporting public policies that are both morally obligatory and politically imperative. Such policies are, I suggest, "politico-moral." Such an attitude dramatically moralizes politics, and politicizes the moral life. It feeds on our instinctive support for good causes. Modern European or Western societies are, of course, immensely varied in their moral sensibilities, and my best hope is to have tracked at least some interesting changes. They reveal much about the way our civilization is moving.

I want to understand the world rather than to change it, and hence my approvals and disapprovals are irrelevant. If they occasionally stand up and bark, I crave the reader's indulgence. Morality is partly about "doing the right thing," but it is hardly news that people disagree about what that might be. Changes in moral sensibility always have some good reasons behind them; equally, very few changes are unmixed blessings. The way these sentiments evolve—which is to say: how we live—is of the first significance for our destiny. The world is a dangerous place, and our moral capacities are the basic equipment on which not only our integrity but our very survival depends.

To those who might object that talk of morality is of little significance because everyone actually makes up their values as they go along, I would merely observe that this is a confusion resulting from the fashion for sociological fundamentalism. The moral world is currently described in terms of "social rules" or "cultural attitudes" rather than of moral commitments, yet no one doubts that moral competence is valuable, even though today some people call (part of) it "social capital." Moral judgments today seem to be essentially contestable, and even in the rhetoric of politics, activists think that condemning something as "illegal" deals a more powerful blow than condemning it as "immoral."

The popularity of this flight from the moral to the social (and the legal) has fostered the illusion that our vices can be reformed if governments send the right "messages." Attitudes, of course, change all the time, and governments are part of the reason they do: part of the reason, but only part. I for one am not dismayed that attitudes have a life of their own, and that the demos in the twenty-first century is not entirely plastic material suitable to be sculpted by rulers. Rulers may get excited about "changing the culture," but modern peoples are usually brutish enough to resist being improved. Being alert to the semantics by which the moral has been transposed into the manipulable is one protection against a gullible acquiescence to the projects of governments. These semantics cannot help but attract philosophical interest. And the philosopher had better start by observing that what we recognize as our "culture" is merely surfaces, the debris left behind from our moral responses in times past. It is out of date even as it is recognized. We never step into the same culture twice.

At the end of a period of civil strife, as Tacitus tells us, Augustus Caesar established peace and security in Rome during the long period in which he ruled, ending in 14 A.D. Augustus carefully preserved the constitutional structures inherited from the Republican period. Rome was still, in a sense, at the height of its power. When he died, however, the Romans discovered that a new system had quietly come into being: they had acquired a master. And what they also learned was that, almost insensibly, over the long reign of Augustus, they had learned the moral practices needed for a sycophantic submission to such a figure. The fate of the Romans under Tiberius, who followed Augustus, was alarming beyond anything even imaginable in our time. But we should not forget the broader lesson that, over long stretches of time, the moral changes that take place only become evident in the light of some unexpected crisis. It is a lesson that ought to make us wary of our easygoing and liberated ways. Our world is infinitely benign, and we are in no immediate danger of falling into the distractions and treacheries that afflicted the early days of Rome under the principate. But we should never forget that moral change takes place below, and often deeply below, the surface of a culture.

The Servile Mind: How Democracy Erodes the Moral Life is an argument: it takes for granted a certain amount of sophistication in political theory and intellectual history. I have no doubt got some things wrong, but to have provided the scholarly apparatus that would justify in detail the certainly arguable judgments I am making would have turned the book into a quite different enterprise. I have simply noted a few references that might be useful to anyone following this or that particular trail. Nor did I want to present a list of the vast number of people to whom I am indebted for a thought here, a turn of phrase there. The test of whether I have got anything right, or whether I live in cloud-cuckoo land, must be left to the judgment of the reader, for any such analysis of lived experience "admits of no other demonstration."

—Kenneth Minogue
June 2010

DEMOCRATIC AMBIGUITIES

1. DEMOCRACY AS A PROCESS OF CONTINUING CHANGE

My question is whether the moral life is compatible with democracy. Since both democracy and the moral life refer to dynamic entities, their compatibility is clearly a matter of history no less than of any philosophical concern with ideas. As democracy came increasingly to dominate British constitutional procedures in the century after the First Reform Act of 1832, little evidence of incompatibility could be discerned. The political and the moral were distinct, even if intersecting, spheres of life. The various political parties in Britain, and in other countries as they democratized, generally knew that their political enthusiasms were quite distinct from their moral responsibilities. Nonetheless, some forms of social liberalism were already tending to advance moral arguments for redistributionist projects,[*] and on the periphery of politics could be found ideological doctrines, most notably Marxism, that actually explained the entire moral life (as then conceived) as being a set of behavioral conditions demanded of people in order to sustain an oppressive system called "bourgeois society," later becoming "capitalism."

Moral ideas must thus be recognized as evolving over time. There is some element of paradox here, in that right and wrong are in principle the same at all times and places, but this is plausible only at an abstract level; moral convictions depend on beliefs and contexts, which both have unique features.

The obvious question to ask is whether the varying features of European civilization exhibit a pattern or whether they are merely random—"one damn thing after another," as it is sometimes put. The answer is not only that we may discover a great variety of patterns or trends in the development of modern European civilization but also that we use the patterns we think we have found in orienting ourselves. Our admirations and contempts are closely aligned with what we think has happened in the past, both to each of us individually, and to the nation whose identity we share. Some thinkers have taken recourse to patterns of human nature in order to discover the ubiquity of such things as the desire for freedom, or of the temptation to seek domination over others. Sometimes strands not only of technological but also of moral progress are detected in the history of mankind, and some believe that in declarations of human rights, our time has discovered— at last!—the true foundations of human felicity. Ideologists such as Marx trace a pattern in which the dynamic of an evil system works itself out, sometimes leading to a welcome synthesis as a form of true community. Some philosophers discover in history the working out of the human drive to freedom. Historians often construe the modern world as a sequence of capitalized chapters

---

[*]   For example, in the work of T. H. Green, L. T. Hobhouse, and Bernard Bosanquet. Nor should we forget Bentham's greatest happiness principle as a political criterion for moral conduct.

in their history books—Renaissance leading on to Reformation, Enlightenment, Romanticism, and onward. Pessimists think that our civilization is declining, while the elderly often regret the loss of the gracefulness they remember from their youth. What all of this reveals, however, is that the modern West understands itself in terms of the basic idea of change. Sometimes we may congratulate ourselves on progress, or alternatively, we may recognize our condition in terms of the things we may regret disappearing— belief in an afterlife, perhaps, or "jobs for life."

This sense of being immersed in a process of change is what distinguishes modern European civilization from the cultures of other peoples. We have learned to welcome change; everything with us has its fashions, but other cultures are often characterized by a resistance to change based on the belief that they participate, however imperfectly, in a right way of life. Such a "right way of life" was in the past encased in a religious or at least in a dominantly ethical way of life. And I take it that this feature of the way people have always lived is as true of notable civilizations, such as the Hindu or the Islamic, or indeed the Confucian, as it is of smaller tribal groups. One of the great divisions in the human world is between people who think that they know the one right way of life, and those (mostly in European states) whose moral responses take their beginnings from the recognition and acceptance of change as inevitable, indeed inescapable.

That word "civilization" may raise specific difficulties, because some people feel that it makes an unwarranted claim that some cultures are superior to others. I certainly want to claim that civilizations are *different* from cultures, though every civilization is, of course, itself a network of different cultures. Superiority is a different question altogether, and if anything sensible can be said about it, the claim must be very closely focused on the abstract aspect for which special value is being claimed. How do you decide whether a business executive in a suit is superior to an intrepid hunter with a deep local knowledge of where he lives and finds food? Indeed, in romantic periods, Europeans have identified the intrepid hunter as a noble savage, dripping with authenticity, and much superior to the nervous ambivalences of our own lives. These judgments are themselves matters of fashion. Most questions of superiority are not only irresolvable, but also tedious. Civilizations are certainly cultures, but not all cultures are civilizations, though the distinction is hardly clear-cut.

I would suggest, however, that those peoples that have evolved their own written scripts have acquired a capacity to manage abstract thinking, which is one mark of a civilization. A grasp of abstract ideas, something found in literary cultures, makes possible adaptive capacities often lacking in those cultures that have evolved an intimate relation with their own local world. There are certainly many ways in which abstractions mislead us, but they also have the power of liberating cultures from the specific environments that nurtured them. Any individual from any culture can of course respond in unpredictable ways to new situations, but cultures are very slow to change. I take this to be an element in the situation of the so-called "indigenous" peoples of the world, who find modern life presents them with problems from which civilizations suffer much less. The specific features of tribal cultures are recognized as distinctive in, for example, the UN Declaration of the Rights of Indigenous Peoples.[*]

We shall thus misunderstand the character of the contemporary world unless we recognize civilizations as distinct types of culture, but we should also recognize that we are all whatever we are because we participate in one culture or another. We all speak a language and live according to habits and values different from those of other peoples. In advancing the argument of this book, I am evidently judging things from a specific historical location. But I am also advancing a universal understanding of human affairs such that people from any culture, understanding the terms I set up, might in principle agree, or alternatively contest, the truth of what I am arguing. I write early in the twenty-first century in one of the centers of the English-speaking world, but what I shall be describing (if I get it right) will also be found wherever modern European modes of thought and life have established themselves,

---

[*] Adopted by the United Nations in September 2007.

or even been marginally influential. The modern West, as I shall for convenience call it, has left some mark on virtually everybody except perhaps a few remote tribes in the Amazon jungle. My pool of evidence will largely consist of what is happening in Europe, America, and those areas of the world where the usages of modernity have most strongly taken root.

Let me now remove one possible if rather unsophisticated misunderstanding of my project. People who talk about morality and the moral life often have a specific form of conduct they wish to recommend. I certainly have opinions on better and worse conduct, but my view of the moral life, as elaborated in later sections, is almost entirely descriptive. The same is true of my view of democracy, though my argument is in part designed to remove certain illusions about it. And to that task we should now turn.

2. HOW TO ANALYZE DEMOCRACY

As with any complex social practice, we may ask many *types* of question about democracy and can thus develop a variety of accounts of it. It is in the first instance a constitutional change in the electoral arrangements of countries that were already constitutionally governed. In their long history of civil development, democratic practices in many European states could meld more or less coherently with the attitudes and practices already in place. Democracy is thus part of constitutional law.

Most people, however, would think that it is centrally studied in political science, though some might feel uneasy about the use of the term "science" as covering any study of human affairs. In political science departments in universities, democracy is studied with particular attention to changing power structures as fitting in to the rules and conventions dominating the national political process at any given time. The way democracy works can be studied comparatively, and sometimes lessons are drawn about how the successes of one national tradition may be followed in another.

Sociologists attend to the politics of democracy by analyzing the relation between power, political support, and social structures. Political theorists investigate the relation between democracy as an ideal and the way in which the ideal relates to the realities of current politics. Historians, again, study the events of political life and their relation to time and context. And perhaps overarching everything else is the practical interest those who live in a democracy have, from day to day, in the way it works.

It is as part of that practical response to living in a democracy that we begin to attend to its psychological and moral features. Here we find what might be generalized as the experience of democracy, by contrast with what it is like to live in those states and cultures, many of them ruled despotically, in which some dominant idea of a right way of life is the basis of both the actions of rulers and the social life of the people. The contrast here is particularly between what people take for granted living in democratic states, which means under the rule of law, and what is taken for granted in states whose collective life is based on other assumptions. It is a striking feature of Western democracies that they exhibit very little corruption at the lower levels of administration (for example the issuing of passports, or the provision of welfare payments) than in other forms of collective life.

There is no doubt that the French are preeminent in the study of this area of social and political life, and that Montesquieu and Alexis de Tocqueville are the most notable figures. This focus of attention in political life generates a concern with what might, somewhat pretentiously, be called a *phenomenology* of democracy. In modern times, those concerned with the place of the "media" in modern democracies—for example, Jürgen Habermas in his work on "communicative action"—exhibit this focus of attention. The acute Tocqueville understood democracy as a complete way of life contrasting with the experiences of an aristocratic country such as France. He did not think it entirely admirable, but he certainly thought that he had seen the future, and indeed that it worked, in some ways, rather well. His concern was with *les moeurs*, and there can be no doubt that the viability of democratic constitutions is crucially related to the consonance between these attitudes and assumptions on the one hand, and the practices (especially inhibitions) that respond to them on the other. Incoherence here between ideal and reality is the reason why democracy is so hard to establish in non-Western states.

In turning to democracy, however, we need to distinguish between "democracy" as denoting a kind of political arrangement, and its denoting a moral, social, and political ideal. The most remarkable fact about Western political development in the last two centuries is how a relatively slight change in electoral practices, namely an extension of the franchise, has evolved into a comprehensive criticism, and in many cases a rejection, of the inherited mores of European states. In Britain, for example, the First Reform Act added quite a small number of voters to the electoral roll, and politics was for the rest of the century largely an aristocratic sport. It was not until the end of the century that a party specifically devoted to improving the condition of the poor established itself as a serious player in British politics. Yet by the time Clement Attlee's Labour Party came to power in 1945, that small technical change in the constitution had blossomed into the remarkable idea of democracy as the critic of an entire civilization. Ranks, classes, formalities, forms of respect, habits of clothing, and much else were swept aside in what one might in retrospect call an "orgy of informality," and elections became forms of voter seduction, in which specific classes of voters were promised concrete benefits resulting from the use of political power to redistribute wealth from those who had acquired it in the economy. In 1832, it would have been absurd to invoke Plato's conception of democracy in Books VII and IX of *The Republic* as having any relevance to modern political life. By the second half of the twentieth century, the Platonic characterization was well advanced. Democracy is the form of government that responds to what its subjects approve, or can be persuaded to approve.

It is this development of democracy, from a relatively minor constitutional change in national politics into a comprehensive ideal or dream of a society in which everyone would enjoy happiness in membership of a true community, that I am calling "the democratic revolution." Revolution is a bit of explanatory hyperbole we commonly use in dealing with modern change, and it may refer to a set of events happening within a very short space of time (such as France after 1789, or Russia after 1917) or it may refer to an accumulation of changes in our form of life such that life has been entirely transformed, almost without people realizing what has happened.

Democracy thus revealed itself, over time, to be not a condition but a process, and in some versions, a process with no terminus short of a perfect way of life. Democrats of one sort or another increasingly found the social, political, and economic arrangements of the states in which they lived to be incompatible with the full flowering of democracy. Some democrats objected to monarchy, some to economic inequality, most to aristocracies, and nearly all to the "gaps" detected in the advantages (or benefits, or privileges) enjoyed by some members of society but not by others. A state itself might be democratic, but its economies, left free from political regulation, were powerful generators of inequalities, while societies were often criticized as being marked by intolerable forms of divisive social distinctions. A rolling program of reforms over the last century, often advanced as "democratization," has brought us welfare provision in many places, republics in some, and human rights everywhere. An increasing range of legislation designed to guarantee full social acceptance of social groups (called "minorities") had become part of a program of making society into what was thought to be a real community.

How do we explain this remarkable new situation? A relatively simple change in political arrangements (extending the franchise) turns out to be a project for the entire reconstruction of society. Here is the sense in which democracy "presides over" a kind of revolution in Western experience. Further, new projects of reconstruction seem to turn up with each new generation, responding no doubt to the increasing wealth of modern states and to new tastes and sensibilities in the people who live in them. Thus there is no such thing as "democracy" abstractly considered, because the meaning of the term changes significantly with each passing generation. Walter Bagehot in the nineteenth century argued that the wisdom of no reform could be seriously judged in the generation that enacted it because people still retained the habits of the earlier conditions, and only time reveals the truth about how they will respond. In each generation, the progress of reform seems to generate projects of social change that would have astonished the previous generation. The shape of politics in twentieth-century Britain resulted in part from the passing of the three Reform Acts in the nineteenth century (and also of course from the admission of women to the franchise in 1918 and 1928), while the shape of Britain in the twenty-first century has been powerfully affected by the welfare state, whose essentials were laid out under Attlee between 1945 and 1951. In each generation, responses to past changes evolve, and new passions arise. These things cannot to any serious extent be predicted before they happen. Generations, no less than individuals, will always find ways to surprise us. The future is largely inscrutable; indeed we may count ourselves exceptionally fortunate if we acquire much of an understanding of the past.

In taking my initial bearings from democracy, then, I am doing, no doubt with rather less flair, something similar to what Tocqueville did in exploring the character of America in 1831–1832. He began with analyzing the social and political experiences of Americans, and ended up with an analysis of a mode of conduct and sensibility that he recognized as democracy. But this was not entirely democracy as the political scientist described it; rather, it was a mode of living, a form of experience, a collection of habits, sensibilities, and expectations of a kind difficult to assimilate to the characteristic questions of the political scientist. Tocqueville did indeed recognize democracy as a new political system, but his main interest in it was in the attitudes and sensibilities (for example its curious subservience to majority opinion) that were transforming human responses to living with others, and to the world in general. My interest, like his, is basically in the morals and manners of contemporary democracy.

But in taking democracy as central, at least for the moment, I am (no more than Tocqueville himself) making the mistake of thinking that everything may be attributed to democracy. In modern life, we all participate in economic, religious, legal, civic, and national activities, and the way these activities affect each other is immensely complex. The relation between technology and the moral life, for example, can hardly be avoided by anyone who gives the least attention to these matters. Above all, many people think that the most significant causal force in our lives is the set of changes usually discussed under the name of "capitalism." The spirit of commerce is detected in explaining everything. But in addition, the student of human affairs must remember that whole countries may be swept by influential doctrines—such as that of progress, or race, or evolution—and by passions, such as the passion for collective moral immaculacy that has induced many Westerners to apologize for what they rightly or wrongly think to have been historical injustices. Democracy is thus a transforming ideal of social life. How do we make sense of it?

3. SOME BASIC CONDITIONS OF DEMOCRACY

The principle is easier to grasp than how it works. Democracy is a constitution in which public policy reflects the will of the people—government, in Lincoln's admirably crisp formula, of the people, by the people, for the people. Trouble begins when one tries to spell out what we understand by "the people."

We can, of course, make a daring leap from essence to actuality by pointing to actual democratic states such as France, Sweden, Australia, and Britain, and I don't see any problems in doing so. The world contains democracies, they are pretty clearly recognizable, and we like what we see. Whatever the theoretical problems, successful liberal democracies seem to demonstrate that democracy works, and indeed that it works rather better than the alternatives. Theorists may quibble about how public opinion translates, or fails to translate, into public policy, but reality always treats concepts pretty roughly. No doubt politics in these countries may on occasion be less than reliably democratic, but practical blemishes are inseparable from human affairs. This range of examples, however, already suggests that exemplification of democracy is safest if we stick to examples from European cultures. There are no doubt many admirable states and constitutions elsewhere (Japan, perhaps, or Mexico, or, in certain of its phases, Ghana) and they seem reasonably well based on popular support, even though they might not be confidently identified as democracies. The basic test, I suppose, is whether individuals can lead tolerable lives in such states. Great Britain before the nineteenth-century extensions of the franchise was an admirable liberal state in many ways, but it certainly was not democratic.

Can we base the desirability of democracy upon the passions of "the people"? For if we look back over recent history, we shall find cases where "the people" have made some very eccentric judgments indeed. These range from the Weimar Republic putting the Nazi Party within range of constitutional power, to the American people judging that they could solve the problem of drunkenness by banning alcohol. Governing states requires wisdom, and the people are no more to be relied on for wisdom than any other ruling group; in some respects, even less so. But exploring this judgment pushes us back to a more fundamental question, both in theory and in practice: who counts as constituting "the people"?

Most nineteenth-century democrats had no problem in identifying "the people" with adult men, or adult free men, if one wishes to take the idea back to its etymological origins in classical Greece. In some countries it took about a century before "the people" (as a political idea) included adult females. Next, "adult" became the problem. The young traditionally attained adult status on reaching the age of twenty-one, but young men of eighteen could be called up to risk their lives in battle. Was it not unfair to deny them a say in the political policies that brought them to this situation? Some reformers today seek to lower the qualifying age from 18 to 16. But then more complex problems arise. It has to be recognized that some individuals have mental problems, and some of them live less than independent lives. Should they therefore be denied the vote? Some enthusiasts for this kind of inclusion have in the past organized transport to polling booths for people suffering from Down Syndrome.

In this and other cases, democracy has evolved beyond its constitutional functions so that it may serve other purposes—such as symbolizing social inclusion. Here we have the overriding political function of wisdom in government being subordinated to another presumed desirability. The vote itself, whose value in any case diminishes as increasing classes of people are granted the franchise, now becomes further devalued as it must perform another function at odds with its constitutional significance. Some social reformers, for example, are concerned about rehabilitating those convicted of crimes. Should we not, then, extend the franchise to those convicted of less serious crimes? Would it not be a denial of human rights to exclude them from the franchise? Some democrats have worried about the representation of children whose interests are bound up with those of their parents. Should parents perhaps be accorded two votes in order to represent the interests of those children? These questions have in fact led to endless tinkering with the franchise, leading to reforms that sometimes extended it—and thus, of course, diminished the value of each individual vote. Both in theory and in practice, the issue of how perfectly to represent the will of the people turns out to be a continuing and insoluble problem of democracy. Every solution to it generates further problems.

Why, we might well ask, should anyone fuss about entirely marginal and numerically insignificant inclusions in the franchise? Is it not likely that the foolish will cancel each other out? The answer can by found by turning our attention away from what the essence of democracy affirms, and toward what it denies.

Democratically speaking, any version of "the people" less than the whole population is a case of the part dominating the whole, and therefore a form of oppression. No oligarchy based on a limited franchise can be tolerated: all must have the suffrage. Even kings, who in principle symbolize the whole state rather than a single interest within it, have fallen foul of this criterion. Thus Immanuel Kant in the eighteenth century plausibly argued that the insulation of kings from the consequences of war explained why states so often engaged in it. Whatever the sufferings of the people in areas ravaged by armies, the king remained secure in his palace. Get rid of kings, replace them by republics, Kant argued, and the result would be peace, because the people had no interest in killing each other. Many contemporary democracies do in fact have a monarch, of course, but in Kant's terms they are essentially republics. Kant's argument is unconvincing, but it is not refuted by the case of democratic monarchies.

Democracy is, then, rule that reflects the interests of the whole of society rather than merely some part of it. But here, as often in exploring the idea of democracy, we have solved one problem only to face another. Do the people always agree with each other on the right thing to do? Since they often do not, a rule is needed for aggregating their judgment in the (almost universal) cases of disagreement, and abstractly speaking philosophers agree that the rule must recognize the rights of the majority. It would seem to be the only rational procedure to adopt, because to advocate minority power would throw open the whole irresolvable issue of what superiority of wisdom could possibly justify such minority power. In practice, these issues are mediated by political parties, periodic elections, and the search for policies that can finesse disagreements between majorities and minorities. No competent government in a real modern state will often be tempted to enact legislation that will be entirely rejected when the opposite party comes to power. Majority rule cannot be mere domination. A polity lacking this kind of wisdom will not remain a democracy for very long. Such wisdom, however, is not to be taken for granted, because it depends largely on a cultural homogeneity not commonly found outside Western states, and not always reliably even there.

The principle is, then, that no state should be governed by any minority within it, and bad things will happen if it is. The most lethal charge that can be made against a state is that it is actually run by the rich, Big Business, the Jews, the Old School Tie, Enarques, the Eastern Establishment, or any other partial and sinister interest. In a democracy the people rule, and public policy reflects their interests.

Or at least it should. There is a sense, of course, in which this whole account of democracy resembles wish fulfillment. A persistent strain of realism in the study of democracy suggests, very plausibly, that every democracy is in the end an oligarchy in which officials and politicians, as controlling the agendas and the rhetoric of public discussion, actually determine what happens.

Democracy, in other words, is merely a superficial gloss over the realities of oligarchy. Such realism certainly points to ways in which the ideal of democracy is defective, though it should also be recognized that a more or less democratized oligarchy is different from other oligarchies and is by no means to be condemned out of hand.

In any case, the ideal of democracy has little purchase on plausibility unless "the whole people" is a relatively homogeneous set of people who "speak the same language" (even if it is only in a metaphorical sense, as in states such as Spain, Switzerland, and Belgium). The United States established its cultural homogeneity as virtually a condition of admission to its shores. A *pays politique* can hardly exist unless individuals share similar sources of information and talk to each other in mutually comprehensible terms.

The recent past of European states in this respect is strange. They all created a shared culture by deliberately marginalizing local dialects and diffusing a common language in order to create the conditions of a modern state. Much of this homogenizing responded to democratic pressures, and occurred as late at the nineteenth century. The resulting condition of mutual comprehensibility turned out to be precarious and temporary. Hardly had it been achieved than these states became a magnet for migration from Asia and Africa. Coming from cultures largely alien to those of Europe, these migrants soon became numerous enough to resist demands that they assimilate to the host culture, and were often accorded a collective status and specific rights distinct from the established inhabitants of the state. The doctrine of multiculturalism rejected the policy of assimilating the whole population to a common culture. In this way, the homogeneous states of Europe turned back into structures rather more like empires than traditional states.[*]

The idea of democracy and the idea of cultural diversity (as promoted by multicultural doctrine) are thus contradictory ideas.

---

[*] For a critical view of the resulting cultural accommodations, see Brian Barry, *Culture & Equality: An Egalitarian Critique of Multiculturalism*, Polity, 2001.

The classic cases of democratic failure have been states composed of radically different tribes or sets of people in which the possibility of accommodation under a rule of law will not work because one group can only understand rule by the other as a form of oppression. African states have been marked by endless civil strife as a result of tribal dissension. Lebanon is another interesting case where this condition is lacking. And in Europe, the Basques in Spain, and the conflict between Catholic Republicans and Unionist Protestants in Northern Ireland, further illustrate the problem. You cannot, in other words, have democracy without having a *people*, and they must be a population that treats each other as individuals rather than as collective enemies and rivals.

Cultural heterogeneity thus tends to make democracy difficult or impossible. But there is another condition that is equally in tension with the very idea of democracy. This is the case of a traditional society in which the role of government is believed to be that of sustaining a form of life immemorially right for all human beings. Just such traditional governments were over the centuries the way most people were in fact governed, and the rulers were usually some established class of nobles or priests thought to have a superior understanding of that way of life. In such conditions, evil is easily recognized as deviation from custom. Such was long the condition of China, of various empires in India, and of the Islamic world. One might think that such a universal belief would at least guarantee long periods of stability, but (as in considering any ideal model of a constitution) we should not be too easily misled by aspiration and appearance. Internal crises or foreign conquest were seldom absent for long, though in predominantly agricultural societies the circulation of rulers often made little difference to the details of life. The point for us, however, is that in such societies democracy would be excluded not because some partial interest had taken over control of the state, but because the people had no business expressing their will at all. Such an arrangement would subject the higher purpose of the state to the ignorance of the lower orders, a possibility explored and rejected in theory by Plato in *The Republic*. The business of everyone in a traditional society is to cultivate virtues as they were embodied in the local structure of authority. Traditional regimes ought to be models of stability in a changing world. In fact, they are often strikingly unstable, as the history of contemporary Islamic states may illustrate.

Democracy as a political regime thus postulates a relatively homogeneous population with both the capacity for expressing its demands and a tradition of doing so. The "legitimacy" of such a regime notionally results from the fact that public policy responds to what the people as a whole want, and that is why the laws of a democratic government have authority. In the past, the authority of governments commonly rested on a claim of authorization by God, and usually in addition the claim to a specific sort of wisdom for their actions. No such claim to possession of the *arcana imperii* is made by democratic governments. Democracy seems on the face of it to be a system of government in which the question of political wisdom has been put to one side because the wisdom of the people, as knowing what they want, is taken for granted. We shall see, of course, that there are other claims to superiority in this system, but we may note that a basic axiom of democracy is that, in principle, what the people want is what ought to be done.

4. ILLUSION AND PARADOX

Democracy is, then, a set of desires in search of coherence. This hardly distinguishes it from pursuing happiness, falling in love, or any of the other things humans get up to. And when humans judge things desirable, illusion cannot be far behind. By an "illusion" here, I mean a false belief about the world that is in part sustained by the fact that we wish it (or perhaps fear it) to be true. All practical activities involve some elements of unreality, and often, looking back on them, we can realize with hindsight the illusions involved, especially those that persuaded us to think important some things to which we are now indifferent. Even better than the wisdom of hindsight, however, is a certain detachment from these misleading signs at the time we act. Hence it is important in understanding politics to consider whether we can detect specific illusions that hover over our political admirations and practices. All constitutions do in fact generate characteristic illusions that help to sustain them, and widespread skepticism can be a sign of coming trouble. Monarchies, for example, rest upon beliefs about the wisdom and benevolence of the ruler (often thought to be surrounded by bad counselors), and aristocracies generate beliefs about the natural wisdom of the elite. What might we point to as the characteristic illusions generated by democracy?

The first illusion must be that those who proclaim themselves democrats actually believe it. I am not thinking here of sinister people who might want to establish a dictatorship of some kind, nor of those realists who think democracy is merely the least worst of constitutions. Most people these days bow the head to democracy, and Western thinkers and politicians advise all peoples to take it up, but what they are actually supporting is a package of liberal and democratic practices in which "what the people actually want" is regarded with some suspicion. Intellectual liberal democrats are dismayed that the public at large often has "unsound" or "reactionary" ideas about the punishment of criminals, especially after some exceptionally vile crime has been reported in the newspapers. Liberals are thus keen on entrenching a whole apparatus of rights designed to limit not only what governments might do, but also what a vibrant popular opinion might want them to do. There is even a vocabulary to distinguish good democratic opinion from bad, the latter being denigrated as "populist." It would indeed be foolish to think that the demos is always right, if only because polling data reveal how unstable its opinions often are. It would be no less foolish, of course, to think that those who mistrust popular opinion possess a superior kind of wisdom. One of the most basic principles of life must be that human folly comes in all shapes and sizes. Those who imagine they are wiser than others may well be the most dangerous.

Realist critics of democracy—and realism is a doctrine that takes its name from proclaiming itself superior to illusions—often take the line, as we have seen, that all democracies are fundamentally concealed oligarchies. The famous suggestion is that of Robert Michels who posited an "iron law of oligarchy," while such theorists as Pareto and Schumpeter emphasized the inescapable element of elitism in any activity. Modern electorates consisting of millions of voters clearly cannot make policy, and visionary projects that might permit this to happen (such as buttons available in every home to be pressed regularly on the questions of the day) merely reveal that the depth of ignorance and incomprehension about the business of governing among electors is bottomless. The activity of ruling requires a great deal of experience of the world, combined with specialist knowledge in economics and other areas. The result is that it is conducted by professional politicians and experts. Considerations of this kind suggest that what we think of as democracy is actually some form of accountable oligarchy, one that we the people can get rid of every so often. That is, however, rather less satisfactory than the promise of democracy, which was to release us from *all* partial determinants of public policy.

Here again we run into the question of how the will of the people might realistically issue in public policy. It is a problem so widely recognized that a whole literature revolves around attempts to deal with it. Philosophers sometimes dream of an ideal speech situation in which the fact that the opinions of press barons are vastly more influential than those of others will no longer distort democratic debate. The dream is of a "deliberative democracy." Here and elsewhere, as we shall see in the next section, the problem, if it is a problem, is construed as one of inequality, and inequalities come in many shapes—financial, educational, and so on. That each member of society should count for one, and none for more than one, is a defensible criterion of democracy so long as we are thinking merely of voting rights. The absurdities, fantasies, and incomprehensions of the many people in the state on whose wisdom no one could rely would be likely to cancel out—though twentieth-century history might well caution us against relying too heavily on this optimistic assumption. Alternatively, the problem may be taken as one of connecting popular support with representation in the legislature. That problem inclines many democrats to embrace the idea of proportional representation as a system more democratic than the eccentricities of "first past the post." Proportional representation may solve one version of the representation problem, but only at the cost of creating a politics of endless compromise. It is excellent in some circumstances, and not in others. As with all projects of constitutional perfection, the solution to one problem merely creates another problem somewhere else.

One current way of formulating the illusions attaching to some complex practice is by constructing paradoxes or contradictions out of the principles implicit in it. The philosopher Richard Wollheim once argued for a democratic paradox by suggesting that in voting, the democrat wills whatever policy he supports, but as a democrat also wills the policy that has majority support. Is this incoherent? It is a common situation in life that we may prefer A to B, but B to C, and so on. There is, however, one paradox that does seem to me to generate profound problems not for democracy itself, but for democracy as it is currently practiced in Western states. Let us call it "the wisdom paradox."

The activity of governing a state deals with matters of life and death, of justice and internal peace. These require wisdom. The case for a very limited electorate is that it ought to be composed of those with experience in the law and other practical activities, and it would therefore be a source of prudence and wisdom in civic affairs. The wisdom claimed in past times was sometimes hard to find, but no practical activity can be free of misjudgment, and Europeans rubbed along with arrangements of this general kind for a long time. But with the coming of democracy, the question arises as to whether we can expect anything better—or indeed as good—from an electorate consisting of everybody. The basic democratic claim, after all, is that universal suffrage expresses all interests; it leaves aside whether it can express these interests *wisely and prudently*. Could we imagine it to be a repository of wisdom and good sense? It seems unlikely, for who are "the people"? Politicians may well say they are sound and we should trust the people, but their business involves them in flattering their patrons. Psychiatrists often tell us that about a quarter of the population suffers from some kind of mental disturbance at one time or another. Like all statistics of this kind, you can make up your own numbers to taste, but common experience certainly supports the general point. Again, as the old joke has it, half the population is of less than average intelligence. And educational-ists periodically freeze our blood with reports of the high propor-tion of people who cannot recognize their country on a map, or think that Winston Churchill or George Washington belonged in the Middle Ages. These, then, are the people who choose the team of politicians who govern us from time to time. Here, then, we have a notable problem of democracy, but not yet a paradox.

The paradox emerges as democratic governments begin to involve themselves in the details of social life. Members of society commonly find themselves afflicted by misfortunes such as single parenthood, debt, adult illiteracy, obesity, and a variety of addic-tions, and they commonly entertain attitudes toward other people that will get them in trouble with the law if they are not careful. Many people, it seems, do not have the right feelings toward women, homosexuals, and members of other races. The govern-ment thus comes increasingly to recognize the lack of wisdom found in the ordinary lives of its subjects. Many members of the electorate seem to be incapable of making rational judgments; similarly, significant numbers cannot take responsibility for many aspects of their lives. The taxation policy of modern governments conveys the same judgment. Between 30 and 50 percent of the wealth of modern democratic states is taxed and addressed to poli-cies that the government judges necessary. Some of these poli-cies supply collective goods such as defense and justice, things that any government must supply. Much of this taxation on the other hand redistributes wealth to the needy and the incompe-tent, something that, in earlier times, the rich (intermittently) did themselves. Governments feel that they will make a better fist at helping the poor if they take into their own hands the power to supply charity to those who need it.

The inescapable conclusion is that the rulers of democratic states judge the populations of democratic states to be incompe-tent over a whole range of important matters—yet these are the very people who are charged by the constitution with deciding who should have the power to rule them. The paradox arises because the foolish are deciding who the wise are. People often legislatively judged foolish may determine who as our governors shall have the vast powers of deciding the conditions under which we today live. And we might say that this is a problem whose salience increases over time because democratic governments have revealed an almost continuous drive to take more and more control over the details of society, and particularly to judge more and more people unable to live their own lives.

Indeed, the problem today seems even worse. The more power and resources of which a government disposes, and the more extensive the area it seeks to control, the more important it is that governments should have a high level of wisdom and competence. But what rational person, contemplating his or her rulers in current democratic states, could think to himself or herself: "These are marvelously rational people, and it is good that they should have taken out of my hands so vast a store of resources and such a wide range of duties that might otherwise fall to me." The people in democratic states are thus constitutionally declared to be wise, and administratively declared to be venal and stupid. It is a remarkable situation.

5.   DEMOCRACY AS PROCESS AND IDEAL

Democracy as a constitution aims to eliminate oppression. What counts as oppression here is notably difficult, since the liberties enjoyed by those living in Western societies vastly exceed what other cultures might even dream of. For some enthusiasts, however, almost any kind of inequality counts as oppression, and in those terms, it is difficult even to conceive what a completely non-oppressive society might be. But however defined, oppression is what democracy as an ideal eliminates. This is no mean ambition, and it seems to adumbrate a fully democratic society as one that makes available to each of its members the full panoply of benefits possible in, and appropriate to, a modern society. They range from material things on the one hand to respect and attention on the other. Indeed—that's barely the half of it. The real aim is to make not just our Western states but the entire world conform to the current bourgeois image of consumption in our times. It is indeed true that an underlying austerity common in radical programs would surface as a rejection of what is called "consumptionism" in our world. Saving the planet is thought to require cutting back on the use of many kinds of resources currently utilized by Western populations. This means that the benefits projected for non-Western societies would be significantly less than those disposed of by the rich of today. They would still be considerable, however.

This is a program of such vaulting ambition that only satirical exaggeration can begin to grasp its scope. How, for example, will one equalize the sexual pleasures available to attractive and less attractive people? But satire here borders on reality, because with each new generation, new and ingenious ways of making advantages or benefits available to everybody, ways that no one had previously conceived of, can suddenly become real political issues. Examples would be fertility treatments for lesbian couples, gay adoption rights, or a right for atheists to teach in religious schools.

"Democracy" in this role has become a portmanteau standing for a variety of programs, and some components of the project are likely to be advanced under other names—social justice being probably the most common, corporate social responsibility another. In its political and constitutional role, democracy refers to a *process* by which the ideal is thought to be advanced, but in its role as a moral or social idea, it stands for an *outcome*, a criterion of what is morally desirable by contrast with which our current world is regarded as dramatically deficient. Indeed, the moral ideal here covers the entire spectrum of whatever happiness a human life is thought to be capable of, and the contrast between how we actually live and how we might (in terms of this program) live is so dramatic as to cause many people in Western states to experience a kind of moral nausea or perhaps hysteria, as they contemplate the widespread indifference other people have to this ambition. The nausea is particularly acute because the technological inventiveness and the wealth of Western societies convey the idea that these possibilities of universal human happiness might well be seized by us, were it not that our blindness and venality prevent it from happening. It is a strange fact that the very success of Western societies in achieving so wide a diffusion of benefits no other civilization has dreamed of should generate so passionate a hatred of that society itself. It is not merely that we enjoy those benefits; it is that we have *invented them as conceptions of benefit* in the first place. They were not at all the pre-established dreams of impoverished cultures.

Equality and inclusion are the slogans under which the democratic program and its many analogues are advanced. Modern societies are in fact pretty inclusive, and an immense variety of possible activities is now available to all, activities that were in the past limited to a few. But that is to miss the point. We are indeed much more open than states had been in the past, but the scandal lies in contrasting present facts with the visions of what would be possible if only we had the will. A realist critic would certainly want to ask whether such an idea of possibility could be distinguished from fantasy.

In contemporary societies, anyone can do more or less anything as long as he or she has the requisite skill or dedication. Access is thus conditional on capacity. The project of democracy as a telos, which is to say as an ideal embracing the whole of mankind, is to remove these conditionalities. The proud ant must be no more "advantaged" than the indolent grasshopper. The people who become rich commonly have invested a good deal of effort and intelligence in their enterprise; those who get into universities must have passed examinations, and the very word "industry" refers to the work and enterprise without which wealth cannot be created. These considerations are brushed to one side, partly by pointing to the large element of chance in genetic endowment, and partly by emphasizing the inter-generational elements in the distribution of goods. The basic idea that some people deserve more than others is rejected because it entails that other people deserve less. Only a failure to understand the role played by social conditions in distributing advantage and disadvantage in our societies is thought to sustain the morality of deserving.

Social conditions, then, both reveal and explain the injustices by which modern societies are characterized. Contemporary argument finds the evidence above all in a variety of statistical "gaps" between what one set of people (generally the rich, the middle class) enjoy, and what the other set does not. There is a "gap," for example, in life expectancy between rich and poor, a gap in university entrances between social classes, a gap in medical treatments available, not to mention the immense "gaps" in available goods between nations and cultures. The gaps get larger the wider one casts one's empirical net—the gap between the poor in underdeveloped countries and the rest, for example. The range of the democratic ideal is certainly not limited to contemporary states. The ideal's ambition is vast: today our own society, tomorrow the world.

The question then becomes: why do these gaps exist? The answer might be that the rich, or at least quite a lot of them, work harder and are more careful about the consequences of their actions. Machiavelli thought that political success (and to some extent human life) depended on two things: *virtu* (or smartness and excellence) and *fortuna* (the goddess of random unpredictability), with *fortuna* determining about half, or perhaps a little more, of the outcomes. The classical liberal tends to see desert as determining the current distribution of goods in modern society, while the dedicated democrat sees nothing else but *fortuna*. For according to the emerging democratic ideal, benefits are a function of those things called *social conditions*. It is time to consider them a little more closely.

F. A. Hayek once argued that the adjective "social" was capable of reducing any expression to vacuity, and he was largely right. Everything is in one way or another social, so we should focus on the term "conditions." In the radical doctrine we are considering, a "condition" has two distinct meanings. The first refers to the benefits, advantages, and resources of which any particular person or group disposes. The "social condition" of the rich is in this sense different from that of the poor; they dispose of vastly more "advantages." I have put quotes around "advantages" because it is a characteristic feature of democratic reasoning that terms such as "advantages," "privileges," and "benefits" are taken to be absolute, and absolutely desirable. In fact, of course, no social condition is significant except in relation to some human response to it. But in this rather limited manner of thinking, the social condition of the successful is radically different from that of the disabled or the unemployed. In these terms, every society is composed of a variety of social locations that may be abstractly specified in terms of the advantages or disadvantages attaching to them. Any given society, then, is made up of a variety of social conditions, and some are—unjustly—more attractive than others.

The second meaning of a "social condition" is causal. It supposedly determines what goes on in society. The poor are more likely to commit crimes than the rich, and the favored explanation of this averaged distribution of crimes is that they do so as a direct response to their social conditions. The explanatory form is that crimes are committed to achieve benefits, and the rich who have them don't need to, but the poor, lacking benefits, tend to take to crime. Again, some people are of course naturally more intelligent, more engaging, more energetic than others, but they have done nothing to deserve such qualities, and it is unjust that, as well as enjoying these advantages, they should also enjoy higher prestige and more money.

Here then we have an entirely consistent form not merely of determinism, but virtually of fatalism. Everything follows from the distribution of social conditions, and even the moral qualities that might lead one to challenge and overcome such a distribution of *fortuna* are themselves social conditions. Incentive structures can be recognized (they are themselves social conditions), but moral autonomy cannot. There is, of course, a logical difficulty in this doctrine, for the democratic critic is himself behaving morally far beyond what his social condition might seem to mandate. How does the social critic achieve release from the dread grip of social conditions? Where does such a person come from? It seems as if the project of using the power of the state to transform the human condition and redeem humanity from an unjust social system is the one thing that floats free of the dread grip of social conditions. Here we touch on the dangers of self-refutation inherent in many forms of ideal radicalism: everything is determined, but I am free! This was a problem that Marx solved by moving the moralizing drive out of individuals and entrenching it in the whole dialectic of history. The idea that a fully democratic or communist or socially just society is being incubated in the womb of history is remarkably improbable, but it does at least solve the logical problem that has been raised.

Democracy as an ideal contrasts dramatically with the moral and religious conceptions that dominated European thought until recent times. Classically, human beings were prone to a form of overreach called "hubris" that was liable to result in nemesis. In Christian terms, human life is essentially imperfect, for human beings are sinful creatures. Many ways of construing such imperfection have been suggested. Traditionally, original sin stemmed from the disobedience that destroyed the perfection of the Garden of Eden. Pride and willfulness kept erupting into human affairs. In the modern world, some philosophers have recognized individualist practices as potentially disruptive of social harmony, while others (such as Adam Smith) have argued that individualism was a dynamic on which vibrant economies depended.

Indeed, we may diagnose two conflicting views of modern Western states. In the first, divergent human projects and aspirations could not help but clash with one another, but such conflicts could be kept within limits by the rule of law. In the second view, individualist disruptions of harmony result from moral faults such as selfishness and willfulness. In the familiar rhetoric of contemporary politics, classical liberals are to be found espousing the conflict view of modern states, while social democrats and other radicals are focused on the hope of an ultimate harmony. The hope is that the plural society in which we live might be transformed into a true community. The idea of democracy is clearly a version of the second view, as is, of course, the philosophy of Karl Marx in which capitalism is diagnosed as the fertile source of all evils.

Democracy as an ideal is thus a version of the hope that a radical transformation of modern states could bring them into conformity with this ideal. The ideal is that of a cooperative form of human life in which mutual helpfulness supersedes the competition on which modern societies are based. Class struggle, imperialism, ignorance, prejudice, and many other evils have been suggested as accounting for earthly imperfections, and what they all have in common is the view that the resolute use of rationality and civil power might overcome these (often sinister) barriers to a better world, and that this should be the overriding moral and political imperative of modern life. There is little that is new about this ideal; much of it derives from earlier Christian views of such virtues as love and charity. What is new is the idea that the ideal can be actualized on Earth by moral, social, and political action. As we have seen, this is a breathtaking ambition: nothing less is involved than the project of transforming the human condition, man taking human destiny out of the hands of God and into his own hands. It is the Titans storming Heaven. Historically speaking, it is a modification of the ideological endeavors of recent centuries, in which men fought against such essential evils of the world as capitalism, imperialism, nationalism, and other forms of so-called false consciousness. But grand ideological experiments are understandably less attractive since the fall of communism, and what we now have is a set of piecemeal revisions that will, it is hoped, guide us along the right road.

6. DEMOCRACY AS COLLECTIVE SOCIAL SALVATION

Western politics—which is to say the whole political tradition, because politics as a manner of ordering a society is essentially a European development—is marked by the imprint of theological doctrines. A reliable way of getting politics wrong is to ignore this connection. The basic idea of Christianity is salvation, a life lived in terms of divine commands that might—but might not—influence one's destiny in the afterlife. An almost instinctive response to Christian doctrine is to think (as Pelagius did) that one may earn one's way to heaven by being good, but in the more muscular variations of the doctrine, salvation depended on God's inscrutable will, and who would be saved, and who not, had been prefigured long before our earthly lives. However we lived our lives might indeed reflect such a divine destiny, but certainly could not influence it. The important thing for the pious Christian was to live in accordance with divine will, and in hope. The rest was none of his business.

In early modern times, the emergence of individualism as part of a much greater concern with secular life evolved a moral vocabulary distinguishing between self-interest and the interests of others, between selfishness and altruism. In these terms, a concern with personal salvation might be construed as a merely selfish aspiration, and one political tradition, which included Rousseau and Marx among its exponents, took this line. In doing so, of course, they were also rejecting the whole idea of salvation in an afterlife. In the modern world, ideas about survival after death lost much of their force. These were among the changes from which emerged a modified idea of salvation as merely a condition of things beyond the frustrations of our present condition.

From this point of view, it was the very idea of individuals seeking salvation by pleasing God that pitted man against man and itself constituted in part the oppression of imperfect societies. A new belief in salvation as a collective good thus took on a morally superior character because it was an unselfish aspiration. What had in earlier times been human life understood as a drama involving both heaven and earth now came to be simplified as a drama of earthly concerns alone. Indeed, a common if rather simple criticism of radical utopians was to suggest that belief in heaven had merely been transposed to earth. Like most new developments in moral opinion, this change claimed to be morally superior to what it had superseded: atheists and socialists saw themselves as exhibiting both an altruistic concern for others as well as a realistic courage not found in earlier generations forever on their knees before God. Pride in adhering to collective ideas of salvation has indeed been a recurring feature of much modern thought. The fall of communism was accompanied by a comedy in which those for whom that particular social dream had collapsed nonetheless prided themselves on the fact that, unlike most people lost in the endless search for merely personal satisfactions in life, they had cared enough to seek to improve the human condition. No doubt they had backed the wrong horse, but at least they had faced up to the big questions.

The idea that the business of life is to work toward the creation of a new and better society is from one point of view a political version of the immemorial occultist doctrine that the world is divided between an enlightened elite and a sleeping majority.

Most human beings are heedless victims of the succession of appetites and aversions, but a few—the saints, the philosophers, the Sufi, the guru, the possessors of the true understanding of the world, perhaps—have alone recognized the realities of the human condition. The doctrine is sometimes identified with the Gnostic heresy of early Christianity, and it shares with that heresy the basic conviction that the society or world in which we actually live is essentially evil and that salvation lies elsewhere. In modern versions of this powerful idea, the conditions of salvation turn out to be collective, while what constitutes enlightenment is of course quite different from the religious ideas of much earlier times.

In earlier versions of the modern idea of social salvation, the new radical belief was thought to be revealed science superseding the superstitions of the past. The elites who thought to navigate us through the evils of modern society in order to get us to a better place had analyzed the evils of the moment—class division, imperialism, gender stereotyping, racial confusion, and much else—and looked forward to a form of salvation that almost invariably depended on the enlightened acquiring the power (in fact, usually a plenitude of power) to lock the new system into place. In more sophisticated versions of the endeavor, such as Marxism, science might itself prove also to be part of the evil order, and enlightenment thus became a higher-level form of wisdom. It all sounded intellectually sophisticated, but in the cases where elites of this kind did in fact come to power, their conduct largely consisted in the most brutally simple technological addiction to actually *making* the new society happen. A new set of rulers telling subjects how they ought to behave was about as sophisticated as these elites ever got, and it usually involved considerable violence. They understood technology as magic, because all they really understood was power. They all turned out to be a gang of sorcerer's apprentices.

The ideological frenzies of the twentieth century have largely disappeared, except in universities, but the basic impulse in our civilization toward collective salvation has not. An elite of the enlightened continues to orchestrate endeavors that aim to make us better, though fortunately in less violent and melodramatic forms than those of communists and Nazis. Today, the problem is often diagnosed as our propensity to indulge our individualist passion for consumer satisfactions and the solution now lies not in the change of political conditions espoused by the ideologists of the nineteenth and twentieth centuries, but in a change in the hearts and minds of human beings. The ideological term for the masses lost in their ideological sleep had been "false consciousness," something explained, of course, in terms of social conditions. The new version pointed to unregenerate prejudices and antipathies of many kinds. Much of it was to be dealt with by enforcing at both legal and rhetorical levels the attitudes called "political correctness." In the earlier version, false consciousness was a set of mistakes about society, mistakes that humanity's elite vanguard saw through. The new mistakes were antipathies to abstract classes of human beings, such as other races, women, homosexuals, and others. False consciousness could be recognized in terms of the true theory of society understood by Marxists, nationalists, feminists, fascists, or other ideological believers. Political incorrectness—a term seldom used in this negative form—depended on a shared moral conviction about the absolute evil of racism, sexism, homophobia, etc.

A perfect society would have to be entirely inclusive. All forms of racism failed this test, and had been irredeemably refuted by the Nazi experience. Even communism, which looked forward to an ultimate union of the whole of humanity, was undeniably discriminatory in its struggle against the bourgeoisie. The new version of salvation was, as we shall see, less systematic than piecemeal. It involved a string of separate projects such as the winding down of many capitalist endeavors in order to save the planet, the diffusion of corporate moral responsibility in closing gaps between rich and poor, governmental aid to further the equalization of conditions between the West and the Rest, and the movement of sovereign power increasingly away from states to international bodies. And it included, of course, the use of legislative power to bring these things about. Education, in this case, took on increasing elements of propaganda.

Two questions become important here. The first is to ask how this project of social perfection is to be connected with what the people want. It might well be an ideal, but does it happen to be something the demos wants? Is it, in other words, democratic in the basic sense of the word? The obvious problem is that the divisive prejudices blocking collective salvation are evidently located precisely in the hearts and minds of the people themselves. In other words, democracy as an ideal of universal happiness might seem to collide with the judgments of the people themselves. It is people themselves, after all, who want to exclude women from clubs and foreign people from top jobs, and who may be unfriendly to those of other races and religions, etc. If the people wanted to behave differently, nothing in a democratic system would stop them. We have here one more version of the old elite fallacy—or perhaps pretense—that what is (arguably at least) rational must also be democratically irresistible.

The ideological versions of this problem were solved by such brutal dogmatism as rejecting "false consciousness." The enlightened had to take control of the way the masses thought and bring a little reality into their confused lives. Relatively little has changed. One common solution to the current version of the problem is called "education." Perhaps the people are merely the victims of bad people with bad ideas. They need to be re-educated. Sometimes they are thought to have been stirred up by evil forces such as demagogues or tabloid newspapers. Some invoke the Rawlesian argument that rational choosers, if they lacked certainty that they would be accorded rights in a future social structure, must rationally favor an equal distribution of goods. The enlightened view is that we live in a corrupt and materialistic society, and the people are understandably corrupted by it, though in moments of clarity they will overcome these defects. And since salvation is collective, the basic evil may be recognized as individualism, understood (against its actual history) as consumerist and self-indulgent.

The second question to be asked is: what is the principle of this new project of social perfection? How is it to be brought about? The answer is, evidently, right belief leads to right conduct. One might think that this is so obvious that it could hardly come as news to anyone, but that would be a mistake. In earlier centuries, no one believed that being good resulted directly from having the right beliefs. On the contrary, the moral life was recognized as an arena in which human beings could not avoid having to fight against temptation, and the rules of good conduct were guides to help them in that struggle. These rules of conduct had to be applied to constantly changing circumstances. They required judgment. Confidence in the effectiveness of a standard schedule of beliefs—about preferring the good of the community above all, about treating other kinds of people always the same, about valuing diversity—would have been regarded as an oddity. The idea that a moral agent, programmed as it were with all the right beliefs, could be nothing else but a good person would have seemed fantasy. The crucial point, of course, is that the moral agent entertains no other beliefs than those that are correct. The doctrine is one of salvation by overwhelmingly correct belief.

The democratic ideal thus depends on the idea that the ultimate causes of evil are locked in the hearts of men. Social conditions do indeed often determine thought, but "education," attitude-changing, raising consciousness, and other direct operations upon hearts and minds must be part of the transition to a better society. As the ancients had it, opinion rules the world. The basic solution to the problems of the world is to change the way human beings think about each other. The problem is constituted by the way in which we think about other races, about men and women, about homosexuality, about who deserves to be rewarded and in what way. These problems have been popularly spelled out as a set of "-isms" to be removed, perhaps by criminalizing them—racism, sexism, etc.

Collective salvation, then, is the aspiration toward a world harmony in which human conflict will have been superseded by cooperation and compassionate feelings toward everybody. Could anything, one would have to ask, be more desirable? As Augustine pointed out, the aim of all conflict is peace, and here is, if not the peace that passes understanding, at least as close to it as an earthly version might manage. But before we join up to this charming utopia, we need to look much more closely into the nature of this revolution in human affairs. The question is: are we to regard it as a moral or as a social transformation of human life?

The point is that if it were a moral transformation, it could not guarantee the peace that is its explicit aim. Moral conduct is essentially indeterminate; it is the judgment of free agents responding to ideas of right and temptations of personal advantage such that the intention to do the right thing will sometimes fail. Indeed, the conclusion toward which we are driven by this line of thought is that human salvation will have to be a post-moral condition of things. For if human beings did reliably believe the right things, and act upon them, then a perfect harmony could at least be imagined. If, on the other hand, they merely struggled to abide by the rules of good conduct, no such outcome would be possible. Those who are merely trying to be good sometimes fail.

Here, then, is one dimension of the problem of democracy and the moral life. It may here be focused in terms of the distinction between the social and the moral. As we have seen, that little world "social" is deeply interesting—or perhaps profoundly uninteresting. But it is certainly a predicate whose reach never ceases to expand. Thus young people who have been brought up to behave morally are currently described as exhibiting something called "social capital," which dissolves the moral into both the social and the economic. Corporations doing what some people at least think they (morally) ought to be doing are described as exhibiting "corporate social responsibility." In other words, there is a clearly definable kind of behavior in relating to other people that can be understood mechanistically as a determinate component of conduct. The moral is being subsumed within the social. The problem with "the moral" is that it is always an arena of discussion and contestation. "The social" is discussed as a set of imperatives that do not invite controversy and contestation. This is very strange, since one of its key technical terms is "unacceptability," which would seem to wear its contestable character on its sleeve. What we have before us is thus unmistakably a doctrine, and it may come recommended in many ways. Christian clergymen often affirm it on theological grounds, and politicians use its language in extending their power to implement some element of it. It is certainly the supreme piety of our age.

And let me briefly anticipate at this point the argument to come. The supreme piety of the age is that a set of available right principles will guide us into a better world. And these principles are always one term of a duality that has hitherto dominated human responses to problems. War and peace must be replaced by peace; competition and cooperation must give way to cooperation; punishment must be abandoned in favor of its partners forgiveness and rehabilitation; and universal altruism must replace its immemorial shadow self-interest. The question might well be put as follows: Does this commitment to these soft virtues point the way to a better world? Or does it merely turn our civilization into a bird with only one wing, forever flapping helplessly as it attempts to keep us airborne in a highly dangerous world?

THE PROJECT OF
EQUALIZING THE WORLD

I. DEMOCRACY VERSUS THE DEFERENCE WORLD

"Democracy" is, then, the name for a set of political devices whose aim is to make public policy correspond to what the people want. It is also, however, the name for something much grander and more significant: namely, of an ideal society or telos, sometimes thought to be implicit in that political structure. Yet even this extended sense barely scratches the surface of its significance. For the term "democratic" clearly also refers to the view we most commonly take about what is "right and proper" in social, and thus also in moral, life. To understand these *mores*, as it were, we must consider the manners (and broach also the moral life) of an earlier time. Democracy emerged as the critic of that world, and as such critics often do, it has made its mark in part by exaggerating its own contrasting virtues.

The Europe that emerged from the Middle Ages in the fifteenth and sixteenth centuries was ordered in terms of rank, order, and degree. Individuals did indeed relate to each other in terms of individual likes and dislikes, but they did so within a framework of associative rules that tended to keep each of them in his or her sphere of life. In Tudor England, towns had become the arenas of social and economic opportunity we would now recognize. Individuality was becoming more prominent. For precisely that reason, ideas of rank and order were in everyone's thoughts. It was this sense of degree that Ulysses elaborated in the famous speech from *Troilus and Cressida*:

> Take but degree away, untune that string,
> And hark what discord follows. Each thing meets
> In mere oppugnancy.[3]

Without degree, Ulysses argued in a long speech, man becomes a wolf to man. This was the condition of things Hobbes was later to call a "state of nature," in which no man could be sure whose hand might not be against him, a "war of all against all." The significance of rank and degree was that people knew where they were. Rank generated authority, and called forth deference. Deference was the key to manners in those times because it demanded more or less automatic respect. Indeed, deference properly understood might well be taken as the essence of manners at any time. In this early modern period, however, everyone understood gradations of rank, and respected them. To encounter a person was no doubt to encounter an individual, but that individual was always to be made sense of by way of responding to the signs that revealed his or her position in society.

In these respects, early European societies resembled the civilizations of the East where, in a similar way, social intercourse required a close attention to nuance. Understanding these matters was a form of education that inculcated considerable subtlety in human relations, and may be contrasted with the bluff complacency of modern encounters between individuals. The deference world required constant wariness; its signs were revelations of power. How one behaved to others, addressed them, even the language one might use in addressing them, depended on one's place in a hierarchical order. In England, deference was a less formulaic element of manners than it was in some other places in Europe, but it was owed to anyone who might be construed as a "governor," a class of person that included not only aristocrats and the gentry, but also employers, masters of servants, schoolmasters and dons, ladies, priests, judges, women of a certain age, and many others. For as Sir Thomas Elyot remarked in advising this relatively new class of person, "where there is any lack of order needs must be perpetual conflict . . ."[4] Here was the complex system of social gradations that was to mature in later centuries into what was misleadingly described as the "English class system" and into the "English obsession with class." It was a complete system of social relations in which the young deferred to the old and men in chivalric ways to women. The feudal presumption that everyone should have someone above him or her had become the modern view that whoever acts must do so under the constraints of some system of authority. No man, as it was put, could be above the law. This was how what we admire as the rule of law emerged from medieval manners. At the apex of this system was the king, and the king himself, of course, was notionally under God. We democrats might well have found some, indeed perhaps most, elements of this form of life constricting, but it was the world, and perhaps the only world, from which our own conception of liberty was able to emerge.

The lower deferred to the higher, in all spheres of life. In this purely formal sense, some of "the higher" no doubt hardly deserved this form of respect, but that was not the point, for there was a reverse direction of respect corresponding to noblesse oblige, or what was due from the higher to the lower. Contempt for the lower orders was in the manners of the time a deplorable form of arrogance. Deference thus supplied the standard by which impudence or insolence, the refusal of due deference, was to be judged. It is a system not easy to reconstruct, because so much of it depended on evanescent features of life such as tone of voice, carriage, and demeanor. And there was, as Lord Melbourne later remarked of the Order of the Garter, "no damned merit" about it. Rank for the most part was something inherited. It was the polar opposite of meritocracy.

The absence of any definite correlation between rank and ability might be thought its defect—or alternatively, its saving grace. As a defect, it might exemplify what medieval thinkers regarded as the worst of evils—"a fool set in a high place"—or it might be thought something relaxing, in that low rank need not mean lack of self-esteem. But in any case, this criticism should not be pressed too far, because when this order of things most nearly corresponded to the ideal, those who reached the top were by no means generally incompetent. Indeed, even in later times it became evident that if a career open to talent in such areas as the civil service or the army meant the rise of careerists who could pass examinations, then the performance was not always notably superior to what had gone before. Deference was thus a principle of order that allowed European societies to function quite efficiently and to develop a very notable culture.

It is always important to remember that no ideal form of order ever corresponds to its reality. Signs of ranks were aids to orientation of conduct in this world, but they could never be adequate to all occasions; besides, we are dealing with a dynamic society and it kept on changing. An apparent solecism might thus turn out merely to be the harbinger of a modification of manners. Further, the formal beneficence of such an ordering of society could and certainly did accommodate unkindness, arrogance, and contempt. Nevertheless, it could also accommodate plenty of patronage, friendship, and charitable endeavors across the divides. The reason it could do so was that paralleling this structure of deference was a completely different form of manners: an egalitarian order based on the Christian view that all human beings are equal in the sight of God, and reinforced in England by much of the common law.

In this crucial respect, the manners of early modern Europe were in stark contrast with much of what is currently believed today, when a single set of democratic manners is thought to be the ideal. This ideal, too, is far from corresponding to our reality, but it illustrates one of the central facts of contemporary life: that we are often persuaded that there is one right principle of social and ethical life, and it is egalitarian. In early modern Europe, the reality was a balance—one is tempted to say a dialectical balance—between two competing ways of understanding human beings: as graded, and as basically equal. This complex pluralism in manners corresponded to the dominant political wisdom of the time: that the essence of a good constitution was a balance between the competing interests of the state, a balance in England between the institutions of king, lords, and commons.

Deference required formality of address, the point of which was to sustain the distance between people. The insight sustaining such formality was that distance is a necessary condition of respect. One great achievement possible as a result of formality was, paradoxically, an intensification of the possibility of intimacy, for intimacy was a privilege and never a right. Like all forms of inclusion, intimacy made one vulnerable. We are talking here of the relations between individuals encountering each other in the wider world, and that was different from the intimacies of family life, which sustained the emotional lives of most people. A customary distance between individuals was not only the condition of real intimacy, but also facilitated independence of mind and judgment. It was a practice in which classes, families, localities, and even professions could cultivate a certain collective individuality in areas such as taste, manners, and even morality. It was a world of secrets and initiations, and it was (in my judgment) a necessary prelude to the modern state. Whole topics of conversation developed—such as the weather—that would allow people to exhibit a limited friendliness without compromising their inner lives.

The sharing of inner lives constituted intimacy as one of the arts of the time. Unlike other peoples, the English allowed the grammatical barrier of the intimate "you" to fall into social disuse, something that might suggest that English life always tended to be less formal than that on the Continent. Intimacy could be revealed in many ways, but was a privilege; formality might be found even in the way in which husbands and wives addressed each other in the wider circle of the family. Democracy has set itself up above all as a critic of this formality and against the distance that it protects. In our current democratic world, individuals are often known even to strangers by their Christian names, and this has made a kind of friendship instantly available to everyone. A recent prime minister of the kingdom went so far as publicly to insist that he should be referred to as "Tony." In the deference world, by contrast, friends were fewer (as they also were in totalitarian societies) but more was at risk in the intimacies of friendship. A major secret of life has always been the art of knowing whom among one's friends one might rely on.

Why, we may ask, did democracy turn out to be so destructive of this way of life, so hostile to elites and above all to anything that might be understood as "hierarchy"? Part of the answer is that it misconstrued deference as a form of servility. For is there not something demeaning, or servile, in deferring to another human being? Are we not all basically equal to one another? And is it not often the case that many people of rank are far from being our superiors in wisdom, knowledge, or ability? Deference could be expanded into the notion of "knowing one's place," and knowing one's place became a problem as society came to be less and less a complex of "places." "Pulling one's forelock" as a sign of respect to the squire was a much-mocked form of respect that survived in some places into the twentieth century. As the deference world in its decline became generalized, class distinctions, accent, and manners might sometimes claim deference, but they would be just as likely to generate hostility, especially if upper-class indicators were combined with any sign of arrogance. Status tended to converge on wealth, but Britain remained throughout these changes a highly mobile society. In the United States, traditional forms of respect were rapidly worn away, since the world of the pioneer was one that could not work unless superiorities were merely functional, and temporary.

The attack on the deference world came from diverse sources. One such attack developed as political scientists picked up the notion that deference was an irrational hangover from feudalism, and therefore also a derogation from democracy. They commonly assumed that rational voters followed their interests, and that the interest of the working class must require more socialism. They therefore became puzzled that many workers voted Tory. How could this be? Their solution was to posit something called "the deference vote" as a specific form of political illusion. The deference voter supported the "toffs" out of a misguided belief that the upper class knew better about arcane things such as politics.

One might well judge this a rather defective theory of how democracy ought to work. Worse than that, in positing a mechanical antagonism between the interests of the rich and the working class, it notionally divided society into the kinds of automatically antagonistic collectivities that make democracy in principle unworkable. Socialist doctrines often assumed this kind of basic political antagonism by denying all complementarity to social groups. Class conflict, distinguishing oppressor and oppressed, was taken to be a form of war between elements of the state. The point of Marxism was precisely to persuade the working class that they constituted a totally distinct set of people being oppressed by the bourgeoisie, thus reproducing in Western states the conditions that later made democracy unworkable in African states, where the collective antagonism was tribal. Marxism was a mobilizing theory designed to destroy democracy and prepare the way for an enlightened elite to take power. In what may be regarded as "mature" democracies, a variety of voters make diverse judgments not entirely about their interests, but more broadly about what the good of the country requires.

This indifference to any mechanical idea of class interest was the kind of judgment for which Montesquieu admired the Roman plebeians. In the great days of the Republic, they secured the right to participate in the election of the patrician magistracies. He remarks that it would be natural to think that flatterers would persuade the plebeians to elect their own kind to these magistracies, but they continued to elect patricians, and Montesquieu adds:

> Because the people were virtuous, they were magnanimous; because they were free, they scorned power. But when they had lost their principles, the more power they had, the less carefully

they managed it, until finally, having become their own tyrant and their own slave, they lost the strength of liberty and fell into the weakness of license.[5]

In judging the past, the starting point must always be: "The past is a foreign country. They do things differently there." And in looking to the deference world of the past, we need to guard against the common but foolish assumption that we today have at last arrived at the right basic set of normative rules that should govern intercourse between human beings. Have we entirely abandoned the sentiments of past time? Is "knowing one's place" so outlandish a sentiment that it cannot possibly arise today? The answer is that our conception of a "place" is indeed often different, but the general maxim remains the beginning of wisdom. The bumptious conversationalist who won't keep quiet is someone who does not know his place. To be a guest, or a host, or a chairman at a meeting, or a new acquaintance, indeed taking a recognized role in any social situation, requires as a matter of good manners that one should "know one's place." Such functional deference, as we may perhaps call it, is not quite the same as the deference of good manners, but they often overlap.

We sometimes pride ourselves in thinking that our manner of direct contact between individuals removes the servile temptation to please others by deferring to them, but that would be a mistake. The strict codes of past times limited rather than facilitated the obsequious ways of the careerist, and flattery is so ingenious a contriver of ways to please that servility is no less a feature of our life and manners than it ever was. Indeed, social scientists study a variety of ways in which we seek to ingratiate ourselves with others.[*]

What actually limits in some degree the servile temptation to please a superior is something far more profoundly lodged in the Western psyche than egalitarian manners: namely, our taste for dealing honestly and straightforwardly with others. The power of

---

[*] See *Private Truths, Public Lies: The Social Consequences of Preference Falsification*, by Timur Kuran, Harvard University Press, 1995.

this tendency can be measured by the vocabulary of disdain for those who seek to curry favor—toady, creep, sycophant, etc. An enjoyment of free relations is a tendency essential to the carrying on of business in European society, for it mandates judgments in terms of who has the ability to do the job rather than who has the power to please. To recognize a subordinate as someone forever trying to say what he or she imagines will please is widely found intolerable. The folly of King Lear's fatal moment of making his daughters articulate their supposed love for him stands as a powerful parable on this question, and shows that our preference for the honest and straight goes back well into the deference world. Shakespeare's exemplary prince, Henry V, disdains any temptation to exploit the fear his accession to regal power might cause those who knew him only as the roistering Hal:

> This new and gorgeous garment, majesty,
> Sits not so easy on me as you think.
> Brothers, you mix your sadness with some fear:
> Not Amurath an Amurath succeeds,
> But Harry Harry . . .[6]

And he goes on briefly to tease and then to reassure the chief justice, who had punished Prince Hal for his delinquencies. It is a model account of one of the roles or "places" of a deference world.

2. FORMS OF INSTRUMENTALISM IN DEMOCRACY

Here then is the deference world that, in a very broad sense, democracy destroyed and superseded. Our next question must be to consider the character of the new democratic form of life that has superseded the deference world. But in pursuing this inquiry, we need to keep a number of qualifications in play.

The first and most basic of them is that the moral life of any modern society is a palimpsest, layer upon layer of modes of life going on side by side and often in conflict with one another. The latest moral fashion as it settles will always be modified by the survival of earlier beliefs, and some quite remarkable moralities can still be found, moralities that echo very distant centuries, especially where they are sustained by religious beliefs that will be widely seen as eccentric in modern circumstances. The Amish communities in the United States are a vivid example of this, but less distinct forms of spiritual austerity will be found in all European countries. In the behavioral buffet of Western life, distant religions such as Buddhism jostle alongside self-improvement groups cultivating occultist secrets, while long-abandoned paganisms are revived and druids roam the land. Families and regions have traditions of their own that modify the workings of the latest morality that is commending itself to a restless population. Over the last century or more, most of these new moralities present themselves to this public as things called "liberations," something that conceals many underlying continuities. "Liberation" is one of those interesting negatives of democratic life that serve to conceal their positive content. What is it, exactly, that we are being liberated from? Is it always from old and outmoded taboos? And what are we being liberated *into*? In the moral world, things are never quite what they seem, and there are few liberations without some undertow of a new servitude.

The vogue for dressing up "change" as liberation (and even more commonly as something called "reform") leads us to a second qualification of the limits of democracy as an overarching scheme of morals and manners. In our time, the rhetoric of change vastly exceeds the fact. It exaggerates greatly how much has actually changed, as against how much has merely been a reshuffling of old elements, a huffing and puffing of moral fashion. Christopher Booker once characterized our civilization in terms of neophilia, or the cult of the new,[7] a paradox brilliantly summed up in the *New Yorker*'s cartoon of the magnate telling his advertising consultant, "New's an old word. I want a new word!"

The passion for liberation has generally been accompanied by undercurrents pulling in the opposite direction: sexually speaking, for example, anything may be recognized as admirable self-expression, but pedophilia has become increasingly detested. Disciplining the young corporally is out, but a whole apparatus of punitive social orders has had to be constructed in its place.

The self characterizations of "lady" and "gentleman," remarkably, manage to survive current liberations in unpredictable corners of Anglophone life, and people who take themselves seriously in this role often proudly resist all the invitations to throw off their inhibitions and live. Decency has little place in the current litany of virtues (compassion, charitable self-sacrifice, charity, etc., drown it out) but it remains a touchstone, however difficult to define, in early twentieth-century moral practice. Even recessive versions of respectability lurk behind the scenes and domesticate themselves within households.

So much, then, for qualifications. If we now consider the general character of this new world, the most striking feature is how instrumentalist it is. Our contemporaries are above all concerned with outcomes, with bang for the buck, with getting what they want. The modern democratic citizen is a vulgar utilitarian. The point of any utterance or act is usually to achieve some specific end in the most direct possible way, though the end may not always be some contribution to the agent's own happiness. Techniques for mastering oneself and the world are the staple of endless books of self-help concerned with getting on in life. The techniques are often managerial in that they rely upon some generalization about human behavior that works best if the subject to be influenced is not fully aware of what is happening.

The critic might well say: surely this is merely human nature. Why else do we act if not to produce some desired effect? Yet there is a difference. In the deference world, individuals often acted in order to sustain and declare a valued identity they had, and this could often conflict with personal advantage. There is a large difference between performing X in order to achieve Y, and performing X (or even more commonly, not performing X) in order to sustain an identity or role, because it is one's duty. To sustain one's identity as a lady, or a gentleman, or even as an honest person, the most likely way of doing so is to refrain from doing something otherwise advantageous.

In what we have been calling "the deference world," advantages are often thrown away in the most insouciant fashion. The novels of Jane Austen, for example, are full of virtuous young women doing the right thing against what would seem to be their immediate interest in satisfying their current passion. In such novels, indeed, virtuous behavior is recognized as a value in itself, distinct from advantage, and in happy turns of plot (not altogether unknown in real life) virtue can turn out to bring advantages of its own. But the point of such acts, or refusals to act, is precisely not to gain an advantage. These acts are performed in defiance of evident advantage because they are the right things to do. This is an issue that will reappear when we discuss the moral life. The deference world in this respect was so distant from the casuistries of our own that a general sense of virtue could be indicated by such a term as "not done" without further specification. And the things that were "not done" were almost always advantageous, but demeaning.

The purposiveness of the democratic world can be seen not only at the level of personal conduct, but also, indeed supremely, in its public policies. A democratic assembly tends to understand legislation as a command addressed to the people. This accords, no doubt, with our common talk about "obeying the law." We talk of laws "forbidding" certain kinds of conduct and "encouraging" others. Sometimes, indeed, laws are thought to be a signaling system, entities that "send a message." Strictly speaking, however, these ways of thinking constitute a simpleminded misunderstanding of the rule of law. A command *means* an imperative addressed directly from a commander to an addressee, and the point of the command is extinguished with that situation or with that type of situation. A master of slaves commands his slaves. An employer can command an employee but only, of course, within the limits of an agreed relationship of employment; such a command is conditional. Indeed, in modern societies, it usually has a form somewhere between a command and a request, and there may well be cases in which the employee refuses, perhaps deciding he wants to get another job.

A law is something quite different. It is a hypothetical imperative specifying a form of conduct that attracts certain sanctions should any particular instance of the conduct be defined as an offense by a court. The law does not "forbid" murder; it simply specifies a variety of penalties for a variety of different kinds of killing. This view of law provides the formal sense in which living under law is what we in the West understand as freedom, and the point is thus very far from being a piece of legal pedantry. The creativity of Western societies in part results from pursuing one's interests by finding lines of conduct that do not incur the sanctions of law. From a hostile point of view, freedom consists in the search for "loopholes."

The really spectacular case of a demos in hot pursuit of a practice it sought to prohibit was the Prohibition Amendment passed in the United States after the First World War. Its popular point was to stop people drinking. It was famously a disaster, and was repealed by the Twenty-first Amendment in 1933. It failed for a reason that we can generalize. Legislation as command assumes that an obedient population will accept the command, but will also carry on doing everything else as before. It is of course an illusion, as we shall see later, to imagine that a government can change one component of social life without affecting the incentive structure to which populations respond, but it is an illusion remarkably resistant to experience. The prohibition of liquor sales created a boom industry in illicit liquor, and the result was that opportunities for gangsterism in 1920s America proliferated. Though the Amendment was repealed, many of its evil consequences are with us to this day.

Redistributive taxation in Western democracies is another example of the way in which some governments assume that a society is a mechanical contraption that can be manipulated to produce any required result. As taxation rises in order to fund increasing welfare for redistribution to the poor, the productive parts of the economy adjust to the new situation, sometimes by avoiding the law, sometimes by cutting back on enterprise because the rewards are less satisfactory, and sometimes by moving resources to lower-tax economies. Here we are in the territory of the famous Laffer Curve, which formalizes that area of taxation in which the taxing authority (counterintuitively) gets a larger net sum when it cuts rather than increases the tax demand. The worst consequence of the reckless use of governmental taxing policies is their encouragement of tax evasion. Such a consequence erodes the very fabric of a civil society, for it not only brings the law into contempt but also erodes the habits of compliance on which civil order depends. Redistributive taxation is often defended as socially just, and therefore as being a moral as well as a civic obligation, but no one who observes the incompetence of governments in first raising large sums by taxation and then spending so much of it wastefully is likely to be impressed by this invocation of morality. Since the crisis of the welfare state toward the end of the twentieth century, opinion has increasingly recognized the force of the empirical finding that lower taxes correlate strongly with prosperous economies.

In our time, however, there remains something that seems irreducibly dirigiste about what we might call "the psyche of the demos." The traditional balance between evils that we may change and evils that we must put up with has been lost in the public imagination. In the popular view, *anything* can be achieved that governments decide to do. Our sense of reality has been seriously disrupted by the vast augmentation of the power available to Western governments. One consequence of this development has been the propensity of politicians to curry favor with the electorate by promising to solve everyday problems. One needs to distinguish between the two kinds of power generating this dream of governmental omnipotence. One kind of power is technological, and another kind stems from what states learned about the uses of authority during the world wars of the twentieth century. Western populations think, then, in terms of "abuses" occurring in society and the power, and the responsibility, of governments exercising popular authority to remove them. This power has been used in various countries to "forbid" smoking, hunting with dogs, smacking children, and a variety of other activities previously left to the discretion of individuals.

This disposition of democratic governments to exercise their authority by command has, then, expanded the size of the law codes of Western states enormously. The situation, however, is even worse than this might suggest. For democracies have now taken over what was once a celebrated device of despotism. The device consists in suggesting that some group in society ought voluntarily to limit its activities in some way, with the additional threat that if the group fails to act satisfactorily, the government will exercise its power to legislate. This is among the devices that are now coming to be recognized as "soft totalitarianism."

Instrumentalizing legislation may thus be counted as a corruption of our civic life. And the question we must ask is: where does this corruption originate? The answer is that in the democratic world, one principle alone is thought to hold the secret of the right thing to do—namely, democracy itself. And that principle itself only makes sense on democratic assumptions—namely, that there is a democratic will and that it agrees on the desirability of the one right policy. It follows that the test of democratic authority is democratic desirability. A law is legitimate to the extent that it has been validated by democratic decision. Here we clearly have a problem, in that if desirability is the test of legitimacy, those who contest the desirability of a policy might be thought justified in rejecting its authority. It is particularly a problem in the attitudes of migrants coming from lands in which the full workings of democracy are poorly understood.

Confusion about the legitimacy of democracy and its limits has resulted from rejecting the principle on which Western states have previously been governed: namely, the principle of a balance between desires sustained by a law. That inherited principle has traditionally sustained the British constitution as combining the unity of a decision-making ruler, the wise council of an aristocratic assembly, and a representative chamber charged with expressing the people's will. And the advantage of a system of checks and balances, by contrast with a democratic system, is that it can recognize conflict between ways of life as a standard feature of modern states rather than as a defect in need of remedy. Conflict is creative: the conflicting parties and ideas generate sparks from each other. Unanimity, were it ever to be achieved in practice, is merely debilitating. And the pretense that uncontested agreement on any general issue might be found in a modern state merely entrenches illusion at the heart of authority.

3. RIGHTS AND THE SOURCES OF DEMOCRATIC LEGITIMACY

The twentieth-century vogue for grandiose declarations of rights is the most influential version of the belief that there is a simple world of moral correctness to which all human beings "ultimately" ought to give allegiance. The significance of rights is a huge subject, but we cannot avoid it because it has become an inseparable part of the package called "democracy." And the first thing to note is how odd this is. To codify moral and political life in terms of rights is to remove judgments from the competence of the demos and transfer it into the hands of governments, judges, and lawyers. In other words, the assumed legitimacy of rights has a different source from democracy, and may often come into direct conflict with the will of the people. The early point of declarations of rights was to establish an independent moral realm, independent, that is, of politics, and also, of course, of religious orthodoxy. Rights became a central part of the project, of which democracy was also part, to create a good, indeed potentially a perfect, society, on the basis of reason alone, reason being taken (by contrast with religion) to be able to transcend merely partisan or sectarian disputes.

What actually is a right? "I have a right to X" makes a right seem like an object that each individual may possess. One has only to advance the most elementary questions about rights to recognize what odd things they are, and if one remembers how over the last century individuals have been killed, dispossessed, and oppressed in so many imaginative ways, one might well think the whole idea that we *have* rights a ghastly joke. Most current declarations of rights originate in some grandiose international body such as the United Nations, and their scope is, on this ground alone, thought to be universal. They are binding on the whole of humanity. But the only place where rights more or less correspond with reality is, of course, in the countries of the West.

This is no doubt the reason why other cultures often repudiate rights as a form of moral imperialism in which Western values are exported to, and imposed upon, other cultures and civilizations. This charge is made particularly in the case of the rights of women, for these are the rights that clash most dramatically with the customs of other cultures.

To repeat: what is a right? Grammatically it sounds like a possession we have, on a level with skin, eyes, feet, and so on. This is confused, for a right is evidently, if understood in such empirical terms, a mere phantom. One cannot smell it, touch it, feel it, etc. What is clear is that a right is a complex relationship holding between the individual possessor of the right, the authority declaring it and also perhaps enforcing it, and any third parties who might want to violate it. My right to life is asserted and protected by the state, which applies sanctions to anyone who kills me. Property is a right of a similar kind. It is notorious that I can have a right to property without actually having any property, something that socialists have long thought a major defect in the whole idea of rights. But it is precisely this disjunction between the abstract right and its instantiation that is the essence of the matter: only the simplest kind of instrumentalist thinks that a right to property is valueless unless one actually owns some. Nevertheless, it is virtually impossible to find anyone who owns absolutely nothing; Mr. Gandhi had his loincloth, and would no doubt value protection against anyone tempted to take it away from him by force. But then, as critics commented at the time, it took a lot of money to keep Mr. Gandhi in appropriate poverty.

Other rights are rather different: they involve receiving benefits, such as food, money, or medical care, under defined circumstances. Back in the 1940s, the United Nations brought itself into disrepute by entrenching the right to holidays with pay as a universal human right, something that most workers outside the West could barely conceive of, much less enjoy. Here, then, we have a set of rights that operate in two ways: they satisfy a need in cases where the bearer of the right cannot satisfy that need out of his own resources, and they also entrench a status. The element of status is involved, for example, when an employee cannot be dismissed by an employer unless a tribunal can be persuaded that dismissal has good cause. Here is a striking development of the idea of a right, because the costs of its implementation are off-loaded by governments onto employers. Here is the state's authority to coerce being used in a new way. The right in this case imposes a duty, and also a cost, on a separate party, namely the employer. And this is a significant move, because it turns what in one sense is a contractual relationship between employer and employee into a kind of *status*. It will be remembered that Sir Henry Maine in the nineteenth century had interpreted the evolution of European states out of the Middle Ages into the modern world as a move from status to contract. What we seem to have in rights of this kind, then, is a reversion to a society consisting of "places" that are enjoyed not quite unconditionally, but certainly irrespective of the judgments of one of the parties to the relationship. And this is a highly significant feature of the way democracies are evolving.

In fact, the more one looks at the idea of rights, the more they seem to reveal contemporary assumptions about human life that otherwise might be obscure. Early formulations of rights were the playthings of philosophers whose aim was merely to formulate a core of rationality underlying the moral practices of Europeans. Locke thought it plausible to do so in terms of the rights to life, liberty, and property, and it is clear that no benefits come attached to this formula, and the only duties on others are not at all specific. The same is true of the Jeffersonian formula about life, liberty, and the pursuit of happiness, even though in the American case, rights were making their fatal move out of the philosopher's lab, as it were, and into the hurly-burly of politicians, lobbyists, and judges.

I say "their fatal move" because, as it happens, I spent most of my life without any rights at all. I grew up in the Antipodes and have spent a large part of my life in England, and it was only with the Human Rights Act of 1997 that I acquired a set of rights. No doubt this is to put the matter in a misleading way. I had no rights, but I did have freedom under the common law, a form of freedom that could be rationalized as the possession of only one basic right: namely, to do whatever I felt like unless there was a law restricting it. This was what was in those parts understood, correctly, as freedom. It might be thought that declarations of rights would advance my freedom because they would codify the details of the freedom that I so long enjoyed. The difficulty, however, is that while specifying one or two basic rights, as Locke and others have done, is harmless enough, specifying lots of rights immediately sets up the problem of how these rights relate to one another. How much should my right to privacy limit the freedom of the press? The more rights are multiplied, the more helplessly I am delivered into the hands of authority. My unselfconscious enjoyment of freedom before we fell into a world of rights seldom raised these issues.

Declaring rights has other bad effects, and they have been widely noted. In the past, moral life was understood basically in terms of the rather stern dictates of duty. This was, among other things, a relaxing opinion, in the sense that having done one's duty, one was free to enjoy oneself. Rights, which correspond to duties over much of the moral terrain, but not all of it, lack this benefit. Enjoying rights does not at all tell one what other things one ought to be doing. Further, rights have psychological effects. They often make people aggressive and contentious. Rights can be the vehicles of a tiresome form of egoism and self-advancement. The result is that moralists today constantly complain that we need to restore our sense of duty.

There are more serious problems. One is that, like all codifications, declarations of rights engage in a hopeless battle against custom, taste, and circumstance. Many governments signed up to the European Convention on Refugees in 1951 and now find that it lands them with obligations that have become inappropriate to their current political life. The enthusiasm politicians have for traveling to faraway places and signing up to virtuous commitments whose impact will fall on their hapless successors is an important weakness of modern constitutions. Such commitments not only circumscribe the power of the relevant rulers, but also that of their constituents. It is a strange illusion to believe that we in our generation have finally arrived at the morality that will fit all human beings for all the time to come. No doubt, in terms of the realities of world politics, affirmations of the right to life, to be free of torture, and so on are beneficent and sometimes have an effect. They certainly had an effect on the weakening of Soviet tyranny, in the form of the Helsinki accords. But they will soon come to feel as restrictive as an ill-fitting suit.

Rights are commonly thought to codify and entrench freedom, but freedom cannot be captured in a rule. Among many other things, it depends on imagination. It is in using liberty to do things not previously contemplated that one enjoys it. Freedom, as we have noted, is essentially doing any of the infinitely many things that are not sanctioned by law. Rights threaten this understanding, for after a generation or so, peoples living under a schedule of rights are likely to think that they are free only to do those things they have been given as rights. In other words, rights have a tendency to slide into being understood as permissions, and this is a cast of thought appropriate to servility, not to freedom.

These points are important, but they do not quite get to the heart of the matter. If we consider Locke's rights—to life, liberty, and property—we note that they do not confer benefits. What good are they then, the eager radical may ask. The answer is that they are rules of the game of life. They express a ludic conception of how people live: not all people, of course, but those who live in freedom, and value living that way. And this may be illustrated in terms of English history. Magna Carta conferred no benefits on anyone. It merely restated the rules governing how the barons related to each other, a set of rules that had been disrupted by a thug called John who held the office of king. Such declarations tend to formulate the point in abstract terms that go beyond the immediate interests of those involved, which is why all the English look back to Magna Carta as a foundation of certain freedoms. What, again, is the Habeas Corpus Act of 1671? It certainly confers no substantive benefits on anyone. You might, perhaps, transpose it into a right not to be subjected to arbitrary arrest. But it is best understood as stating clearly a long-standing rule about the relation between the citizen and his rulers. Let me repeat the basic point, because it is central to my argument: The life of Europeans in modern times has been strongly marked by their addiction to understanding human beings less as creatures having needs than as participants in what we may call the game of life. And this, as we shall see in later sections, is central to their idea of the moral life.

This ludic conception of the human condition runs right through European life, but is perhaps most purely seen among the English. The Christian religion was developed and elaborated by critics, often philosophers, whose ideas commonly got out of hand and threatened what any religion of belief must have—a settled orthodoxy. Christianity, in other words, emerged out of conflicting views of its truth, and to some extent it is still changing in that way. Our view of science is as a competition of hypotheses. What we respect as "science" is the set of hypotheses that has, perhaps only for the moment, stood the test of criticism. The economy, again, has emerged out of the competitive endeavors of individuals and corporations to make a profit by satisfying wants. And it is the English who in the late nineteenth century codified the playing of many different games in terms of a set of authoritative rules. Above all, perhaps, justice in the common law is not the outcome of an Inquest or Inquisition conducted by experts, but the result of a competitive game argued out by lawyers.[8]

The problem with games, of course, is that they usually have winners and losers. The games may be inclusive, but the outcomes are certainly not. The winners in economic games have a good deal more prestige than the losers, and are generally rather richer. It is true that Western civilization has ingeniously created such a variety of winning posts that losing in one sense becomes winning in another. The poor were often thought to be closer to God, and these days are often thought to be more authentic than the rich, but these spiritual benefits, if taken seriously, have not been thought to weigh heavily on scales dominated by materialistic and egalitarian concerns. In any case, even the most ludic of characters will conduct himself in other ways, in dealing with his family, his friends—and also with "the needy." In other words, charitable endeavors will play, and have always played, a prominent part in European life. But what we find in schedules of rights is that rules formalizing the ludic world have been run together with the desires of love and charity, so that formal rules turn into substantial entitlements, and both are confusingly called "rights." A procedural right to property is not at all the same thing as a substantive right to a quantity of money if one should be unemployed. And it is this confusion between needs and the game—concealed by the description of all these relationships as "rights"—that opens the door to the ceaseless advance of governmental management of the way we live.

The very idea of democracy is, it has to be said, at the root of the illusion that all rights are benefits conferred by governments. It may well be argued that a welfare benefit paid by a government is indeed conferred by the state, though the resources for paying it must previously have come from the people themselves by taxation. All political bribes are financed with our own money. But where we are concerned with rights to life, to liberty, to freedom of speech, to free assembly, and other such basic assumptions of a free society, we find firstly that we are dealing with rules and not benefits, and secondly that these are rules responding to dispositions prevalent in free societies. The problem with universalizing rights is thus that other cultures frequently lack the basic ludic disposition on which the successful world of rights depends. They do not consider that life is a game, any more than did Marx and other socialists, who thought that the business of governments was satisfying needs rather than enforcing the rules of the game. Without the ludic disposition of Westerners, rights will always be a mismatch with other cultures.

In this abstract world, things that seem to have one function or significance can turn out to have a quite opposite effect. Democracy is the idea that the state responds to what the people want. But as the demos grows accustomed to receiving substantial benefits from the state, subjects begin to conceive of the state not as an instrument of their own will, but as an independent source of benefits. The abstraction of rights is a powerful and sometimes useful idea, but like all abstractions, it can turn reality upside down. And as a right expands beyond signifying a freedom and begins to signify an entitlement to some substantial benefit—sliding, that is to say, from life conceived of as a game to life conceived of as a collective endeavor to satisfy the needs of human beings—it begins to turn into the blueprint for a static state.

4. CULTURE AND THE DEMOCRATIC WORLD: WOMEN AND POLITICS

The selling point of rights, if one may put it that way, is that they benefit the weak and vulnerable. The strong, by contrast, might seem to have no need of rights because they have the power. If rights do indeed signal a transfer of power from the strong to the weak, then the centrality of rights in the democratic world does signal a change in the human condition. Nietzsche hardly exaggerates in talking of a "transvaluation of all values." We ought, however, to recognize that such transvaluations are slippery things. A little doubt may be in order.

That the weak should have displaced the strong as the evaluative center of contemporary liberal democracies would seem to be the ultimate triumph of the democratic hatred of hierarchy. Those at the bottom are now equal, it seems, to those at the top. But it is one of the givens of radical theory that no mere reform seriously reduces the power of the strong, who are in contemporary circumstances usually identified with the middle classes. Only a revolution would achieve that, for, as the radical slogan goes, if democracy changed anything, "they" wouldn't have let it happen. Aristocrats, landowners, warriors, capitalists, and priests have always dominated law and custom. They formulated official beliefs and religions, and appropriated a large share of the surplus production as necessary to help them sustain these onerous responsibilities. Is it likely that this basic human condition has really changed?

Democrats in the twenty-first century distance themselves from this basic radical skepticism that demands the complete overthrow of the liberal democratic powers that be. Such an idea was too closely identified with ruthless twentieth-century totalitarian regimes. Democrats are far more patient, and ready to work by using the steady infiltration of ideas of social perfection

as instruments of social transformation. They identify their political ideal instead with the rolling program of normative development we have recognized as the democratic telos. And the welfare
state is recognized as one step along the road on this journey.
But in taking at its face value this self-characterization of democratic states as being engaged in a process of empowering the
weak, we are also touching on one of the most basic objections to
democracy: namely, that it takes its standards and bearings from
the lower rather than the higher.

This may seem to be a pretty abstract criticism, because it
means little without careful specification of what is meant by
"higher" and "lower," but such specification is soon forthcoming.
One version of it may be found in Plato, whose properly ordered
state depended on the wisdom of the philosophers, and for
whom disorder and tyranny could be the only result of allowing
the lower elements of the state into the process of rule. In the
Republic, any displacement of wisdom, of the higher faculties,
from the seat of power became a slide leading first to anarchy
and then to despotism—the ultimate triumph of the lower over
the higher. Another version of the same move will of course be
found in Islam, in which democracy is thought to turn upside
down the right ordering of life derived from divine sources. These
examples make clear that democracy is likely to be rejected by any
group that believes it has access to wisdom superior to that of the
mass of the people. Different enthusiasts have judged that such
wisdom will be found in philosophy (or some version of it), or
in the true religion, or from that cocktail containing elements of
both religion and philosophy often called "ideology."[*] And all of
these claims to superiority are in conflict with democracy because
democratic legitimacy depends not on any claim about wisdom
but upon the assumed correspondence between democratic policies and the popular will.

---

[*] I have analyzed the structure of ideology in Kenneth Minogue, *Alien Powers:
The Pure Theory of Ideology*, 1985, new edition ISI Books: Wilmington, Delaware,
2008.

Democrats, of course, will instantly smell elitism in the accusation that democracy and the extension of rights amounts to handing the state over to the "lower" rather than the "higher," and indeed some skepticism about the claimed qualities of the lower and the higher will certainly be in order. Some skepticism, perhaps, but not a great deal. For the danger that the state will fall into the hands of the morally lower—of bad people—is not at all a mere imaginary fear with which to frighten democrats. The Nazi movement was certainly a movement of "the lower" and they managed to take over a more or less morally respectable European state. Communist movements often led to the entrenchment of unbridled megalomania at the heights of the state. Marx was one of the theorists of this analysis of modern politics, talking of French Bonapartism after 1848 in terms of the "lumpenproletariat" being reborn at the height of French society.[*] Marx, of course, is no one's idea of a democrat, but his argument had had a long history in the tradition of political thought, in which it is a given that a revolution bringing slaves to power could produce nothing else but a new version of a despotic state. The explanation is that the slave's only conception of liberty is what in modern life is called "liberation"—namely, the removal of restraints that previously frustrated impulses. The "lower" are thus in the most abstract terms to be identified as those pursuing the nastier human impulses toward pornography, obscenity, blasphemy, etc.—the reign of indulgence over self-restraint. Even those who take democracy to be a sacred principle had better take the question seriously.

And in doing so, they need but to take notice of opinions commonly held until about a century ago, and which retain considerable life today, even though some of them are barely entertained

---

[*]   "The French bourgeoisie . . . has brought the lumpenproletariat to power . . .";
"The Eighteenth Brumaire of Louis Bonaparte" in *Karl Marx and Friedrich Engels: Collected Works*, Vol. 11, 1851–1853. At the end of this brilliant pamphlet (pp. 195–6) Marx suggests that Louis Napoleon would like to take over the whole wealth of the country as a "patriarchal benefactor," give it back to the French, and convert it into a personal obligation to himself. It is a brilliant formula that uncovers the corrupt passion democratic politicians have used to replace the idea of authority with rule resting on the gratitude of the ruled.

in our time, and others have now been consigned to the realm of unthinkabilities. In this well-entrenched tradition, men, as rational beings, had authority over women, parents over children, and teachers over pupils (including university students whose teachers were explicitly *in loco parentis*). These were the respectable givens of the world in which everyone had a "place," so that we are now looking at the other side of our own democratic world. Here was indeed a kind of hierarchy at odds with democratic egalitarianism, but it was based on a plausible view of a division of labor responding to evident differences between the sexes. Men were the hunters and warriors, women the nurturers of rising generations, and the system was essentially complementary. A vague notion of general respectability held this set of hierarchies in place, and all of it was sustained and limited by the rule of law.

So strong is the contemporary dislike—often indeed derision—of this conception of social authority that one must emphasize several of its crucial features. It was one that allocated to men and women alike a sphere of life in which each was, in principle, dominant. In the management of a family, a decision procedure giving precedence to fathers was incorporated in cases of disagreement, and its effect was to generate in men and women different ways of influencing decisions. Men as breadwinners and women as household managers certainly gave ultimate power to men, but ideally (and often in practice) it was a form of authority that carried its own self-limitation. The relations between Wotan and Fricka in Wagner's Ring Cycle are a brilliant image of the idea. How it worked out in practice varied enormously, of course, and that indicates the most basic qualification that must be applied to understanding it, as well as to understanding any successor principle: namely, that human relations are so complicated that there is no conception of social and individual authority that will not produce both good and bad consequences.

The crucial break in this formidable view of society (it had, after all, lasted in most societies as far back as records go) was made by feminists as they responded to the new conditions of modern life. As societies became wealthier, the need for women to devote their entire lives to nurturing the young became less pressing. Birth control technology facilitated this move. Women now sought to participate further in education and began to go to universities. Physical strength became less necessary over large areas of industry (not to mention household life) because technology created push-button power. An electorate of male citizens might previously have been thought to comprehend the interests of women within the family, but feminists argued that women had different interests than men and that they, too, should have the vote. Given Voltaire's view that history was the story of crimes and follies, perhaps an input of feminine judgment might give us a more peaceful world: here was a modern version of Kant's argument that certain classes of people had an overriding interest in peace. None of these, and other such considerations, would have had very much effect had it not been that women had long been playing in some degree an independent part in the life of Western societies. "I have been frequently surprised and almost frightened at the singular address and happy boldness with which young women in America contrive to manage their thoughts and their language," Tocqueville wrote, ". . . a philosopher would have stumbled at every step along the narrow path which they trod without accident and without effort."[9] Hence new tastes, and a changing sense of justice, were important contributors to this highly complex development.

A critic of feminist ambitions, taking the line that women tend to be less rational than men, would regard these developments as indeed a move toward enthroning the lower over the higher, even though nobody had ever imagined that *all* men were more rational than *all* women. But even those who thought that there was no difference in the rational capacities of the sexes had to face the fact that the new feminist version of equality between men and women was producing, as changes always do, unforeseen consequences. The decision procedure that sustained the so-called patriarchal marriage, in which the man's decision took precedence over that of his wife, could not continue once women had been accorded fully equal rights relating to voting and property. Lacking a formal decision procedure, husband and wife were left to negotiate a settlement of their disagreements. Negotiation might have many advantages, but what it certainly did not do was to strengthen the marriage bond. It was not merely that divorce became easier and more common, but that very large numbers of people ceased to get married at all. A major danger facing those who married was ending up in a divorce court with a judge determining who got what. Judges were not really equipped to make sensible judgments on these questions. Probably nobody is. Genies are hard to put back into bottles.

The drive to democratic equalization, then, resulted from many things: sexual and other new technologies, market freedoms, and the evolving implications of the central idea of equality. Increasingly, this took the form of an attack on something called "discrimination" in a whole variety of forms. Discrimination took the ideas of the lower and the higher with deep seriousness, and the point of anti-discrimination was to destroy all such distinctions entirely. The lower was to be raised to the level of the higher, and all the echoes of the deference world were to be ruled out of court. This development had very important consequences for the idea of personhood to which we shall come later. What we find is a new attack on inequalities under such slogans as anti-discrimination and its many developments. This new development has both logical and practical aspects, and insofar as we can distinguish them, we shall deal with each in turn.

5.   THE LOGIC OF ANTI-DISCRIMINATION

The democratic telos identifies inequality as the source of all imperfections in a modern society, and while inequality of wealth remains a central concern, the basic drive from the late twentieth century onward has been against a thing called "discrimination."

In broad terms, the democratic telos inherited the long-standing concern of modern thinkers with "the poor." These were the Europeans who had been displaced from the land and moved to the cities, in which survival depended on finding employment, and in which starvation and homelessness were always possibilities in hard times. In England a minimal safety-net called "the workhouse" had long existed, and was regarded with dread by those likely to end up in it. The welfare state in all its forms was the response of increasingly prosperous societies to this condition of things. These were all sets of people defined in terms of their needs, and it is appropriate to observe that they also had votes (though in fact, contrary to their interests, they often did not vote in large numbers). The arrival of immigrants from other cultures clearly fit into this picture, but the immigrants constituted a slightly different problem, which we may characterize in terms of *exclusion from society*. The drive of the democratic revolution was to focus attention on, and generate policies to respond to, both these classes of people—*the poor* and *the excluded*. The two classes clearly overlapped in many ways, and they were sometimes bundled together along with a number of other groups (for example, children) as *the vulnerable*. It is in this context that the anti-discrimination movement may be seen as generating policies aimed at social inclusion.

The fate of the term "discrimination" is an object lesson in how new conditions, and new theories responding to them, can overturn English semantics. Discrimination used to be what students of English literature learned to do. To discriminate used to be the act of a cultural connoisseur; within a generation or so, the word had been turned upside down. Only narrow xenophobes discriminated, and they threatened social peace by doing so. Here then is a complex and immensely powerful movement in society, politics, law, and culture, and it is one that has been so rapidly domesticated among us that it is worth spelling out and seeing whole. Such is my concern with what I have called "the logic of anti-discrimination."

a.   Discrimination as a Category

Discriminating against another human being on grounds of group membership is caused by a psychological deformation called "prejudice," or in some cases "bigotry." The act of discrimination disadvantages others in one of many areas, and it is directed at specific groups in modern societies. The groups are sometimes called, in a technical sense, "minorities," though some members of this category are in fact the majority of the population. Discrimination is an act typically performed by employers, but it may be done in any of the situations of life by anyone at all. In extreme cases, discrimination becomes an element in crimes of "category hate" such as race hate, or homophobia. Women may suffer disadvantage because of their sex, blacks on grounds of race. The disabled are seen by those who discriminate against them as rather less than "fully paid up members of the human race." Each direction of discrimination is stigmatized as a specific attitude, as sexism, homophobia, and so on, but it is perhaps racism that carries the most basic charge of passion, because the Jewish experience of the Holocaust in Nazi Germany counts as the paradigmatic case of racism. Racism is thus closely related to such international crimes as genocide. Jews as victims of Nazism are thus the founding victims of racism (though the same claim is also made for Armenians). On the other hand, Jews are not widely thought to be the victims of contemporary discrimination (though they may suffer specifically from anti-Semitism, which has a somewhat eccentric place in discrimination theory when it is understood as a social pathology.) This view of racism coalesced with the civil-rights rejection of racist attitudes toward blacks in the United States, generating a powerful charge of feeling.

The charge of racism is thus the trump in the anti-discriminatory creed, yet remarkably little attention has been paid to quite what it means. Is it an idea, such as animated the Nazis, or the Dutch Reformed Church in its view (long since repudiated) of blacks as descendants of Ham? Is it a sentiment, a feeling of dislike for some particular group of people? Is it perhaps a preference for others, in employment or friendship? This lack of precision in how to specify racism might seem a defect, but in fact it makes the term "racism" all the more useful as a tool of forensic attack, and great caution is needed to avoid being charged with it. It can lead to sackings and expulsions, and in some circumstances to a jail sentence. Jokes are a particular danger, but so is anything else—as an administrator discovered in Washington some years back, who used the word "niggardly" and found himself accused of denigrating blacks.

Perhaps the basic point to be made in exploring the idea of discrimination is that it is impossible to avoid. That we are all guilty is a deep Western conviction, perhaps assimilating discriminatory conduct to the Christian idea of original sin. There is a sense in which this might be true. It is a highly plausible inference from what we know of the past that *peoples do not like other peoples*. The emphasis must be on the plural here; we are talking of distinguishable groups, races, or sects. The history of the world is full of dramatic examples of mutual ethnic dislike, and it will be found in all regions and at every level of culture. Even relatively similar peoples—the Scots and the English, for example, or the Quebecois and the English Canadians—exhibit dislike for each other. The same is generally true of different religions, and even of sects and movements within what might, from the outside, be thought the same religion. Western societies, of course, are individualistic, and therefore the relation between individuals is not at all the same as the relation between peoples. Montagues have a remarkable tendency to fall in love with Capulets. Individuals across any such divide can and do like each other, marry, associate as professionals, get on as fellows in universities, and so on. This fact might suggest that the anti-discrimination movement should be seen as trying to compel all peoples to behave the way Europeans often do— namely, to respond to others in terms of their individual personality and abilities. The paradox of anti-discrimination, however, is that in many respects, it goes in the opposite direction. Individuals can only achieve victimhood by class membership, and victimhood within the context of anti-discrimination is a benefit not to be lightly discarded. The anti-discrimination movement thus has the curious effect of locking everyone into his or her specific category. The language of anti-discrimination is a process of learning that the success in some field of a member of one's category is something the whole category may cheer and feel good about—the first woman, black, etc., to become this or that. Recognition as a member of a victimized category involves learning to feel collective unhappiness at exclusions, and a corresponding joy at occasions of newsworthy success. And all those claiming to suffer discrimination can be mobilized in a "struggle" against it.

Anti-discrimination is thus a collective attempt to change the nature of human beings, comparable to making water run uphill.

It might seem that a doctrine, ramifying into the set of patholo-gies collectively known as "political correctness," and amounting to a project of turning human nature around about 180 degrees, would have no chance of succeeding. How can people be per-suaded of any doctrine that runs so obviously counter to the way most of them can hardly help thinking and feeling?

This objection underestimates the curious moral capacity of the Western mind to discover ideals that require contortions of the mind not only unusual but barely possible. That "we are all racists, sexists, etc.," points to one universal if intermittent senti-ment in human beings: when combined with the conviction that we ought not to be, it becomes a powerful device instilling a salu-tary sense of guilt in every human breast—salutary, that is to say, if the promoters of these doctrines are concerned (as some of them certainly are) to exercise power over people. And there is very little possibility of escape. Racism, for example, if it means anything, has to be an idea in the mind of the racist, but the idea of "institu-tional racism" has evolved to cover cases where inequality is still thought to exist without anyone ever intending it. It is, as it were, a fault that can be committed, or perhaps can merely happen, without mens rea. Here discrimination becomes a sort of "objec-tive" event, and it can only be overcome by authority taking power to correct it.

The human race is distributed over the Earth's surface in terms of different cultures, minorities all over the place finding some sort of modus vivendi, often precarious, within the majority dominating a state. Separating different peoples into independent political units does help (one might say) to keep at least some people out of each other's hair. Mixing peoples up together does not usually enhance their happiness. This generalization is just marginally less true of individualistic European states, and we may well ask what is the mechanism that impels everybody in some degree toward sexist, racist, etc., attitudes. Are we actually all racists? Or sexists? Is this the original sin to which we are help-lessly prone? The answer must be, I think, that these attitudes emerge because human beings, or perhaps it is merely Euro-peans, cannot help generalizing any experience they have. They are natural inductivists. It takes only a few good or bad experiences to generate a positive or negative response to one category or another. Difference soon turns into liking or disliking. Where we come into contact with some set of people frequently, as the British do with the French, we commonly have complementary images of the good French and the bad French, each available as a response to whatever may happen.

Here then is the basis of the anti-discrimination movement: the observation that difference soon leads to disdain, and often to the judgment that some members of society are less equal (perhaps in some particular respect) than others on the basis of category membership. The explicit aim of anti-discrimination is to make the expression "member of society" the basic category in terms of which each individual will not only be recognized but also *included* (in a sense to be considered) in the whole range of activities in a society. All those holding the national passport must now be understood as components of the national identity.

Difference was to be understood as "diversity" and advanced as something to be welcomed (or "celebrated" in the terminology of the movement.) Society must be a club in which we are all equal members. That would have been a conception almost impossible to make actual even in the nineteenth or early twentieth centuries, when European states were relatively homogeneous, but in the second half of the twentieth century, when this ideal of equality was growing legal and moral teeth, it was a hope soon to be mocked by the rapid arrival in all European countries of large numbers of migrants coming from very different cultures indeed. Differences were exploding just when Europeans were being schooled to regard them as things of no significance. Multiculturalism was the version of liberal doctrine that had evolved to provide a normative understanding of the tolerances that now became necessary to assimilate this new influx of strangers into Western states. That doctrine became the theoretical basis that required a higher sense of political correctness and laws against discrimination.

The Western world has acquired a new form of *piety* derived from what we might call "the religion of equality." Christianity no longer benefits from a condemnation of religious impiety, even as a matter of good manners, but today a regular stream of unfortunates is forced to resign, or be sacked, for the most astonishingly casual breaches of this piety, while the massed ranks of incompetents working in Britain have become virtually untouchable.

b.   Who Are the "Minorities"?

Let us now consider the basic categories, sometimes called "minorities," who have claimed, and been accorded, status as victims of discrimination. As we have noticed, Jews may have been the founding paradigm of discrimination but, for a variety of interesting reasons, they were not to be the beneficiaries of the new equalizing of rights. Having been too successful in getting on in Western societies without being accorded any special status, they had been drummed out of the ranks of the "vulnerable," though anti-Semitism remains a problem, but one of a different kind.

The basic category of victimhood today, I think, is women, though again many women would repudiate such a role, regarding it as demeaning. The female status as victim, however, is entrenched by the promotion of a terminal point—known technically in Equal Opportunity Organizations as "justice for women"—at which 50 percent of all the "power positions" in society are held by women. Until we arrive at that happy moment, women will be able to claim victimhood.

Women clearly raise no question at all of cultural assimilation. By contrast with women in any other civilization, Western women already enjoy extensive freedom to construct their own identity and to play any role they might like in the activities of the modern world. Already in the nineteenth century they were participating in schools and universities. But some women, at least, felt marginalized in a domestic role, and some were the victims of the brutishness of stronger males. Discrimination is to a considerable extent a matter of image, and is focused on abuses rather than usages.

The feminist movement has always been torn between claiming that women could do anything men could do, on the one hand, and the claim that women were different, bringing a distinct and superior understanding to human affairs ("emotional literacy," it was sometimes called). Both these claims had a certain limited validity, and led to the demand that women should be incorporated into the economy on the same terms as men. On the other hand, women were different, and their involvement with children and with household life clearly resulted in difficulties for employers. To discriminate against young women who might become pregnant was obviously a rational option for an employer, and was made all the more so by the growth of onerous legislation guaranteeing women rights that were costly and inconvenient for trading organizations. They were guaranteed maternity leave, as well as a return to their old jobs—often, indeed, also to benefit from promotion procedures on the same terms as men who had been continuing in the relevant job. Women have been, throughout the Western world, with minor variations, accorded an economic status having some characteristics of both a right and a privilege. The status is always described in terms of rights, but being accorded a legal advantage not available to males, it constitutes a form of privilege. And as with many other entitlements accorded by the authority of government, this one imposes serious costs on third parties, namely employers. Those who speak for women are also keen to diminish this element of privilege by advocating "paternity leave"[*] for fathers. Employers understandably have slight enthusiasm for this scheme.

The difficulties of employing women have also included the demand that employers should become responsible for preventing sexual harassment by other employees, and thus to sustain what is curiously called "a safe environment." A rational employer, faced with these burdens, would clearly prefer not to employ women except in rather limited circumstances. No one doubts, of course, that women having children (and also caring for them in their early years) is unmistakably a good thing. These enactments, however,

---

[*] The anti-discrimination movement has, of course, a metaphysical dimension. Essences can be shuffled about. It was reported in 2007 in Britain that a lesbian schoolteacher had been awarded £20,000 as compensation for being refused "paternity leave" by the Roman Catholic school in which she had been teaching. Her "partner" had been expecting a baby.

raise the issue of how costs should be assigned. They used to fall on the one-breadwinner family, but are now being reassigned by the state to others; this is no doubt a way of garnering votes. So far as women are concerned, these benefits are a "free good." Any government threatening them would hemorrhage votes.

Women as oppressed victims raise many questions that lurk below the surface of public discussion. Above all is the question of whether women should serve in the army, the police, or other jobs requiring the kinds of aggression and physical strength not commonly found in women. The problem would be less pressing if there were separate female battalions with their own traditions, but women always want to serve alongside the men, which raises problems of chivalry and team spirit. Some women are, of course, stronger and indeed more aggressive than many men. Further, a great deal in these occupations today is bureaucratic, and in any case technology has made much of it a matter of pressing the right buttons. Further, above the levels of service at which strength is needed, there are managerial "power positions" of the same kind that feminists lust after everywhere. Women could hardly be promoted into these positions without having at least some exposure to the heavy work done by "grunts" on the ground. The real problems, however, lie deeper than this. The point about being a soldier, or a cop on the beat, has often been that men in some moods regard women as weak and emotional. The self-image, indeed self-respect, of being a soldier or participating in other such rough trades is thus precisely that women cannot do them. Only men can do them. If women are insinuated into them, necessarily with the concessions inseparable from feminine physical weakness, then the whole "ethos" of these services is transformed. They sink to the level of other service industries. All of this is part of the broader domestication of democratic men who must learn never to indulge these curious moods of sexual superiority. (They are, of course, also sometimes found in women.)

A second major category of victimhood consists in ethnic minorities. They are sometimes distinguished in anti-discrimination literature as the "visibly distinct." Most of them have migrated to the West from dysfunctional Third World countries in order to live less impoverished lives. Some have suffered from the attentions of repressive authorities and are "asylum seekers." The paradigmatic category of ethnic victims of discrimination is that of blacks, and in the American case, of course, they are mostly the descendants of slaves. In the United States, the civil rights movement of the 1960s led to "affirmative action" as a notional corrective of centuries of discrimination against blacks. We shall later discuss the issues raised by this response to ethnic discrimination, but its significance at this point for my argument is that the response to discrimination against blacks in the United States became the model for responding to discrimination against other groups. In Britain, for example, ethnic groups, and religious groups without deep roots in Western culture (such as Muslims), tended to congregate together in the same parts of cities, to present themselves as a distinct "community," and to equip themselves with spokesmen to represent their interests and allow them to use the opportunities of lobbying and "politicking" in Western states.

The emergence of new ethnic victims of discrimination is in part a function of how the relevant ethnic population gets on in society. We have already noted that Jews have largely worked their way out of this class because they have little trouble getting jobs, and Jewish children do well at school, partly no doubt because, as the noted black economist Tom Sowell has observed, they arrive in class with a well-entrenched respect for books. Sowell notes that this is not commonly the case with black children. Again, Chinese immigrants have seldom been the object of specific help because they and their children do well in the economy, and their "representation" in prisons is low. On the other hand, Hispanics in the United States have often been the legislative beneficiaries of federal help.

A third important category of victimization is that of "indigenous peoples," who have been recognized by international organizations such as the United Nations as a separate class of person, and whose numbers early in the twenty-first century

were sometimes estimated at 250 million. Such round numbers clearly need to be treated with a certain suspicion. The
category includes Canadian Inuit, New Zealand Maoris, Native
Americans previously called "Indians," and the Aborigines of
Australia. Many individual members of this class have silently
disappeared into the white population, but there remain many
of the indigenous living in cultures that do not easily assimilate
to the modern world. They are therefore heavily dependent on
outside financing.

A fourth category of victimhood is a good deal more miscellaneous. The dominant group would certainly be homosexuals.
Once denigrated as a pathology by the American psychiatric profession, they have had their psychiatric profile turned upside-
down, and the new pathology of "homophobia" has taken its
place. In the exuberance of "gay pride," homosexuals have
become an important presence in Western states. They are sometimes classed in legislation, along with transsexuals, as victims
of prejudice. But it will be clear that victimhood is a moving
target, and can create an almost indefinite number of new categories. There is, for example, an articulate "minority" called
"Deaf," which consists of the congenitally deaf. They communicate in sign language, and their exponents are hostile to the use
of medical technology to offer hearing to those who lack it. To
improve the hearing of the deaf is taken to be a form of cultural
oppression, and some extreme exponents of the doctrine identify
it with genocide. Another large and influential class recognized
as victims of discrimination are the "disabled," a highly miscellaneous set of people that includes those in wheelchairs, the blind,
those with mental illness, those with learning difficulties, and an
indefinite number of others. Their numbers in Britain have been
estimated, by those lobbying on their behalf, at 10 million out of
a population of 60 million.

Here is a formidable list of how much suffering goes on in
modern societies, and it is notionally suffering that could be pre-
vented by policies of inclusion. It is important to be clear that no
list such as I have given could be exhaustive. What, for example,

of the class of convicts, of whom it is said that many should not be in prison because they have been the victims of child abuse, illiteracy, and "learning difficulties"? And then there are the victims of the drug culture.

The anti-discrimination movement is thus nothing less than a complete theory of modern societies, and a remarkable one. Some indication of its scope may be given by the fact that the number of oppressed, by some counts, greatly exceeds the entire population of Western states. This happens, of course, because of the multiple counting of symptoms of vulnerability—the proverbial one-legged black woman counts as three. But even if we leave these statistical frivolities behind, the number of people who count for one or more reasons as victims of discrimination is large—by one count, about 73 percent of the population of Britain.[10] Women, at 51 percent of course, get the figures off to a good start. And all of these people are victims of one kind of oppression or another. The obvious question to be asked is: who is doing the oppressing?

We male white Caucasians can hardly avoid being herded into the dock, but some of us might be allowed out of the dock because we are poor, or perhaps disabled, or mentally disturbed. The rich are certainly under indictment, and they render the position of wealthy women highly equivocal: are they oppressors, or oppressed, or are they, probably like most of us, a bit of both? Such an account of oppression and class warfare necessarily gives a tinge of melodrama to a conception of society in terms of inclusion and exclusion. What is more natural than hating one's oppressor? There is, however, a (slightly) more sophisticated view by which we are *all* victims of a wrongly structured society. It is the thought that lies behind the muddle about "institutional racism." Middle-class Marxists in the past often took the view that the alienation of the capitalist rich was itself a moral distortion that the revolution would correct, and thus that the revolution was therefore in the basic interests of everyone in a capitalist society. The French social theorist Michel Foucault advanced a view of modern societies as so "structurally" oppressive that any actual oppressor disappears, like the smile of the Cheshire cat. Even this mere hint of a real oppressor is enough for a bit of melodrama and indignation, however.

c. The Vocabulary of Anti-Discrimination

Let us now examine a little further the terminology in which this view of modern Western states is explored. As we have seen, it includes two branches, that responding to the poor, and that responding (in so far as they can be distinguished) to the excluded. The welfarist branch concerned with the poor is commonly concerned with aspects of inequality. The second, responding to the excluded, is generally formulated in terms of the idea of rights.

The poor in the past were specified in terms of several negations: they were "disadvantaged," "deprived," and "underprivileged." Sometimes, they were the "less fortunate," as if society were a giant casino, showering gold randomly on a few and leaving others with a few tinkling coins. "Underprivileged" is not a felicitous term because "privilege" cannot be equalized: having a benefit that others do not have is what the word means. "Disadvantaged" is perhaps the standard term in use, and it assumes that there is a standard set of conditions that are always advantageous in human life, and that the poor don't have them.

It is in terms of this description that the abstract character of the welfarist attitudes to the poor becomes most evident. The lives people lead are complicated responses to extremely varying circumstances, and misery is no more confidently to be inferred from poverty than happiness from wealth. The important logical point is that the assumption that any condition of life constitutes in some absolute sense an advantage or a disadvantage is false. It is the infinite adaptability, one might almost say creativity, with which people respond to their condition that marks out a European society as dynamic in a way other societies are not. The idea of the absolutely "disadvantaged" is thus a remarkably static, unimaginative, and indeed reactionary understanding of the world, because it assumes that the lives of such people will reliably be enhanced by supplying the absent things thought to be advantageous. Many critics have plausibly argued that welfarist policies leave the happiness of the poor untouched but certainly succeed in creating a "dependency culture." The beneficiaries tend to lose their autonomy and become, one might say, "addicted" to the benefits offered.

Nothing, then, is unambiguously advantageous. Modern technology constantly produces new forms of advantage—from computers to medical advances—and defining the poor in terms of an ever-changing set of "advantages" has allowed the very idea of poverty to change its meaning. The poor used to be under-nourished and live in slums. In modern society, however, they live in public housing and the only undernourishment they suffer is caused by choosing a bad diet. The paradoxical result is that the poor are no longer the thin waifs of the past, but the obese. The threat of the social problem of poverty (on which a whole social-service industry rests) disappearing—before our very eyes, as it were—galvanized theorists to come up with a new concept of it, and the result was "relative deprivation," which, by "defining" poverty in terms of the general rise in living standards, guaran-teed its continuance far into the future. It was not quite what Jesus meant when he remarked that the poor are always with us. In fact, the only solution to poverty as relative deprivation would be absolute equality, if such a condition of things could be imag-ined. (There would be impossible problems, for example, with "positional goods.") "Disadvantaged" is thus a technical term for pointing to one of the essential elements of what we have called "the democratic telos."

"Deprived" has, however, a claim to be the most interesting of these abstract terms, because over it hovers the question of whether it refers to a mere state of affairs (that of not having something) or to an event in which some person or group has actually deprived the victims of something to which they were entitled. If the victimhood were merely a condition of things, it would be a social problem. If, on the other hand, it resulted from some act of exclusion by the powerful, we would be back with the melodramatics of class warfare. It would be a suitable subject for indignation, an incentive for political activism.

Those who suffered discrimination could be, and often were, assimilated to these basic categories of inequality, but the anti-discrimination movement created new signs of presumed disadvantage. The most powerful idea was that of "representation." Ethnic members of society ought to be "represented" across the spectrum of occupations in proportion to their demographic profile. This was clearly a lobbying device, because no one was interested in the ethnic proportions in industries such as rubbish collection or furniture removals, though a British cabinet minister once deplored the number of girls going into hairdressing. More of them should have studied plumbing, was the message from on high. Nor was there any concern with the "overrepresentation" of blacks on highly paid soccer teams or in other athletic contests. The idea of ethnic representation was a concern with opportunities for becoming managing directors, professors, media presenters, bishops, and suchlike. And indeed the media has responded to this lobbying by making those who front its programs just as representative of "minorities" as the crews of spaceships in Hollywood movies. They have, so far, hesitated to give way to the demand of Muslim women to have a Muslim lady reading the news in a hijab or even a burqa, but we must await the outcome of this demand: media folk are highly responsive to pressure; they enjoy sensations. That would certainly cause a sensation.

The logic of the idea of representation (in this debased sense) depends on the assumption that each human group generates the whole range of abilities found in modern societies and necessary for it. The assumption is so powerful that no one ever seems to deny that categories are in fact equal as collectivities of ability. The empirical evidence, however, suggests that, with individual exceptions, categories do tend to specialize—Jews in chess, East Africans in long-distance running, blacks in football and other sports, and so on. Nobody runs a Mafia like southern Italians. The problem of supposed discrimination is that different occupations are widely thought to yield different quantities of categorical prestige. Football and other sports for blacks are no match for chess and science among Jews, just as the nurture and beautification that women bring to modern life lack the prestige of more intellectual pursuits. The point of these categories for the anti-discrimination movement, however, is their role in boosting self-esteem, as we shall see.

These distributions of "power positions" in any society are, of course, merely empirical. In a generation or so, they may well change. They also raise the question of whether such differences result from cultural and environmental causes, or whether some of them have been "hard-wired" into certain sets of people. Psychologists may have much to say on this question, but all I can do is record a certain skepticism about anything at all that they may say. We simply do not know. When employers consistently tend to favor some ethnic groups against others, they may well have their reasons, though they may not be able to formulate them. Preferences often have a point even when people cannot explain why they have them. Many people, for example, can certainly profit by legal studies and pass examinations, but it does not always follow that these tests guarantee a real understanding of all legal situations. Some ethnic lobbyists for rights and freedom, for example, can sound as if they are advancing the interests of some industrial product rather than understanding the subtle balance between freedom and the national interest in the British tradition. It is in interfering with judgments of this kind that a modern government becomes oppressive and lowers the standards of contemporary life. They do so, no doubt, in following the idea that the imperatives of social policy override such considerations. And again the costs of dealing with these uncertainties are off-loaded onto employers, because they are assumed to have the deep pockets.

We may well suggest that there are two distinct problems of discrimination. The first of these responds to a genuine difficulty immigrants have in getting jobs against a common preference to choose those whom the employers are familiar with as workers. The second is a lobbying operation designed to benefit people who are reasonably good but not quite good enough to succeed on their own. The outstanding seldom have problems getting on; it is those on the margins of mediocrity who constitute the problem. It is here that we find that the logic of anti-discrimination is in the highest degree opportunistic. Women were very keen in the past on the idea of "equal pay for equal work," as it affected such people as teachers and office staff. Then they grew more ambitious, and wanted equal pay for work of equal worth. But how was "equal worth" to be judged? A variety of experts were invoked to advance the case that so many hours of carpentry were equivalent to so many hours of taking dictation. Feminists have in more recent times demanded that their prize money at tennis tournaments should be the same as that of men. There may be a case for this (perhaps in terms of audience interest) but it certainly cannot be advanced as a case of equal pay for equal work. Women play best of three sets, men sweat it out over the best of five. Women in dangerous occupations raise the same problem.

Anti-discrimination certainly targets a perfectly real problem in modern societies, one that has largely arisen because of large-scale immigration from non-European cultures and from the imperatives of liberal democracy. As a form of social engineering, it creates an industrial mixing of ethnicities that no doubt facilitates social peace and order, and some of the people appointed will find in themselves abilities previously latent. In forcing employers to take on people whom otherwise they might have thought unemployable by virtue of disability, for example, the governments are, up to a point, forcing employers to rethink what employability means in their own particular circumstances. The problem is that other pressures—those of trade unions, governmental insouciance about increasing the costs of others, extensive regulation, and so on—militate against a purely beneficent outcome. Western societies might certainly have been less troubled and difficult had they been able to avoid the massive influx of desperate Asians and Africans from dysfunctional societies, but given that they have found this to be impossible, active measures to incorporate the newcomers in the workforce can hardly be avoided.

The overall cost, however, has been a general diminution of competence throughout society. Limiting the power of employers to hire freely and sack at their own judgment has certainly not increased the effectiveness of most endeavors. Other factors, such as the state taking over many things that used to be the responsibility of individual prudence, have moved society further in the same direction. In earlier generations, immigrants such as the Jews and the Poles managed to succeed in British life without the benefit of an anti-discriminatory apparatus. The same thing happened over a much wider ethnic mix in the United States. These earlier immigrants no doubt met with many problems that might be construed as prejudice and injustice, but they also had the benefit of a powerful incentive structure that led them to overcome many difficult obstacles. It may have been unjust—or it may have been a distinct advantage—that they had to learn to run faster, to work harder, to be more amusing, in order to get on in the world. Their successors in the anti-discriminatory world of today lack this interesting incentive structure, and are much more likely to succumb to querulous discontents if they do not succeed. "Playing the race card" and other forms of exploitation of anti-discrimination are well-known responses to this new situation. There is a price to pay for every reform, especially where the reform extends the coercive power of the state. Further, many of these immigrants come from cultures so distant from those of Europe that they test to destruction the liberal passion to find a place for every culture within the privacies of a liberal democratic society.

d. Sentimentalism and Anti-Discrimination

We have so far been treating anti-discrimination largely in the context of employment opportunities. This is to ignore the fact that it is more than that: in fact, it is a major enterprise in social and psychological engineering. Disadvantaged people are judged to suffer an affront to their feelings, and damaged self-esteem tends (it is argued) to cause the problem to continue over the generations. "We," in treating "them" as different, and thus as less than fully competent and human, have taught them to internalize these feelings and thus to despise themselves. A good deal of intellectual abracadabra has been played with themes of this kind in universities, and it has been suggested that our sense of identity depends on how we constitute "the other." Whole books have been written about the way in which Western theorists have not taken as fully human the cultures of other civilizations (especially Oriental cultures).

In other words, the anti-discrimination movement concerns itself not merely with the issue of opportunities of social advancement, but also with issues of feeling. The structure of Western societies amounts to a systematic assault on the feelings of the excluded; indeed, the whole of European civilization has found itself up on a mental-cruelty rap. The remedy for this deplorable state of affairs was soon codified in terms of avoiding the sins of insensitivity, a codification known as "political correctness." Some of these insensitivities were, one might say, old friends, such as racism and sexism; others were additions to an ever-growing index of sins, and promoted beyond being deplorable "isms" to the more serious status of pathologies, such as homophobia and Islamophobia.

Here we find ourselves dealing with a new and powerful movement in Western civilization. We may call it "social sentimentalism," and its reach extends far beyond the issues of anti-discrimination that are our central concern here. It will already have been evident that we have so far been touching on admirable forms of benevolence toward other human beings, of a kind often packaged as the virtue of compassion. In calling this new form of compassion "sentimentalism," I am pointing to the abstract character of the feelings commonly involved. They are feelings that relate not to specific cases, but to abstract categories, and the actual circumstances of those people who find themselves in these categories will be very various indeed. To experience emotion on the basis of images and descriptions of abstract categories is a form of unreality, rightly called sentimental because it often involves considerable self-indulgence rather than real feelings. It may be not the less virtuous for this reason, and can generate real acts of philanthropy, but it is also a basis for shallow posturing.

Sentimentalism is clearly spun out of the Romantic movement, which I am inclined to date from Jean Jacques Rousseau's propensity to burst into tears at the ills of the world. In one of its many aspects, sentimentalism is the dream of a nicer world shorn of the brutality and nastiness of which so much history is composed. One common account of its founding assumption is to say that it is the belief that human beings are naturally good, and that their evil acts result from misery and desperation induced by a disordered society. This, however, would be a perilous bit of metaphysics, and the actual substratum of sentimentalism in politics is the less ambitious doctrine that human beings are the creatures of their circumstances. They are, as it were, the raw materials of society, and their moral quality depends on the character of that society. In good social conditions they will be good; otherwise, they may not be. What, then, are we to make of evils that seem to emerge from human beings in perfectly good social conditions? Not all villains have had abusive and twisted childhoods. The cause must lie (runs the belief) in some inner derangement, some addiction or mental disorder that ought to be subject to professional help. Here is the line of thought, then, that leads to treating all human ills in therapeutic terms, and crimes and sins as disorders requiring rehabilitation rather than as moral acts deserving punishment.

One current version of this doctrine holds that the punitive elements of the society we have inherited are themselves the cause of the very evils they aim to eradicate. They generate not remorse, but alienation from society. Capital punishment has been abolished, and corporal punishment in school rejected on the ground that it "sends the wrong message" to children subjected to it. The message supposedly sent by the use of corporal punishment is thought to be that violence pays, but the idea that human beings understand one fixed "message" from any human act is marvelously absurd. As with other concepts in this area, responses to circumstances have been absolutized under the illusion that such responses can then be controlled. The doctrine of people learning right or wrong messages treats law and the moral life as one vast signaling system, social problems being taken as failures of communication. To this we shall return.

Sentimentalism has had a serious impact on language. The very idea of punishment, for example, now signifies an unmerited pain that affects an innocent victim. The friend of a prostitute who had been murdered while working to fund a drug habit said of her friend's fate: "She fell in with the wrong crowd, but she shouldn't have been punished for it." In the ideal sentimentalist world, problems are dealt with by talk, by negotiation, and bad things ought not to happen.

They would not happen, the doctrine continues, if our society were differently organized. We must abandon the immemorial assumption that human beings have a propensity to evil acts and must be kept in check by authority. Authority can only work if it is sustained by a certain element of fear. The essence of sentimentalism is the aspiration to remove fear and other uncomfortable emotions from human life. The stick and carrot combination of the past is to be replaced by a diet solely composed of carrots. A more brutal way of characterizing this doctrine, which is a major revolution in human affairs, would be to say that discipline has been replaced by bribery.

This elementary doctrine has certainly had dramatic effects in unlikely areas. In teaching, for example, it rejects not merely any kind of physical discipline, but even any idea that the teacher, having more knowledge, is in a superior position to the pupil. Equality replaces hierarchy, and children must thus be persuaded rather than coerced into getting on with the more tedious bits of education—French irregular verbs, chemical formulas, strings of dates, and so on. The outcome has been the turning of education into popularization; every lesson is tethered to a beginning point, fatally limited by the interests of the pupils themselves and by whatever sense of relevance they have picked up. This is not an ideal way to convey the importance of formal aspects of learning, such as spelling, and it shows in the levels of literacy in pupils emerging from national school systems. A population of students who can only be persuaded to take an interest in anything if they can be convinced that it will be useful to them is at the mercy of its own limitations. The aim of the doctrine is to base education on what the children themselves actually want to learn; the effect is to atrophy their capacity for self-movement.

The principle of democratic egalitarianism constituting the democratic telos thus removes the respect pupils have, or used to have, for someone wiser and more knowledgeable than they are. In the extreme formulation, the teacher becomes a "resource person," which is to say a mere *function* in the *process* of transmitting knowledge. Teacher and pupil cease to have a specific kind of personal relationship, and the teacher loses his special role, becoming merely someone without authority and with no claims to any special respect in our informal world. In the worst cases, the teacher tries to become a "pal." Indeed, the full development of the democratic telos is to standardize all relationships as those of a "pal." The child has thus been liberated from authorities, the general reason being that authority is a hierarchical relationship. And what, we may ask, follows for the respect that ideally is felt for the teacher by the pupil? That specific kind of respect must, of course, be distinguished from the mutual respect that good manners impose on both of them as human beings. Respect due from pupil to teacher is distinct from that and depends on the fact that the teacher has vastly more knowledge and experience than the pupil. More than that, however, respect incorporates, as we have noted, a certain element of fear. The pupil fears the disapproval of the teacher, and seeks, by good work, to please him or her, which means also seeking to avoid the pains of censure. Not all respect involves fear, but most does, and that is precisely the emotion that sentimentalism seeks to eliminate.

In the parallel case of the matron in a British hospital, much feared by the nurses under her, fear was a major element in sustaining cleanliness and discipline. And matrons were, in effect, abolished, because nurses thought life would be improved without that old dragon breathing fire at them. Given recent nation-wide crises of infection in hospitals in Great Britain, the cry has gone up: bring back matron. It is not possible. The extensive authority with which matrons were trusted—and trust is the crucial concept here—cannot be restored because employment legislation makes every change in the status of a subordinate an exhausting judicial risk. This process by which authority has been, as it were, "defanged" by the removal of any element of fear sustaining it, runs rights through the democratic telos. A strong movement, already established in some European states, wants the state to pass laws punishing parents if they should smack their children.

Authority does not, of course, disappear. It merely moves away from parents to the state.

The sentimentalist assault on respect has been transforming society for at least two generations; it began even before the major assault on authority in the 1960s, and modern societies are now, with the benefit of experience, able to judge its consequences. One major consequence has been the disappearance of respect for "governors," at every level of society. Respect remains in some degree alive and well in "middle-class" families, and is a crucial part of what today is called "social capital." Without it, conduct deteriorates everywhere, and education goes into steady decline. States recognize these problems, and attempt to use the prestige of the state to remedy it. A British prime minister—Tony Blair— even had a "respect" agenda in order to restore this essential bastion of civil order to its earlier place. Respect without fear, however, is an empty thing. You cannot bring it back easily. Society comes to reverberate with the clatter of stable doors being banged shut long after the horses have bolted.

In terms of the democratic telos, the young have been "liberated" from the sometimes-oppressive ordering of these authority figures. But it is an almost universal rule of life that the desuetude of one ordering principle in society necessarily calls up a compensatory principle to do similar work. Nor is the change always a desirable one. In the case of the decline of respect for "governors," there is no doubt where this new ordering principle comes from: namely, the state. Teachers, parents, and all other such figures now find themselves subject to increasing bureaucratic regulation.

e. The Positive Entailments of Anti-Discrimination Negations

Our analysis of the anti-discrimination movement so far finds itself immured in negations of many kinds. The poor are disadvantaged, the vulnerable suffer prejudice, and these facts generate the moral ground of political correctness, which, as a moral theory of a kind, presents itself as a duty to avoid bad things rather than an opportunity to do good ones. No one in general would be inclined to denigrate women because they are women, or ethnic people because they belong to a different culture. The sensitivities codified in political correctness are widely accepted because they intersect with good manners, but their very codification gives them a quite different character. Codification, it cannot be too much emphasized, caters to a less sophisticated population that lacks the inner sense needed to guide manners and morals, and it turns the moral agent into a casuist. Codes are crudely indifferent to tone and circumstance.

This may well be the reason why political correctness comes largely packaged as a set of prohibitions. Disadvantage and exclusion are ideas that tell us what the vulnerable and the oppressed do *not* have—advantages and memberships. They leave the positive character of these victims, and of society itself, mysterious. Those who guide the movement have a curious lack of interest in what it is that the beneficiaries of their concerns are actually like. Their positive characteristics are a complete blank. But human beings are not blanks. Instead, they have opinions, attitudes, practices, sentiments, reasons, and everything else that furnishes a human mind.

A conception of society as a set of people relating to each other only as active and passive agents in the activity of excluding, disadvantaging, underprivileging, etc. each other, is no basis for understanding European societies. And this is the way in which the state—by virtue of its legislation and its "educational" projects designed to change attitudes—presents us to ourselves. The state, in other words, has nationalized the poor and the vulnerable, while the poor and vulnerable have taken over morality by supplying the moral terms in which modern states ought to operate. What the ubiquity of negative characterizations suggests is that the state is concerned with the vulnerable—the vast majority of the population—merely as *materials to be transformed*. It is a conception of an entirely servile world—and yet, as we shall see, democratic governments are increasingly dismayed by the character of the people they rule, and keen to change them. What we need to understand at this point, however, is what, according to the morality (if we may for courtesy call it that) of political correctness, ought to be our *positive* relation to the poor and the excluded.

So far as the poor are concerned, our positive duties are to help them with money and with a range of charitable endeavors such as youth clubs and sports-coaching that will keep their younger members off the streets. So far as the excluded are concerned, our duty is in the first instance *tolerance*. They may look funny, and behave funny, to put it in the demotic, but we must enjoy them all the same. Tolerance is often presented as the archetypal virtue of Western states, and one that ought to be taught as part of an induction into citizenship, particularly to such ethnic groups as Muslims who are deeply unsound on such questions as homosexuality, the status of women, and the proper place of religion in society. What this means, of course, is that the ethnic population is not merely at times a victim of discrimination, but that in many areas it is itself an enthusiastic discriminator against others.

It turns out, however, that tolerance is not enough for some victims of discrimination. They want a much more serious thing called "acceptance." This is the position of gays, who want, indeed often demand, that their sexual preference be judged as no less admirable than that of the heterosexuality that is commonly taken as the norm. Such a demand brings them into direct conflict with those Christians who believe that God judges homosexuality a sin. The problem arises where, for example, some proprietor of a hotel refuses a double room to a same-sex couple and finds, these days, that he has broken the law by such a refusal. Again, anti-discrimination legislation in Britain is requiring that Christian adoption agencies should accept same-sex couples as adopters.

But even acceptance may not be enough. As we have seen, the logic of anti-discrimination is closely linked to the inclusion/exclusion nexus. Merely to tolerate (for what attitudes might not such a policy conceal?) or even to accept (which still permits a certain distance) cannot be enough. The ultimate in anti-discrimination would thus seem to be *inclusion*.

What is the moral model being invoked in this tolerance cycle on which Western societies have embarked since the arrival of ethnic migrants? It assumes, I think, that society itself is a party, or a club, or perhaps even a domestic hearth, and our duty is one of hospitable accommodation of those who come to live here. This is no small demand.

There are two important observations to be made about it. The first is that the bland surface of anti-discrimination turns out to impose some quite onerous, indeed freedom-threatening, individual responsibilities upon us. One might well sympathize with the idea that we have a duty to accept and include everyone living in our society, but how far does inclusion go? In Britain the Commission for Racial Equality has complained that the integration of the ethnic communities is not advancing fast enough, because not enough of us have ethnic friends, and the level of intermarriage between the indigenous population and some of the ethnics is low. The commission speaks for the state, of which it is, of course, an agency. A little way onward, a duty to make friends with ethnics may surface as a moral duty.

The second observation is to recognize one notable unreality of this area: it is that the ethnic population is taken to be a part of the population previously not assimilated to liberal norms. It is a problem understood abstractly and un-historically. The unreality here is that this population has very recently arrived on European and American shores, and continues to come in very large numbers. It enters European states in pursuit of its own interests, not because any serious number of the indigenous Europeans actually thinks they need such an augmentation of their populations. The issue is one of numbers. Giving succor to individuals threatened with torture or death is one thing; accepting whole communities into our society is quite another. That the one leads to the other is an obvious point obscured, and sometimes deliberately obscured, by both the state and those who seek to encourage this migration. The fallacies involved in this understanding of migration will be discussed later. But it is a sentimental error to think that people persecuted by bad governments must themselves be merely victims wanting nothing else but a quiet life. Some of them are terrorists and political activists in their own right, and Britain has long since found itself with international problems because it has given refuge to those with terrorist ambitions, and it can often find no legal way of sending them on their way.

6. THE CIVILIZATIONAL SIGNIFICANCE OF THE DEMOCRATIC TELOS

Let us now consider the broader significance of the anti-discrimination movement as a central component of the democratic telos. The most remarkable thing about it is the overturning of immemorial beliefs that there is in society a natural hierarchy on which order should be based. The details varied, of course, from culture to culture, but women and agricultural laborers have almost invariably been low on this universal totem pole, while warriors, priests, and scholars have tended to dominate. The basis of any such hierarchy is, I suppose, productionist: it is a judgment of how important the activities combined together in society are. Defense and good relations with the gods are always important, household life and the continuance of the society from one generation to the next have usually been taken for granted. The new democratic egalitarianism rejects any such view of the supposedly natural importance of some activities as against others. Society, guided by the government, can deal with whatever has to be done, and deciding on that question depends on what the demos wants. The basic criterion of what has to be done is the satisfaction of human needs. We thus seem to have moved into a "consumptionist" rather than a "productionist" view of society, and the new order is (among us) largely a function of our power and prosperity. More or less according to taste, we may regard this as a catastrophic triumph of the "lower" over the "higher" or a final triumph of social justice after millennia of oppression. In a very rough sort of way, the Nazis provided a caricature of the reaction against the first idea, and the communists a very rough blueprint for the social justice view. These two gruesome examples should alert us to the fact that things may not always be what they seem.

An important component of this skepticism about what democratic governments declare themselves to be is that they are very far from being responsive agencies of the popular will. In fact, we may mark this down as one of the illusions of the epoch, if not the main one. For well-known reasons, some of which we have discussed above, "the popular will" is largely fictional, and any modern society is a vast complex of opinions, ideas, and interests. These things are forever changing, and it would be logically impossible for all of them to be actualized. In the process of discussion, formulation, and representation, the policies emerging from modern governments contain a large component of ideals remote from the lives of the demos and sometimes directly at variance with them. Modern states, for example, have a practice of signing up to international treaties promising action to deal with some current ill, and in the consequences of these commitments, in the declaration of rights that often emerges from them, and in the judicial decisions and bureaucratic implementation of these highly abstract policies, the popular will is often left on the sidelines. Indeed, governments often embark on persuasive campaigns to bring the people into line with the national commitments that have come into being to limit democratic sovereignty. At the explicit level of ideals, these ideas are abstract tokens of justice and benevolence. Their actual consequences will only be discovered a long way down the chain of implementation, at which time a new government will explain that it has no option but to implement what was so long ago decided. That giving asylum to those in danger of torture and death comes to entail a general citizenly duty to include as friends a proportion of the ethnic population, for example, is one case of "blue sky" aspirations having highly specific "implications." In much less discussed areas, the whole apparatus of anti-discrimination is expensive to fund and onerous to regulate.

These considerations are sufficient to suggest, even if elementary political experience does not, that the apparent disappearance of an elite at the top of European social and political hierarchies might not be quite what it seems. It was a notable contribution of the eighteenth century to political thought that the path to a better society lay through education, and modern governments are nothing if not tutorial. They are eager to encourage us to be responsive to whatever is presented to us as training or instruction; education ought to be, they often say, a lifelong process. In the past, we became educated at school, and some of us became reflective at university, and that was quite enough, because we could now make our own judgments, and we did. But in this new phase of democratic egalitarianism, we should submit ourselves year in and year out to unceasing courses of instruction and training. In some countries, judges have been subjected to something called "sensitivity" training should they be found unsound on the question of race, or rape. This sinister element of tutorial overreach to which contemporary governments are prone is, among other things, the re-emergence of the natural hierarchy of the past, and at the top of it will be found politicians ruling us, experts instructing us, and highly bureaucratic agencies all combining to smooth out our deficient understanding of what modern societies require. Some of us smoke, for example, others eat too much and don't take exercise, and many are incapable of getting their children to go to school. And all of this is before we come to the sexism, racism, homophobia, and other pathologies infecting society, many of which have become the territory of well-staffed agencies set up to enforce the relevant law. In principle, the demos rules society, but in fact it seems to have been set a multigenerational curriculum of improvement, and serious power for the telos must be postponed until our lessons have been learned. Only then will democracy converge with wisdom. It will be remembered that I have already criticized the demos on the score of wisdom, and pointed to the paradox of democratic legitimacy inherent in this situation, and it will be clear that I do not judge modern governments to be necessarily superior in wisdom to their peoples.

Remarkably, then, modern Western societies are evolving into the same kind of rigid pattern of society, based on a notional right ordering of life, that previously was found only in traditional societies. The imposition of democratic egalitarianism upon society is a notional "right ordering of life" that now parallels the rule of Confucianism in China, or the Hindu caste system, or various kinds of Sharia, as things used to flourish in earlier centuries. The only difference is that we have replaced natural hierarchy with equality as the essence of rightness.

The period from the beginning of modern times until the last part of the twentieth century was a new kind of society, dynamic because it responded to the creativity of Europeans released by individualism and the rule of law. The future could never be predicted. Second-rate theorists like Marx who thought they had solved the riddle of historical development were object lessons in futility. The rigid class divisions that Marx wrongly thought characterized capitalist societies were then imposed on the societies unfortunate to succumb to communist rule. And today, a rather similar meritocracy (but without the merit!) has evolved among us, as if we were too tired these days to support the dynamism and creativity that led to our greatness, greatness that has so dramatically swept the world. The telos of democracy turns out to be a static perfection of happy people with satisfied needs.

On general grounds, of course, we know that the nightmare of rightness will not happen. The human condition is not like that. A more general reason, however, is that the character of Western populations runs directly counter to the proposal that we should devote ourselves entirely to the satisfaction of needs. No doubt the idea of a harmony of happy hedonists has been an attractive fantasy in European life for many centuries, but the actual character of Europeans is that of competitive game-players. Further, there is a significant problem with the conception of the moral life involved. Dealing with this issue will take up our third chapter, but we may indicate here one form of the basic problem.

Political correctness is not merely the imposition of rules of sensitivity on us; it is also the demand that incorrect thoughts expressing the forbidden attitudes must be stigmatized and abolished. For reasons I have given earlier, this seems virtually impossible, but impossibility has never discouraged moral reformers. And the basic assumption of the politically correct moral reformer is that the moral life is essentially imitative. That is part of the reason why the anti-discrimination movement is so preoccupied with creatures called "role models." The assumption is that the young (particularly) will imitate those they admire, so the state attempts in the first place to control the people called "celebrities" by imposing the responsibilities of "model-hood" upon them. It relies on the psychology of imitation to control the way people behave.

One way of understanding this strange project is to say that it is a version of the story of the fall of man, played backward, so that fallen men return to their pristine condition of moral goodness. The fall of man, it will be remembered, is a myth about the emergence of self-consciousness in human life, a change that modern writers have often found admirable and described as a "fortunate fall." Eve was persuaded by the serpent to eat of the tree of knowledge, and thereafter Adam and Eve knew that there were alternatives to the way they lived. Nakedness, for example, might be the way to live, or it might be shameful. The point of original sin is that although human beings sometimes do the right thing, they cannot help conceiving of a lot of attractive wrong things as well, and they sometimes do them. This self-consciousness is precisely what poses the questions that have generated the moral order in which, inescapably, we live. But if we belonged to a world in which our sentiments precisely mirrored those of society at large, and if our thoughts had been so circumscribed by correctness that we could barely conceive of any other form of conduct than doing what society prescribed, then we would be back in the garden, before the fall, doing naturally only what we ought to be doing. It would, in a sense, be a perfect human condition, because everybody always would do the right thing, and there would be no distinction between the good and the bad. But it would also be a triumph of the servile mind.

7.   DEMOCRATIC DISCONTENTS

Democracy is, then, a transvaluation of values in which the immemorial reign of the strong over the weak seems to have been broken. At last, human beings are animated by the satisfaction of need rather than the pursuit of power. This must surely be an *hal-*

lelujah! moment in the history of the world. Radicals had merely dreamed, but here we are, imperfect still, no doubt, but on the way to a better world. A democracy that at last puts government at the service of solving the problems of "ordinary people" must, you would be tempted to think, be blessed each day by its beneficiaries. You would be mistaken. The sad fact is that much of the demos has become an ungrateful mass much given to grumbling. The popularity of democracy seems to vary inversely with its success.

Contrast, for example, the condition of Britain in 1897 with its condition at the beginning of the twenty-first century. Queen Victoria's Diamond Jubilee was marked by an outburst of national pride. Such outbursts might, of course, be cases of shallow exuberance, but the reality of this devotion to Britain was triumphantly confirmed in the volunteering spirit evoked by the Boer War and in the crisis of 1914. Britain in 1897 had pretty much universal male suffrage, but it could hardly be counted much of an advertisement for democracy. Its rulers were unmistakably a collection of toffs, though also never without a contingent of talented upward mobiles. The state provided virtually nothing for the poor, though old-age pensions were on the horizon. In our time, a little over a century later, the situation has changed out of all recognition. Vast amounts of national wealth (well over 40 percent) are now disposed of by the government, and much of it is distributed as welfare, medical services, or compulsory education to the people. About one third of the population is sustained by public money rather than by its own efforts. Ministers of the Crown understand how popular this condition is and they boast about it, competing, indeed, to spend even more of the public purse on resourcing desirable activities. In public statements, they plaintively affirm their passion to help "ordinary people" deal with the problems of their lives. All this public largesse is certainly valued by its recipients. A snarl of fury can be detected from far off should there be any proposal to discontinue it. Yet political comment and public talk is dominated by a powerful contempt for the whole political class in their role as our benefactors.

One cost of exercising political power in our time, for example, is the contempt of interviewers on radio and television, often asking dim and aggressive questions, but hardly concealing the fact that they regard those they interrogate as weak and evasive. The state showers its subjects with benefits, and scatters new and more arcane rights with a free hand. It is never without a hand on its heart as it declares how much it cares for "the most vulnerable in our society"—a class of person that has, as we saw, expanded remarkably since 1897. And where, these rulers might well demand, is the gratitude? Why is the demos conducting itself like a kept woman, addicted to flattery and benefits and never, in its caprice, satisfied?

The demos, then, is not very happy with democracy. But the question that follows from our argument is: which of the elements that constitute "democracy" has provoked this hostile response? Certainly not the democracy of informal manners and casual conduct. That, for the moment, has plenty of impetus left in it. Just as hats for men (and mostly for women) disappeared decades ago (taking with them the possibility of certain old-fashioned signs of courtesy), the collar and tie is now moving toward its sad desuetude.* Nor is it the democracy of the ideal telos. Every expression of discontent with the present aims toward a society in which we make sure that this or that bad thing from which we have just suffered should never happen again. Where would we be without our dreams? The ideal telos promises ever more of those benefits that we seem to like, however much we might despise ourselves for taking them. No, the contempt is unmistakably directed at the basic democracy of elections and politicians. And perhaps we may hope to explain it slightly better if we look at one or two factors that seem to be implicated.

One would certainly have to recognize a variety of factors contributing to this result. One of them is semantic. A Christian tradition such as Europeans have inherited is based on gratitude for the many blessings that God is presumed to have showered

---

* I have a photograph of a large audience of undergraduates at a talk given at Sydney University in 1949. Every one of the young men is wearing a jacket and tie. You dressed "proper" if you went to "varsity" in those days.

on us. The virtually abandoned practice of saying grace at meal-times is a training in being grateful for the many things we now take for granted. Rights are different. No one need be grateful for a right. Rights are not the result of charity; they are not gifts, they are things you may bang the table about if there should be any problem of implementation. Rights demand to be taken for granted. Indeed, it is one of the consequences of the decline of Christianity and the rise of secularism that a standard posture of gratitude for what one enjoys has gone. Instead, the common atti-tude to life is a somewhat querulous demandingness. Politicians certainly did not create this world, though they have contributed to it, and it is not surprising that they have also become the vic-tims of it.

Another part of the explanation for alienation from politics—indeed from democracy—is that the British government has handed a great deal of its power over national life to international organizations, and especially to the European Union, whose regu-latory passions (for how else can they pass the time if they are not busy dreaming up new ways in which regulation would improve our lives?) constantly disrupt British life. It is one of the curiosi-ties of contemporary politics that a political class eager to hand its power over to unelected officials of a supranational body are also rather shamefaced about admitting the real origin of measures they have to implement, measures that often require seriously unpopular legislation. British politicians thus find themselves acting in a political charade. They go through the motions of Commons debate and Whitehall implementation of legislation, but for much of the time, they must obey their masters in Brus-sels. Rule by political eunuchs is never an inspiring condition, and may explain the strange passion national politicians have to manage in detail those areas of British life over which they have not actually yielded their power.

Here, as in much that we discover if we think seriously about democracy, is a political tendency that seems to be "against nature." We all know that politicians are in the business of power, and cannot get enough of the stuff. Yet here we find them handing over nothing less than the preponderance of their power to other bodies and leaving themselves without, as the vulgar saying goes, "clout." How can this thing be? The problem is indeed genuine, and the answer can only be speculative. A very small part of the answer lies in the fact that politicians are actually human, like us, and occasionally cherish an ideal or two. Some believe that "global governance," a new term that means being controlled by rules and laws issuing from international bodies seemingly untouched by the sordid compromises of national politics, is the path to a better world. The European Union, not to mention the United Nations and other international bodies, would seem be the agent of this advance in world happiness.

A second and perhaps larger part of the answer is that the politicians who hand over elements of democratic sovereignty to this alien rule are posing before the bar of history, and imagine that they are, as believers in the global ideal, participating in a historic moment by signing up to another stage in the dilution of the sovereign power to which the wars of past times are attributed. Politicians have a weakness for leaving a historical legacy behind them. But a third and even larger part of the explanation is that they themselves are evolving into a new class of world-historical rulers. The move from national to international power would thus be a case of *reculer pour mieux sauter*.

Many modern politicians belong to a new class that John Fonte has called "trans-national progressives," or "tranzies" for short. I have elsewhere called them "Olympians,"[11] in honor of their contempt for the democratic voice. Lawyers are prominent in their ranks, because they think that a new legal order will be able to solve the problems of violence, war, genocide, and other forms of oppression. The new class also includes large numbers of academics, intellectuals, and journalists in all Western countries who have detached themselves from any serious patriotic allegiance and regard themselves as critical citizens of the world, as open minds uncluttered by local religious or political commitments. And wider public opinion has been seduced by the prospect of a new order that will solve the problems of the contemporary world and (perhaps) issue in a new era of peace. All of these are people who may pay lip service to democracy (so long as it moves in the direction they approve) but whose real allegiance has moved from the actual democracy in which we live to the ideal of democracy as a telos. For democracy as a telos is an essential component of a more perfect world order.

These factors are all important, but another is no doubt also present. The essence of a state is that it is the exercise of authority, and that requires two closely related features. The first is distance between the holders of authority and those subjected to it. It may seem like a triumph of democratic informality that we may recognize that our rulers are people just like us, people whom we have elected to act for us. It also means, however, that we no longer attribute to them a superior category of political understanding. We do not attribute to them any such things as *arcana imperii*. One might well think that belief in such a mysterious kind of understanding is entirely an illusion, and perhaps it is. To be a politician, however, is in some degree to have a skill whose point outsiders often miss. It is hard to exercise it when the difference between the reason for a decision and the justification for that decision are so constantly being run together in public discussion. One cannot doubt that the impact of incessant media attention is shallowness. And if politicians were less often boxed into a corner from which the only escape is evasion, it might even be possible that their electors might be just a little less confidently opinionated.

The second feature of authority is related: it is a certain mystery. It does seem to me that the formality and theatrics of judges in court and lawyers wearing wigs is an independent, and also a valuable, element in the tradition of justice. Underneath those wigs, judges are no doubt ordinary human beings pretty much like us. But when wearing those wigs, they become slightly but significantly different, and that difference is an element of authority both in the law and in politics. No doubt a monarch is but a human being just like us, as Montaigne so forcefully remarked, and meeting a monarch generates no great prodigies of wit or wisdom. But a monarch is also (as F. Scott Fitzgerald once remarked in a different context) different from us. A society homogeneously human and democratic, lacking in these accoutrements, is a rather debased thing. Democrats, of course, disapprove of these theatrics, and there are periodic proposals to abolish all symbols of difference,[*] but that is because democrats do not believe that authority is a necessary part of social order. They think it is an irrationality surviving from a less educated past.

Like those teachers who want to get rid of the cane (and therefore of fear), many liberal democrats want social order and good conduct to result from discussion and negotiation. They believe that a real, critical discussion of public issues must in the long run reveal the kind of general will Rousseau thought would be generated by a just state. The rationality thought to be superior to authority is hoped to lead, at an abstract level, toward liberal virtues such as freedom and tolerance. It would incorporate social justice (on the Rawlesian ground that if you can't be sure that you won't be at the bottom of the heap in the future, you'd better opt for the most equal condition.) It incorporates also social responsibility, an area commonly subsumed under the "ethical" in our time. Rationality, it is assumed, would only be contested by a surviving rump of the prejudiced and the bigoted. No one quite imagines a world in which these virtues would be uncontested, but the teleological democrat retreats to a higher level in which these liberal basics are meta-virtues permitting lower-level beliefs so long as they are consistent with what is "ethical."

Democracy, then, is full of laments. The electors often feel that they no longer really govern themselves, the reason for which is probably that governments seem to resemble a voracious octopus forever extending its tentacles into civil society, and talking about "partnership" when the reality is unmistakably domination. The responsiveness of government has been lost in the creation of endless agencies (known in Britain as "quangos" or quasi-autono-

---

[*] In 2009, John Bercow was voted Speaker of the House of Commons, and abandoned the traditional dress and accoutrements speakers had always hitherto paraded.

mous governmental organizations), which exercise an unaccountable power with a remit over large areas of social life. The authority of national governments, which the electors can at least influence, has been handed over to international bodies, which they cannot influence. The flexibilities of freedom in Anglophone countries is giving way to the judicialization of rights and increased power of lawyers and judges. We used to respect the rule of law, but so many things now count as "laws" that authority has retained little respect. The range of government is now so vast that a citizen can barely grasp one issue before another is demanding attention. The decline of cultural homogeneity in European states has left many people complaining that the country is no longer the one in which they grew up. And the flow of information and argument is so continuous that the people employed by governments as "spin doctors" can switch items of news around in such a way that it becomes difficult to know what is happening in the political world. This may be the reason why membership of political parties, and turnouts at elections, have both been falling in recent times.

A century has thus made a vast difference to Western civilization. In 1897, the presiding moral concept was duty, and our self-understanding was that we stood for progress. At the beginning of the twenty-first century, the presiding moral, or rather politico-moral (a concept we shall be advancing) idea, is rights, and we are busy apologizing for our civilization. Amidst all the tensions, paradoxes, or perhaps merely contrasts that we may discern, reality is hard to fathom, but there is one contrast that cannot fail to strike any observer. In intellectual circles and among the elites, a cosmopolitan allegiance to an ideal world has replaced the necessarily ambiguous love for and allegiances to real Western states.

The educated identify their integrity with criticism, and the criticism is more concerned to denigrate our supposed faults than to analyze our virtues. But this is only one kind of judgment on our civilization. Another is to be seen out in the Third World, where millions of poor and downtrodden people are in no doubt whatever about which societies are to be preferred. The immigrant trail goes from Asia and Africa to European civilization; it never goes in the other direction. And the enthusiasm for it is so overwhelming that the process of migration (which cannot help also being a migration of cultures) threatens the very uniqueness that has made our manner of life, for all its defects, so popular.

One must repeat: where lies reality? Is it in the judgments of theatrical folk keen to dramatize all those faults that the anti-discrimination movement has so relentlessly laid bare? Is it in feminists claiming to be oppressed when their condition is the envy of sisters elsewhere? Can it really be found in Muslim refugees from dysfunctional societies who get angry at our tolerant and satirical ways, but never angry enough to go back to where they came from? Or does it lie in the judgment of peoples who in migrating toward us are gambling with their whole lives and futures?

There is, of course, a precedent for this contrast between the beliefs of the elites and the movement of refugees. It is to be found in reactions to communism in the twentieth century. While the elites in large numbers rather admired communist societies because they claimed to be superior to the vulgar consumerism of the West, the miserable creatures actually subjected to this superior system were in no doubt which way they wanted to go.

Where lies reality? This is, of course, always the basic question. Leaving aside the wispy abstractions that float through the minds of so many of the elite, abstractions that change each generation with the onset of new fashions, what is it that those who want to get out of their hell holes and live among us actually value? Why is it that they want to come and live among us and, in a sense, live as we do? This is an important question, not only for them, but also for us. Is it democracy? Is it liberty? Is it merely our affluence? Is it perhaps the individualism that might release them from the bondage of custom? Is it perhaps even Christianity, which has so totally shaped the culture of Western life, and which has now in its broad ecumenical tolerances almost begun to merge with Western life? The West is all of these things and a great deal more. Modernity is, at the very least, a historical moment exhibiting a pattern of life that very few people in the world do not wish to join and to emulate. Our very popularity with millions who do not understand freedom may doom our time to being a mere historical moment that we shall fail to be able to sustain. The irony is that while we have banished most of the immemorial oppressions of history, we are weighed down by shrill voices complaining that our own modern world is itself based on oppression.

It is, as I say, a moment. Human history is very largely the story of despotic elites, and the human condition is always likely to relapse into folly. The important question is: What it is that has allowed us to achieve the condition of things that outsiders find so overpoweringly attractive? We cannot, of course, ever be sure we have the answer to this question. It is equally vital that we should keep it before our eyes.

I hope the reader will forgive this indulgence in grandiose polemics. It is not really my basic concern, but every writer needs to be let off the leash sometimes. The theme of this chapter has been the emergence of a new understanding of society generated among us by various aspects of the idea of democracy. We like its informality, and it has so far failed largely to dent our prosperity, but these things change. To this I shall return. But in the next chapter, I want to characterize the moral life, which is, I shall argue, being transformed by these developments.

THE MORAL LIFE AND
ITS CONDITIONS

I. MORALS AND POLITICS

Democracy is one player in an intellectual dialogue—often a blazing row—called "morals and politics," but as we have seen, it can, confusingly, adopt either the moral or the political voice. The Machiavellian problem posed in this universal dialogue results from the claim that political decisions can never be purely virtuous, and must often involve "not being good."[12]

Democrats are often to be found straddling this issue: to be democratic in politics at least hints at a claim to stand for a higher moral status than would be possible for any other kind of regime. How can "what the people want" collide with morality? Such an apparently rhetorical question sustains many current assertions about the superiority of democracy, such as, for example, that democracies never go to war with one another. The real world is evidently more complicated than these abstractions would suggest. Virtue and civil prudence commonly point in different directions.

Even when they seem to be closely aligned—as is thought to be the case, for example, in policies such as redistributing wealth to the poor—they also involve trampling on the rights of property, and the closer we get to the details of supposedly virtuous political policies, the less virtuous the actual bureaucratic mechanics of the operation will seem. One of the most notable discussions of the larger problem came from Aristotle: Can the good citizen also be a good man? Aristotle's answer[13] brilliantly explores this question in terms of the many subtle (and time-bound) features of citizenship in a Greek polis and here we need not follow him, but his basic answer is the same as ours is likely to be: it depends on the regime.

The business of a good communist citizen in the Soviet Union of the 1920s, for example, was to report criticism of the regime even if made by one's own parents, and that is what made Pavel Morozov a briefly famous figure. He denounced his parents (they were "executed"), became a Soviet hero, and was killed by his enraged uncle. He scored high on citizenship but certainly flunked goodness. Similar examples could be taken from other twentieth-century totalitarian states, especially Nazi Germany, the very model of a state in which goodness had been entirely detached from the policies of the regime. Thus Philippa Foot, in discussing the rationality of moral action, cites the case of a young man, referred to only as a "farm boy," who, imprisoned with a friend in Nazi Germany in 1944, wrote to his parents: "I have been condemned to death . . . We [his friend and he] did not sign up for the SS, and so they condemned us to death. Both of us would rather die than stain our consciences with such deeds of horror. I know what the SS have to do."[14] We hardly need such horrifying instances in order to be clear that the good man could only be the good citizen under some particular constitutions, if indeed even then. As Aristotle remarks, "the good man is a man so called in virtue of a single absolute excellence." Such excellence would often fail to correspond with what the state demands, especially given the highly specific demands made by the civil associations in which Aristotle was writing. Ancient Greek cities required particular investments of public spiritedness from their members, and the likelihood of collision between moral and political judgment was correspondingly high, as Socrates found out, fatally.

Socrates was executed because his philosophical inquiries were thought to be incompatible with the demands of a democratic regime, suggesting that the basic moral problem in politics is the collision between personal judgment and public policy. Whatever else moral judgment may be, it is also irreducibly personal, and this is a concept of the moral life we shall discuss in the next section. The moral life, as we shall see, concerns care of the soul, self, or whatever element of identity is thought to constitute an individual; politics has the different responsibility of caring for the state and its interests, sustaining peace, order, and security. The two realms can perhaps be distinguished; they cannot be separated. Following my conscience in personal life may not be compatible with what the regime demands of its subjects. In early modern Europe, rulers commonly believed that civil order required unanimity about how God ought to be worshipped. John Calvin and Louis XIV alike demanded the right kind of Christianity. It took about two centuries for this principle of government to evolve into John Stuart Mill's idea of a liberal society, and then only at first in limited areas of Western Europe.

But evolve it did, and the result has been that modern Western Europeans have been able to live in liberal democracies in which freedom to speak and act according to their own lights (within the rule of law) has been exercised to an extent never before enjoyed. Whatever else may be wrong with liberal democracies, they are evidently a triumph of personal freedom, and it is a triumph resulting partly from doctrine (especially the European self-understanding of what it is to be free), and partly from observing the misfortunes that have resulted from trying to make everybody believe the same thing. The interesting question is whether this evolution of freedom reflects the grasping of a deep truth about the rationality of freedom (as Hegel argued), or whether it is a contingent benefit resulting from a great variety of complicated social circumstances, circumstances that have a lot further to go and may well produce some surprises, possibly nasty.

One not implausible argument about Western states in the twenty-first century, for example, is that their freedoms have gone too far. They are characterized by rampant individualism. Selfish impulses predominate, an attitude some have called "hyper-individualism." We think too much of rights rather than duties. Our dominant passion is to consume, leading us to grasp for short-term advantage, and we become heedless of tomorrow by getting into debt today. This diagnosis of our current condition takes a high moral tone and identifies goodness and right conduct with philanthropic and "socially responsible" activities.

Such a diagnosis clearly descends from critical attitudes toward a free-market economy, and one cure has entrenched itself as the result of generations of public discussion. Improvement rests upon the young, who must be taught the folly of these ways. The solution to social problems is to be found in something called "education." Educating the young is the key to perfecting the future. The name is misleading, for it is not, as the simple reader might imagine, a call for greater immersion in Latin grammar or quadratic equations. It is rather the inculcation of improving beliefs, initially aimed at the young in schools, but also increasingly directed toward the adult population at large. It is the attempt to change attitudes thought to be undesirable; it aims, as people say these days, "to change the culture." It is propaganda, benign no doubt, but still propaganda. The term "education" is being lost to the familiar process of political debasement.

The really important point about this common and—one must say, plausible—diagnosis of our current moral troubles is that it has bypassed the dialogue of morals and politics altogether. We have moved into a new area called "social criticism." I find this significant because it illustrates a rather common disposition to ignore the question of how individuals ought to behave in favor of rather grandiose remarks about the supposed condition of our society as a whole. The reason for this switch of rhetoric is, I think, that the conventional moral critic has become an absurd figure, since "everybody knows" that moral judgments are merely matters of opinion. They are "values" and people value lots of different things. This is, indeed, a pretty unsophisticated view of things, but it has attained such currency as to transform altogether the terms in which we respond to these important matters, and in this common belief we have one formulation of what concerns me in asking whether democracy is compatible with the moral life. The moral question, which in this area is the only question that takes us seriously as moral agents, has been transposed into a remarkable ambition to legislate the kind of society we want, or think we want. This rather God-like ambition belongs unmistakably to the realm of politics, indeed of democratic politics. The assumption is that what the people want, the people get. Again, we are obviously involved in a world of illusion, but it is remarkably influential.

In responding to questions about the character of the society "we" live in, democracy is the only kind of politics that might be relevant. We no longer believe in philosopher kings, or that some class of people possess superior political understanding. More democracy, and perhaps better democracy, is thought desirable. The problems of democracy may be many, but they are not generally thought to be problems affecting what I am calling "the moral life."

Liberal democracy is almost universally regarded as morally benign, and for very good reasons. If we consider the variety of regimes that have flourished in modern European states from about the sixteenth century onward, we shall certainly be impressed by the range of official demands they have made about how their subjects should live. Some rulers were haunted by the fear that no state would be governable unless some uniform Christian confession prevailed. Masterful rulers demanded that their subjects should worship God according to their own convictions, and some feared that the Lord would punish populations delinquent in any such respect. Treason and sedition might result from dissident minorities, and they were brutally suppressed. Later, the dominant enthusiasm thought to sustain the state came to be political rather than religious, and sometimes led to demands on Europeans vastly more onerous than the religious passions of the past. The emergence at last of liberal democracies from this turbulent passage of modern life certainly suggests that the people

have at last escaped from the tiresome tutelage of their governments. We believe today, with some plausibility, that we have liberated ourselves from priest and commissar, and from any of the
bullying variants of these functionaries that history remembers.
If history is the story of freedom, as political philosophers have
sometimes argued, then we have come through! We can express
our thoughts, and act on our moral choices, with virtually no fear
that some interfering authority will make any serious attempt to
interfere.

Qualifications and doubts may well crowd in on the critical reader, and we shall come to them. For all that, however, it
is worth emphasizing that liberal democracies constitute an
immense advance over the practices of even the quite recent past.
And it is worth recapitulating how we have arrived at this enviable
situation. The philosophers understood the point early, as philosophers often do. Thinkers such as Montaigne and Hobbes recognized that a modern state was a new kind of association in which
a considerable divergence of views about goodness (and particularly about how God ought to be worshiped) was no mere unfortunate accident of the moment, but a constitutive feature of modern
life.* It would hardly be an exaggeration to say that most of the
power and creativity that modern European states have exhibited
has resulted from the recognition of this absolutely central fact.
Conflict and disagreement, even religious, which were at first
deplored as something that had to be accepted through gritted
teeth, in time became recognized as essential to our freedom.

It is important to be clear about the place of Christianity in this
history of the growth of tolerance, because a great deal of current
legendry sees only the protests against demands for conformity.
Church establishments certainly played a highly repressive role
in seeking to sustain their monopoly on the care of souls. They
were, of course, responding to a real problem. Christianity, as a

---

* In *Leviathan*, Chapter 31, Hobbes deals with what natural reason tells us
about our duties to God (which largely amount to conforming to the laws of
nature) and in Chapter 43, what in Christian terms is necessary for salvation. It
simply consists in the affirmation that "JESUS IS THE CHRIST."

religion based on belief, cannot do without an orthodoxy, since it is forever threatened with dissolution into incoherence by new understandings, or misunderstandings, of its basic doctrines. The temptation has been to turn orthodoxy into an iron fist. This feature of European spiritual life has often been a social and political disaster, provoking war and repression, but it has also been a marvelous stimulus to the intellectual life. Christianity has been closely involved with philosophy since its beginnings.

In a religion of this kind, a tradition of doubt and skepticism could hardly be avoided, and it has also come to play a central role in science and philosophy. An unmistakable feature of European life has been this undercurrent of skepticism and dissidence even in the most regulated states. It was never lacking in the Middle Ages, which we tend to regard as more intellectually homogeneous than they actually were. In English life, skepticism is clearly an element in the practices of the common law, and exhibited very notably in the assumption that a man is innocent until found guilty. The late emergence of the distinction between a government and an opposition was another case where skepticism undermined the instinctive monism not only of those holding power, but also of a widespread sentiment in the people they ruled. It was particularly the needs of Christianity for a recognized version of its beliefs that was long in conflict with the skeptical trend in European life.

A powerful theory of the modern states that emerged from the complex realms of feudal times was that they consisted of associations of individuals joined together essentially in recognizing the sovereign authority of law. This was clearly a view skeptical of more high-flown claims to allegiance. And the very idea of "law" in this understanding was fairly strict, excluding anything so specific that it might seem to be a command pretending to be a law. A law was a hypothetical proposition enabling certain sorts of things to be done (such as making wills or contracts) or invoking certain sanctions, and it operated within a structure sustained by courts and other institutions operating in predictable ways. Such a view is the very essence of what we mean by the rule of law. This is civil association in the strictest sense. But this view must be qualified by the fact that no actual state has ever been exclusively "civil" in this fashion. Most of the time, their members have also been involved in some grand enterprise—winning a war, creating the right religious establishment, spreading revolution, or increasing national prosperity, for example. Nevertheless, many of the subjects of any state will not care much about such grandiose national projects, or may even be hostile to them. The implication, as Hobbes spelled out very clearly in *Leviathan*, is that states could never be united around a single overriding project.

Hobbes, in construing the basic character of modern states, certainly thought that one impulse actually did unite individuals in their submission to civil power, and that was a universal recognition of one overriding evil—death, especially violent death. A civil society (the term preferred to "state" by most English writers till recent times) was a form of law-governed order replacing the insecurities of what Hobbes called "the state of nature." The aim actually was to achieve a world in which the good citizen might coincide with the good man, and that ideal has in some impressive degree been achieved. It would not, of course, be the absolute goodness Aristotle described, because no such idea of absolute goodness has survived, or indeed could survive, the dominant skepticism of modern times, nor indeed would it be compatible with our pluralistic practices. Hobbes's negative solution to the problem of a psychological basis for civil society was generally replaced by ideas of security and mutual need in social contract theory. But the fear of death might well be thought even more persuasive in our own times, when our sensitivity to the evil of death has become positively morbid. We may indeed ask the question: "What kind of society do we want?" But "we" don't agree on a lot of things. The most basic achievement recognized by political philosophers these days is that "the right" (the conditions of civil order) must have priority over the many conflicting goods that will be pursued in any modern society.

Both the theory of our freedoms and its practice are genuinely impressive. We no longer live in fear of arbitrary actions by the state, though nasty exceptions to this generalization sometimes occur. No alert reader will fail to recognize, of course, that qualifications to this rosy picture do demand attention. Contemporary states do in fact impose uniformities on us, but they are usually not terribly onerous. They do, however, reveal a tendency in our civilization running counter to its basic liberal assumptions. The whole complex of demanded attitudes popularly known as "political correctness" is a significant qualification of freedom in liberal democracy. These attitudes are a codification (and therefore vulgarization) of conventions previously understood as good manners. As a demand for a semantic conformity of attitudes, this attempt to homogenize opinion requires from us a servile rather than a reasoned response. A certain reservoir of derision for the pieties enforced by egalitarian bureaucracies alone these days sustains our independence.

In one or two countries, Austria for example, denial of the historical reality of the Holocaust has been made criminal, and there have been proposals that those who deny climate change should be treated in the same way. These may well be portents of a strong movement in contemporary Western states to make some agreed doctrine no less compulsory than versions of Christianity had sometimes been compulsory in the past. The persistence of this basically ideological cast of mind is unmistakably a revelation of a very powerful drive within our civilization. In one of its meanings, the 1960s slogan that "the personal is the political" expresses just such a project. It suggests that there are some personal desirabilities (especially advanced by feminists) that can only be achieved by employing legislative power. It invites the government into the bedroom and the drawing room, and the rising tide of legislation affecting family life suggests that it has been taken very seriously. Feminists, for example, have succeeded in passing into law measures whose point is to move women out of tutelage to fathers and husbands and into the tutelage of the state. It remains tutelage, however. That the personal is the political is an important corollary of the more general doctrine that every social arrangement is basically political, in the sense that virtually no public policy fails to have implications for the interests of at least some people.

One might have thought that the point of a free liberal world would have been to solve most of the major problems of civil order precisely so that the citizens could make their own arrangements about how they wanted to live. Such an outcome is most easily achievable in homogenous European states that very largely "speak the same language" in both the metaphorical and the literal sense, because they share a general agreement on the basic conventions governing conduct. European states had largely achieved such a condition, not without difficulty, by the twentieth century. The British had achieved it centuries before; other states were still becoming culturally unified into the nineteenth century. The arrival in Europe of large culturally distinct populations unaccustomed to the usages of freedom has destroyed this civil unity, and opened the way for compromises of custom that qualify our freedom. Sustaining civil order in states containing a variety of very different cultures requires increasing use of regulation and guideline by governments.

One striking consequence of Western involvements with other civilizations is that the familiar skepticism of Europeans has generated as one of its fruits a variety of forms of relativism, most notably perhaps the postmodernist doctrine that the very concept of truth itself makes implausible claims to objectivity in a world in which only a variety of competing perspectives is to be found. Philosophical doctrines are dangerous things, with a capacity to unhinge the wits, and an unreflective skepticism is a case in point, because it illustrates how abstractions can get out of hand. One of the eccentric uses of philosophical skepticism in the past has been as an instrument of dogmatism. Thus seventeenth-century fideists practiced skepticism about both reason and experience in order to conclude that one should live by nothing else but the dogmas of Catholicism. Postmodernist skepticism itself seems to lead to a similar form of dogmatism. It might imply that the state ought to be excluded from governing the details of social life because any such interference would be the oppressive imposition of one perspective against the people involved. Modern academic relativism, however, is combined with a dogmatism about social life. Is the Western view of the rights of women, for example, merely one of those perspectives? If it is, have we no right to impose it on others? If we do not have such a right, then the very different views of the position of women taken by Eastern migrants must be just as valid as our own free and easy ways. In fact, Western states have striven to protect migrant women from arranged marriages, honor killings, female circumcision, and other things that we, with our narrow Western perspective, do not tolerate. In other words, postmodernism seems to have generated a binary off-the-shelf choice of skepticism or dogmatism, available according to convenience. A dogmatism about ethics consorts with skepticism about our own European traditions.

The remarkable fact, then, is that liberty of opinion may well turn out to be not the climax of freedom after centuries of censorship, but merely a way station along the road to some idea of larger perfections. And those "larger perfections" (of which more later) seem to include a repressive dimension intolerant of free discussion. Politics has always been a scene of changing alliances. Law and freedom have always gone together, but judicial activism now casts a shadow over that connection. "Rights" have in the past been a formulation of the essentials of freedom, but utopians have learned to turn a vast range of rights into the blueprint for some supposedly larger social perfection. That is why vigilance and political connoisseurship are necessary in sustaining the practices of our free world. As the English politician Chris Patten once remarked: "In politics, as soon as you take a trick in diamonds, you find that hearts have become trumps." Machiavelli's realism in arguing that the politician must at times know how not to be good is rejected in favor of a moral fundamentalism demanding that the state must be brought fully into line with our new and superior understanding of rights and social justice. But in political life, there is no such thing as a moral imperative that does not have large implications for power. When social justice meets political correctness, the old liberal idea that relations between individuals are a purely personal matter is overridden. There is a right thing to do, and the state will make sure it is done. Democracy today is becoming rather intolerant of moral and political disagreement. A servile perfection has become the way we think, or perhaps ought to think, and politics seems to resolve itself into technical issues of how to actualize the one true policy of international harmony and social justice.

These are some of the considerations that make it worth asking whether the moral life is compatible with democracy. But what actually is "the moral life"?

2. WHAT IS THE MORAL LIFE?

The moral life is that element of our experience in which we cultivate the duties we have to ourselves, duties to sustain a character we approve of, and one that will not suffer justified reproach from others, or from our own inner sense. A character of thievery or lying is widely thought reprehensible, while one of being courageous and helpful is admirable. The moral life is, then, our concern to do the right thing. Does this sound a little unreal? The reason it might is that I am concerned with the formal character of such a life. People often fail to do the right thing. It is also an elementary fact that people have the most astonishingly varied ideas of what actually is the right thing to do. It is further true that while no one is likely to approve of thieves or liars, the content of these terms is a matter of the highest ambiguity. Am I a thief in taking away the shampoo sachets provided in hotel rooms, or a liar when I pretend to have enjoyed something so as not to hurt people's feelings? At this level, the moral life is a morass through which we trudge with difficulty. But in everyday life, we usually manage to do the right thing, by our lights, as we go along. Frequently, of course, we fail, but failure is also part of our moral experience. And the moral dilemmas that make us scratch our heads are fortunately rare for most of us.

One rather elevated view of the moral life is that it consists in caring for the soul, caring for our integrity as moral beings. If we follow Socrates, we are likely to think that this is the most important element in the lives we lead. In this sense, it is the activity of caring for goodness, our custodianship of that inner core of continuity in our lives that has many names: soul, self, reputation, character, will, identity, and so on. In this meaning, other things such as success or failure, even happiness, are largely trivial, and some people think that this is true of life itself. Self-sacrifice may become the highest cultivation of the self. On the other hand, the very word "moral" has acquired rather dire associations in contemporary life. It often connotes some severe moralist invoking principles that stand between us and the pleasures we enjoy, especially sexual. As against this, a powerful popular view is that we have the right to decide for ourselves what "values" we hold. These are questions of substance on which, fortunately, I do not have to pronounce. My limited aim here is merely to sketch the moral life as an element in our experience.

And that means a brief excursion into the perilous territory of saying what "moral" is. In self-defense, let me say that no one is very clear on this. If the moral life consists in the attempt to do the right thing, then the moral thing would have to be one possible answer to the question: What is the right thing to do? The "moral thing" in our civilization responds to the sentiments and rules we acquire early in life, and it varies from individual to individual. Whether there is an imperative principle on which everyone ought to agree is a matter of great dispute. This situation, however, is (I would suggest) almost uniquely Western. The question "What is the right thing to do?" in non-Western societies has a variety of answers that need not be "moral" in any sense we might recognize. One possibility is that the right thing to do consists in following the custom of the tribe or the country. Another answer is that it is doing what is pleasing to God. In both these cases, there is, at least in principle, a specific right thing to do, and correspondingly not doing that right thing is a specific kind of badness. Nor are these answers absent in Western life, which is also marked (but not exclusively) by both custom and religious judgments. Conventionally, following custom is the avoidance of shame, while doing what is pleasing to God is avoiding sin. In parallel we might say that doing the moral thing (whatever it may be) is the avoidance of guilt. This schema would, I think, be fairly widely accepted, but my next step would probably not be. It consists in suggesting that the moral life in its purest form is almost entirely a European idea.

Most human beings, in doing the right thing, are guided by custom, for there is in most tribes, cultures, and civilizations an overriding conception of a right ordering of things, usually in terms of youth/age, male/female, and ruler/subject. No such system of the right ordering of people can, of course, be entirely transparent; all will at some point require interpretation. In many cultures, ideas of the right thing to do are determined by what are thought to be the commands of God. Custom and religion commonly reinforce each other, but they must be distinguished because the same religion will be "spoken," as it were, in a variety of different idioms, leading to great variations in ideas of what is divinely commanded. Europeans are not much less influenced by custom (though probably less by religion) than other peoples, but in our form of life, moral ideas have in much greater degree detached themselves and begun to lead a life of their own.

One plausible view would be that this detachment of rightness from both custom and religion begins with Socrates, who rejected the customs and the gods of Athens in order to make the care of the soul a free-floating concern whose content would be elaborated in philosophical criticism of the received ideas of his milieu. Philosophy was clearly a necessary element here in facilitating the project of detaching the right thing to do from its religious and customary encrustations, and some capacity to isolate the moral from the customary and the religious has lived an intermittent life in Western experience ever since. A great deal of philosophy in the Hellenistic and Roman periods was concerned with how one ought to live, and Stoic, Epicurean, and Skeptical ideas have seldom been without influence on modern thought.

In early modern times, a new terminology developed to allow the autonomy of the moral life to evolve. The most celebrated of these conceptions was, of course, conscience, a relational term connecting the will with the integrity of the individual. One view of the right thing to do is that it must always be something that conscience approves. The problem is that conscience, when a purely subjective conviction unconnected with more public moral ideas, is as likely to be the vehicle of lunacy and fanaticism as it is of right and rational conduct. We tend to admire dissidents purely for their independence of mind, but some of their doings are far from admirable. Admiration for conscience has not usually been shared by philosophers, or indeed by governments. In the moral life, guidance by conscience as being a person's own conviction happens, however, to be consonant with current unreflective modern ideas. In more recent times, the project of morals without religion has been a popular version of the morality of conscience.

The moral life as we understand it has certainly been spun off from religion, and most notably from the Protestant reformers of the early modern period, who rejected monastic asceticism and transferred some at least of its embrace of spiritual value to the ordinary conduct of life. Max Weber takes the view that this move picked up some of the tendencies of medieval Christianity, but "one thing was unquestionably new: the valuation of the fulfillment of duty in worldly affairs as the highest form that the moral life of the individual could assume."[15] Fulfilling the obligations imposed upon the individual by his position in the world was his "calling" and was the only way of living acceptably to God. And here, the crucial term is that of the "individual," because the correlate of the moral life as we understand it is (as we shall see) an individual with his or her own sense of the right thing to do. The right thing to do in this context is individual, but it is never *merely* individual. It cannot avoid picking up some of the features of a complex moral tradition.

What actually is the right thing to do? This is a question of substance that I cannot answer, nor, I think, do I need to, since I am merely concerned with the formal aspects of the moral life. All I need say is that philosophers have commonly elaborated three types of answer to the question. The first is the utilitarian answer that the right thing to do is always that which most effectively maximizes the happiness of all the people involved. The second is a Kantian argument to the effect that a series of absolute values or categorical imperatives are objectively binding upon us if we are to exhibit goodness of the will. And the third type of answer, sometimes called an ethic of admiration, is that the right thing to do is an authentic expression of the character of the moral agent concerned. None of these proto-philosophical formulas exhausts the possibilities, nor is any of them likely to be of serious help to the person in a quandary. Who, on learning from Aristotle that virtue is a mean between extremes, would find his moral quandary solved? A reader being told by an ethical skeptic that moral terms are merely expressions of feeling will be even be worse off than before.

My argument, then, is that the idea of the moral life is essentially part of our European world, having emerged from classical philosophy and Protestant worldliness along with other sources, including the many currents of thought often today packaged together as "the Enlightenment." The striking thing in this development is the way in which our moral life has detached itself from custom and become a kind of independent tradition of moral experience in parallel with those other more universal sources of human order. The condition of this uniqueness is the Western sense of individualism, as distinct from the social conceptions of custom and religion, both of which also continue to operate in Western life. I am sure that those who know vastly more about other cultures and civilizations than I do will find this an absurd judgment, but I think it worth advancing as a hypothesis that would cast some light on what makes our form of life different from that of other cultures.

I am not suggesting, of course, that there is no moral element in the experience of non-Europeans; merely that the moral element as distinct from the customary and the religious is very much more developed among Europeans. There is no doubt, for example, that Confucian ethics has many of the features of our moral life, and certainly there is even more vibrantly a sense of honor operating than among us in the deliberation of those in Confucian lands. But the sense of honor attaches, I suspect, vastly more to a social role (as Samurai, as Mandarin, as father, etc.) than to a distinct individual. The opposite side of this argument will be found in Western philosophers who think that moral judgments merely express forms of generalized approval or disapproval, and if moral phenomena have no more substance than this, then it would, indeed, be plausible to assimilate them without remainder to religious and customary attitudes. When I speak of the moral life without qualification in this argument, however, I shall be taking for granted that it necessarily involves individualism. For it is from the self-conscious individual as a moral agent that European self-respect emerges.

The individual round whom the moral life revolves is, if I may use the vile jargon of the moment, a "construction." We don't come by it naturally. When we do, we often construe the moral life as a succession of problems in which we respond to circumstances (as understood in terms of our moral sentiments) by the use of rules. Rational moral agents take stock of their circumstances and consider practical questions in terms of the moral rules and sentiments that seem appropriate. This familiar account of the moral agent is, of course, highly abstract. Certainly deliberation is an activity that focuses the mind to an unusual extent because our conscious experience is commonly rather diffuse. The best descriptions of our inner life in general are those given by skeptical philosophers. Thus Thomas Hobbes remarks:

> For, I believe, the most sober men, when they walk alone without care and employment of the mind, would be unwilling the vanity and extravagance of their thoughts at that time should be publicly seen; which is a confession, that passions unguided, are for the most part mere madness.[16]

David Hume takes a similar line in searching for some reference for the idea of a soul or a self. Introspection, he thinks, fails to reveal such a thing. Setting aside some metaphysicians, he remarks dismissively:

> I may venture to affirm of the rest of mankind, that they are nothing but a bundle or collection of different perceptions, which succeed each other with an inconceivable rapidity, and are in a perpetual flux and movement. Our eyes cannot turn in their sockets without varying our perceptions. Our thought is still more variable than our sight . . . The mind is a kind of theatre, where several perceptions successively make their appearance; pass, repass, glide away, and mingle in an infinite variety of postures and situations.[17]

We generally present to the world a coherent character, and we mostly utter sensible words, but these things are constructions out of rather inchoate materials, constructions that respond to our awareness of an audience, and they exhibit a trained recognition of what is sane, sensible, and acceptable. The "audience" need not be an actual presence, and for believers, it is often God judging their thoughts and actions. Hegel characterizes the educational disciplines required of children in schools as "liberating" them from the arbitrary and random sensations of the child mind.[*] Schooling and custom give most of us some elements of rational direction of the mind, and those who entirely miss out on such a discipline in youth, such as the odd feral child who has grown to maturity without human contact, can never recover it. In other words, the moral life in any form is not "natural." It is something we learn, and it seems we must learn it at an early stage of life, or not at all.

The moral life cannot help but find itself revealed in the explorations of character we make every time we read a novel, for the novel is the aesthetic correlate of the individualist moral life that has developed in Western parts. That life consists of the daily flow of thoughts and feelings as we navigate our way between what Hobbes called "appetites and aversions." In doing so, we are making sense of what happens to us by interpretations that can range from the subtle to the mad. The moral life is Don Quixote convinced that the windmills he encountered were wicked knights, and ought to be put to flight. It is Emma feeling ashamed at the way she had treated poor Miss Bates in *Emma*, and Jim in *Lord Jim* jumping ship. It is Merton Densher and Kate Croy in *The Wings of the Dove* using Milly Theale for their own purposes, and discovering the destructive effects such moral corruption can have. Novelists deal with dramatic moments that feature very much less frequently in everyday life but they do capture

---

[*]   "The necessity for education is present in children as their own feeling of dissatisfaction with themselves as they are, as the desire to belong to the adult world whose superiority they divine, as the longing to grow up." Hegel's *Philosophy of Right*, T. M. Knox (ed. & trans.), Oxford: Clarendon Press, 1952, Para. 175 R.

the way in which morality is an aspect of the continuous flow of our experiences and our actions. We often think of the moral life as setting us problems to solve, but actually most of the time we do the right thing (or fail to do it) according to our lights from custom and habit. This is why the moral life has sometimes been understood as a "language" of practice that we mostly speak fluently, though occasions sometimes arise in which we don't know, quite, what to "say," or to do. At such times, we have a problem to which we may respond by deliberation, and it is in the process of deliberation that "morality," as a coherent set of ways of solving moral problems, appears.

The moral life consists, then, in doing the right thing, in that intermediate arena where no legal sanction generally applies, and also where the gracefulness of manners is not the point. It is, in one formulation, a matter merely of following appropriate rules, but following moral rules is a complicated activity. Why is it so difficult? The reason is that circumstances often tempt us to do the wrong thing because it yields a pleasure or an advantage that the rules, or our sentiments, forbid. Evading those rules or sentiments often leads us to interpret the world conveniently rather than dutifully. It is often said that all political lives end in failure; similarly, it is hard not to think that moral lives are not only a challenge, but also a challenge that in the long run we always fail. One powerful psychoanalytical tradition takes the view that civilization imposes almost intolerable burdens upon us. It is hardly surprising, then, that a gap may open up between inner desire and outward show, and that we may do the wrong thing but conceal the fact that we are doing it, or at least conceal our real motives behind some respectable pretense.

One value of moral conduct in the lives we lead is that it orders our lives so that we can rely on other people, and other people on us. This is a supremely valuable basis of cooperative enterprise in social life. Confident expectation of the responses of others is the basis of much of the enterprise that distinguishes our culture. Whatever its defects, the moral world may be accounted a success to the extent that we manage to lead orderly and fulfilling lives. Yet we are often excessively concerned with the extent to which people fail to live up to our expectation, not understanding how much more dramatically other societies fail this test. The reason they fail is in part that they lack our *civil* order, which rests on moral foundations. The freedom of our civic life allows us a space in which we are largely secure from arbitrary and casual despotic interference, and this grounds our practice of moral deliberation. But since it inevitably has its failures, it is understandable that many people dream of a better way—a form of social life that avoids the failures of virtue we cannot avoid. Those failures, however, are the price we pay for freedom, which is thus logically incompatible with perfection.

A disciplined moral life does not come easily. Moral education is a process of evolving out of a condition of egocentricity in which we are mere victims of impulse into a condition in which we recognize objective features of our situation. As Adam Smith puts it, man desires not merely to be praised, but to be praiseworthy, and in order to be so, "we must become the impartial spectators of our own character and conduct."[18] Such a spectator has the effect of correcting the constant pull toward self-partiality in human life. In a religious idiom, God may be for many people the spectator in terms of whom they construe their moral experience, even where doing the right thing is not understood as obeying divine law. Plato makes the same point in his story of the invisible man who by nefarious conduct kills a king, seduces the queen, and takes over a kingdom because he can do these things with the furtiveness of invisibility.[19] In other words, the moral life is acted out on a stage that includes both visible and invisible spectators.

In the moral life, then, we are challenged to achieve a kind of life in which we are able to sustain a character that is both good in itself and can be relied on by our associates. Human beings understand themselves as creatures that can and often must morally resist the call of temptation, and temptation may be understood as a feeble propensity to be the victim of some external stimulus. Money in the open till is stolen, the pretty girl one meets is groped, a sunny afternoon means that the worker slopes off to see the sporting match, and so on. The Mafioso who breaches the code of silence when arrested is hoping for the short-term gain of being released from confinement. But just such a Mafioso illustrates the contention that the moral life is virtually universal among us. A notable capo in Sicily arrested in 2007 was found to have written down a set of moral commandments, such as telling the truth to associates, refraining from seducing the wives of others, and respect for their property. A commandment is not, of course, the same thing as a rule, but this case illustrates very well the contention Socrates affirmed in talking to Thrasymachus, namely that even a band of robbers must behave morally.[20] The defect of criminal associations is the range over which the good conduct operates.

The Greeks understood this element of the moral life as the distinction between the moral autonomy of a real (i.e., rational) human being, on the one hand, and a slavish character on the other. The essence of the slave was that he would not get on with his duties unless watched, and would not work without incentives, whereas the free citizen could be relied upon to do his duty without supervision. As a mere creature of his circumstances, the slave hardly counts in these terms as a moral agent at all. Corruption (accepting or demanding bribes, for example) is thus an expression of slavishness. Ancient writers such as Polybius were in no doubt that the strength of Republican Rome resulted from the fact that the Romans took their oaths very seriously, even oaths extracted under duress, as when Scipio forced Romans, at the point of a sword, to swear to fight on after their defeat by Hannibal at Cannae.[*] Similarly, the great moral heroes such as Thomas More and Martin Luther are those who stood firm, even at the risk of their own lives. But in these examples, we have drifted toward the familiar mistake of identifying the moral life with the rigor of some widely admired versions of it.

It is but one of the many complexities of the moral life that rules, being abstract, may be in conflict with each other, and that

---

[*] A matter of central interest to Machiavelli. See *Discourses*, Ch. IX. Polybius discusses Roman religion in Book VI of *The Rise of the Roman Empire*, trans. Ian Scott-Kilvert, Penguin Books, 1979, p. 349, where he writes that ". . . the very phenomenon which among other peoples is regarded as a subject for reproach, namely superstition, is actually the element that holds the Roman state together."

exhibiting one virtue may prevent us from exhibiting another. Philosophers recognize that identifying "the right thing" to do may well depend on how it is described. One can play lots of amusing games wondering whether one's civic duty should override one's loyalty to family or friends. But exploring competing descriptions of the same type of act is often a way of introducing moral reality into the complex situations to which we must respond. Certainly abiding by the rules may entail exhibiting a vice, and the demands of virtue may require us to violate some moral rule. These problems arise because human motives and social situations are complex. In some concrete experiences, the admirable and the disreputable may be almost inextricably combined.

It is but one aspect of this complexity that Western moral attitudes may include admiration even for the bad, if the bad is grand or heroic. Satan in Milton's *Paradise Lost* is one example of this, and even Don Juan the seducer can be taken as a morally ambiguous figure. Should we the more admire a remorseful sinner, or a defiant sinner who sins with panache? It depends, no doubt, on the sin and the personality. But this contrast between the submissively good and the heroically bad is one dimension of ambiguity in our moral understanding picked up by Nietzsche's view that morality is a conspiracy of priests. In some moods, he thinks that Christian-derived moral rules prevalent in Europe express the morality of the herd. It is in these elevated philosophical speculations that simple people may lose their grip on reality, as did the two Chicago students Loeb and Leopold, who read more Nietzsche than their tiny understandings could absorb, and went in for murder as an act of elite bravado.[*]

Nietzsche deplored morality, but thought it made man an interesting animal. Animals, we assume, don't deliberate; they just do what comes naturally. Human beings may choose because they have a quality commonly called "freedom of the will." They choose, and in such choices, duty is often more painful than incli-

---

[*]   This event became the basis for the play "Rope," which in turn became an Alfred Hitchcock film.

nation. This sometimes leads to the question: "Why should one be moral?" If the question assumes some particular set of moral rules or admired virtues, then it provokes one kind of answer, but if it asks whether we should participate in the moral life as I am describing it, then the answer is simply that we have no choice. We are individuals whose inner lives are inextricably involved with sensations of obligation and compulsion. It may be, as the psychiatrists suggest, that there are some people called "psychopaths" who are entirely without a moral sense, and do not know "the nature and quality of their act," as the old legal definition of insanity had it, but they must be very rare. Delinquent or supposedly immoral behavior often responds to highly eccentric moral admirations. Governments periodically run public relations campaigns designed to discourage their subjects from dropping litter in the streets. By contrast, in some teenage circles, it has been reported, the disposition to drop one's trash in a litterbin is thought to be conformist and "sissy." No red-blooded youth would be seen doing it. Gangs, fashions, and peer groups are sources of eccentric and usually short-lived variations, often deplorable, about what it is right to do. In traditional societies, it is perhaps not quite impossible to generate a virtual uniformity of practice, but in an individualist society such as our own, it cannot be done. Hobbes recognized this point in arguing that in modern European states no summum bonum, or highest good, could be agreed on, though most men might agree on a summum malum, or highest evil, which as we have seen was violent death.

We have said that doing one's duty is often painful, and the whole structure of law and morality may be regarded as a burden that civilization places on creatures that have evolved over millions of years out of very different conditions. Individuals become moral beings in part as a result of painful experiences—denials, disappointments, frustrations, slaps, shoutings, and the rest. Admirations, or "positive reinforcement," are obviously also part of this development. Punishment is the basic device for enforcing both legal and moral rules, and Europeans have acquired a moral sense as a result of centuries of often-brutal enforcements of some version of the right thing to do. When we punish people for crimes, we assume, and indeed force on them, the assumption that the person we punish is the same person who offended. We do indeed have machinery within the moral life for recognizing repentance and remorse, but we also look to the characterological underpinnings of offenses and judge offenders by their record. Here we encounter another modern response to the moral life, most commonly associated with Sigmund Freud. This response argues that modern societies are essentially repressive, and that the whole apparatus of condemnation and punishment ought to be replaced by greater understanding, indeed ideally by forms of therapy. It is, as we shall see, an opinion influential in our current practices.

That the moral life is a burden is often how we feel, and certainly how people have felt in times past, especially in the early centuries of the Christian era when a particularly severe interpretation of the doctrine of original sin was in vogue. But toward the end of the medieval period in Europe, a new disposition emerged in which many people understood moral choice less as a burden than as an opportunity. This change is at the heart of the emergence of individualism that we shall discuss presently, but for the moment my concern is with another feature of the moral life as it developed at that time: namely, that it is profoundly argumentative, indeed casuistical.

It can supply for some people the pleasures of a highly sophisticated connoisseurship. It provokes us to reflection, and for some people this kind of high seriousness will be a pleasure rather than a burden. It will certainly be a great source of intellectual subtlety in anyone's life. The characters in novels by such writers as Joseph Conrad and Henry James are often virtuoso moral reasoners. The heroine of James's novel *Confidence* may find virtue "boring," but her young man merely raises his eyebrows in wonderment at this idea. Moral reasoning can crop up in remarkable places. Bertie Wooster has just been invited to dine with a man who had seriously misjudged him, but has now discovered that he was wrong about Bertie. Wooster says that he regards the invitation as:

"'The *amende honorable*, sir?' supplied Jeeves.

'I was going to say "olive branch."'

'Or olive branch. [Jeeves continued] The two terms are virtually synonymous. The French phrase I would be inclined to consider perhaps slightly the more exact in the circumstances—carrying with it, as it does, the implication of remorse, of the desire to make restitution. But if you prefer the expression "olive branch," by all means employ it, sir.'

'Thank you, Jeeves.'"[21]

The problem with the moral life is that morality is so powerful a drive in human nature that almost any kind of conduct can be fashioned into some kind of morality responding to what, in a general way, some people are inclined to admire. This we have seen to be the point of the band of robbers Socrates talks about in Book I of *The Republic*. Evil as those robbers no doubt were, their association must necessarily have rested on some form of justice; otherwise they could have been nothing more than a disorderly rabble. The same point may be seen in St. Augustine's admiration for the virtues of the Romans, whose moral strength was to be admired even though he believed that it rested on false beliefs.[22] Nietzsche detested the bourgeois morality of his time, but few men were more passionately involved in issues of the moral life.

Because many kinds of conduct can be fashioned into some sort of moral system, moral admirations and approvals never seem to stand still. It has to be admitted that there is an element of fashion about the way in which they change from one generation to the next. Certainly the twentieth century offered a positive frenzy of moral revision. Most societies have regarded sex as a drive likely to disrupt good order in society, and therefore as requiring strict control, but the twentieth century has largely swept this fear away. Sexuality in response to desire is now regarded as a natural impulse that must not be frustrated or denied, unless it risks dangerous consequences such as disease and abortion, and sometimes not even then. This basic conviction lies at the heart of many of the moral revisions in our time. Homosexual liberation and the greater ease of divorce were alike consequences of this new idea. Expressing these changes in old-fashioned terminology, we may say that sins of intemperance lost much of their sting, but sins of pride (especially collective or caste pride) were all the more passionately rejected as violating the principle of equality.

The many changes in moral sentiment (and often also in legal enactment) during the twentieth century were accompanied by (but not, I think, caused by) a growth in beliefs about moral relativism. Those beliefs were generated only partly by an intense interest in the variations of moral practice found among the various inhabitants of our planet. Moral relativism in the "anything goes" idiom was part of the rejection of any form of oppression, part of the egalitarian spirit. Once moral conduct lost its anchorage in custom or religion, many people argued on quite general grounds that no one had any right to impose "his" or "her" morality on anyone else; each must decide for himself or herself. Morality, one might say, was bounced out of the retail trade and became a cottage industry.

One might imagine that such moral dynamism would have stilled the propensity to make grandiose declarations of moral rightness, but the opposite has happened. There has been no illusion more powerful in human history than the belief that we in our enlightened time have at last arrived at the true understanding of morality. Even today's popular relativism has not saved us from succumbing to it. On the basis of this remarkable illusion, governments have been signing up to international schedules of rights, and social institutions in liberal democratic states have been implementing rules and practices intended to enforce moral desirabilities such as the equal treatment of everyone and politically correct forms of social intercourse. The power of the illusion of timeless universality has followed from another conviction no less remarkable: namely, the belief that, in making the changes we have, we are rationally triumphing over the prejudices and superstitions of past ages. We thus combine a rhetoric of rights and freedoms and a reality of attitudinal engineering. The result is a powerful moral project to relax the punitive sanctions of the past—the schoolteacher's cane, the parental slap, the magistrate's custodial sentence, the moralist invoking self control—in favor of a program that emphasizes communal involvement and rational understanding as getting at the "root causes" of bad conduct. Whether this attempt to "negotiate" moral order has been a success or a failure is a question that only time can answer.

In insisting on the illusory character of our fancied superiority to the moral opinion we inherited from the past, I am not taking a position on whether or not some moral structures are better than others. I am not even denying that some moral principles, or at least some formulations of them, might be plausible candidates for universality and absoluteness. There is, however, no denying that human societies are immensely variable in their moral sentiments, and that many such sentiments respond to local circumstance, and hence cannot easily be compared, if indeed any reasonable comparison between concrete practices can be made at all. Good lives of one kind or another are possible under many different "moralities." It is certainly true that the popular conviction of our time that our ancestors suffered from prejudice and superstition, and that we have broken through into the peaceful pastures of reason, is one that would have had the skeptics of earlier times splitting their sides.

And justifiably: a notable paradox of twenty-first-century Western life is that while our moral sentiments tend to follow the principle of "anything goes," institutional life has never been more tightly controlled. Tolerance is the foundational liberal virtue, but bad trouble awaits the slightest hint of attitudes that might be described as racist, sexist, discriminatory, xenophobic, or homophobic—a bestiary to which additions keep on being made. Intolerance is thought to be the fertile mother of vices. Speech must be free, but not discriminatory speech. Rights grow in every corner of life, yet every liberation we acquire augments the march of regulation.

There is a solution to this paradox, and we shall be exploring it in depth later. The solution arises from the fact that the punitive structure enforcing law and morality in the past has been rejected as being both repressive and ineffectual. Just as many formal features of dress and of social manners have been relaxed, so also do we find that the strict application of moral rules has been liberalized. From Freud and others, we have acquired the idea that if people were able to express their feelings, and understand better the reason of rules and forms, then the repressive ordering devices of the past—punishment and authority most notably, but also morality itself—would be unnecessary. If people could express their feelings honestly, they might learn to deal with them rationally, and therefore learn how to fit in with other members of society. Human beings will thus find their highest happiness in such accommodation to their fellows. In this way, we shall be able to arrive at the immemorial dream of combining spontaneity with good social order. A project of this remarkable kind seems to lie behind much that is otherwise puzzling in the moral beliefs of our time.

3. A CONTEXT OF THE MORAL LIFE

Democracy and the moral life go together, in principle, because each is an element in the freedom we enjoy. Democracy is the political system of freedom because it is self-government: the people rule themselves. They are not subject to a despot. Similarly, in the moral life, each individual is self-moving in the sense that no one is his or her master. We all rule ourselves, and live with the consequences. Such autonomy does not exclude a variety of situations in which the agent's duty is to obey another, but beyond the tutelage of childhood, any subordination is the result of choice, and is functional to some agreed purpose. In the classical world, as Hegel put it, some were free, but now we are all free, all self-moving moral agents.[*] And moral agency, I have been

---

[*] "World history is the progress of the consciousness of freedom—a progress whose necessity it is our business to comprehend . . . Orientals know that only one is free, the Greek and Roman world knew that Some are free, and our knowledge is that All men as such are free, and that man is by nature free . . ." Hegel, *Lectures on the Philosophy of World History: Introduction: Reason in History*, trans. H. B. Nisbet, Cambridge University Press, 1975, p. 54.

suggesting, is the stream of inner feelings that seem to oblige us to do the right thing, and to which we cannot help but respond as we go through life. But we need to say a little more about the moral character of this experience.

Emerging from the Latin *mos*, which also gives us "mores," morality takes its rise from the idea of customary conduct as guiding our lives. And so far as most human beings are concerned, the customary (as we have seen) has nearly always been the right thing to do. The point about custom is that it was usually associated with religion, which provides all the authority that custom might need in order to "feel right." Custom generally rested on both divine sanction and what Burke called "prescription." It was the thing done, and the thing "not done." In Muslim lands, guidance comes from the Koran, from traditions of the Prophet, from the Sharia, with a considerable variety of local forms of living. It seems largely the case that doing the right thing in this world is a matter of conforming to some particular structure of tradition, and doing the wrong thing is deviating from it. Obedience and disobedience are the key ideas. Similarly in Confucian culture, conduct was prescribed for a variety of social roles ranging from the emperor to the youngest sister in a family. In Hindu society, complex distinctions of caste generate a general assignment of duties. These are cases of what sociologists have commonly assimilated to each other as "traditional" societies, by contrast with the modern societies of the West. In such a traditional world, a distinct sense of "moral" is likely to be rather fugitive. A right action would be whatever has religious and social approval, and would have no need of any further justification. The moral could be little more than some individual variation in the distribution of the virtues each person brings to his encounters with others.

In Western experience, I am suggesting, the moral aspect of things has been uniquely able to disentangle itself from both religion and custom. Socrates was famous for raising the question "How ought I to live?," and refusing to answer it in terms of local custom, or (what amounts to the same thing) of what the majority of people think. Socrates argued that rational inquiry was not merely a preparation for right conduct, but was itself the beginning of the moral life. The famous story of the Delphic oracle that declared him to be the wisest of men became a ground for his declaring a kind of tabula rasa or clean sweep of customary beliefs about conduct. Everything, including stories about the gods, was up for rational consideration. As a philosopher, the Platonic Socrates, being wise in that he knew he knew nothing, refused to take either religion or custom as being authoritative. A good man might find himself at odds with custom, with the gods, and even with his city itself, a position dramatized in the events that led to his own trial and condemnation at the hands of the Athenian court. In *The Crito*, Socrates explains that had he fled Athens to avoid trial and condemnation, he would have betrayed a lifetime commitment to his city. This was a judgment we might well call "moral" because it rested on the idea that a good life should be coherent, but it was certainly not in accordance either with custom or divine command. Here was a dramatic, indeed a self-dramatizing, challenge to the dominant ideas about how one ought to live. Perhaps any abstract vocabulary describing manners and conduct might generate the kind of semantic friction from which a new and critical conception of a morality could emerge, but here in the unique career of Socrates, we find a remarkable moral illumination. The career and the philosophy of Socrates, itself of course emerging from an already established philosophical tradition, gave this event a salience that set the moral ball of European reflection on its way.

Early Christianity might seem to offer little purchase for independent ideas of right, but in fact it became a major source of such ideas. For one thing, Christianity had to enter into a dialogue with Greek and Roman thought, and in the process became a religion entangled with philosophy. This made the early Christians remarkably disputatious and liable to internal and external quarrels. For another, the Christian distinction between the secular and the sacred life suggested the possibility not only of different standards, but also of a conflict of authority between them. The basic Christian revelation was of a kingdom not of this world, which adumbrated a dualism given classic status in St. Augustine's two cities. To be a Christian was to belong both to the *civitas dei*, and also the *civitas terrena*. In later medieval times, tensions periodically erupted between the priestly teaching of peace and the enthusiasm of feudal nobles for armed conflict.

The dualistic structure of Christian thought had the effect of facilitating the emergence of independent moral ideas within the secular world, a morality that eventually came directly into conflict with religious authority. In the republics of medieval Italy, a love of one's city might be found in conflict with the Christian's focus on individual salvation. Machiavelli admired a time when citizens "preferred the good of their country to their ghostly consolations."[23] With the Renaissance in Italy came an efflorescence of individuality and, in the course of the early modern period, the creation of modes of conduct and of government that allowed (as we shall see later) individuality a recognized place in the governing of modern societies. A further element in the emergence of this pluralism was the fact that the word of God as expressed by the clergy came to be challenged by the inner light of conscience as felt by many believers.

In an individualist world, then, the moral might stand on all fours with the religious and the customary; indeed as we approach the modern world, new versions of morality bid fair to taking over the entire guidance of European conduct. But for the moment, our focus is on the moral life itself as an aspect of our conscious and self-conscious experience. We have argued that the moral life is to be located in those feelings of obligation and duty impelling us to do the right thing. One problem is how to distinguish this moral sense from the immense variety of other inner compulsions that we all experience.

Our felt obligation to obey the law of the land, for example, overlaps with our moral sentiments without being identical with them. The rule of law is, of course, a major achievement in the rational ordering of a human society. In despotic societies, humans find themselves suffering from caprice, and the only response is an entrenched wariness about anything to do with rulers and their arbitrary ways. But in our Western liberal democracies, compliance with the law is something we internalize in such a way that we rarely feel directly constrained by the law's demands. We may guess that without this relaxed condition of civil confidence we would not have the moral life playing such an important part in the way we conduct our lives. Where civil order is weak, the sense of duty gives way to a short-sighted opportunism, as it has in many contemporary African states.

Again, many compulsions arise from our involvement with superiors whom we must please on pain of losing a job, failing an exam, or suffering some other check or frustration to our desires—the whole range of compulsions that Kant called "hypothetical imperatives." We learn from experience that we had better not express some opinions or indulge in some actions on pain of consequences we shall find unpleasant. A rule of conduct dictated by the need to please superiors is one of the central forms of servility and corruption found almost universally in despotic states. On the other hand, a tactful prudence sometimes eases social relations, and it is an acute moral question deciding which line of conduct would be appropriate.

Another set of compulsions arises from conforming to the set of manners current in our circle. We must not rush out of a room in front of a lady, or use vulgar language on a formal occasion. Handbooks of manners from earlier centuries introduce us to a totally different world of coughing and farting, a world very far removed from the genteel compulsions of our own time. If you blow your nose, as Castiglione noted in his advice to courtiers, do not examine the contents of your handkerchief "as if they contained rubies." That word, "compulsion," itself has been domesticated in the language of psychiatry, and suggests that the more neurotic we are, the more we shall be enslaved to compulsions arising from our obsessions, phobias, and anxieties. Superstition tells us not to walk under ladders or entertain thirteen guests.

Moral obligation may thus be specified negatively in this manner. It is a sense of obligation that can be independent of religion, custom, and felt practical necessity, though any of these may be contingently involved with it. Such a free-floating sense of what is right depends directly on our approvals and admirations for types of acts. It may be that we can press this explanation one stage further, and discover that our approvals and admirations rest upon objective foundations, such as rationality, happiness, justice, duty, and rights, or some other conception. I think we can say with some confidence that no such foundation has yet been established by philosophers, but I like the very idea that it might be possible, and it is certainly worth discussing. Here, as often, it may be better to travel than to arrive. Retreat to a mere relativism on morals is certainly in our time a symptom of superficiality and obtuseness.

At the beginning of the twentieth century, the exponents of ethical relativism gleefully collected a whole anthropology of moral variations. Monogamy for Christians was to be contrasted with Islamic polygamy, and Eskimos were discovered to have some remarkable customs involving husbands hospitably offering wives for the pleasure of their guests. In another part of the forest, ideologists were at the same time reducing moral rules to forms of false consciousness functioning merely to facilitate the domination of men over women, bourgeois over proletarian, Jews over the capitalist system, and other such oppressions. These doctrines came to constitute a large part of the intellectual sophistication of the educated classes in the twentieth century, and undermined the sense of absolute moral obligation that had previously been so cherished a condition of an orderly world. Moral skepticism was even presented as an intellectual breakthrough of modern thought, a triumph over the prejudices and superstitions of the past. But what had largely been the same debate had been a lively issue back as far as Socrates and the Sophists. Few things are more destructive than pseudo-sophistication in morality, and one can only say of most of these ideas what R. G. Collingwood said of the realism he so detested at Oxford in the first half of the twentieth century:

> If the realists had wanted to train up a generation of Englishmen and Englishwomen expressly as the potential dupes of every adventurer in morals or politics, commerce or religion, who should appeal to their emotions and promise them private gains which he neither could procure them nor even meant to procure them, no better way of doing it could have been discovered . . .[24]

Collingwood was far from the only philosopher in his century who despaired of morality. G. E. Anscombe argued that morality in contemporary life was a religious inheritance from an earlier time, and that it depended upon legislation from a source that was no longer taken seriously. "This word 'ought,'" wrote Miss Anscombe, "having become a word of mere mesmeric force, could not, in the character of having that force, be inferred from anything whatever . . . [and ends as] a word retaining the suggestion of force, and apt to have a strong psychological effect, but . . . [it] no longer signifies a real concept at all . . ."[25] Miss Anscombe suggested that we should abandon the idea of morality altogether, and something rather like this has been happening, piecemeal, throughout Western civilization. The very term "moral" invites derision as suggesting preaching in favor of some set of prescriptions, often identified as the vice of dogmatism. On the other hand, the moral life (I have been arguing) is inescapable, and politicians prescribing desirable conduct to us (as we shall see) are often accorded a quite astonishing amount of respectful attention.

4.   A STRUCTURE OF THE MORAL LIFE

Our last section, I am afraid, turned into a kind of prolegomenon, though a necessary one, to answering the question posed: What is the structure of the moral life? Let us, then, pose the question again. Like all human practices, the moral life takes a variety of forms, but it will already be clear that it cannot be resolved simply into a situation in which a moral agent encounters a problem and solves it by following (or not following) a rule, or pursuing an ideal. In a concrete moral act, many things are happening simultaneously. The moral agent conforms to a rule, but in following the rule, he or she is revealing the kind of character he or she has, or is. The idea of character is of something continuous over time, and might be construed either as a kind of essence, or as a set of dispositions "possessed" by some notionally higher element of agency.

In recognizing this complexity, we commonly distinguish motive from intention, or the spirit in which the act is done from the intention in doing it. The essentials are often illustrated by a famous couplet from T. S. Eliot's play *Murder in the Cathedral*. Beckett is Archbishop of Canterbury and in exile in France because of his quarrel with his sometime friend Henry II. He decides that duty requires him to return to England, however dangerous this may be. He faces two tempters who outline various agreeable possibilities that could result from his becoming reconciled with the king and repudiating what he has hitherto taken to be his duty. Beckett's resolve is unshaken. Then he must confront the third tempter, encouraging him to take the path of martyrdom as promising the glory of immortal fame. But as he recognizes:

> The last temptation is the worst treason
> To do the right thing for the wrong reason.

The moral life is thus dualistic in the sense that it involves at least two sets of considerations. The first set arises from the motive of the agent, and the second from responding to the question of what is the right thing to do. Ideally, of course, these considerations will cohere, but it is part of the complexity of the moral life that they sometimes do not. Indeed, it is this discovery of human self-consciousness that is dramatized in the Biblical story of the fall of man, as original sin.

An analysis of moral conduct in terms of this kind is given by Michael Oakeshott, whose argument starts from the premise that human beings are always intelligent agents, and that human actions can only be understood in terms of intention.[26] Oakeshott rejects a whole repertoire of explanations of human conduct, explanations that take it as "behavior" and therefore to be understood as caused rather than reasoned. Acts construed in that way come to be seen as non-rational—driven by reflexes and instincts, social structures, historical causes, the dialectic of the class struggle, the chemistry of glands, or any other instance of mechanical causality. These abstractions may be useful ideas for many purposes, but they do not correspond to moral conduct because moral issues have been assumed away before the analysis begins.

Conduct is not behavior; it always rests upon some sort of understanding (which may, of course, be a misunderstanding) of the agent's situation. Oakeshott's model of human interaction is a conversation, in which no utterance can be understood except as a response to the utterances preceding it. Human conduct, similarly, is not the effect of some cause, but a response to a precedent situation. In these terms, Oakeshott argues that in acting, human beings both "disclose themselves" and "enact themselves." By self-disclosure he refers to the evident meaning of the act as communicating a desire to others, and by self-enactment he points to the motive or the character the person is revealing in acting as he does. The ideal character to be inferred from the action might be anything that human admiration or contempt might conceive, and obviously different cultures and different activities have a varied repertoire of such conceptions. The Mafioso, the crook, the martyr, the monk, and the good-time girl are all very different kinds of self-enactment. Right action amounts to following the rules of right (as the actor understands them), while good action depends on the conception of good that might be entertained.

Oakeshott's analysis of conduct recognizes the essential fact that human beings are self-conscious creatures. When they act, they know that they are acting, though they don't, of course, understand every aspect of their situation. They have a particular purpose and a universal dimension of self-understanding. The point is clearly illustrated in another celebrated analysis of self-conscious activity, that of so-called speech acts offered by John Austin. Austin was exploring the theme that "for far too long the assumption of philosophers [was] that the business of a 'statement' can only be to 'describe' some state of affairs . . . which it must do either truly or falsely."

Utterances in fact function in a great variety of ways, and he called them "speech acts" or "performatives." He was particularly interested in such cases as a person uttering words like "I promise," or a bridegroom saying, "I do." His analysis went on to discover a performative element in all utterances. A policeman, to use a famous example, tells some skaters, "The ice over there is very thin," and he is (in Austinian terms) performing no less than three acts. His "locutionary" act is the proposition about the ice, and is either true or false. His "perlocutionary" act is the effect

THE SERVILE MIND 155

he seeks to achieve by making this utterance—to discourage the skaters from skating in a dangerous area of the pond. And finally, in making this remark, his "illocution" is to issue a warning. Moral speech and action exhibit an analogous structure. They exhibit a principle, reveal a situation/character, and produce an effect.

When, for example, I help a blind person cross the street in heavy traffic, I am following some such rule (no doubt internalized and barely conscious) as that one should always be helpful to those in need. But at the same time, I am contributing to bringing about a good end—helping someone avoid an accident. And finally, in helping such a person across the street, I am revealing myself (and perhaps enjoying the image of myself being expressed) as a considerate and decent human being. The attraction of this analytical structure is that it illustrates the emphases that have generated three common types of moral theory. Deontological morality is founded on the idea that moral conduct is the implementation of rules and principles. Teleological versions of moral analysis such as utilitarianism look to the consequences of a moral act: are these consequences good or desirable? Finally, so-called virtue ethics is concerned with what moral agents reveal about themselves in acting as they do.

Anything to do with human conduct is complex, and the moral life cannot be separated from a variety of considerations that arise in the course of deliberation. Moral agency has many dimensions. One of them is that of sincerity and authenticity, a criterion explored in terms of the danger of hypocrisy, and of the extent to which a moral act flows freely from the nature of the actor, or responds to a deliberate attempt to follow a rule. Some moral acts are pure pretense, engaged in merely so as to project an impressive image.

Another dimension is that emphasized in the Christian doctrine of the fall. When we act, we commonly contemplate or imagine less admirable possibilities that we construe as temptations, and which (when construed as such) we sometimes reject. But the mere fact that a temptation has been entertained reveals something about the character of the agent and the extent to which he could be relied on to do the right thing if the temptation were more powerful. What is the motive underlying the calculation on which the agent bases his action? It may be doing the right thing, or it might be fear of the consequences of transgressing. Here we encounter something that may seem irrelevantly old-fashioned, but is at the heart of the modern world. In merely contemplating, even if rejecting, a temptation, a moral agent is no longer innocent. Such innocence was often greatly valued in, particularly, young girls in past ages. Today such innocence is derided, and no child gets very far in the world without acquiring some knowledge of a syllabus of available temptations. We even think this a possibly desirable situation. The strange thing is that one of the dreams of communism was to create a world of innocents—one in which each person would unselfconsciously behave as a member of a true community, without even the possibility of thinking selfish thoughts. Innocence, in other words, is at the heart of modern *political* conceptions of a true community. In this idea, there is a direct and unmediated move from correct doctrine to right action.

Just as the victims of torture generally have a breaking point, so a great deal of virtue would be helpless against dramatic inducements to do the wrong thing. Modern entertainment sometimes toys with the question of whether a woman would sleep with a stranger for a million dollars. Or two million? Modern legal systems do not countenance the use of "entrapment" as a technique for securing evidence of the guilt of people the police believe to be bad. There are circumstances in which most people would succumb to temptation, and there are complex situations in which no one without exception could avoid moral imperfection. Here we are, of course, in the world of the modern economy, in which the essential basis of order is doing the right thing, from whatever motive.

The usefulness of Oakeshott's dualistic account of the moral life is that it establishes a criterion for the recognition of what is moral. A great deal of attention is paid in modern times to the ethical aspects of public policy. Authoritative advice, usually from philosophers and statesmen, is often sought on such issues as euthanasia, cloning, abortion, stem-cell research, genetically modified crops, and others. In these cases, the ethical question is different from the moral, for it is concerned only to find, or perhaps merely to decide upon, the right public policy. This specialized question arising in judging the right thing to do is no doubt part of the reason why in modern usage "ethical" and "moral" are no longer synonyms. Questions of general public policy commonly arise because part of the population has religious reservations in these areas, and governments seek authoritative advice as an alternative to offending such groups by the policies they adopt. Public policy is also concerned with the desirability of the courses of conduct that might attract people under whatever laws might be enacted. We all have sympathy with people who in great pain would prefer death, but we worry about the possible misuse of a right to euthanasia by relatives eager to enter into their inheritance. A Christian view would reject euthanasia on the ground that human life is the gift of God and human beings must not preempt divine decision, while a secular view would look to the likelihood of misuse of such a right. In such cases as this, the ethical element in the recommendations to be made seems to be nothing more than taking what emerges as "the right decision." That is to say, those making the decision are not themselves involved in exhibiting a moral character except in terms of the intellectual cultivation they may bring to the task. The element of self-enactment, if it is to be found at all, is found in merely having the right opinions (whatever they may be) rather than in exhibiting a virtue. My argument, in other words, is that the moral life is structurally different from any ethical element in the issues discussed in public policy.

Investment in supposedly benign economic enterprises is also often claimed to be "ethical." It is ethical to avoid making money out of the arms trade (it kills people) tobacco (bad for health), alcohol (leads to crime and other bad things), and from whatever other enterprises that from time to time become popular with activists. In these cases, it might seem that there is at least a notional component of virtue that might be claimed for this particular version of doing the right thing. The virtue might be thought to be compassion directed at those who might suffer from the activities of these enterprises. Yet it seems to me that we are here slipping over the borderlines of morality into what I shall later be calling the "politico-moral."

The problem is that the right thing involved here is a policy using authority, and often coercion, aimed at imposing an abstractly desirable ideal and attitude on other people, thus foreclosing their own judgment. These are enthusiasms cultivated by activists in Western states, and enthusiasms with an appeal wide enough to be able to present themselves plausibly as moral rather than merely political. Yet some arms supplies are needed for legitimate defense (as we assume to be the case with the policies of liberal governments) and alcohol and tobacco are freely chosen and often benign choices of other people. In other words, the claimed moral dimension of such public policies is intermingled with the objective of making others conform to some demanded standard of behavior, and here indeed we have moved into the political. There is thus about these forms of collective activism, advanced as ethical enterprises, a project of social control that goes far beyond what may be construed as morality. The term "ethical" reveals itself as a persuasive gloss on the ambition to manage the lives of supposedly vulnerable people.

5. INDIVIDUALISM AND THE MODERN WORLD

The moral life, I have argued, concerns our duties to ourselves as individuals, something quite distinct from the duties imposed by any system of a right-ordering of life found in non-Western societies. The characteristic moral idiom of the modern West is individualist. The dominance of custom has been so close to ubiquitous that it is not easy to imagine anything different. The emergence of individualism in Europe could hardly look as anything but a form of selfishness, of willfulness. Yet something different did come into being in Europe. It had not been designed by anybody, and resulted from the confluence of many circumstances. It had momentous consequences.

Certainly nothing about the way we live in the West can be understood without taking individualism into account. It is the form of conduct that created in the fullest sense the thing we now call "the economy," and it entrenched a taste for novelty and change at the heart of European life. But individualism itself is no more changeless than any other aspect of human life. It never stays still. Whatever form it takes over time, however, individualism has always seemed to outsiders a dangerous and destructive moral mode. On the surface, it seems to be nothing less than a surrender to the impulses and desires people have, and impulse and desire are precisely what every other form of social order is designed to control. Individualism is thus widely regarded, even by Europeans in some moods, as profoundly destructive of the moral restraints without which the world would slip into anarchy. How can we make sense of such a strange idea?

To do the right thing in customary or religious terms could be characterized as a form of obedience, or perhaps of conformity. Individualism was, in these terms, a form of non-conformity, and its internal principle took time to become evident. That principle was the idea that a coherent moral life depended on one's fidelity to commitments one had made oneself. It was in these terms that later philosophers could emphasize autonomy (contrasted with heteronomy) as being at the heart of European moral life. Such an institution common in most cultures as an arranged marriage, for example, stands condemned in these terms, for it is a case of parents and kin imposing on individuals commitments they may not be willing to make for themselves. We might well today think that the idea of romantic marriage itself stands condemned because modern marriage commitments so commonly collapse, but this was not at all true in the classic period of individualism, in which marriage as a sacrament involving a life-long union was sustained by law.

To be an individualist is to think and to act on the judgment that what one admires and what one desires should, within the bounds of law and moral rules, legitimately lead to action. As with all moral doctrines, the practice emerged long before it had a name or a theory. A common view is that individualism could first be seen emerging in the city republics of northern Italy during the later medieval period; indeed, this is a large part of what we mean by the Renaissance. Individualism was first to be detected among merchants, rulers, and those closely associated with them, such as artists.

Individualism is not at all the same thing as individuality, for all human beings have a certain individuality, and it is a form of uniqueness quite likely to be at odds with custom. But individuality, when at odds with custom, is exactly what custom and tradition treat as evil. It is the intrusion of will, indeed of willfulness, into a settled order, and it is therefore destructive. But in Europe, the idea slowly emerged that, in certain areas, individual choice, even when at odds with custom, had a legitimate moral claim to recognition. And in the long term, this moral innovation turned out to have created a form of social order that was flexible, adaptable, and astonishingly powerful. The experience of individualism often runs counter to our superficial intuitions about it. Those intuitions—that individualism liberates the disorderly in people—might seem to have been vindicated, as in the early modern period when individualist cultures battled over religious observance and other practices, but the long-term consequences were different.

Individualism could only have arisen in a civilization that had long domesticated the idea of living under law. Individualism and law are thus correlates, inseparable partners. The reason is that law, by contrast with custom, and by contrast also with the arbitrary character of the despotisms often associated with custom, is abstract, and an abstract rule requires compliance rather than obedience. Whereas custom adumbrates a whole manner of life, rules and principles leave open the mood and the manner in which compliance can take place. The person who looks to be frustrated by the application of a rule looks for a loophole, but a loophole is not a violation of the rule, or a rejection of it. It is the discovery of an unusual implication of the rule in new circumstances. The abstract character of law thus opens up scope for innovation in every sphere of life.

As it happened, loopholes came to be scarce in the Europe of the later Middle Ages, which was suffering from a surfeit of law. Customary law, the statutes of parliaments, cannon law, the local laws of fairs and forests, natural law, not to mention the rules generated by Biblical precedents, constituted a framework of social life that had succeeded in taming the violence of the earlier feudal period, but at the cost of circumscribing to an intolerable degree the actions of later generations. In a world increasingly eager to prosper in temporal life, the frustration led to an outburst of will and violence, the breaking of rules, and an expropriation of ecclesiastical property. The remarkable outcome was the emergence of powerful sovereign governments equipped with a largely unprecedented authority: that of being able to make law at will, given that there was adequate consent. Much more importantly, this sovereign power was able to unmake law without actually violating it. Such an unusual civil power turned out to be what a population dominated by individualism required. They demanded the power to change the world, and sovereign states gave them not only the power but also the authority to do so.

The period in which individualism emerged was, not surprisingly, a period of great violence and instability, as faith fought faith and local magnates contested the power of the emerging sovereign rulers. The Catholic Church was seriously weakened even in those countries that resisted Protestantism. And Protestantism equipped the individual with the remarkable law-making capacity called "conscience," which we have already discussed. Conscience, especially where sustained by wider belief, could stand against established authority and generate sects of believers convinced that they had found the right manner of worshipping God. Christianity, understood as a liberation from the Mosaic Law, as coming to set men free, led to an efflorescence of ingenious beliefs and practices. Given the immensely destructive effects this new form of conduct had throughout Europe, it was hardly surprising that individualism was widely believed to be fatal to good order. Many people felt that Europe was declining into decadence, and some of them were convinced that the end of the world—to be presaged by a time of troubles—was near. There was certainly no doubt about the troubles. Nor was there any mystery about the fact that churches and rulers of that troubled period incessantly demanded from their subjects the most passive obedience to rulers and to those in authority. St Paul's remarks in Romans

13 that the powers that be are ordained of God were a particular favorite of the preachers of the time. A population that had been as insanely active as that of early modern Europe could certainly benefit from a spell of passivity.

The more or less conventional view I have just been offering of religious dissension in the early modern period suggests that something called "individualism" caused those violent episodes of religious violence. "Causing" in this kind of story-telling is a powerful idea, and we need to remember that "individualism" itself is an abstraction that merely summarizes much later interpretations of what happened. The actual thoughts of these turbulent people were often limited to a rejection of what they thought to be the sacrilegious imposture of church dignitaries. Individualism, we must at least say, was as much a by-product of the conflicts of those times as a cause of them.

Historically speaking, the period after 1648 (when the Treaty of Westphalia ended the Thirty Years' War) marks the emergence of a new mode of thought and conduct, in which some elements of tolerance began very fitfully to play their part in helping Europeans to live together without being at each other's throats. Classicism in literature and politeness in manners became dominant fashions. It was not that violence was abandoned, merely that it found somewhat less destructive channels. During the "long" eighteenth century (1689 to 1815), European states were at war with each other during half of the entire period. Historians sometimes explain this period as the rise of the bourgeois social class; more exactly, it was a time in which more customary forms of the moral life were being increasingly superseded by modern individualism.

The modern individualist was essentially a will. The will issued a stream of responsible judgments by which the individual would guide his (and to a lesser extent her) life. The decisions were based on the individual's interests and desires, but this was not at all to say that these decisions were always self-interested, or even that they were selfish. Often, of course, they were both, but this was also a self-consciously moral population, following rules and inner inspirations that might well be quite remarkable, if not indeed bizarre, but could certainly not be explained in terms of mere selfishness.

The individualist will was the essential organ of personal responsibility, and therefore the organ on which punishment could be based. The basic problem of punishment, of course, is the assumption that the person punished is the same as the person who committed the offense. A whole casuistry of mitigating circumstances recognizes moral faults resulting from temporary psychological derangement or eccentric circumstances. These are problems particularly acute in an individualist culture because the individual is assumed to be forever developing. And that assumption itself results from a central feature of the logic of individualism that we shall meet again. Whereas traditional systems of morality are based on obedience to command or custom, the individualist moral life is primarily a matter of the moral agent sustaining a coherence within the set of commitments he has grown up with, or has himself chosen.

Early Christians had often been weighed down by the burden of original sin; these later Christians were burdened by an intense sense of moral responsibility. Internalization lay at the heart of this moral experience. Individualist societies were successful because individual desires were not—ideally!—let loose on the world in their raw and violent shape. They were shaped by an internalized morality and governed by a conscious and deliberate compliance with the law and with morality. It is thus not at all paradoxical to observe that individualism was far from being a liberation into willfulness; on the contrary, it demanded remarkable powers of fortitude and self-control from those who embraced its permissions.

There is no doubt that individualism constitutes a large component of the reason why European life must be regarded as distinct from that of other civilizations. It is the moral fact that lies behind the European preoccupation with freedom, which in turn spun off the popular currency of human rights. Without individualism, European technology could not have been the creative force it has been. Further, it is far from being a mere moral fashion, but is deeply rooted in European life. Without some recognition of these roots, we cannot understand its character. Where then, in historical terms, did this remarkable practice come from?

Clearly many things contributed to it—the consultative practices that had developed among the rulers of the Vikings and other tribes that invaded early medieval Europe were part of it. Social arrangements facilitating the developments of markets, and of the wider possibilities of commerce across Europe, were important. In England a distinctive common law, along with the practice of juries, contributed a notable variant of the "idiom" in which individualism was "spoken." But two intellectual influences are also germane to the argument.

The first was the philosophical tradition of the Greeks. Philosophers there set themselves up against the "hoi polloi," understood as immersed in appearances rather than reality. Ordinary people were inhabitants of the Platonic cave. Plato's Socrates was certainly a remarkable individual whose example inspired many to follow him. He had no patience with the idea that something believed by everyone must be true, and he thus supplied the most elementary mechanics of a doctrine that would encourage the individual to stand against his society. Plato's presentation of him conveys both his physical presence and his psychological individuality. Here was unmistakably an individual whose spring of action was internal and who brought to the customs and usages of his society just the kind of critical attitude individualists later came to admire.

Yet Socrates also believed that the passions by which we are in fact individuated are defects in our rationality, defects to be overcome by the philosopher. The Greeks commonly understood the world in terms of norms of physical and psychological perfection. The philosophical aim was to become entirely rational, an ideal within which individuality as such had no place. The Greek idea that man is a rational animal is often invoked by modern secularists, yet its meaning is at odds with the moral sentiments of modern Europe. That man is a rational animal entails that we are human in proportion to our rationality, and the Greeks commonly inferred from this that women were less rational than men, and slaves were perhaps hardly rational at all. No Greek (except perhaps Diogenes the Cynic) would have followed Oliver Cromwell in demanding that his portrait should be "warts and all."

The basic individualist notion that man is essentially a creature of the passions came in fact from Christianity, which is the direct and essential progenitor of European individualism. The Christian distinction between the spiritual and the secular powers lies at the heart of Western civic pluralism. It no doubt seems odd that a religion of humility warring against the snares of the world should have evolved anything so apparently fatal in our time to religious observance as individualism. Yet such inversions and reversals are in fact a staple of human experience, no less than of the theological imagination. The Weberian derivation of capitalism from Calvinism (to the extent that it is convincing) is merely one example of this: an unworldly attention to spiritual salvation led, remarkably, to success in laying up treasure in the world below.

Christianity is the source not only of individualism, but of the spiritual egalitarianism that individualism also involves. Each soul is unique and is valuable to God, with whom it has a central if (in many versions) mediated relationship. The particular element in a human being that does relate to God is not reason but the soul, which is believed to respond only to the grace of God. Christian philosophy took some centuries to construct its complex doctrine out of the materials available in reports of the life of Jesus, and the great architect of the construction in its first complete form was, of course, St. Augustine in the fifth century. In this new understanding, the limitation of the classical civilization was, precisely, its pride in reason. The transcendence of that limitation was by way of faith—the will to believe, by which the earlier defiant *credo quia absurdum* of Tertullian became the *crede ut intelligas* of Augustine. The ancients, in this view, had attempted to create out of reason a doctrine without assumptions. This is a logical impossibility. For St. Augustine, basing thought on the Christian account of the creation was an assumption that allowed everything to fall into place.

Augustine did not reject reason. He merely recognized how limited the part it could play in the full range of human experience was. In the *Confessions* he talks of existence, knowledge, and will (*esse, nosse, velIe*), and goes on:

> I would that men would consider these three, that are in them-selves . . . For I am and know and will; I am knowing and will-ing; I know myself to be and to will; I will to be and to know. In these three, then, let him discern who can how inseparable a life there is, one life, one mind and one essence; how insepa-rable a distinction and yet a distinction . . .[27]

This line of thought reflected a solution to one of the basic problems of Christian thought—how to make sense of the doc-trine of the Trinity, and to reconcile that theory with the belief in one God. They anticipate Descartes in their use as putting aca-demic skepticism to flight, and they lay the groundwork for the later modern conception of man as a desiring creature, a creature of the will. Such a creature is not cut off from reason, but the reason available to him is not at all the same thing as the *logos* of the Greeks. It is, rather, an instrument by which human beings may orient themselves in the world. Much later, St. Thomas Aquinas would attempt a synthesis of *logos* and revelation, a highly notable construction, but not one that modern philosophers have gener-ally found convincing.

6. SOME INDIVIDUALIST LEGENDS

Many will reject the idea that individualism derives from Chris-tianity. Surely, it will be argued, individualism was a form of self-assertion in revolt against priests, bishops, and authori-ties. Liberals will look back to the Enlightenment revolt against Christian orthodoxy, while socialists will route their history back through Marx and his sources. Liberalism and socialism are the dominant political doctrines of modern times. Liberals embrace individualism as "a good thing" because it expresses free choice and thus underwrites both liberalism and libertarianism. Socialism, by contrast, rejects individualism as a mistaken belief in the autonomy of individuals, a mistake that locks our civiliza-tion into the selfishness of capitalism. Socialists dream that contemporary societies will transform themselves into something that could be recognized as real human communities. In such a perfection, cooperation would replace the competitive drives of the modern world. Each of these beliefs tells its own story of how we in the West got where we are. Let us take each in turn.

Liberals value individualism as moral independence; they fear it will be suppressed by states and other authorities. They are therefore liable to confound individualism with the emergence of individual rights. The modern world can then be interpreted as resulting from revolt against medieval authority, and against orthodoxy in all its forms. Copernicus and Galileo take their place in this story as scientists challenging implausible inherited beliefs about a flat Earth. Anglophone versions pick up the story by incorporating the seventeenth-century Whig opposition to the passive obedience of the Tories and culminating in Locke's 1689 theory of the conditions under which a people might legitimately overthrow its government. For many of these Whigs, the enemy was "priestcraft." In this narrative, individualism is the power of reason struggling against enemies in specific areas—most notably against Anglican orthodoxy and governmental hierarchy. It must also be contrasted with the threat to liberty arising from popular prejudice and superstition. The "party of humanity" as the eighteenth-century Enlightened have been described, was also the party of modernity. In other words, the liberal story selects as being the whole story one specific part of the history of individualism—that aspect of it that anticipated the autonomous individual who rejected both religious and monarchical authority in order to bring forth the secular democracies of the modern world. It will be obvious that the liberal story has been stripped of any disreputable theological ancestry. Its forefathers are heroic rebels bringing reason to bear on the bigotries that surrounded them. The history of a changing moral practice has been simplified into the emergence of an admirable doctrine. Liberals prefer not to remember that individualism in many of its early versions was primarily concerned with the right way to worship God. It sought the freedom to worship in some unorthodox way, and many of these dissenters migrated to the new world in order to escape compulsion. It was these people who played such a large part in the American founding.

The capstone of individualist legend is the Darwinian theory of evolution, for until Darwin provided an account of how human beings came into existence, an account based on a plausible body of evidence, and thus to be taken as scientific, secularists found it difficult to shake off the philosophical arguments for the existence of God and the origins of the universe. After Darwin, however, "science" had demonstrated that man was not a fallen angel but a promoted ape. Indeed, history itself was turned into an evolutionary story in which modern rational beings were the culmination of a long process of moral evolution. And what that signified was that the many patterns of human life could be explained as resulting from human interaction without the need to postulate a designer.

In the eighteenth century, the economics of Adam Smith, along with the critical spirit of Voltaire and the philosophes, were central elements of the liberal story, and in one of its versions the march of progress culminated in the French revolution. At this point, liberal thought often merged with the classical republicanism that had been simmering in European thought since the late Middle Ages. The basic idea being that men are free only in standing on their own feet, some liberals looked forward to the coming of a republic in which servile monarchical forms had been swept away as man stepped forward into his full inheritance of freedom. For some liberals, progress required nothing less than the overthrow of the *ancien régime,* as happened in France, but failed to happen in Britain. As a monarchy, Britain is often thought to be an *ancien régime* that failed to achieve the bracing excitements of a real revolution. Some liberals, now and then, still regret this failure.

In philosophical terms, both Kant and the utilitarians feed into the liberal story, though they give a different tone to liberal movements in Continental and Anglophone countries. Mill's *On Liberty* became the key text of Anglophone liberal individualism, and was to lead on to the more welfarist inclinations of the "new liberals" in the late nineteenth century, for whom the business of "society" was to provide the necessary conditions for individual self-fulfillment. The question was: what did individual self-fulfillment require? At every stage in the story, many people thought that the process was essentially complete, but in the twentieth century, liberalism began to erode the supposedly oppressive conventions of respectable bourgeois society, rejection of which was taken to be a further advance in liberty. The story of liberty turned into the story of successive liberations, one after another, each overthrowing some newly discovered oppression. Among the fruits of these new ideas was an enthusiasm for the codification of freedom as a set of human rights. Such codifications were mistaken for specifications of the minimal condition of individualism, and their embrace by governments was thought by rather simple liberals to demonstrate that civil oppression was at an end. The great advantage of abstract rights was not only that they sounded impressively philosophical, but that they could be exported to other civilizations as a central element in the progressive advance of democracy.

Such is the liberal account of individualism, and its defect is that it provides no explanation of why this new dispensation should arise at all, much less why it should arise in European states rather than in some other place and time. Hesiod tells us that Athena was born straight from the head of Zeus, and Whig history often presents a comparable account of how liberalism suddenly and largely unaccountably emerged into the modern world. Human beings have a weakness for ancestor worship, but here we have an interesting case of ancestor denial. Yet the emergence of liberalism and modernity in Western Europe rather than anywhere else can hardly be fortuitous. Can it really have been the case that in a world dominated by custom and orthodoxy, prejudice and bigotry, a spontaneous freedom-loving disposition, supposedly universal in human nature but previously suppressed by hierarchical oppression, at last burst forth and transformed our Western values? The real history of individualism is, as we have seen, more complicated, and more interesting, than this rather sterile legend.

The second or socialist version of individualism at least has some answer to this central problem of how individualism actually came into the world. It explains individualism as part of a commercial mode of life emerging from feudalism, and gives it a sociological form by identifying this moral idiom with a specific class in European life, namely, the bourgeoisie. They are, as it were, the "carriers" of this community-threatening infection. Individualism in both its moral and sociological forms is rejected as the false belief that each human being is a social atom separate from, indeed isolated from, other members of society. Such an individualist self-conception is in Marxist terms a distortion of reality thought to have been popularized in the interests of the bourgeois class. The essence of collectivist movements such as socialism is the belief that individuals, supposedly isolated under capitalism from real community with their fellows, are mere alienated fragments of humanity. They are unreal fictions that only begin to take on human reality as they recognize that man is a social being. Society endures, whereas individuals come into existence at a particular moment, reflect the culture that forms them, and as the generations come and go, they are replaced in their turn. Hence although (in the Marxist system) individualism was in a limited sense progressive by contrast with the unfree societies of the past, it is essentially one element in a bad system, and it imposes the cost of revolution on late capitalist generations as the condition of bringing real community to birth on the grand stage of history. Individualism is the mark of a "bourgeois society," or "capitalism" as it was later called. Capitalism depended on turning man against man, which it achieved by focusing the passions of human beings on an illusory salvation in the afterlife. Christianity thus lay at the heart of the competitive character of modern economies. Salvationist belief in such a fantasy future enfeebled the natural class solidarity of modern workers in their essential character as producers and turned them into mere consumers of fantasy. A great deal of this body of thought had been generated by Enlightenment philosophes in the eighteenth century, but it was given definitive form by Marx in the 1840s as he adapted Hegelian philosophy to the purposes of political agitation. Marx regarded individualism as an element in the modern explosion of human technical inventiveness, which had the historical function of generating the technology that would allow capitalism to be superseded by communism as the perfect form of human life.

Both of these stories suggest that the basic moral question of our time is: what is the future of individualism? Is it the wave of the future, or a mistake we must transcend? Is it to be perfected in the creation of societies in which everything is subject to choice? Or is it perhaps to be superseded by a world in which the struggles of the past give way to the spontaneous recognition of the real sociability of man? We will have much to say bearing on this question later, but for the moment, our concern must be to continue our focus on the moral life. And that brings us back to the issue of religion.

For it will be clear that both liberalism and socialism are remarkably comprehensive doctrines about the human condition. They each call on profound emotions about how human beings should live, invoking loyalties that go far beyond such political questions as the best policy for sovereign liberal democratic governments. To be a liberal, or a socialist, is often to participate in an identity that determines a whole range of admirations and antipathies. It incorporates a righteous belief in its own moral superiority. In the case of Marxism, this element of socialist competition with religion was generally quite explicit, and was carried through into establishing atheism as part of the official doctrine of the Soviet Union. Some Western Christians, however, still thought they could combine Christianity with communism. They called it "liberation theology." In some Continental countries, liberalism has also taken a form explicitly hostile to religion. In the pluralist bazaar of Western ideas, almost anything can be combined with anything else. Believers will be found espousing almost any combination of these beliefs, and many others. Nevertheless, we may say with some confidence that the dynamic of both liberalism and socialism is secular rationalism. The issue is confused because Western thinkers commonly assimilate their rejection of Christianity to a rejection of religion in any form. And what is meant by this is a rejection of any belief about entities that cannot in principle be subject to some sort of empirical investigation.

What is certainly true is that each of these stories includes in its program the desire to supersede the terms of our inherited moral life in any Christian form. Both tend toward some form of humanism. Many liberals and socialists will indeed recognize that many of our moral convictions have been inherited from one form of Christianity or another, and that is exactly why such moral beliefs ought to be subject to new critical scrutiny. These beliefs need to be purified of whatever is "outdated," especially in the area where moral convictions intersect with sexuality.

We thus find ourselves faced with two questions. The first may be put as follows: does the secularity of liberalism and socialism tell us that a new human form of life has come into being, its novelty being that religion, as it had commonly been identified in earlier times, must be relegated to the class of outmoded superstition? Or is it the case that we have here a belief system that inherits much of the religiosity of the past, yet advances itself (for complex rhetorical reasons) by the paradoxical move of refusing to recognize itself as a religion? Such a question requires some attention to the issue of what we mean by the term "religion," and I shall postpone it to Chapter IV. The other question that we must now consider is: what becomes of the moral life without its implicit Christian underpinnings?

7. ELEMENTS OF INDIVIDUALISM

The Moral Life is a continuous experience of self-understanding and self-discovery, for the individual is responding not only to external pressures but also to reflections on his own inner life. Our passionate interest in our own inner lives has led to the creation of the literary form of the novel, which gives such scope for understanding the complexities of individualism. People vary enormously in the richness of their inner experience, but everyone shares in some degree a cultural repertoire of stories, proverbs, phrases, formulations, and historical legends. It is a tangle of good Samaritans, fairy godmothers, admirals putting telescopes to their blind eye, chickens in pots, and vastly more. The encounter between experience and this evolving repertoire has generated the immense variety of conduct found in European life.

A further complexity is that individual self-management demands that the moral agent must cultivate his attachments to family, firm, school, club, regiment, friends, state, and any other responsibilities he or she may have undertaken. These attachments are direct and personal, and each relationship has some kind of moral dimension. This simple fact is what rules out of court—not merely as wrong but as a hopelessly incompetent understanding of modern states—any suggestion that the individual is a "social atom" isolated from society. Indeed, this curious error, found particularly among Marxists, leads to another mistake. It is to imagine that "man is a social being" because of his relationship with the thing called "society." For while we have direct and tangible relationships with many associations and institutions that are "within society," the grandiose thing called "society" is not something to which one can be related in the same way at all. To imagine that one can is to commit what philosophers call a "category mistake." Those making this mistake are usually identifying "society" with the state; it sounds more inclusive, after all. But we are certainly closely related to the state. Often, these days, too closely related.

It is in fulfilling these commitments and responsibilities that individuals sustain their self-respect, both in their own eyes and in the eyes of others. A project of recent times has been to treat individuals in ways that are thought to generate the self-esteem and self-respect supposedly lacking in their lives. This is a typical enterprise in that it mistakenly tries to provide from the outside what can only come from within. "Self-respect" is an achievement word that can only be experienced by those who have successfully responded to something they recognize as a responsibility. You cannot "buy in" supplies of it from outside parties seeking to improve your life. In its more elevated forms, self-respect is a matter of honor, of duties recognized by the individual to himself and successfully fulfilled. In less admirable forms, this sentiment sustains our feelings of superiority to others, and may be a perilous bit of self-indulgence. It is perhaps a vice, but as with quite a number of vices, it may also sustain virtues.

Our basic source of self-respect, however, is simply competence. Our moral lives are intimately involved with the skills we have and the work we do. With greatly varying degrees of success, we sustain families, practices, professions, obligations; we indulge in hobbies and volunteer for public and charitable duties, and the main source of moral fulfillment and self-respect lies in the simple love of the work itself. That is the reason why, up until the twentieth century, manuals of moral advice were almost invariably focused around the idea of duty, for there was no unhappiness like a duty one recognized being unfulfilled. Even where we are concerned with someone merely doing a job because he has to live, a certain sense of integrity (which usually increases with age) impels individuals to perform their duties with at least some attention. Where little satisfaction comes from the work itself, the individualist acts from the integrity of commitment, and it is precisely this possibility of detaching the duty from the task itself that makes modern individualist societies both tough and flexible.

Individualists are usually, at need, prepared to try their hand at a range of tasks, and can set up cooperating units (for example in emergencies) with remarkable speed. This is something about modern societies that the sociologist Ernest Gellner called "modularity,"[28] and it is possible because individualism allows but does not necessitate a complete disjunction between the individual and any particular task he engages in. The flexibility of the individualist contrasts with the rigidity of those cultures in which a person, on the basis of rank, age, or station, is accustomed to a narrow range of tasks and usually to the prestige and respect that goes with those tasks. Where there is a fixed connection between work and status, the individual is often reluctant to do anything that might be "below him," or no doubt her.

Modern individualists, by contrast, are usually ready to do anything needed to meet an emergency. It may well be that expectations of this kind help to explain why individualist societies are relatively free of corruption, in the sense of officials using power or authority to demand money or benefits before they will perform their duty. It is a common charge leveled against individualist societies that they are filled with self-interested people largely incapable of sinking their own interests into those of the larger group. On this view, being "self-interested" amounts to being selfish to the exclusion of the common good. If this rather common theory had any serious grip on reality, then it would follow that European societies, and perhaps Anglophone societies above all, would be the most corrupt in the world. They remain, in fact, less corrupt, especially at the lower levels, but the increase in servility is steadily assimilating us to the rest of the world.

The remarkable thing, however, is that the worst corruption happens in traditional and in post-revolutionary societies whose official doctrines are in one sense entirely self-denying and communitarian. By contrast with this very widespread problem, anyone with the right to a passport, or a license, or any other kind of official permission in Western states will generally get it without the demand for a bribe. We might well take as a further piece of evidence for my thesis that Russians, after three generations of bombardment by doctrines promoting altruistic collectivism, turn out to be a good deal less reliably guided by duty than those in the selfish capitalist West. That Western firms and bureaucracies are often to be found behaving in undesirably self-interested ways is no doubt true, but these moves in the game of advantage usually collide in time with media critics and competitors whose interests run counter to them.

The basic charge against capitalist states is that desire generally trumps duty. An increasingly heedless individualism must be reined in by those states in order to protect the vulnerable left behind in the race for advantage. An individualist is actually *defined* as a selfish consumer with little or no concern for others, especially for vulnerable others. It is easy enough to see what makes this view of contemporary life plausible, but to understand why it is dangerously wrong, we must consider rather more closely what we mean by "desire" in the context of individualism.

In philosophical treatments of the moral life, a desire turns up as something quite different from a mere passion or impulse. It is a highly rationalized entity in which the individual considers the broader context of a situation and the likely consequences of satisfying one desire rather than another. A desire, in other words, is a *rationalized passion*. It expresses an appetite (or, negatively, the implication of an aversion), and is distinguished from an *impulse* by this element of rationality. As Hobbes put it in *Leviathan*:

> From desire, ariseth the thought of some means we have seen produce the like of that which we aim at; and from the thought of that the thought of means to that mean; and so continually, till we come to some beginning within our power.[29]

Here we have a conception of reason as instrumental, a conception quite different from the Greek notion of reason as an insight into the nature of things. In this modern understanding, reason is merely a "scout to spy out the land." It is an essential component of individualist desiring, in which a movement of the will is explored in terms of its context, of the coherence of the expected satisfaction with other satisfactions in view, and with commitments already undertaken. It is, one might say, a psychological drive that has been given a reality test. No doubt such a process of reasoning, which considers among other things the rational interest of the individual self, could lead to a decision to do the selfish thing, but in other cases it would not. An insouciant negligence is always a possibility. The outcome depends on many things. The crucial point, however, is that a desire is quite distinct from an impulse.

An impulse, by contrast with a desire, is an unrationalized passion demanding immediate satisfaction—perhaps for food, sex, or money. An impulse might well be confused with a desire, because we often use the two words almost interchangeably to cover the supposed ground of an individual's act, and it is not easy to discriminate them. An impulse, however, seeks a satisfaction uncomplicated by the rational tests the individualist brings to judgment when he deliberates. The essence of the moral life is to turn impulses into desires; correspondingly, the decadence of the moral life may be measured in terms of the spread of impulsiveness. We might, in the most abstract way, distinguish "desirers" from "impulsives" as different kinds of characters, and we often assess conduct in this way. The commonest confusion in this area would be to mistake impulsiveness for selfishness, and it is a mistake because strictly speaking an impulse is neither selfish nor unselfish. It is like an instinct. Road rage and drunken aggression are contemporary illustrations of impulse, and so is a good deal of credit-card debt. To judge by the abortion level, a great deal of sexual conduct is governed by impulse, and of course always has been.

I have argued that desire entails rationalization, but what kind of rationalization is involved? The answer is that the test of whether a desire should be satisfied depends on a judgment of the coherence between the various elements of a context—a judgment of the commitments, consequences, and likely outcome of the act. The whole point of the autonomy of an individualist as he or she leads a moral life is that there is no master to be obeyed, so that the contrast in logic distinguishing individualism from religious or customary forms of order is that between *coherence* and *obedience*. We conform to religion or custom; it depends on an external consideration. It is in this sense that the individualist may be described as free; but that freedom is not at all the same as irresponsibility. On the contrary, it is highly accountable.

Finally, let us consider what an individualist state looks like. The first thing a visitor might notice about such a state would be that individualism involves an immense amount of "busyness." Each person in an individualist society has his or her own projects and is busy getting on with them. It is an etymological curiosity of English that the term "policy," derived from *polis*, was not limited to institutions (as in Continental languages) but was also a term that could describe the projects of individuals. This makes them purposive, much less formal in their dress and manners than other cultures. They tend to become impatient with ritual. These days, relations between men and women are even more dramatically equal and direct in the West than they have been in the past, for European women were always in some considerable degree "liberated." In such a society, at least until very recently, a great deal of voluntary activity goes on, sometimes charitable, sometimes participatory, as when adults lead groups of children in sport or activities such as scouting. And there is, or used to be, a striking sense of what would now be called "social responsibility." Some patriots during the First World War, for example, bequeathed their wealth to the state, which needed it. Given the level of governmental profligacy today, we certainly shall not see their like again, but such generosity stands for a kind of virtue not usually associated with individualist societies.

It is common to observe that the freedoms we enjoy result from the struggles of earlier believers in freedom, but this, I suspect, is a misleading piece of moral athleticism. Freedom belongs to a whole way of life, and it is there to be enjoyed. We sustain it in using it and enjoying it. No doubt occasions arise in which some real or fancied threat rouses a population or part of it to take a stand. This happened in 1215 and in 1642, to cite two famous occasions in English history. Americans would perhaps wish to invoke 1776. But our actual situation in Anglophone countries has largely been one in which we have enjoyed the practices of freedom from generation to generation without any grand dramas. We think of our freedom as being the untrammeled ability to do whatever we choose to do unless there is a law against it. Other inhibitions will also operate—for example those of decorum, manners, morals, and (it is important to observe) a sense of what is often called "social responsibility." Isaiah Berlin[30] has largely persuaded us that it is important to define freedom in negative terms, and to resist smuggling into the idea elements of virtue that have no place in it, however desirable they might otherwise be. This argument no doubt saves us from various kinds of semantic confusion, but it is misleading as an explanation of the conditions of our freedom.

For the freedom we enjoy depends on a certain distribution of virtues and tastes. The taste for dealing with honest and independent people, for example, is something we have already met. Few would deny that courage is central to freedom, both in the sense that we must be ready to defend the state against aggression, and to defend our own legitimate desires and opinions against the disapproval of others. Fear of looking foolish, or offending the powerful, is a source of the servility that is the opposite of freedom. Without a vigorous political life, we succumb to the power of bureaucrats, a development to be observed in the current spread of more or less unaccountable quangos as agencies of the state. And civic life itself is a vast network of spontaneous connections essential to governmental policy. Political life, most obviously, is sustained in a free society by support for one or another political party. Without the volunteer, ready to give time and money toward civil society, life in the state would be reduced merely to economic activity on the one hand, and family life on the other. The incorporation of women into the workforce in the latter part of the twentieth century was a major blow to the creativity of civil society, for it had long rested on the enthusiasm of women. It has been suggested that the inroads on free time made by television and computers have also badly affected the vitality of civil society. Family life has also commonly been recognized as an obligation needed to project our civilization into future generations, but the pleasures and obligations of family life are very much less recognized in the twenty-first century. In past centuries, individualism was a self-regulating order of society, but its success in this function is inversely proportional to the level of impulsiveness in moral conduct. There is quite a lot of evidence today that we desire less, but are subject to impulse a good deal more.

8. CONFLICT, BALANCE, AND THE WEST

Let us now widen the focus and locate individualism and the moral life within broader issues in the character of our civilization. And we may take our clue about this from our sketch of the moral life itself. "Doing the right thing" turned out to involve two elements, those of act, and those of motive. Starting from a single idea, we found ourselves with a duality. And if we extend the context of this observation, we shall be struck, I think, that the duality merely reflects the Christian distinction between Caesar and God. Order is the business of authority, goodness the business of spirituality and the inner life. We have not here stumbled upon a pure point of origin, of course, because we might trace this distinction back both to the constitutional practices of the Romans and the philosophical disputes of the Greeks. The drive in most human life is to find some basic principle that will satisfy all demands, and yet our imperfections tell us we have not found it. We may yearn for a single coherent harmony of things in the world, but something in the practice of European life, especially in the modern world, prevents our achieving it. Instead of harmony, we find conflict. This is to restate the problem of the early modern skeptics, and we may ask, as they did, is this a misfortune?

From this perspective, European history is a graveyard of grand projects of intellectual and political union. Both papacy and empire overreached themselves in medieval times, and more recently hegemonic ambitions afflicted Hapsburg, Bourbon, and Bonapartist. They all failed. The Prussians and the Nazis have been the most recent powers attempting to turn Europe (and indeed the world) into a single entity. And the Nazi case is instructive because it was based upon a project of ordering the world in terms of comprehensive notional superiorities of race. Communism is another typically ideological project for creating a single world community in which everybody lives the right way of life. Nationalists have also often had such transcending ambitions. Christians sometimes dream of reconciliation of all the faiths, but for rip-roaring religious monism these days, one must go to the Islamist project of uniting us all in submission to Allah and Sharia law. In all of these cases, the project depends on the idea that there is a single right way of life we all ought to be living.

Europeans have turned out to be profoundly unsuitable material for grandiose unifications of this kind. And here we face one more version of that interesting criticism of individualism that has long been a standard *topos* in our European self-understanding: namely, that taken abstractly, the individualist moral life would seem to be so destructive of peace and order as to be on the verge of collapse. The much-hated thing called "capitalism" is always generating crises that encourage its enemies to hope that the end is near, but they suffer endless disappointment. Individualist societies have turned out, in fact, to be astonishingly stable. They may well not last forever: indeed, it is the argument of this book that they are currently under serious threat, but they have so far been remarkably successful. Individualism in European experience has an indispensable partner in law, and a rule of law is a further essential ordering element of Western life. But law here is not merely a book of rules. Like every other abstraction supposedly explaining Western modernity, it is seriously underspecified, because the law operates not only in the mouths of judges but in the minds of men. It has been internalized in the feelings and judgments of individualists who have a very good sense of the practical limits of what they do.

What is striking is that wherever perfection might suggest that a single authoritative conclusion ought to emerge, Europeans generally manage, as Hobbes once put it in another context, "to see double." If an offense has been committed, judicial proceedings ought in principle to discover the truth of the matter and decide an appropriate punishment. Instead, the process has turned into a debate between prosecution and defense, and the outcome is merely a "balance of probabilities." For centuries, the ideal political system was a ruler, wise because well advised, protecting his subjects and guiding them to lead the right way of life. Rulers themselves have often had a weakness for just such a conception of civil order. In Europe, such harmonies seldom lasted long. Medieval kings were surrounded by highly independent vassals, and there was a limit to how much the vassals would put up with. The signing of Magna Carta in 1215 was merely the most dramatic and best-remembered occasion in which the essential character of the government of England, as resting basically on a balance of powers, came out into the open. In time, this conception of government as the outcome of discussion could generate the paradoxical ideal of a "loyal opposition," and a new form of balance was created through the operation of a great variety of constitutional conventions.

Conflict and balance are thus the realities of European civilization. It is almost as if the principle had been: "Many (i.e., pluralism) is good, but two (i.e., dualism) will do." It is a principle to be found no less in religion than in the workings of the economy. Monopolies can sometimes be established, and prosper briefly, but they will be challenged before long, either by competitors or by changes in taste. In international affairs within Europe, conflict was mediated by the idea of a balance of power. As the current hegemon becomes more threatening, the others will find grounds for cooperating with each other so as to counter-balance any threat to them. The essential recognition generating these balances is that power corrupts in all its forms, and that includes the power to declare what is true or false. Power must indeed be used, but only in terms of constitutional constraints. The counterpart of this European restlessness about ideal unities is rejection of the capricious and the arbitrary.

This point is implicit in Montesquieu's analysis of the three possible regimes. The fear on which despotism rests and the public spirit available to the rulers of republics are both direct motives for doing the right thing. Monarchy, on the other hand, is based on honor, which is not a motive leading to any particular action, but a principle that mediates between what order demands and the motives the actor may invoke in performing the act (or refusing to perform it). Instinctive monists, such as the anarchist William Godwin, considered that this is a corrupt ground for doing the right thing. In a good state, in his view, doing the right thing and doing it for the right motive would be a single act.

Other cultures generally deplore the Western taste for conflict and balance, but in one area, European ways have swept the world. I refer, of course, to the institutionalization of sport in which games are played according to fixed rules, and individuals, teams, and players compete with each other, or used to, about nothing more serious than prestige and reputation. Indeed, sport today is the source of a vast industry absorbing the energies and the resources of thousands. It is a source of money and fame. And that, one should perhaps say, is the tragedy of its diffusion into the world. It has conquered the world, and lost its own soul. Sport and games are expressions of human playfulness, and human beings, like kittens, are all naturally playful, especially when young. Professionalization has destroyed the playfulness from which the games began. As an industry, it is subject to corruptions alien to its original spirit.

European cultures are, then, marked by conflict and founded on balance between competing powers and interests. They are not in any way the expression of a purely rational harmony into which everyone and every interest can be fitted. And that may provoke us to ask a further question: what underlies this disposition to engage in conflict?

Later, we shall discuss the central part played by human ambivalence, but here we may look to the field of moral dispositions. The tendency toward conflict lies, more particularly, in a conception of the point of human life. In Europe, we have inherited from our religion the view that the point of life is to meet the challenges posed by experience, welcoming these challenges as opportunities for demonstrating the qualities we have. In other words, life is a kind of game to be played according to the rules, in which the important thing is less winning or losing than doing one's best. In saying this, we are virtually in the territory of the school prize giving address, and for a very good reason. In England, sport has long been part of education and its point has been explicitly seen as moral development. The game of cricket may these days be no more free of corruption than any other game, but for the English it long featured as a paradigm of life itself. And the English experience here is merely one example of the way in which Anglophones drew out more effectively than other Europeans what was at stake in their practices. The same conception of life is to be found throughout European experience. It was indeed the Dutch historian Jan Huizinga who wrote *Homo Ludens*, one of the best accounts of this conception of human life.

In spite of the vast success of what one might call the European "model" of conflict and balance, the pull of the idea of harmonious monism remains extremely strong, and we may well wonder why this should be so. The broad answer is that our model of conduct is moral, and morality, or doing the right thing, is a hit and miss affair even if we could get some agreement on what the right thing might be. One may entertain utopian dreams, as communists and others have long done, of a society so much the more perfect than our own that moral failures would not occur. In a perfect community, which might require the abandonment of private property, individuals would live in a world warm with love and mutual consideration. Moral problems would not trouble this perfect world. It would be a kind of prelapsarian dream, but it would not be for us—if indeed it would be for anyone constructed out of human clay.

More specifically, however, the point is that in cases of conflict in the real world, some win and some lose. Children often race against each other, and only one of them can win. Some will come puffing in a good deal later than the winner. In one view of the world, the point of life is to minimize pain, and competitive failure is painful. In a better society, no one would fail. Everyone would be praised for effort, and all would get prizes. *Homo Ludens* takes a different view: failure may hurt, but like many other common forms of pain, it is an important, indeed an essential, learning experience. We should welcome it, just as Socrates (somewhat disingenuously) claimed to welcome being refuted because a philosopher's only care should be exposing the false and finding the true.[*]

9. SERVILITY AND THE MORAL LIFE

The moral life consists in doing the right thing from a motive related to some virtue we believe we admire. Being the conduct of autonomous agents, it is the essence of freedom. The servile mind, by contrast, is marked by an extreme dependence of judgment on outside powers, and particularly a concern with the substantive benefits (money, food, sex, etc.) that might result from an action whatever the moral considerations might be. Both forms of conduct will be found in modern societies at all times, but the remarkable thing is that many aspects of contemporary life, since early in the twentieth century, have tended to facilitate servility rather than independence.

---

[*] The Hobbesian version of something like this idea is that life is a race, which "we must suppose to have no other goal, nor other garland, but being foremost, and in it. In this game . . . To consider them behind, is *glory*. To consider those before, is humility . . . To see one out-go whom we would not, is *indignation* . . . Continually to out-go the next before, is *felicity*. And to forsake the course, is to *die*." (Thomas Hobbes, *Human Nature: or the Fundamental Elements of Policy*, in R. S. Peters (ed.) *Body, Man and Citizen*, Collier Books, New York, NY, 1962, p. 224.)

Contemporary market economies are increasingly dominated by modes of communication featuring sophistry, exaggeration, unreal promises, evasion, and the cultivation of fears and alarms useful in inducing customers to spend money. In this sense, all of us are being "managed" in one of the basic meanings of that omnipresent activity: namely (to quote the Oxford dictionary), "The use of contrivances for effecting some purpose: often in a bad sense, implying deceit or trickery." Ours is an opportunistic and often crudely utilitarian world. The remarkable thing is the extent to which so many of us do sustain a certain independence from the endless manipulative messages amidst which we live. In a generalized way, deceit is everywhere. Given the hyperbole of advertising and a celebrity culture devoted to what is currently called "hype," anyone who took seriously the endless flow of words and images emanating from politicians, advertisers, and governments would very quickly find himself dazed, perplexed, and probably penniless. Just such an outcome is sometimes dramatically exhibited by simple people who suddenly come into vast quantities of money. But most of us seem to take it in our stride.

One reason we take it in our stride is that, at any given period, there is usually some general agreement about what virtues constitute doing the right thing—paying debts, not deceiving people, sticking by one's commitments, and so on. Sexual mores have in recent times been the most unstable arena, and that is the main reason we tend to think that the moral life is a matter of choosing "values" for ourselves. That there is some general agreement on what is decent and respectable behavior does not itself guarantee virtue. Many right acts follow from the narrower kinds of self-interest, arising from fear of punishment or damage to reputation.

Whatever the actual motives, however, a great deal of modern experience consists of people leading lives in which a continuous stream of low-level disappointment is mitigated by the hopeful illusion that tomorrow will be better. The remarkable thing, perhaps, is that most of us develop a protective shell of skepticism in which we regard the promises and inducements of the advertising industry with appropriate derision. Such things we regard as entertainment, and familiarity protects us from the worst consequences of gullibility. Yet it would be a mistake to think that a rational and morally sophisticated population was untouched by the pervasive falsities by which we are surrounded. This condition has many bad effects, and one of them may well consist in accustoming us to the possibility of getting what we want by means of the deception, fraud, and relatively low-level dishonesty by which we are surrounded.

Many people plausibly identify this temptation with the commercialization of every aspect of modern life. Sport is a notable example. Cricket when played by amateurs in earlier times became, for the English in particular, the model of honest and gentlemanly conduct, but its commercialization has brought corruption. Athletes and horses in show jumping are alike subject to instances of using performance-enhancing drugs. Artless fraudsters in Rugby Union have been known to fake injury by the use of blood capsules. And all of these sporting figures today exhibit those absurd parodies of joy and excitement that signify the scoring of a goal or some other token of winning. They do this, one imagines, for the benefit of those watching on television, whose dull lives must be artificially enlivened as they sit. Even in more serious areas, the story is mixed. The lower levels of contemporary bureaucracy in Western states do not operate on the basis of corruption, but the higher levels are by no means without some elements of it. There are, in fact, very few areas of life that have not in some way been affected. It is very clear that the context I am describing is that of a servile rather than a free society. Servility is, of course, the psychological correlate of despotism.

One of the central features of a free society is trust between individuals. In the high Victorian age, trust was high and verbal contracts between those who knew each other, or merely belonged to the same social context, could be relied upon. Today, all parties call in the lawyers. More generally, trust in professionals is declining. One reason is that governments sometimes impose the duty of reporting confidential facts about their clients to the authorities. Some departments of the government currently supply "hotlines" to be used by those willing to report to appropriate authorities instances of "welfare fraud" or evasion of taxation. The spread of litigation in tort mandates a high level of wariness between employer and employee, client and professional. Politicians, now being subject to aggressive questioning in media interviews, are even more disposed than their predecessors to shade the truth, and indeed to say almost nothing at all. We regard the "whistleblower" as a heroic figure these days, and no doubt whistleblowers are often admirable. In the past, however, the duty of loyalty to associates figured much more highly than some general defense of the public interest—but the crucial point is that the loyalty of earlier times partly resulted from the fact that our forbears lived in a more honest and trusting world.

This breakdown of general trust is typical of despotically ruled societies in which fear is the basic motive by which social order is generated. Despotism (and totalitarianism in particular) is an order of political life that fragments a population, because where undercover surveillance is extensive, one cannot trust strangers. Each individual will tend to trust only a much more limited set of people—family, tribe, co-religionist, or "community"—and the broader society tends to become a concealed (or sometimes overt) contest for power between these groups. European societies marked by civil practices in earlier times were not usually subject to such conflicts except in times of political tension. One ought not, of course, romanticize these earlier periods of the European past. Dishonesty can and does appear in all environments, but the low levels of crime and fraud from the nineteenth to the twentieth century is well documented. Many factors would seem to be implicated in the evolution toward our very much less trustful world. We are now a much wealthier society, and the more wealth we have, the more we seem to want. Abundance of anything, no less than scarcity, creates problems. Another dangerous abundance is that of communication, for the more we communicate with people, the more likely we are to be led into deceiving them in one or other respect. Entertainments provide abundant opportunities for promoting products or messages.

Given that, for these reasons, we are a long way from any kind of austerity of the moral and political life, such as was promoted by the classical Greeks and the Roman republicans, how is it that we still characterize ourselves as free? Rousseau's program for reviving such austerities and making citizenship the essential basis of modern society came in time (and especially after 1789) to look positively sinister. Exploring a line of thought that had been developed by the French, Adam Smith advanced the notion that self-interest is an admirable motive on which a prosperous society might be based. He certainly did not mean to identify self-interest with the vice of selfishness. It was, rather, a legitimate recognition of one's own interests, so long as they were part of respect for the interests of others. Smith, we may remember, thought that our conduct should meet with the approval of our inner spectator, but much conduct in our market societies would fail this test. The motives from which modern citizens act are likely to be mixed. Fear of punishment or decline of reputation may well be important. Hypocrisy is no doubt deplorable, but some good acts result from it. Mandeville's earlier *Fable of the Bees* (last edition 1732) offers a satirical development of the French view that an entire social order could, and perhaps actually does, depend on vices.

The element of realism in such judgments reflects the account of modern conduct given by British philosophers such as Hobbes and Hume. In this view, conduct could be based on nothing else but desires, and the element of reason in good conduct was not (as the ancients had largely believed) the dominance of the passions by a faculty mandating the right way to behave, but rather a coherence of commitments, principles, and passions cultivated by self-conscious individuals. In such a view of conduct, judging the right thing to do is a good deal more relaxed than in the classical model because a coherence of different things can be understood in a number of ways, though not so much that "anything goes." Direct contradictions can occur. Modern European societies have clearly worked quite well in spite of many people doing the right thing for arguably wrong or debased reasons. The tradition of economics in modern times tends to lower the moral temperature considerably. But the danger is, of course, that the sources of self-restraint found in this view of the passions might, over time, become eroded. The sheer plurality of desires found in a society of individualists is part of what we understand by freedom, but unless it is grounded in sophisticated moral understanding, it takes us to the edge of disorder, and perhaps beyond. This is a possibility that is open to the changing explorations of each new generation in an individualist society. The danger is that desiring, in this special sense, might give way to that less deliberated thing called impulse. And just such a development in recent times has come to be legitimated in the idea of liberation.

An essential part of our modern conception of the moral life is its assumption that every individual is entirely capable of judging what is best for his own life. We are all, morally speaking, "masters" in the classical sense. In other words, there is no such thing as a natural slave, and even more emphatically, no European state can rest upon the rule of a supposedly superior class of masters. Hobbes is perhaps the most emphatic philosopher on this point. The assumption that each individual is capable of competently managing his or her own life is, of course, as unrealistic as its classical alternative that some people are natural slaves. Many people on many occasions lack this competence. In the past, families largely accommodated the less dramatic forms of incompetence, and criminal sanctions took care of the rest. Today, we have a whole industry of social workers whose task is to direct the lives of a class of persons whose incompetence in the business of life is likely to damage either themselves or those dependent on them. Although their manners may not be servile—many are confidently assertive—these people constitute a servile class periodically dependent on the state.

Servility must therefore be recognized as a matter of degree. Its essence is to be found in a specific sort of dependence on others, particularly on either a peer group or on those with power. Servility is not so much the absence of reason as a lack of thoughtfulness, and this may be found no less among intellectuals than among the intellectually limited. Some ideological enthusiasts in the last century had a servile relationship to those guiding whatever movement they belonged to, and chose to become the instruments of what they imagined to be some higher power. Such people were characterized in the past as "true believers," and they managed, as it were, to abandon some features of "personhood" in order to become instruments of a cause. For these reasons, the expression "activist" is highly ambiguous, since activism may be the expression of a critical and independent attitude, or may equally be a rather passive submission to group ideas.

It will be clear that this is an extremely difficult idea to operate with, because much ordinary conduct, ranging from being in love with someone to succumbing to one or other spiritual enthusiasm, will look like an abdication of independence without necessarily being servile. But it is characteristic of these situations that they are usually temporary, and that in time a certain reflectiveness will break out. We all take most of our ideas from others, but independence of mind consists in making the ideas one has picked up one's own.

Servility in this basically collective sense has been examined in great detail by twentieth-century critics of totalitarian enthusiasm. Critics often focused on the collapse of personal independence that was revealed by the idea that horrible acts could be justified by the defense of "superior orders." Here was the moral life betrayed by an erosion of the basic moral idea of duty itself. Yet not all servility is collective in these ways. It may express itself no less influentially in the corruption that results from an opportunistic concern for one's personal advantage. The individual prefers an illicit benefit to the rigors of performing a duty. This form of corruption is especially prevalent in non-European parts of the world. It seems to be a common response to political despotism. We have argued that in many parts of the world the normative structure of life, arising in social roles generated by custom or by religious belief, and usually by a combination of both, has little or no place for what we understand as a moral life. Our European notion of the moral can and should be distinguished from both custom and religion, though it is related to both. By contrast, in many parts of the non-European world, whatever is not determined by custom, religion, or fear is an opportunity to aggrandize oneself. This is a disposition that often defeats policies seeking to supply aid to the poor in other parts of the world.

It is a disposition that also helps to explain the instability of some of these states. Where corruption facilitates servility, any kind of power becomes dangerous. Military power, even the mere possession of a weapon, may be used to take advantage of others through intimidation. Again, a bureaucratic structure in which an official has the power to permit or to forbid something desired can evidently become an instrument for personal advantage. Attempts to reform such systems have usually foundered on the fact that the same corrupt practices flourish at higher levels, and notably at the level of sovereign power itself. In such states where constitutional formality is little respected, sovereign power becomes itself an opportunity of corrupt conduct. Western states are, as I remarked, by no means free of corruptions of various kinds, and they are certainly increasing, but one very notable exception is the reliable restraint of European armies in resisting temptations to overthrow governments.

Corruption is servile for many reasons, and almost universal as a response to a tradition of despotic government. Despotic government itself is a complex power structure being rather capriciously exercised by rulers, much of the time for their own advantage. European states are therefore likely to exhibit increasing levels of corruption, and therefore servility. The more governments take power over the workings of society, the more capricious their actions must become. Parsimony in law-making restricts regulation to things widely thought indispensable to society, but the more governments interfere in social life, the more complicated will be the details of regulation and the more capricious official judgments will come to seem. And caprice, as we know from despotic states, is itself a factor in the spread of corruption.

Again, corruption expresses the unexamined impulse to seize an immediate advantage with no concern for either moral commitments, such as duty, or for broader interests. It is the part determining the whole. Plato regarded the despot as the most slavish of men because he was at the mercy of his own impulses, and impulse is always the most evident mark of the occurrence of servility. In the cases of collective servility, the servile character is at the mercy of outside forces; he is being managed by others, and management must be distinguished from rule. In a European civil society, by contrast with despotic structures, citizens comply with the laws because in doing so they are not having some particular project imposed on them, but merely participating in an association of law-governed individuals, each of whom is free to engage in whatever projects he or she happens to support. It is this basic commitment to freedom in a European society that leads free men to be extremely wary about yielding obedience to authorities over whom their power of accountability is remote or non-existent. The relation of European states to the European Union is, in these terms, an abandonment of the power of self-government. Free men demand accountability. This is especially true if the abandonment of power is not limited in time. The tradition of freedom requires great wariness in doing whatever may circumscribe the independent judgment of future generations.

We may summarize our account of a servile mind by observing that we have arrived at a rather Aristotelian idea of what it is: we define it as the abdication of moral autonomy and independent agency in favor either of some unreflective collective allegiance or of some inevitably partial and personal impulse for illicit satisfaction. The independence of mind that distinguishes the individual who is not servile is found in a kind of mean between these two abstract extremes of the collective and the impulsive. The moral life, we may say, reflects some deliberative attention to the whole of an individual's context, both psychological and social. Servility is a collapse of independent judgment into partiality, and it is an aspect of what I shall presently be discussing as the "politico-moral."

A free society is one in which each individual complies with the law and may be relied on to conduct his own life in an orderly fashion. Many of course do not, and free societies certainly do not depend on large numbers of citizens likely to cry, "Give me liberty or give me death." But even the ordinary citizen of a European country believes that he or she lives in a free society, and that this has conditions in which the authority exercised over them has clear limits. He or she is, as it were, self-regulating. In respecting the rule of law, the laws involved are in principle the conditions of good order. They are, in Oakeshott's phrase, "non-instrumental,"[31] which means that they do not impose any arbitrary project upon citizens who are recognized as having their own enterprises to conduct. No state quite fits such a specification, and perhaps none possibly could: taxes must be collected, defense organized, and a certain patriotic concern with the national interest had better be sustained. The idea of civil society nonetheless may be taken as perhaps the criterion by which we may usefully judge how we ought to respond to the powers governments take for themselves.

The power that modern governments claim for themselves is generally justified as necessary for bringing some benefit to electors. But the very idea of government as a source of benefits, rather than a fount of order, is itself a retreat from the characteristic judgment of a free society. That governments give us good things is powerful rhetoric in the armory of rulers seeking power, and we have come to take for granted that it is the state that supplies good things such as medicine, education, and welfare subsidies. It takes considerable simplicity of mind, however, to believe that such policies are straightforward gifts of the state, because governments have nothing of their own to give: all they can do is redistribute what some people have so that it may benefit others. This manner of thinking has, however, become part of the public attitudes of citizens of European states over the last few generations. Here is the cast of mind that leads populations to be content with authority taking ever-increasing powers to itself. It is part of this world of illusion that the increased power that governments demand generally becomes evident only at a point later than the benefit supposedly supplied. It seems sensible to agree that subsidies to good causes such as education or the arts must itself be subject to the rules of accountability applied to public expenditure. In time, the expense of such things as nationalized medicine induces governments to move on to a new stage of control: it begins to regulate our lifestyles, or to put the matter more plainly, to tell us how we should live our lives. Obesity, smoking, promiscuity, and other such activities generate costs for the state, and thus justify extending the control of rulers even further than before. Similarly, governmental provision of education by the state soon leads to demands that schools should have a special character pleasing to authority (being non-selective, for example, or teaching what the government thinks desirable). Making exams easier is pleasing to people, and standards begin to get looser. A recent problem has been that fewer candidates from state schools, whose standards are declining, are accepted by universities, and the government solves the problem with a further extension of its power: by imposing on universities a duty to accept students whom they previously would have rejected. In a servile world, institutions also become cheapened and corrupted.

The rhetoric of governmental absorption of the institutions of civil society is to talk of "partnership" with the institutions, but control lies with the money, and the money comes from the state. The end of institutional independence is an important element in the advance of servility in European societies. Universities, hospitals, professions, charities, and many other elements of a free society were in the past, as industrial firms to some extent still manage to be, self-governing. They were able to manage their own affairs as they saw fit. But few can resist subsidy, which is perhaps the point where servility takes over from independence. The result is that many have been suborned by the money promised by government, and the pill has often been sweetened by talk of justice or social justice or equal access or some other bit of rhetorical sweetening in which servility is disguised as a form of virtue.

Government agencies often seem to control society by the light touch of issuing things called "guidelines," which in fact determine how much money hospitals can spend, which drugs doctors may prescribe, what ought to be the conditions of admission to schools, or the limits judges must respect in sentencing criminals. Most of these bodies have been given powers under law to determine a range of conditions, but they are held on a loose rein of democratic accountability. Here we have, unmistakably, the march of despotism, in which one central power, and one central policy, comes increasingly to dominate our free and plural society. And the decline of institutions in this way is paralleled by the collapse of the psychological independence of the individuals who manage them. They lack the sense of freedom that would alert their understanding to the fact that governmental control is a slippery slope from which it is difficult to escape.

In other words, the advance of a servile mind results from a pincer movement, in which the almost "instinctive" drive that states exhibit to expand their powers links up with a popular (and democratic) disposition to value easy enjoyments whatever the cost. This disposition is one that has been nurtured by our technological inventiveness in making such an easy and pleasant world for us to live in. The object of desire is some concrete outcome, and we want it—we often think we even have a right to it—irrespective of any constitutional, formal, or even organizational conditions that might get in our way. We might call this development a "culture of convenience," in which easy satisfactions will always be chosen above form and discipline.

The abiding image in our time of this convenience culture has been in sexual practices. The powerful drive of sex was traditionally formalized in terms of romantic love, marriage, and chivalry. These things were disciplines and restraints; they slowed things down. The most comprehensive evasion of these forms will be found in pornography and sexual liberation. Sex as liberated from all disciplines except the hygienic has advanced to the point where it is often thought a "right," the denial of which is against nature. Such denial is certainly against convenience. But sex is merely the centerpiece of the culture of convenience. Other instances will be found in the casualization of dress (especially among men), the ever-open supermarket and the decline in rituals, ranging from family meals to church attendance. To the secular mind, the rituals of the Jews derived from Leviticus, or those of the Muslim Ramadan, are absurd restraints on our pleasures because they do not rest upon any rational foundation. No doubt, but rationality in this limited sense is not really the point. These rituals are disciplines that generate identities. It is significant that people without much in the way of a clear sense of their identity are the most helpless when faced by the plausibilities of political regulation. It is in this sense that the culture of convenience facilitates a servile mind.

Some people regard this collapse of discipline as inherent in the logic of individualism itself. We need to remember, however, that classical individualism, far from being a carefree indulgence in impulsive conduct, expressed the most solicitous and disciplined concern for one's moral and personal identity. It was essentially self-disciplined. To think that our current passion for convenience is an outcome of individualism is a highly significant mistake, because in this vulgarized sense of the term "individualism," its opposite is social involvement. The individualist is misunderstood as someone with no other concern than his own interest, whatever the social consequences might be. What I am calling "the culture of convenience," and which concerns other critics of our time as heedless selfishness or "greed," is pretty universally recognized as a defect of our civilization. To advance as a solution some collectivized endeavor is, however, to slide from one version of servility to the other. And while responsible conduct is no doubt always to be admired, "social responsibility" and its many pious analogues play directly into the ambitions of masterful governments. For it is characteristic of governments to justify themselves by claiming a monopoly of what may be thought "social" virtues.

It follows that the defect on which critics nearly all agree ought not to be identified with any corruption of the moral practice of individualism. For what we mean by "individualism" is so complex a practice that we may only talk about a "logic of individualism" if take our bearings from some limited aspect of it, and aspects are, of course, abstract and partial. A real individualism does, however, survive in our world, even if elements of it are sometimes described in odd ways, such as "social capital." My inclination, as will already be clear, is to attribute the supposed corruption of individualism itself to the idea of liberation misunderstood as the essence of freedom and human rights.

The decline, and in some cases the collapse, of institutional independence in our societies reflects a more general decline in formality and constitutionality. The morality of liberation expresses the demand for some desirability to be immediately and usually costlessly available, and the effect has been a widespread collapse of the formal processes that previously marked Western life. The idea of liberation was a caricature of freedom because it identified most forms and limits as irrational and unnecessary barriers to some satisfaction. Such things as the self-government of university institutions, or the autonomy of professions, often seemed in this environment hardly worth passionate defense when some grander social project (such as "social justice") was within grasp. Similarly, the conventions of politeness and morality required a self-control and sometimes an expenditure of time that many decided they could not afford. Subsidies from government are alluring because they allow desirable things to be done, and short-term benefit trumps the sense of future threats to freedom. Principle plays a subordinate role to what we have often called "pragmatism." That particular corruption of justice often criticized as "judicial activism" is a practice of nudging law toward the moral and political outcomes one judge or another thinks would be desirable. And it will be obvious that corruption occurs whenever an agent shades a duty in order to achieve something of substance.

The march of servility may also be tracked in the spread of the self-excusing individual. Servility being the collapse of moral agency, any explanation of an action that transfers responsibility away from the actor as a moral agent, and toward some abstract social condition, is servile. Invoking some social condition (poverty, abused childhood, etc.) never actually *explains* a vile act unless every instance of the condition causes vileness, and it never does. It is significant that the inhabitants of prisons very commonly pick up this kind of patter as a way of enrolling themselves in the advantageous class of victimhood. We need not doubt that social conditions often play a part in delinquency, but it is important never to abandon the fact that moral agency is always involved. It is only by doing so that we take individuals seriously as agents. A preference for excuses is merely one step down a slippery slope toward state control.

It may seem perverse to diagnose servility as a rising theme in our free and easy societies of the twenty-first century. For it is possible to think that we are the freest people who have ever walked the planet, able to choose many things that were closely restricted in the past—things such as sexual preferences and artistic proprieties. We are a living utopia in the sense that people from other cultures flock to our shores and wish to live among us, as they never did to the revolutionary utopias of the past. The respectabilities of past times seemed much more intrusive than the benevolence and compassion in our contemporary moral idiom. But freedom, we know, never disappears overnight, and an aspiration to become part of an international world has led us to abandon the sovereignty that used to be our protection against the arbitrary. Only in the United States has the constitutional insistence that only Congress can abridge the rights of Americans so far blocked the increasing European submission to internationalist bodies, and the result is that it no longer means very much to be British, Dutch, Spanish, and so on—though the French and the Germans do seem to have kept a practical if not a theoretical distance from these submissive tendencies. But submissive we have all become in many areas of life, and the increasing passion of reformers to concentrate not just on civil institutions, to which we may respond as we choose, but on substantive conditions of life, such as social justice or happiness, cannot help but make us ever more manageable.

THE POLITICO-MORAL
WORLD

I. THE DEFECTS OF WESTERN CIVILIZATION

Learning from our mistakes is a basic precept of prudence, but it
only works if we understand what these mistakes are. Accident,
death, and injury are, as a rule, unambiguously bad, but what are
we to say, for example, about the drug that solves the immediate
problem but turns out to have unfortunate long-term effects? Success and failure often take time to disclose their character. At one
point in the twentieth century, enlightened opinion decided that
competitive games were bad for children because losing in such
contests damaged their self-respect. Schools therefore changed
their physical training ways, and public authorities often profited
by selling off their sporting fields and facilities. But then attention turned to the rise in obesity, partly caused by children not
exercising enough. The program went into reverse, new facilities
had to be financed and governments proclaimed that we needed
to restore a "ball games culture." This tiny example is instructive,

because it illustrates not only the pitfalls of thoughtless prudence, but also the fact that one basic drive in our civilization is, as we have already seen, to save people from pain—in this case, the supposed pain of inadequate self-esteem.

A sensitivity to what is bad and defective in Western life is, in fact, one of the most powerful judgments we make about the world we live in. We pride ourselves on our critical response to our world, for we think that it demonstrates our virtuous transcending of the more vulgar forms of self-satisfaction. We have many dismissive names for such collective self-satisfaction—nationalism, ethnocentricity, xenophobia, and suchlike. Other civilizations and cultures also have defects, of course, but we are less tolerant of our own defects because we are convinced that we have the knowledge and capacity to correct them if only we have the political will. And these attitudes—a critical spirit, a technological confidence, a weakness for grand moral projects—have been projected onto the world scene, and have created the materials for a whole new view of the world.

We share, no doubt, the defects of the human condition, with its propensity to ignorance, prejudice, violence, massacre, and so on, but our defects are less tolerable because we have available to us the materials for understanding bad things (in the form of reason and science), and also the capacity for dealing with them (in the form of technology). Our defects are thus worse than those of others, because we have the materials of transcending them. And there is worse: we are rich and others are poor. This is perhaps a defect of egalitarian justice. But it might just be the case—some have it argued strongly—that we are rich *because* they are poor. Could our wealth be founded, for example, on the capital gained through the slave trade, even though we abolished that trade two centuries ago? Later, in the nineteenth century, European states created empires throughout the world, from which only in the twentieth century were many peoples freed. Perhaps Africans suffer to this day from the burden of artificial state boundaries drawn on maps by imperial cartographers. There are other theorists who suggest that the West has established itself in the production of wealth as a Center that has reduced the rest of the world to a Periphery.

This idea has been common among activists attacking globalization, and among academics keen to explain the world in terms of capitalist and other forms of exploitation, but I do not think we need spend much time on it. As I suggested in the last chapter, modern Western civilization has evolved a conception of human life and a manner of living that is quite distinct from that of other peoples, and it is not exploitation of others, but the exceptionalism of that achievement that explains the wealth and good order of liberal democracies. European states are the source of a long string of inventions and practices that have, along with economic enterprise and the rule of law, transformed the world and allowed millions to live longer, and better. Nor have we kept our secrets close to our chest, like Venetian glass makers of earlier times trying to defend the monopoly of their skills. The West has been the most open civilization imaginable. Millions of young people from other places come to study at its universities on equal terms with our own young. And the proof that this is a real sharing of skill and opportunity will be found in the fact that other countries, such as Japan, and more recently China and India, have taken up the wealth-producing forms of living that we pioneered. It is a popular option, because in general, people prefer being rich to being poor.

But perhaps that is itself precisely the central term of the indictment brought against our civilization. Our fault may lie not in keeping other peoples poor but in that we have taught them how to be rich. We now know, or think we know, that the electricity pouring out of power stations to power computers and press-button machinery is actually destroying the planet by building up carbon deposits in the atmosphere. We Europeans are profligate users of the mineral resources of the planet. We have corrupted ourselves and everybody else by creating a lifestyle so rich that the planet cannot sustain it. Millions of less fortunate people live on less than what we insouciantly discard as waste. Aircraft are destroying the atmosphere as we enjoy the trivial benefits of international tourism, a human activity as unproductively corrupt for those who enjoy it as for those who serve in it. Like everything else in Western life, it is driven by the passion for profit—often these days attributed to "greed" rather than by any concern for human benefit.

"We" are thus to blame for being involved in a vast historical process that may threaten the future of human life on planet Earth, and that we seem to be powerless to modify. The standard by which we are being judged here is a reconfiguration of the immemorial hatred of the luxury of the rich, a hatred entrenched in Western projects for social equality. In this view, luxury is the greatest of all evils, and Westerners enjoy a level of luxury that even the despots of the past would have envied. The proper way to live is that of the "philosopher" who understands that superfluity corrupts, and that the satisfaction of human needs is all that is required for human happiness. Instead, we have been seduced by the lure of luxury, the capitalist passion for the unlimited satisfaction of false wants and needs. Yet "research" (i.e., replies to questionnaires) reveals that people are no happier now than they were in earlier generations, if indeed they are as happy. In that sense, the modern world is a tribute to irrationality. Our satisfaction at increasing wealth is actually the pointlessness of the treadmill.

It is also a tribute to inequality. In democracies, we ought to be sharing our wealth with each other rather than allowing some people to enjoy an "obscene" claim on the wealth of society while others live with little. But these differences within modern Western societies pale into insignificance when compared with the inequalities we have allowed to grow up in the Third World, where X % of the population lives on less than a dollar a day. (I have not put a figure for X but the reader may, as everybody else does, supply the figure he finds plausible.) Indeed, it is part of the inequality that our food and other things are cheap for us because so little is paid to producers in those exploited countries. At the root of this argument lies the fundamental belief that inequality itself is the same as oppression.

That particular conviction—that inequality reveals oppression—is implied by the postulate that perfection would be an order in which everyone equally shared in the goods of this world.[*] Quite what such a perfection would be like is something not fully elaborated, indeed, probably not to be elaborated at all. To the extent that accounts of a better world are supplied, they depend on negating evil abstractions such as war, poverty, ignorance, and so on. Perfection would be the absence of evils. The important point about this kind of moral ideal, so common in contemporary Western thought and often called "utopianism," is that some of its implications—such as the equality-oppression implication—are powerful moral impulses independent of any problem of giving an account of the basic ideal itself. For what they do unmistakably show is that the current state of Western societies, and *a fortiori* the current state of the world, is very bad indeed.

The large question arising within this utopia thus might well be: how far equalizing "up" the condition of the Third World poor should go. One might imagine that the test is met at the point where they live like us, but at that point the inequality argument collides with the globalization argument. The poor could never attain our luxurious standard of life because, for example, the attempt to equalize the consumption of meat, which is heavy on natural resources, is way beyond what the planet could sustain (so it has been calculated) at present levels of population. In other words, it is a further indictment of Western life that our drain on natural resources is one that could not be sustained if the impoverished millions of the Third World were to claim their share in it.

The reader might now be getting restless. It is tiresome to endure being denounced for more than a short space of time. It is important, however, to spell out and to analyze the indictment that many of our fellow Westerners (and it is overwhelmingly our own kind that advance this case for the prosecution) bring against their own civilization, because this indictment underlies the large shift in the moral imagination whose contours I am attempting to trace. That moral shift arises from the conviction that Western civilization has done great damage to both the planet itself (by its

---

[*] A human rights version of this idea, advanced by Thomas Pogge and others, will be discussed in the next chapter.

industrial techniques and wastefulness) and to our fellow inhabitants (by its arrogance and contempt). And this very broad understanding of our condition generates a whole set of problems, response to which is the basic test of both our rationality and our moral quality. What I am about to call the "politico-moral world" is a structure of thought that rejects the narrow boundaries of the individualist moral life as I have described it in Chapter III, and presents instead a set of aspirations, support for which would begin to redeem the guilt appropriate to the way we as a civilization have developed.

But there can be no redemption without a clear understanding of the sin, and we are by no means finished with the indictment. For we have so far been dealing with the grosser social and economic faults of our kind. We must also consider the narrowness of our thoughts and feelings. Is there not a conspicuous arrogance in the way we understand other peoples, sometimes romanticizing them, sometimes treating them as less than human, but seldom recognizing them as human beings on our own level? We are locked into our own Western perspectives, imposing on others a rigid conception of objective truth that denies validity to perceptions that lie outsides our own range of experience. These faults are at the root of a racial arrogance that goes with a white skin, and was in the past taken to justify imperialist oppressions.

Finally, some critics also bring Western civilization before the bar of history. "We" engaged in earlier times in righteous religious warfare against Muslims living in Palestine. It has to be admitted that those Muslims had themselves only conquered these regions four centuries before, but they had established settled societies, and the Crusades could thus be taken as aggression. Again, for some centuries we profited from the slave trade. These indictments, particularly, attack the political classes, leaving the poor morally in the clear. The rulers are to blame, as also they are for such events as the Irish Famine of the Hungry Forties, for which Tony Blair as prime minister apologized to Americans.

Here then is a brief sketch of the remarkable reasons commonly advanced for that civilizational self-hatred of the West that has long been one of our recognized pathologies. Ernest Gellner called it a "yearning for post-imperial expiation," and went on to analyze the destructive effects that various forms of the resulting relativism have done to Western social science.* Readers of Rousseau often felt rather gimcrack by comparison with the noble savage of legend, who was untouched by our frenzied consumerism. When communism overturned traditional regimes, many people in the West ignored its murderous reality and admired the good intentions proclaimed by its leaders. Those communist despots might have made a frightful mess of it, but at least (as old communists have said in attempts to expiate their misjudgments) they *cared* about the world in which we lived. Lenin, Stalin, Castro, and even Pol Pot did not lack for admirers among Western radicals and intellectuals. Indeed, there remain some whose hatred of the modern West as it has developed is so intense, and whose disappointment at the failures of revolutionary expectations is so intense, that they will support absolutely anything that is violently hostile to the lives we lead—jihadism, for example—in the hope that some day our civilization will at last be smashed.

Alienation from one's own culture is not, of course, unknown in other times and places, but it usually consists not in root and branch rejection of what one thinks and feels, but in rage at the failures revealed in one's own culture when compared with the technological and organizational superiority of the West. Western self-hatred is not of that kind. It is, I suspect, part of Western exceptionalism that the very duality of secular and sacred in the West is the basis on which a self-hating location might be created. For where does the root and branch social critic of the modern West belong? What, as it were, is his theoretical location?

The answer must be that he has an institutional and ideological identity as a member of a self-nominating group of those who share what he takes to be a rational and critical attitude that claims to have transcended the illusions and deceptions of local prejudice. And this possibility of locating oneself in a kind of ideal or utopian "nowhere" was one that became culturally possible

---

* Gellner was writing a long reflective essay on the mood of what he called the coming *fin de millenaire* in the *Times Literary Supplement,* June 16, 1995.

because Christians had long ago learned how to detach themselves from the errors of their place and time and to understand themselves as citizens of the *Civitas Dei*. European self-hatred is individual detachment from patriotic loyalty to Britain, France, Holland, the United States, and so on. In academic life, local attachments can often seem to be a betrayal of one's academic vocation as a critic of the dogmas and prejudices in the society by which one is surrounded. It is in some degree paradoxical that the critics are in no way more dramatically Western than in their hatred of their own heritage. It is an entrenched European tradition, though previously found largely in a religious idiom.

It is an interesting question whether those who reject their civilization on moral grounds exemplify moral abasement—or moral megalomania. The answer, of course, is that the abasement is collective, and the megalomania is personal. Denunciatory prophets are not new, but few fail to leave room for a saving remnant. The critics have cast themselves for this interesting role, and the theory generating the criticism is a form of gnosis, or claimed superior understanding, that is central to any antinomian tradition. The theological analogue of what we are dealing with here seems to be the belief that the world (or "society") is essentially corrupt, except for the saving remnant, who are beyond the laws. It was a notable feature of the Christian antinomians that they felt they were above the law, and our modern antinomians often think themselves justified in taking any step that might weaken the evil power they oppose. They illustrate the fact that the essence of civilizational self-criticism is its capacity to generate righteous emotions. Of this, more later.

The critics of our civilization who have recognized faults to which the rest of us remain largely insensible in our heedless consumerism are not only the saving remnant, but have also come up with solutions to what is understood as the basic problem. The solution consists in three things that we shall consider. Firstly, an ethical revolution must transform our attitudes, and we shall be discussing it as the "politico-moral" in later sections. Secondly, we must spread the universal reign of human rights that have (notionally, at least) been generated not by Western values and prejudices but by a rational understanding of the human condition. And thirdly, an emerging global order must be created in which evil acts (of which genocide is the paradigmatic case) will become legally accountable.

There is, of course, an inexact but suggestive sociology of the phenomenon we are considering. If we ask who the critics are, we shall discover that they tend to come from the pedagogic, the communicative, and the administrative classes. It seems significant that these are not people directly involved in the production of wealth. On the other hand, those likely to have local and national loyalties are those involved most directly in the economy. What distinguishes these two groups from each other is that the critics have salaries largely paid by governments and other bureaucracies, and therefore are to a large extent detached from the actual pursuit of *interests*. The minds of social critics, one might say, are largely concerned with *ideas*; "ideology," to put it brutally, is their trade.

To advance an idea apparently detached from any taint of interest gives the person affirming it an agreeable sense of contributing to universal rationality, by contrast with the mere protection of some interest. The rich socialist feels greatly superior to the patriotic industrialist. Besides, interests conflict with each other, and are the beginning of civil and social dissension. This gives the exponents of ideas, or utopias, an agreeable sense that their opinions are, in the best sense, disinterested, untainted by the vulgarities of interest. The sophists in Greece lived off the idea that "opinion rules the world," but they were not at all disinterested. In modern times, the main doctrines of political science have exhibited politics as an arena for settling conflicts of interest. Now, however, we have a large and influential ideas-producing class for whom reality is mediated either through their evaluative judgments, or through the current ideas found in history and philosophy. Getting one's interests wrong soon leads to disadvantage and pain. Getting one's ideas wrong seldom brings a rapid disillusionment.

Self-hatred in the West is a strange and indeed puzzling thing. It seems to happen when loyalty to one's own cultural heritage is transferred to an ideal location. A common explanation offers guilt as the psychological dynamic of cultural self-alienation, but it is not at all clear what the average European should feel guilty for, and who should be guilty for whatever it might turn out to be. Guilt in this context is seldom defined, but we may suggest, in brief, that feeling guilty is a learned emotion derived from a consciousness, real or imagined, that one has betrayed a moral principle constituting one's identity. It might be possible, for example, that some people have so internalized equality of social and economic conditions as a moral principle that they experience the disabling emotion of guilt merely from the contrast between their own wealth, on the one hand, and the poverty of some reference group on the other. If so, the therapy is clear enough: Sell all thou hast and give it to the poor. Some individuals have in fact done this, but it is rare. If guilt does lie behind the passionate self-hatred of some Westerners, then they seem to have gritted their teeth and with great fortitude learned to enjoy its benefits.

More likely, in fact, would be that they have responded by construing their civilizational detachment as evidence that they belong to the class of sensitive and superior people. Does not self-disgust demonstrate that one's moral attitudes are rational rather than self-serving? In analyzing the views that people take of their place in the world, one is seldom wrong in discovering some element of self-regard in the mix. Those who adopt some abstract moral position commonly admire themselves for doing so. This is especially so in this case, because those proclaiming their own collective guilt have also generated, as we shall see, the political policies that might be imagined to remedy these faults. This demonstrates that they are seriously involved with the problem.

Burke once wrote that he did not know "the method of drawing up an indictment against a whole people."[32] We might well say the same thing about a whole civilization. And in fact the impossibility is clearly a logical one. We shall presently be discussing the logic of the muddle called "social responsibility," and the logical impossibility of being responsible for the thing called "society" applies no less to the idea that we might be responsible to such a thing as a culture, or a civilization. Any serious indictment can refer to nothing else but moral actors, individual or collective, per-

forming identifiable acts. At this level, we certainly find plenty
to criticize in the way Europeans have behaved, though whether
our criticisms are well judged or not always remains an arguable
matter. I suppose it is just possible to repudiate our whole civilization as a ghastly mistake, but even in doing that, one would be
expressing one of the possibilities that the civilization itself allows
to find expression. Civilizational self-hatred is, in other words, a
self-refuting idea, and hardly a very profitable one. But my concern
with this rather strange cast of thought is that Western self-hatred,
in both explicit and implicit ways, has become increasingly influential in generating our ideas about how we ought to behave. Let
us move, then, to consider the moral response it has generated.

2. THE POLITICO-MORAL WORLD AND ITS ETHICAL CLAIMS

This pseudo-historical conception is the analysis out of which a
new moral understanding of our world has developed. We may
specify it by the ungainly name of "politico-moral," because it has
for many purposes rejected any conflict between the (individual)
moral life on the one hand, and the (collective) policies of states
on the other. The politico-moral, as it emerges from the vision
of our global situation sketched in the last section, demands of
us both a moral attitude (particularly toward suffering among
abstract classes of people) and a political commitment to change
a world so morally defective. We who are rich and educated owe
a commitment to serving the overriding project of achieving a
once-and-for-all transformation of the condition of humanity.
Recognizing that we must change the world for the better is the
only moral attitude that can be defended as responding to the
realities of the human condition. The transformation demanded
is to equalize satisfaction of the needs of everyone in our own
society and, in the longer term, to relieve poverty and oppression
in the rest of the world. Increasingly, this project is being subsumed under the expanding concept of human rights.

In the individualist world, moral issues were distinct from
political issues, and it was often accepted that they clashed. As
Machiavelli had so famously recognized, the ruler must sometimes

know how not to be good, and the good man could not help but compromise his principles on going into politics. The politico-moral world, however, has discovered a set of moral and political imperatives in whose pursuit no real conflict need arise. The moral, or to use the term that has come to be domesticated in the rhetoric of the politico-moral, the "ethical," determines the political. A century ago, the world at large was widely understood by Europeans as a place of interest and opportunity. Today, it is a nest of problems to be solved.

Such a project affects us in terms of what might be called "species loyalty," perhaps crystallized during the twentieth century by the currency of John Donne's famous sermon insisting that "no man is an island."[33] Donne's sermon, of course, was intensely Christian, but when Ernest Hemingway gave the idea its modern currency, he was making a political point about humanity's common involvement in the conflict between fascism and democracy. Today, our world conceived in terms of the problems of war, climate change, poverty, and so on is understood as a place of suffering. Those among the modern young who participate in this vision are more conscious of the poverty of others than of the wealth they themselves enjoy. As theoretical egalitarians, they feel that the poverty of others is a betrayal of people with whom they are linked by compassion and empathy. These attitudes are an important element in the larger movement of things called "globalization," and they have been spread in a number of ways.

Intellectual fashion now as always plays its part in diffusing these attitudes, and so too do the pious hopes of civil and educational authorities, who have identified this complex moral and cognitive movement as an important part of educated awareness in the contemporary world. Such a thing is often promoted as "global citizenship." In other words, a vocabulary is developing that adumbrates a conception of mankind in terms of a unified ideal democracy, in which the peoples of the Earth, as in any democracy, are able to enjoy the things they want. The basic conviction is hardly different from what the satirist P. J. O'Rourke called "voting yourself rich."[*] For it is part of the underlying drive of political correctness that unequal patterns of consumption result from inherited injustices that we may abolish by an act of political will.

Let us track the emergence of this new moral world in two sections, the first being a strictly moral development, and the second the response of Western self-rejection. The moral development is often associated with the 1960s, but it had been evolving from much earlier times. It was an understanding of human conduct that we may analyze in three steps.

The first and most basic was the rejection of authority in favor of reason, something most conspicuous in the rhetoric of the 1960s. One reason advanced for rejecting authority was that it was sometimes abused. The common media image of rulers, teachers, policemen, matrons, judges, and others holding some kind of authority came to emphasize that they were human, all too human. Some of them were sadists, many were capricious. This was the time in Anglo-America of the great satire boom, in which anyone holding an office of authority was derided as combining pomposity and stupidity. It soon came to be thought that many of the actions of government were "beyond satire," as indeed quite a number of them were. The general argument was that authority had ruled the world from the beginning of time, and what a mess of the world it had made! We should now give the people a chance. Besides, authority seemed to be a system necessary only for forms of government in which the people were oppressed. But in today's democracies, policies were legitimate not (it seemed) because they issued from an authoritative source, but because they responded to what the people wanted. The problems of political life no longer seemed so complicated that a subtle immersion in a country's tradition was necessary to deal with them. The formula for political success seemed to be "popular will plus expert advice," on which basis the obfuscations of the past would come into the light of day.

---

* As P.J. O'Rourke argues throughout *The Parliament of Whores* (Picador: London, 1991), democratic government is a device for getting your hands on other people's money.

No doubt for functional reasons of organization, there had to be bosses, policemen, matrons, and so on, but their power should be circumscribed by a machinery of regulation, inspectorates, and tribunals, and these institutions were themselves part of the process of broadening power out to the people. This was to be a rationalization of an often-irrational world.

The rejection of authority in favor of reason has been, of course, the rationalist project of European civilization since the time of Descartes, but this tradition had previously been limited largely to an elite versed in science, philosophy, and technology. The slogan of "down with authority" was now animating a much less sophisticated set of people and leading to a whole range of fancied liberations. In fact, it had "plugged itself" in to much deeper layers of European thought, according to which our grasp of technology might be extended—few limits on the process were conceived—to solve social problems and create a notably better world. The rebellious young of the 1960s, in whom these long maturing tendencies burst forth in the most flamboyant way, looked at a world whose complexities (and whose subtle pleasures) they hardly understood, and said: "There must be a better way."

The second prong of this new moral order followed pretty directly from the first. It consisted in the feeling that punishment was merely part of the oppressive past, and that the aim of "social control" ought to be reclaiming a human being rather than imposing pain upon him (and occasionally her). Prisons were thought not to work because many released convicts simply went on to offend again. Great hopes were sometimes invested in projects of teaching convicts skills such as acting and anger management, but the offenders usually disappointed their champions. Nevertheless, criminals tended to be assimilated to the class of the (mentally) ill and the vulnerable, and the problem was thought to be one of finding the right therapy. Criminality, like everything else, was a problem to be solved, and in solving it the moral sphere had to be abandoned in favor of the sociological or the psychiatric. But these remedies could only work if people had been liberated from past repressions so that they might express their real feelings, and deal with them.

The third prong of this moral change was its response to conflict, and especially to war. Conflict is endemic in human life and often leads to violence. We need therefore to institutionalize ways of dealing with it, whether in industrial life, in bullying in schools, in domestic violence, or in the extreme form of war. The basic idea seems to be that, in any conflict, both sides can present some kind of case, and therefore a solution to the problem can only come from compromise, from "give and take." In other words, the solution to any conflict must be negotiation, and in negotiation both sides must give way on some things. There is no room here for the conflicts of principle in which the twentieth century abounded. The instinct of many people in the case of the Falklands War had been to negotiate through the intermediary of the United Nations. How effective a reasonable policy may be depends, of course, on the character of those one is negotiating with. With lots of people, ranging from Attila the Hun to Adolph Hitler, negotiation is not a very serious option. Rejecting force in favor of negotiation through international institutions can often be a sensible thing to do, but there are other times when the best hope is, if we may invoke O'Rourke again: "Give war a chance." Negotiating is a form of realism whose success depends entirely on a judgment of the other side in the conflict. But the basic principle involved here was that cooperation with others could always be made possible, and would always emerge if people had the opportunity to transcend self-interest.

Here, then, as a package of attitudes blending rationalism, liberation, and cooperation, is a moral position seeking to override the eccentricities and conflicts of what we have been calling "the moral life." It is distinguished from the moral life in that it depends on *substantive* commitments that operate to exclude authority, punishment, and violence as responses to social problems. It relies on a rather different vocabulary from those dominant in the first half of the twentieth century. Freedom and the rule of law have been largely replaced by liberations and rights.

The move from traditional freedoms to a rhetoric of rights is a significant development. The point about freedom as it had traditionally been understood was that it incorporated moral limitations within it; liberty was distinguished from license, and those who enjoyed it accepted the conventions and limitations of their duties in respect of family life. Very many of them accepted the duty of volunteering their services in civic activities such as scouting, refereeing school games, youth clubs, etc. A liberation, however, is simply a release from conventions and restrictions; it does not in itself incorporate limitation, as freedom does. The same is true of rights, which are in themselves (as moralists often complain) obligation-free. The result of this transposition of moral vocabulary is that our complex understanding of freedom, as both permission and limitation, has curdled into two separate entities: untrammeled liberation, and a set of rights adjudicated by tribunals solely concerned with conflicts between those enjoying such rights.

Just as the attack on authority soon had many people lamenting the collapse of respect, and a British prime minister tried to create a "respect agenda" in social life by political dictation, so the evolution of freedom into liberations and rights required a counterbalancing concern with "social responsibility," which became in time an aggressive form of moral intimidation directed at the rich and the powerful.

For it is a conspicuous feature of democracy, as it evolves from generation to generation, that it leads people increasingly to take up public positions on the private affairs of others. Wherever people discover that money is being spent, either privately or by public officials, they commonly develop opinions on how it ought to be spent. In a state increasingly managed right down to small details of conduct, each person thus becomes his own fantasy despot, disposing of others and their resources as he or she thinks desirable. And this tendency itself results from another feature of the moral revolution. Democracy demands, or at least seems to demand, that its subjects should have opinions on most matters of public discussion. But public policy is a complicated matter and few intelligent comments can be made without a great deal of time being spent on the detail. On the other hand, every public policy may be judged in terms of its desirability. However ignorant a person may be, he or she can always moralize. And it is the propensity to moralize that takes up most of the space for public discussion in contemporary democracy.

3. THE EMERGENCE OF THE POLITICO-MORAL

As we have seen, politics and the moral life have traditionally been understood as distinct, both in the way they operate and in the considerations that they raise. Clarifying this relationship is an idea associated particularly with Machiavelli, who was remarkably unflinching in explaining that immoral political acts were unavoidable in the business of rulers holding states together. Justifications of political acts, on the other hand, require the justifier to minimize this difference. Apologists usually make some claim that justice is being done, but justice may, on occasion, have to be overridden by necessity, which is an appeal to the public or national interest. In any case, justice is a complicated and contestable idea, and what is just in one way may be unjust in another; or what is just to one set of people may be unjust according to the judgment of others. These are all versions of the incompatibility of politics and moral goodness.

The essence of the politico-moral is the denial of this problem. It consists in the espousal of policies claimed to be both "morally imperative," and also "necessary in the national interest." This combination is made plausible by a number of ideas, one of them being the conception of planetary consciousness we have already introduced. To be alive today is thought to involve us, whether we know it or not, in a massive crisis of global management, and only one basic course of action is thought to make sense. The planet must be saved from man-made degradation, poverty must be overcome, war abolished, and so on. The politico-moral is unmistakably a moral movement, but as we have seen, one that does not usually describe itself in moral terms, for the word "moral" got fatally entangled with sex. The preferred term is "ethics." A person who takes care to minimize his carbon emissions, for example, and thus to lead a climatologically pure existence, is described as "leading an ethical life." The desirabilities of the politico-moral are described in terms of a better society, and in this conception, the social is the ethical, and the essence of both is equality.

A philosophical argument may often be more easily expounded in terms of examples, and many will be familiar from contemporary political rhetoric. Politico-moral projects include saving the planet from man-made deterioration, dealing with poverty in Africa and other parts of the so-called "Third World" (which is virtually defined in these negative terms, as an area of unsatisfied need), abolishing land mines, spreading human rights so that people are no longer oppressed, and preventing war. It will be obvious that these issues compel a great deal of sympathy. Who would want to destroy the planet, ignore the needs of people abroad, support the use of land mines whose evil consequences continue long after a conflict has been forgotten? It is this overwhelmingly plausible goodness that allows the projects of the politico-moral to claim the support of all decent people. Indeed, criteriological reversal becomes inescapable: supporting these causes becomes the test, the criterion of decency itself. The young in particular find in the politico-moral a compass guiding their political direction. The ethical *becomes* the political, in a unified form of life.

In modern times, European politics consisted of two or more parties debating contestable desirabilities. Each party was usually itself a coalition based on internal compromises. Parties were thus in part instruments for smoothing out political conflicts. Liberals, conservatives, and socialists "fought" fiercely as they picked over the policies to be espoused by governments, but they themselves were part of an ever-changing constellation of ideas. The more that national politics had the character of a contest between government and opposition, the more political activists were brought into a national compromise, because they were forced onto a level of abstraction at which a coherent tradition of politics could emerge. Preventing fragmentation in such fragile coalitions was a central element in the skill of politics.

In the twenty-first century, many things have changed. Large areas of what were previously of private concern have become subject to political regulation. New problems have arisen from social changes, such as the emergence of multicultural communities, and these have also become subject to civil regulation. And associated with such changes, new pieties have arisen according to which individuals are able to demonstrate their decency by the political attitudes they adopt. These attitudes are normally correlated with the grand political projects emerging from the politico-moral vision, and the result has been a coercive centralism of attitude and policy on which all right-thinking people agree. We are all, as it were, moderates now. Being in the center of opinion comes to mean that one is both nice and sensible, while criticism of these positions, rejecting "centrism," is to be "extreme," and thus probably to be morally deplorable. The terms "left" and "right" are now often qualified as "center-left" and "center-right" in order that semantics should reflect this basic change in politico-moral attitudes. "Centrism" is the new orthodoxy, and, as ethical, it is both moral and political.

The underlying principle of this change is revealed in the agreed universality of the norms that currently dominate politics at all levels. Most people have been persuaded that the state is a source of wisdom superior to the impulses of individuals, that it alone has the power and knowledge to deal with social problems as they arise. Governments have widely claimed the right to determine the conditions of welfare, health, and education, and that these should be universally provided out of taxation. The argument is that individual responsibility for these things cannot but generate inequality of provision. Some would be left behind. The only way to guarantee minimal social benefits is, it seems, to entrust the state with the power to provide them. The strange ethical foundation of the politico-moral is the worship of power and authority as the agent of human improvement.

It is this basic agreement on the goals of policy that, transposed into the international sphere, gives rise to such conceptions as "global justice." And in this, as in much else, the policies of national states are found to be defective: they are partial and self-interested when they ought to be universal and compassionate.

It was part of this cast of mind that led Western politicians to declare that the age of national sovereignty was ending, and the belief may largely be dated to the end of the First World War. Such statesmen were seldom careful in distinguishing nationalism as a grievance movement on the one hand from the national interest of established states on the other. The national interests of established states are not usually concerned with grievances, and they always incorporate a universal element recognizing that their own state belongs in a system whose interests benefit them all. Nationalist movements have little in the way of such a rational balance of concerns. Political rhetoric is hardly careful about its categories, and muddled logic in these particular cases has often reinforced the "ethical" distinction between being compassionate and being self-interested. The ethical aspiration was that national partialities would be replaced by internationalist universalism. Such a hope came to be realized, in a way, by such institutions as the United Nations and the European Union.

Two things clearly follow from this set of beliefs. One implication is that international institutions are generally, perhaps always, wiser, more rational, indeed more legitimate in exercising authority, than national states. International law therefore comes to be credited with a range and completeness it does not have. The Iraq War in 2003, for example, was said to be illegal in spite of the fact that no judicial process had been argued or a decision given about its lawfulness by any court. Indeed, it is hard to say what body, in terms of what law, could have done so. But such a propagandist use of the label "illegal" is merely one more response to the semantic changes that have robbed the term "moral" of its persuasive power in policy discussions.

The second implication is that rational and rights-based policies can best be achieved by expert bureaucracies rather than by democratic votes. It is the politico-moral movement that explains the remarkable rise in the political salience of international charities, or Non-Governmental Organizations (NGOs). The NGO is the natural habitat of the ethical. The assumption is that these bodies represent the altruism of good intentions. They are therefore free of the dependence on political interests unavoidable in democratic governments whose responsibility is to sustain a national interest.* We thus encounter one more of the paradoxes of this democratic world we are investigating: that the democratic telos leads directly to the subversion of any real democracy.

My argument is, then, that the moral life as I have described it is in some degree giving way to this new form of moral enthusiasm that I am calling "the politico-moral." No moral fashion ever completely supersedes its predecessor, of course, but it is worth asking how the politico-moral is continuous with, and has indeed grown out of, what I have been calling the moral life.

The basic moral difference between these ideal sentiments is that in the moral life, the individual constructed his own identity in terms of personally chosen commitments. In that world, moral questions were distinct from religious ones, though the relationship was obviously close, and in many cases the religious demand foreclosed the moral issue. In our modern world, a remarkable plurality of views about "the right thing" has flourished, and consequently many diverse ways of life. These ideas have taken the form of sentiments, rules, and principles, and they have constituted the materials for the essential core of the moral life—namely, the activity of deliberation.

In the politico-moral world, large elements of this kind of chosen identity have been converted into the standard postures of support for politico-moral causes. Such elements are mandatory because they are thought to be the necessary postures of decency. Such a posture is most obviously recognizable today in the postulates of so-called "political correctness," in which we are required to respond to persons of every race, religion, sex, and sexual orientation with the same standard recognition of common humanity.

---

* In this area, it has been common to confuse nationalist movements, such as that of Basque nationalism, or the Irish Republican Army, or Jihadist terrorism, with the interests of national states. But nation-states are actors in a wider world, and a concern with accommodating the interests of others, and with universal goods, is part of the way national interests are constructed in constitutional states. This is not true of nationalist movements demanding a change in the international structure.

This demand excludes, most notably, the preference for one's own kind that has been instinctive in most human lives.

The practical assumption sustaining political correctness is clearly that if sentiment and belief can be adequately entrenched in the human mind, they will determine conduct, more or less without any intervening (and unpredictable) process of deliberation. To some extent, the distinction between the moral and the politico-moral might seem very slight, because what the politico-moral makes politically correct has often been covered in the moral life by the precepts of good manners, which require the treating of all human beings with appropriate consideration. But this overlap of actual conduct merely conceals the large difference in logic between the two. In the moral life, the agent is assumed to be a rational will whose conduct responds to circumstances as he or she makes sense of them. In the politico-moral, what is rational has been established in advance. It is given in the moral and political package constituted by political correctness, along with a few additional imperatives responding to current fashions, such as smoking, or smacking children. This is a package taking the form of an orthodoxy so complete that attitudes and acts falling inside and outside it can be specified merely as "acceptable" and "unacceptable."

Moral pronouncements using this terminology are commonly made by ministers of state, but they may be heard from anyone with some didactic claim on our attention. They are today's language of authority. It is a form of moral control in which government regulations operate as if they were commands. An example would be the legislation prohibiting "hate speech," or the further march of right thinking found in declaring some beliefs as—well, beyond belief! In some European countries, it is a crime not to believe that the Holocaust happened, and others have suggested that denial of anthropogenic climate change should be criminalized.

It seems plausible to say that there is a large measure of demanded obedience in the politico-moral, not to mention a level of intimidation implemented by a variety of equality officers and other custodians of the correctness vocabulary. The result is that a whole range of statistical discriminations of the qualities of different categories of people cannot be discussed for fear of accusations of xenophobia and other discriminatory sins.

The most important point that distinguishes the politico-moral from the moral life is psychological: it is essentially imitative rather than deliberative. This is seen not only in the coercive aspects I have just mentioned, but also in the preoccupation with "role models." Celebrities who might influence others by their conduct are expected to hold the right opinions, eschew smoking and drugs, and thus be worthy of imitation by the young. They are told of the responsibilities they carry, and severely criticized if they fail.

4. ASPECTS OF THE POLITICO-MORAL

Certain features of the politico-moral will have become fairly evident from this short sketch of it. Imitation as determining conduct, for example, entails an elite orchestrating the process in order to block off deviant models. Again, an imposed orthodoxy cannot avoid great anxiety that incorrect remarks might disturb the thoughts and actions of those who read such things as tabloid* newspapers. But the politico-moral has various aspects that should be highlighted in their own right as helping to compose the mental world of this new phenomenon.

a. Fallacies of the "Social"

First, what should be noted is the salience of the term "social," and the remarkable things that may be done with it. As Hayek pointed out, "social" is a powerful adjective capable of reducing almost any idea to vacuity.[34] But that is not quite right. "Social" certainly carries meanings, and they may be profoundly wrong-headed. The classic definition of justice as "giving every man his due" refers in its legal sense to ownership and title. But by extending the significance of "due," the formula can, as "social justice," become the basis for any amount of redistribution, on

---

* *The Times* is now a tabloid, but this term has been appropriated in *bien pensant* or chattering class circles to refer to downmarket newssheets dealing in the cruder forms of emotion.

whatever principles of equity the speaker may happen to favor. In most of these derivative senses, the term "social justice" is thus a direct contrary of the basic meaning of justice. Terms that can so easily whistle up self-contradiction are marvelous instruments of rhetoric.

Take, again, the term "social capital,"[*] which has come into sociological currency to describe a cluster of virtues such as self-control, punctuality, steadiness in work, ability to learn, and a variety of other virtues. These virtues are all moral. They are what any person properly brought up learns in the process of education, but which contemporary state education, along with those new varieties of kinship associations recognized as "families," has often failed to achieve. One might think that presenting these virtues as "social capital" was merely a bit of modish semantics, a harmless response to the fustiness of genuine moral terms. But that would be a mistake. For moral virtues are the fruits of the moral will, whereas social capital is merely a feature of the world, causally derived from social conditions. In other words, the term "social" here involves a switch of logic, from choice to outcome.

Much more serious is the rhetorical mayhem created by a logically muddled term such as "social responsibility." Here is a real shotgun marriage between the moral and the sociological. One may, as a moral agent, be responsible for oneself, one's family, one's golf club, one's reputation, one's school, and so on. The reason is that all of these entities are in some sense "enterprises" that may set terms of responsibility. They have aims, ends, means, and purposes, and one may behave responsibly in terms of such policies. But the thing called "society," being the total assemblage of all the enterprises going on within any particular state, is not an enterprise at all. The point of the politico-moral is indeed an attempt to turn it into one, so that we all share the same aims and "values," but in the actual modern world in which we live, there is

---

* The term is associated with James Coleman and, later, Robert Putnam. For a discussion of some of its features, see: John Meadowcroft and Mark Pennington, *Rescuing Social Capital from Social Democracy*, Institute of Economic Affairs, 2007.

no single enterprise toward which one might direct one's responsibility, because the various projects of so many individuals and institutions point in different and often contradictory directions.

Is this merely pedantic fussing? The way "social responsibility" is currently used covers any kind of beneficent act or gift, particularly any charitable enterprise clearly benefiting some class of people. But "social responsibility" is also part of the somewhat intimidating rhetoric of the politico-moral. Those receiving "obscene" financial bonuses in their work, for example, are regularly lectured on their duty to do something for "society," and industrial firms are subject to demands to spend money on good causes, rather than on their main business of producing quality goods at the best price. This belongs to a rhetoric of public discussion in which industrial firms feature as generators of a selfish kind of wealth called "profit," and the assumption is often made that these resources really belong in the public purse to be distributed according to "social need." Indeed, one of the more remarkable advances of the politico-moral vocabulary in recent times has been to equip economic enterprises with a set of standard (and deplorable) motives called "fear and greed."

There are two very serious consequences of the nest of fallacies lurking in the vocabulary of social responsibility and its many variations. The first is, up to a point, self-correcting, but the second is a very serious contributor to the political incompetence from which we currently suffer.

The first consequence is that the politico-moral drive to involve economic enterprises in responsibility toward "stakeholders" adumbrates a strange world in which everybody is vaguely responsible for everybody else. The economy and the society become closely entwined, to the confusion of both. The business of enterprises is to be efficient, while the duties of moral agents in society may well be quite different. Politically, this semi-moral and semi-political project leads to an increasing burden of taxation on industry, and an increasingly corporatist and consultative style of government—the sort of thing symbolized in Britain in the 1970s by the disposition of the Labor government under Harold Wilson to settle strikes by late-night sessions of "beer and sandwiches" in 10 Downing Street.

Here was the politico-moral dream in action. Negotiation replaced hard-edged principle. The reality was that the relationship between folly and its consequences had been abolished, and firms could lose money, individuals could borrow, and unions could indulge their intransigence to their hearts' content. In 1978–79, Britain had the immense good fortune to experience directly the real results of universalized sentimental benevolence: A rip-roaring economic crisis followed by a "winter of discontent" in which a variety of industrial disputes collided with each other, reducing the country to disorder and frustration. In these conditions, the evident disasters of one version of the politico-moral were dramatized, and this opened the way for a political appeal to realism. Other countries have experienced less dramatic forms of this self-correction, but Britain remains the model, and Margaret Thatcher, who wielded the whip that restored some sense of reality to British life, has been regarded with increasing respect, even by the many who loathed her policies at the time. The whole episode is currently regarded by some European politicians with a certain element of envy; the issues were so marvelously clear.

The second consequence may be illustrated by a dramatic contradiction between the dictates of morality and the necessities of politics on whose denial the politico-moral is founded. Since about 1960, most European countries have experienced an influx of immigrants from the many poor and dysfunctional parts of the Third World. Immigrants who used to be described as "refugees" in the 1930s have now become "asylum seekers," a sentimental term because the actual motives leading migrants to arrive in huge numbers are extremely varied. Most of them are, in fact, responding to the material incentive of escaping poverty and hopelessness.

Faced with any particular case fitting the description of needing asylum from persecution, the only decent response must be to agree to it. The moral question is, evidently: ought we to agree to admitting X, Y, and Z, etc, who are knocking on our doors and who have suffered, and seem to be in danger of worse things to come? The answer is pretty clearly that we must. On the other hand, in terms of Britain's national interest, the answer of most voters would clearly be negative to the question of whether we support the entry into Britain (and other European countries) of distinct communities, often bearing ways of life and practices at variance with our own. Most voters were, of course, never directly consulted, and were subject to a great deal of public persuasion that accepting large numbers of immigrants was not only a benefit, but a benefit that only bad people would be so "incorrect" as to criticize. Muslims, numbering in Britain about two million early in the twenty-first century, were described as one "community" among others, and became a public issue because of jihadist terrorism. All such "communities," however, constituted problems of one kind or another, by way of education, welfare, health, and other conditions.

In 1970, most European states had the effortless cohesion of a basically Christian or post-Christian population, and this background was the condition for understanding what it was to live in a modern Western society. The same necessary experiences could be confidently assumed about migrants into Britain from most, though not all, of the countries in the European Union. Other consequences are less benign. In all groups, many people are happy to be here, but some raise difficult questions, and the Muslim population has been the most challenging, partly because some of them have become terrorists hostile to our way of life, and partly because many of them regard Western life as decadent and immoral. That very Western way of life, however, is also the source of the benefits that have induced them to migrate, and none of them are sufficiently disillusioned actually to return to their countries of origin.

The issue of immigration agitating the Western world is one clear illustration of the fallacy resulting from failing to recognize that what is morally imperative may be politically disastrous. A kind of sentimental moralism has the capacity in the long run to destroy European culture altogether. There is clearly a limit to how much demographic transformation European life can sustain without destroying the very virtues that made Western states so attractive to migrants, most of whom have been induced to migrate because of the dysfunctional conditions from which they came. Some parts of the ethnic population themselves already have a very firm grip on this point. But the wider understanding

of these realities is crippled by the fact that politico-moral ortho-
doxies (with their associated bureaucracy) block our making any
distinction between some categories of immigrants as more desirable than others.

Britain, for example, contains rather more than a quarter
of a million Chinese. They do not notably feature on the crime
statistics or the welfare rolls, they supply delicious things to eat,
and they have children who fit pretty seamlessly into any school
they go to. The consequences of large-scale Muslim migration,
on the other hand, include a vast increase in the burdens of security, danger from Islamic terrorists, and a pressure group whose
dislike of freedom of discussion and whose broader intolerance
make them a worrying group. Many Muslims, of course, are very
happy to lead their own lives here and present no problem at all,
but others are involved in intimidation, honor killings, and corruption. These things may well change over the generations, but
they are striking current realities that cannot be publicly discussed
without aggressive accusations of evil motives.

One other aspect of this complex question should be mentioned at this point. The freedom of action of European states in
this area, as in many others, has been severely circumscribed by
internationalism. In 1950, European states signed up, under quite
different circumstances, to a set of admirable moral commitments
under the European Convention on Refugees. Politicians commonly have the illusion that they become statesmen by signing
up to such things. The issue of refugees then was quite different
from its modern shape, but the commitments undertaken at that
time now block states from making many changes. A refugee was
anyone in serious danger of persecution or death, a category that
includes untold millions of inhabitants of the Third World. And
in Britain, loss of legislative capacity over a wide range of issues to
the power of the European Union is a further hindrance to most
possible democratic response to this problem.

b. The Concept of "Representativeness"

The issue of immigration has also brought into clearer focus
the politico-moral development of the idea of being "represented."

Multicultural policy has generated a demand that within a generation of arrival, members of each ethnic community should be "represented" in proportion to their numbers, in desirable occupations. This new version of the idea of representation had been pioneered by feminists, who agitated for "more women" in government, the judiciary, business management, and indeed just about everywhere except furniture removalism and abattoir work. Yet there is no obvious reason why there should be more women in government. Like most other commercial and bureaucratic activities, government has been carried on for centuries by men, who have created the terms and conditions under which it is conducted. The call for "more women" is thus, on the face of it, merely the lobbyist's demand for more benefits, without any obvious reason why the demand should be granted. There is equally, of course, no reason why there should not be more women in these desirable jobs. The point is that the sex of the officeholder is a complete irrelevance. What matters is the relevant kind of ability. There are plenty of clever women, and they should have the opportunity to take up such posts; there are large numbers of less clever women, as with men, who can make no claim at all.

The lobbyist's assumption here is that because the proportion of women in such posts is considerably less than the proportion of men, women must have been the victims of injustice. They are "underrepresented." But this is, of course, a merely passive and mechanical sense of the idea of representation. The argument—absurdly—is that women have statistically identical talents and aspirations as men, and that their involvement in family life may be treated as no more demanding than the hobbies men happen to cultivate. What is true of some women in some situations is certainly not true of others. We have here again another fallacy of aggregation: the opportunities that have suited many women good at managerial tasks have so affected the labor market that many more women are forced, or think themselves forced, to take jobs in order to sustain a desired standard of living. The desires of some commonly have consequences for the happiness of others. Justice for one group leads to "injustice" for others.

Feminist assumptions about oppression and social justice have understandably been taken over by ethnic groups on the make. Who could resist bidding for a free good? Why are there few blacks managing investment portfolios in the City of London? Why are there so few Hindus in Parliament, or Sikhs on the judicial bench? It is, in fact, highly unlikely that brilliant candidates in any areas have been passed over; brilliance is pretty widely recognized. This means, of course, that the whole lobby for female and ethic "representation" in managerial life would have to be recognized as being advanced in the cause of privileging those of average or marginal talents. And just such a conclusion may be drawn, as we shall see later in discussing the mechanization of social mobility in many policies of welfare states.

The idea of representation has thus been corrupted by having its active character removed from it. It means no more than belonging to some social category. This corruption forces us to confront the question of differential temperament and ability head on. It may well be the case that most women do not have conspicuous ability in these fields. Path-finding female mathematicians are said to be thin on the ground. Some women certainly contribute with distinction to any profession one might mention. This is especially the case in politics, in which a succession of able women, ranging from Zenobia, Elizabeth I, and Catherine the Great on the one hand to Golda Meir and Margaret Thatcher on the other, have shown that in certain circumstances female politicians can exhibit a distinct kind of skill in politics. On the other hand, plenty of women who have come to the top in politics have proved to be at best mediocre. The argument for opportunity is strong. The argument for representativeness is merely absurd.

The same considerations apply to proposals that the immigration of ethnically different people into a country requires that members of each community should prosper proportionately in all areas. Ethnic groups tended, at least in earlier generations, to specialize in certain types of activity. Blacks are notable in football and boxing, but so far not in brain surgery. Jews shine in law and commerce but are rare on the football field. The caveat always to be remembered is that any kind of talent may crop up in any kind of group, but that in no way invalidates the fact that the statistical distribution of activities and skills in different social categories is one entirely valid but certainly limited basis for practical judgment. It is also true that some professions, such as law in Britain, emerge from long-standing national traditions not immediately available in the lives of immigrants. They can pass the exams in related subjects, but their "feel" for the realities takes time. The language of rights and liberty has been enthusiastically taken up by many ethnic spokesmen, but they speak it like foreigners. They do not understand the hesitations and qualifications that were built into understanding these things long before freedom had become codified, and thus vulgarized.

The theory that in an ethnically plural society, employment benefits should be distributed according to ethnicity is one that political scientists have studied as characterizing "consociational" societies.* Lebanon used to be the classic example before it descended into civil war in the 1970s. The principle also applies in international organizations, such as the European Union and the United Nations. No one has, I think, suggested that the result has been to achieve models of organizational efficiency, and the level of corruption has usually been higher than in European administrations staffed by fellow nationals.

Agitation for this mechanical representativeness intensifies to the extent that the vocabulary of individual rights and social justice becomes involved in it. Something like a collective right to be "represented" in better-paid situations comes to be so widely assumed that observers talk of lack of "equality" if it is missing. Indeed, such agitations may be recognized as a kind of learning process in the politico-moral world: members of ethnic and religious (and "gender") categories are being taught to feel pride in the fact that one of their number has been appointed to some particularly respectable office. In other words, they are being taught a collective version of self-esteem that conflicts directly with the

* The term was developed by Arend Liphardt.

individualist assumptions of the moral life. Such a learning process is an important element in the diffusion of the politico-moral view of the world. But that process is also a debasement of our tradition of politics. This is part of the new version of "social cohesion," in which a state must turn into an empire in which the various "colonies" are "consociationally" represented in appropriate places.

The basic point about the corrupt sense of representation is that it is essentially passive. The beneficiaries of the idea have never been elected but become representative merely on the basis of the ethnic or sexual character to which they belong. What representation actually refers to in European politics is an agent who has been chosen by others to make judgments on their behalf. But the successful female stockbroker has in no sense been elected by any group of women to act on their behalf. We are thus moving from an active and meaningful sense of the term to a mechanical and passive view of it, a minor department of what is often deplored as "the cult of celebrity." This we may see as a typical development of the politico-moral mind set, in which entitlements have been completely disconnected from any active capacity.

Consider, for example, the collapse of that important sense of "representation" on which individuals used to pride themselves, when among foreigners and strangers, in behaving in a way that would sustain credit in their category. That any person mixing with foreigners ought to be responsible for sustaining an admirable image of his people was something that many individualists first learned from wearing the uniform of their school. Indeed, inculcating precisely this particular form of self-respect was largely the point of putting pupils in uniform. It was a matter of not letting the side down. And in the moral life of the individualist, disgrace seldom did happen. The British, for example, long had the benefit of being widely regarded as conforming to the image of the gentleman when abroad. Edith Piaf even sang a famous song about this image, and "Remember, you're British" was an important part of the moral psychology of the country. Times have changed. No doubt this active moral sense of representativeness may still be found, but it has been notably swamped by the conduct of young British drunks, both men and women, spreading liberated Britishness throughout the tourist world.

We have then a move away from the idea of representation as imposing responsibilities on us, and toward representation as a right, a bit of public relations used by bureaucrats pushing for benefits, such as promotions. We have moved, that is to say, away from an active and meaningful sense of representation to a passive and mechanical one. Category is destiny. Paradoxically, this seems itself rather like a kind of racism, and sexism.

A far-ranging change in contemporary European societies has been the widespread abandonment among women of what used to be a self-chosen responsibility as guardians of morality and decorum. Here was a real sense of representation, because it involved duties rather than benefits, and it was self-imposed. In feminist terms, its self-imposed character was merely a bit of false consciousness imposed by an unjust society. What such representation involved was, for example, a demand that the language used by men in speaking to women had to be free of gratuitous vulgarity. It was in accepting and cultivating inhibitions of this kind that women claimed a special role in European moral and social life; it was part of the apparatus of chivalry on whose terms women claimed a particular kind of respect. The basic feminist demand, however, was that women should be freed from this representative burden. They should have the same rights as men, and those rights commonly included a kind of permission to behave in louche and risky ways. This is all, of course, merely one special department of the wider tendency to abandon formality and behave spontaneously.

c.   The Appeasement Tendency

What could induce rational people to take these corruptions of the concept of representation seriously? One important part of the answer is that Western public discourse is excessively prone to judge the world in terms of ideals, and therefore to give those who claim ideal virtue the benefit of the doubt. Hence any absurdity could be passed off as a special kind of "justice," such as social, Soviet, Peoples', and so on. The most spectacular instance of this mistake was Soviet communism, which retained, in some cases up to the actual moment of its collapse, the admiration of many a simple Western idealist. The actual history of death and despotism passed these admirers by, perhaps because of the famous "omelet defense" of gross brutality in the service of an ideal. Even Pol Pot had a few Western dupes supporting him until the horrors became unmistakable and overpowering. The necessary equipment of any alien despot in our own time is to understand how to say what Europeans like to hear.

The obituaries of Ian Smith, who had long resisted black majority rule in Southern Rhodesia because he did not believe that the black population was capable of self-rule, told of the one moment in which he wavered in this belief. It was just after Robert Mugabe had come to power because British and South African support for Smith's regime had been withdrawn. When Smith met Mugabe, Mugabe told him that he recognized what an economic jewel Southern Rhodesia/Zimbabwe was, and that this was the achievement of white enterprise. Smith, it is said, went home and told his wife that perhaps it might be all right. It was at that moment that Mugabe was already planning a vicious repression of the Matabele peoples who lacked enthusiasm for his rule. But he certainly understood what patter should be used in placating a critic. We might call this the "Gee Officer Krupke" phenomenon, after the song in the musical "West Side Story," in which the delinquents mock Officer Krupke by reciting with derision the explanations of their deviancy favored by policemen and social workers. The first thing those who want to exploit the West must learn is how to recite the patter, or "talk the talk," as the current cliché has it.

The reason Westerners have a weakness for taking the idealistic talk of other regimes more seriously than their actual conduct is often put down to guilt. It may indeed be that many Europeans suffer from versions of the collective guilt built into the idea of planetary consciousness as we have earlier discussed it. We must never forget (so the idea goes) that the problems of others may perhaps actually be our fault. Some such irrational emotion may be involved, but I would be more inclined to explain this curious phenomenon in terms of a misunderstanding of rationality, and it may be that this misunderstanding has a collective aspect. It consists simply of believing in the principle that one cannot validly criticize others unless one is free of the fault being criticized. And the "one" in this case is likely to be collective: it will be our country, or perhaps our whole civilization. This is a mistake that rapidly leads to the error of moral equivalence.

Criticism of communist societies, for example, could be deflected by arguing that the West, too, has its pools of poverty, and its injustices. Criticism of jihadism after 9/11 in New York was very rapidly transposed into a rational rejection of something called "fundamentalism," which thus lumped Muslim suicide bombers in with southern Evangelical Christians, who were not blowing anyone up. This is rationality crossed with humility. It takes the form of insisting that "we have our loonies too." No doubt we do, but that is not the point.

Here then is the cast of mind that leads Westerners to appease people who make demands on us, however unreasonable the demands may be. The paradigmatic case of appeasement in our civilization was that of Neville Chamberlain in the face of Nazi demands over Czechoslovakia. "You were given a choice between shame and war," as Churchill famously put it. "You have chosen shame, and you shall have war." Chamberlain's concessions began, however, as appeasement, and ended as a probably necessary play for time. The motive for appeasement here was something similar to guilt, though not, I think, identical with it. The reason was that many people had misgivings over the justice of the Treaty of Versailles, and believed that if arguable injustices arising from that settlement were conceded, then peace would be restored. Here we have in full play the basic politico-moral doctrine that the solution to any conflict must be compromise and negotiation. Obviously such a doctrine is not false, but it also has a restricted application. Where matters of principle are involved, refusal to compromise is absolutely necessary, and appeasement will not only fail, but reveal cowardice in the appeaser. There can be no agreement between one party that thinks it is being rational and another that interprets rationality as fear.

d. The Stick and Carrot Problem

Appeasement misunderstood as rationality, or rationality misunderstood as requiring appeasement, might plausibly be regarded as the basic operational mode of the politico-moral attitude. A violent hatred of all local exponents of political incorrectness (racists, sexists, that lot) is combined with a dedicated openness to non-Western movements and to the local groups that sympathize with them. Part of misunderstanding ideologically sophisticated totalitarians at the level we have just been discussing lies in thinking that others operate in terms of the ideals they declare themselves to be espousing. The politico-moral world is paved with good intentions.

It is part of this mistake to think that others are rational in the same norm-saturated sense of rationality as obtains in Western life. This mistake, for example, was the basis of the 1960s-era conviction that most conflicts result from lack of communication. If only people had communicated more what they really wanted, if they would have just talked to each other, then many of the conflicts of past times, perhaps all, would have been unnecessary. There is, of course, the problem of dealing with the Hitlers, Stalins, and others not notable for a conversable reasonableness, and here the answer would no doubt be agreement that force would have been necessary against these people. In other words, some force in recent times OK, all force in future bad. The politico-moralist would, however, immediately raise the question of why these figures were so brutally intransigent, and the answer would be in terms of social and psychological conditions. No doubt there are bad and evil people, runs the doctrine, but they are disturbed personalities in need of treatment. At bottom, there's no such thing as a really evil human being.

We need not deal with that large question, for all we need to bring out at this point is that human life has hitherto responded to the problem of bad behavior on the basis of sticks and carrots, of punishment and reward, and the new order wants to dispose of the sticks and guide people exclusively by carrots. Traditionally, authorities operated on the principle that the basic human emotions were hope and fear. Carrots mobilized hope in the service of good order, sticks mobilized fear. Some theorists have argued in the past that the main appeal should be to one rather than the other. The passion to be reckoned on, argued Hobbes, is fear, a belief held in an even more emphatic form by Joseph de Maistre. Hobbes believed that fear was the emotion that generated an understanding of reality, while hope merely fostered illusion. Enlightenment thinkers such as Beccaria and Bentham much preferred recourse to hope, but none quite went as far as the politico-moral abolition of sticks in order to run a society on the basis of carrots.

A basic implication of the reliance on hope as sustaining civil order was the rejection of punishment as a rational way of dealing with human beings. Punishment is the infliction of pain or frustration on a malefactor, perhaps as a sign to deter others from similar delinquencies, perhaps out of a belief that such pains, loosely responding to the original offense, would restore a kind of moral balance to the universe. Deterrence, however, was basically unjust because it involved using the delinquent as a means toward the wider aim of discouraging others, while retribution was thought to be merely a version of revenge, and hence rather barbaric. Our response to criminal behavior should be to understand and to rehabilitate the offender. This, of course, is to abandon the principle of punishment in favor of the idea of therapy.

One insidious form of this doctrine surfaced in British teacher training colleges in the 1950s. Educational institutions are vulnerable to the illusion that teachers, charged with forming the minds of the young, have in their hands the material for making a better society. In the 1950s and after, the idea got around, and was diffused to many in the teaching profession, that corporal punishment in schools "sent the wrong message": namely, that violence pays. In any case, physical chastisement of children was an illicit use of power over them. In the spirit of Beccaria, who showed importantly that a society might be kept in order by the use of a much narrower range of painful punishments than had appealed to the imaginative rulers of early modern times, teachers took the view that negotiation, disapproval, and reasoning could all achieve what had previously been done by the occasional use of the cane. From the 1960s onward, the cane and other forms of corporal chastisement went the way of capital punishment. This was a policy that certainly did away with any teacher-initiated violence in the classroom, but in many cases it was followed by a rise in pupil-initiated violence and aggravation. Certainly the level of violence on the playground, and later on the streets, went up rather than down.

The problem of indiscipline in classrooms was only in part the result of the spread of politico-moral ideas. Many influences contributed to it. One was the spread of television, and a situation in which young minds constantly had rather banal distractions available to them—television itself, computer games, constantly available music, and, rather later, mobile telephones. To educate a child requires that the teacher must be able to command his or her attention even for passages of information and instruction that the child will instinctively find tedious. Without such a resource, the contemporary teacher thus finds himself in a situation in which he must bid for the attention of his charges; he must become, that is to say, a popularizer. The result has been to tether most education to the shackles of relevance, precisely the source of immediate unreflective practicality that defeats the real purpose of education. One unintended result of progressive tendencies in education has been to reinforce an elite/mass distinction that had previously been disappearing. Fee-paying schools and grammar schools were able to retain large elements of pedagogic discipline, but the remaining state schools declined in quality. To education we shall return in the next section.

First, however, we must observe that the basic drive to abolish pain, fear, punishment, and other sticks in favor of an all-carrot policy has been the march of democracy itself. This drive may be explained by focusing on two basic concepts of modern politics: interests and ideas.

Interests first. Democratic governments must face periodic elections, and winning largely depends on being able to promise either further benefits or the removal of further pains from life (known in the political trade these days as "helping solve the problems of ordinary people"). Benefits, however, have costs, and the trick (at one level) lies in scattering the benefits over a larger number of voters than the number who have been lumbered with the costs. Many benefits, of course, are economic, and there are far more workers than employers. Hence a large component of welfare costs can be loaded onto businesses, which have low voting power. In particular, governments can legislate (without themselves spending money) all manner of rights for workers, the costs of which will be borne by employers—a right to flexible working time, for example. In other words, modern democracies have come to exhibit precisely the dynamic against which classical writers from Aristotle onward always warned: that the property-less will exploit those with property.

The right to property, however, is not merely a right, but also in some degree a responsibility: that is why constitutional states often in the past operated with a property qualification for the franchise. Those with property are often a source of wise judgment on policy. This is one of the reasons why there is a built in limit to how far this Robin Hood policy can go. Governments engaging in too much taxation and regulation eventually find that the wealth dries up and the entrepreneurs move away. The modern welfare state, however, has so far managed to travel a considerable distance along this road, eliminating the more extreme pains of poverty, unemployment, physical punishment, illness, and fear of dismissal from a job. Pain remains, of course, being part of the human condition, but its extremes have been mitigated. Interests remain important, especially in situational demands to protect industries threatened by foreign competition, but over a large range of classes in a modern Western state, the demands of redistribution and of security have reached a kind of equilibrium such that, for the moment, governments can do little except sustain it. The only problem is that this delightful new order has not produced the leap in happiness that might have been expected.

Next, ideas. These are important, because a significant proportion of a modern society, including most of those employed by the government, has become detached from immediate financial interests. The salaries of state employees generally go on being paid whatever happens. In the experience of a large class of people in modern states—bureaucrats, journalists, academics, and so on—interest is seldom a serious matter. The result is that political judgments are now much more responsive to what voters think is the reasonable or just thing—in other words, the general ideas they have picked up, and which cater to their politico-moral self-respect—rather than to any calculation of interest. The fact that most issues in politics today raise questions of spending other people's money further distances voters from any direct concern with interests. The actual details of policies are often extremely complex, yet voters are expected to have a position on them. Economizing on "information costs," many voters settle for the notionally moral or righteous policy. We thus have here another version of the aggregation fallacy, in which certain features of individual moral judgments can aggregate into politically dubious national policy.

Democracy, then, is a system in which individuals tend to vote either in terms of their interests, or if (as with many classes of people) interests are no longer pressing, in terms of moral ideas, which in our century so far are commonly of a sentimental kind. This is a tendency that leads directly to the removal of whatever is thought to cause pain or discomfort. In education, for example, "research" at one point was thought to have led to the conclusion that failing or doing badly in exams, not being picked for the sporting team, and other such disappointments had bad long-term consequences for the self-esteem of the pupils. A great deal of attention is now paid to the avoidance of stress in schools (not to mention in other areas of life).

Educational "research" has a long history of telling teachers what they currently want to hear, and often collides directly with what we may dogmatically call "sound common sense." Common sense, for example, tells us that failure might well be regarded as a discovery process. It tells people what they are not good at. As the *New Yorker* cartoon once had a psychiatrist remarking to a patient: "You don't have an inferiority complex. You're just inferior." Children protected from information about themselves by such limiting procedures are not improved by it; rather they are led into illusions about themselves. When all must have prizes, prizes clearly cease to signify anything serious.

Similar considerations operate in such a field as industrial relations. It is painful to be fired from a job, and it may occasionally happen for capricious reasons. What could then be more electorally attractive than moves to make such events difficult and costly for the employer who might want to fire staff? The legal rhetoric is already in place for such regulations: it consists in declarations of rights. Employment protection law is thus vaguely appealing to most voters, for most voters are employees. The results of employment protection law, however, include the entrenchment of the incompetent and the aggressive in their jobs, and it does not facilitate the conditions of a society in which most people are both dutiful and competent. Here is one more case where a sentimental moralism leads directly to the entrenchment of illusion in contemporary democracy. It is also a further case where what seems on the face of it to be "a better deal" for individuals leads to a worse result for the society itself. For the pains of life that can be banished by governmental regulation are also those often necessary in the repertoire of authorities in sustaining the efficiency, indeed the elementary competence, of institutions. Abolishing these does not lead to a pain-free world, merely to a world in which the pains are different, and much less under our control.

Here then is a sketch of some of the attitudes of which the politico-moral is composed. The attitudes are not entirely coherent, and certainly different people embrace different clusters of them. If we put them together, however, it should become clear that the politico-moral world seems to be based on a paradox. The paradox takes many forms, but here is a particularly central version of it:

on the one hand, human beings are mobilized by the selfishness/ altruism form of ethics to be the instruments of the social purpose of perfecting the world. On the other hand, as the beneficiaries of free-standing rights, they have been liberated from most frustrations and inhibitions on their right to satisfy all their own impulses. They are, in other words, to be collectively dutiful and individually hedonistic. Here would seem to be a current version of the immemorial conflict in Western societies between morality and inclination, and our moral life in modern times has been an endless quarrel between these two drives. We have been liberated from many conventions that have previously shackled our inclinations, but liberations, obviously, are never quite what they seem. Let us, then, move from the attitudes constituting the politico-moral to its psychology.

5. FROM DESIRE TO IMPULSE

This paradox of collective dutifulness and individual hedonism may be illustrated by an event that occurred in April 2007. A pop concert was organized by two artists called Bono and Bob Geldof, and its point was to "make poverty history," especially in Africa. Corresponding concerts were held simultaneously in various parts of the Western world. This was an archetypal politico-moral event, because although it raised some money for its causes, its real point was to persuade the G8 conference of heads of state, then meeting in Britain, to spend vastly more money on relieving African poverty. And if those statesmen had acceded to this demand (as to some extent they did), they in turn would be spending money appropriated from their own taxpayers. One of the central features of the politico-moral world is its widespread public enthusiasm to spend other people's money.

Thousands of people turned up to the concerts and no doubt enjoyed themselves. If these supporters reflected the demographic features of Western populations in the early twenty-first century, then most of them would have been living with a partner, but they would not have been married. A high proportion would have had one child, if that, and more than a fifth of their children would have been in "single-parent families."

The interest of this event for me lies in the fact that these young participants in the politico-moral world were taking up a posture on a grand, indeed immense, project of world transformation (African poverty), but would also be evading the more serious commitments involved in getting on with their own lives. Of many, it could be brutally said that they were clinging on to the irresponsibilities of youth. Here then we seem to have a new moral situation coming into play. It illustrates many things. One of the most elementary of them is the fact that public policy raises extremely complicated questions that can only be answered by considering (to specify merely a few of the complexities involved in this example) the way in which different African states work, the competing demands on the national exchequers in European states, the future prospects of support for an expensive and difficult project of international charity, and a very great deal else. Very few people have the necessary grasp on reality to make an intelligent contribution to understanding this situation. But in "make poverty history" we have something different from public policy. We have a "moralized" public policy. Not everyone can become an expert on Africa and its troubles. Everybody can moralize. The politico-moral world is thus distinguished from the considerations of national politics in that it is drenched in moral features that demand not mastery of complexities but intensity of politico-moral emotions. And the moral situation is constituted as having the form of a melodrama containing good and bad actors, good and bad attitudes. No one is in any doubt as to the right, or perhaps better, the "correct," moral judgment.

That fact again gives us a further clue to the character of the politico-moral world. We know that the politico-moral is the stepchild of democracy, as mobilizing a population to do a certain sort of right thing. In the case of national politics, the political class discusses and debates the issue of policy. The decision emerges from conflict about what it is best to do, and the outcome commonly reflects a balance of considerations, those considerations being recognized as contingencies whose significance is uncertain and must be made sense of by the best available judgment at the time. This unavoidably is the condition of political action, whatever the simplicities (and not infrequently the idiocies) of actual political judgment may be.

Contrast this with politico-moral judgment. In the African poverty case, the moral issue is its alpha and omega. All other questions (such as the level of taxation, the judgment of the electors, the problem of corruption, and so on) have been occluded. The problem is to be solved by the application of a single principle—equalization, in some degree, of the resources disposed of by Western and African states. Consider, again, the solution to problems such as human beastliness and war crimes. Again, the discussion is generally in abstract terms, without a concern for such issues as the history and future interests of the countries in question. International relations are understood by analogy with the criminal law of states. The single principle of judicialization is to be applied to all cases. The same is true of anti-discrimination policies at the national and individual level. The characteristic of the politico-moral understanding of human life is that it eschews complexities of interpretation and conflict in order firstly to moralize the problem, and secondly to find some technical solution to it. And the solution lies in discovering how to apply whatever single principle by which salvation is to be achieved.

The politico-moral is thus an immense simplification of human life, and it corresponds to a simplification of personality in the people who inhabit this world. That simplification takes the form of a movement away from desires toward *impulses*. A desire, it will be remembered, is the precondition of a commitment and incorporates rational deliberation. The individualist is concerned both with appropriate moral rules and sentiments, but also with what to make of the complex situations we all find ourselves in, along with questions of context and consequence.

An impulse, by contrast, is an imperative passion, such as one for food, drink, sex, or anger, which takes little or no cognizance of anything but its own satisfaction. We may also act from impulse when we are insouciant, posturing, careless, or in any other way inattentive to our situation or our sense of ourselves. Everyone on occasion acts from impulse, and everyone will often deliberate and act from desire. Impulsiveness is often charming in children, and a sign of an agreeable spontaneity in adults, but it is also a net reduction in the level of rationality with which we conduct our affairs. I wish to argue that in the politico-moral world, the balance of human conduct has in the course of the twentieth century moved strongly away from desire and toward the dominance of impulse. Why should this be so?

One obvious reason is the set of liberations we have already discussed. They all have the effect of excluding rules that might have forced us to deliberate. Another powerful reason is that welfare states have changed the terms of our engagement with life. In the past, it was necessary for us individually to think about rainy days and save enough to cover medical emergencies. Most of us, in fact, would before long have families of our own and this would make such thrifty prudence even more incumbent upon us. The provision of state health care has largely obviated this necessity. Similar considerations apply for some people in responding to the expenses of educating their children, and also in facing up to the threat of indigence and unemployment. What the state supplies is not, of course, such as entirely to obviate self-provision in these matters, but it cannot help but lead to a reconfiguration of the virtues, and that can have far-reaching effects. At lower levels of society, for example, it can weaken the family bonds that in the past were based not only on natural affection but also on a canny sense that the family was an insurance policy. As in economics, change at the margins works its way through the system.

The emergence of impulsiveness as a feature of our modern politico-moral world results also from developments in technology and the economy. The central drive of economies is to profit from making things more convenient for customers. Convenience is a function of the diminution of frustrations likely to accompany the satisfaction of a desire. Some supermarkets are known as "convenience stories," and they provide products available whenever required, ready to be plucked off the shelves, and with no need to waste time visiting a variety of specializing shops. The only human contact needed is at the checkout, where conversational indulgence is minimal. The increasing stock of ready-prepared meals in shops further liberates many people from the concrete business of having to cook in order to satisfy the pangs of hunger. Shopping, concretely, used to be a transaction between shopper and supplier; it often involved a personal relationship. An individualist world, for all its virtues, however, is full of people busy about one project or another. They are always attracted by the prospect of a more convenient satisfaction of their desires. The speed and availability of travel in the Western world is a dramatic example of a vast leap in convenience. It is no doubt a further convenience that the traveler can read a book or a magazine, listen to music, and talk to friends on a variety of new devices. Such convenience is purchased, however, at the expense of the time for reflection on events that gave solidity to the lives of our ancestors.

The classic case of abstraction in the service of convenience is no doubt that of pornography, in which the satisfaction of sexual desire is disentangled from complications ranging from marriage on the one hand to the tiresome business of having to chat up the satisfying object on the other. Perhaps the model of heroic abstraction in this field might be the pop singer who when interviewed was asked why he paid girls to have sex with him when he had them queuing up round the block for the honor. Your mistake, he explained, is in thinking that I pay them to have sex. What I pay them for is to go home afterward.

Impulsiveness is also likely to emerge from the experience of relaxed discipline in schools and the home. Pupils have been liberated from the heavy hand of pedagogic discipline, and endless pleasures distract the student from the path of work before play. Liberation, it will be recalled, is a release from rules and restrictions previously thought necessary to good order, and it assumes that the removal of the restrictions will facilitate good conduct because people will be naturally reasonable in doing things that were previously done from coercion.

The result of a liberation in which respect for teachers changes as they become that more equal thing called "resource persons," however, is a decline in the experience of frustration that children are likely to have to endure. If the conventions are that the teacher must be treated with respect, that his or her orders ("learn this" or "learn that") are to be obeyed, then by and large the children learn a form of self-control. Tutorial command in a system of respect overrides the otherwise fluctuating attentions of the young. Such self-control becomes habitual, and often turns into an actual preference to perform obligations, scholarly or otherwise, before settling down to enjoyment. The erosion of this kind of self-discipline may be seen in such phenomena as "road rage," the decline of orderliness in British life, and the conduct of soccer crowds.

Nevertheless, the world of "impulsives" (as we might call them) is highly attractive on its own terms. Impulsives are generally friendly and informal people. And the outward form of impulsive intimacy is symbolized in its tendency to use Christian names and forget family identities. Slave masters used to call their slaves by their Christian names because a slave was merely an instrument in a process of production. Such mere labels or tags on human beings were qualified by no conventions of formal respect. Serfs were referred to in the same way. The universal currency of family names came relatively late in European history, and it signified the rising status of the lower classes. In some cases—Turkey is an example—it came as late as the twentieth century. Family names were significant because belonging to a family, and thus having an honorable past and the prospect of named descendents, was an important step in social life. This kind of respectability was an issue in the French Revolution, in which the Abbe Sieyes defended *hommes d'hier* against what he took to be aristocratic Frankish disdain. Family names were part of human dignity, preserving a certain desirable distance, even sometimes within marriage. On the Continent, distance was preserved by the second-person pronoun—the practice of *tutoyer* in France, for example. Here was an order of manners in which intimacy was a privilege that people might accord each other, and it was greatly valued precisely as a privilege. The violation of social distance in those earlier times, on the other hand, was the source of social vices such as insolence and impertinence. That had all been part of what we called "the deference world," and it guaranteed respect for a whole class of persons such as clergymen, teachers, aristocrats, elderly ladies, and many others. The increasing employment of Christian names alone exhibits a lack of substance in situational relations.

No moral order stands still, and clearly new circumstances are changing the way in which the individualist moral life currently works. "Individualism," like its partner "desire," is an inadequate specification of modern individualism as a self-ordering structure of society. Besides, our inherited moral vocabulary seriously fails to specify important moral sensitivities of which we are seldom aware. A desire can easily be confused with an impulse; we all experience both. Individualism as the coherence of a set of (rationalized) desires is thus not easy to distinguish from a rising tendency to impulsiveness. From the outside, they may well look pretty much the same. Sometimes these conceptual confusions are further complicated by attributing the social problems that result from personal irresponsibility to a hybrid thing called "hyperindividualism." The reader will be in no doubt as to the reasons I reject this view as an illegitimate form of concept-stretching. And the point can best be made by asking: how in fact does a modern society order itself?

The crucial fact about order is that what does not come from below must be supplied from above. Our situation is such that a system long established on the assumption that each adult is a responsible person must now accommodate increasing elements of irresponsibility. But this point must, in politico-moral descriptions, be obscured, because Western democracies like to conceive of themselves as populations of independent moral agents. The irresponsible, however, are not fully moral agents, and they must be assimilated to the ill and the sick, who are always with us. The irresponsibles, in all their spectacular variety, must be construed as "vulnerable people" in need of our compassion and professional help. Yet they retain full democratic rights of participation in the responsibilities of public choice.

A lowering of standards is thus presented in politico-moral terms as the introduction of a superior form of virtue: compassion in social life addressing people who need help. Problems that in the past would have stayed within the family are now to be dealt with by an assemblage of social workers, drug rehabilitation experts, thrift counselors, probation officers, and even people who, with the decline of good manners, might be needed to train us in "sensitivity," or what is currently called "emotional literacy." The legal basis on which these helpful people operate is given in the vast increase in legislation that has been so conspicuous a feature of contemporary life. The legislation is the climax of a process by which, first, an assemblage of personal irresponsibilities turns into a different kind of thing called a "social problem." And, secondly, under such a description, it is but a small step for the government to take unto itself the power to deal with it. If children stay away from school, for example, the state may take the power (and indeed has taken such power) to threaten the parent or parents with imprisonment.

These sanctions necessarily assume that citizens are agents of government policy, and just such instrumentalization of the civil subject has been an important development in the recent governing of welfare states. Governments, for example, sometimes set up "hot lines" on which ordinary citizens are "empowered" (I use the devious bureaucratic term) to supply details if they know of anyone benefiting from fraudulent claims on welfare. The British government was also reported (in 2007) to be funding and supporting an organization that wanted to take an anti-smoking campaign into the schools that would "encourage" (further devious bureaucratese) children to take the message home to their parents and to demand the right to a smoke-free environment. Some of the demands made of the citizens by governments (alertness to terrorist activities, for example) are no doubt reasonable, but enrolling subjects as agents of state policies (often highly contestable policies) cannot but recall the mobilizing tactics of totalitarian states. Even more sinister is the passing of legislation making it a criminal offense if professional advisers (such as accountants, lawyers, or doctors) should fail to pass on to the appropriate authorities suspicions they might acquire that criminal activities may be afoot. Such an obligation directly violates the confidentiality of professional life.

Children are always of particular interest to governments, partly because of a belief that perfecting society must always begin with the young. In recent times, states have been very keen on engineering attitudes and "skills" among the young. The pupils in schools, already rumored to be as overloaded with tests as their teachers are overloaded with ministerial directives, are to be guided in their sexual habits, diet, parental skills, and their manners. Indeed, they are also to be instructed in acquiring the capacity to do something called "express their feelings."

We have, then, a new situation emerging, in which the classic individualism of modern Europe is being superseded by a system in which Europeans are being slowly but steadily trained to live according to a pattern resembling the one true way of life found in most other societies. The one true way of life here is the set of desirabilities that from time to time manage to establish themselves in current opinion as part of "ethics." Virtue is fitting in to an ethical system. The slide can to some extent be tracked in terms of semantics. The very term "government," for example, is giving way to its much broader cousin "governance," which suggests control in terms of a set of rules and conventions having no evident source. They are, as it were, "untouched by human hand." And why is this imposture plausible? Because ethical public policy can be passed off as something transcending mere politics.

6. THE POLITICO-MORAL IMAGE OF A MODERN SOCIETY

To make sense of the flow of remarks, attitudes, proposals, changes, and every other element of public discussion in a modern liberal state, one must consider the conception of the point of human life that underlies it. That conception is also a clue to the way in which moral and social life is developing. In considering individualist moral life, we have already met the conception that underlies it: namely, that human life is a kind of game, in which the point is to exhibit the virtues of a player. Hobbes, we may remember, construed life as a race in which the point was to be in it, and foremost. Within this rather athletic conception, heroic virtues such as courage and honor are to the fore, and everyone has his or her own starting point from which to be judged. It is said that the German general Rommel, on meeting some Australian troops during the desert war, said: "What are you doing here? This is not your war. Are you here for the sport?" It was not an absurd suggestion.

As we saw, modern European societies organize many of their activities, such as their economies and their legal practices, as competitive games, and they have formalized sporting contests so successfully that competitive sport has spread throughout the world. This conception of human life assumes that active human beings strive to overcome weakness and temptation, and in this individualist form, it needs to be distinguished from the much later understandings of society as an arena of struggle between groups and interests rather than between individuals, the groups here being classes and nationalities. In the individualist image of human life, everything in it is contingent. The individual must make something of events requiring interpretation as one aspect of an active life. Success in a variety of guises is no doubt important, but the fundamental basis of judgment of a person is less success than the moral qualities displayed in playing the game. A constitutive ambiguity of the individualist moral life is that individuals may be judged in a variety of ways, and that approval in one set of terms is entirely compatible with disapproval in others. People can find reasons for rather despising both businessmen and saints, and often both. This is one of the standing ambiguities of the moral life understood in individualist terms.

That life is a game means that *homo ludens*[35] must value independence above all, for independence is the currency with which the player goes, as it were, into business. This instinct for independence is the basis of the European concern with equality, and its mistrust of "hierarchy." It is important to recognize that an idea of personal equality is fundamental to the European conception of life, however much that basic idea has in recent centuries been taken over and subverted as a criterion for implementing various versions of a supposedly better society. The point about equality in this basic sense is that it entails independence of judgment. On it is based the European disposition to mistrust sycophancy and to want to deal with independent individuals. There is no point at all in any public deliberation if some of the deliberators desire merely to please one of their number, and hence this propensity, not indeed uncommon where power is involved, is clearly recognized as a corruption of individualist life. Further, this disposition has been widely disseminated through European states. Thus Gertrude Himmelfarb, discussing the history of the Poor Law in nineteenth-century Britain, observes the connection made by the poorer classes between work and self-respect, and remarks that sustenance without work "would have put [the poor] in a condition of 'dependency,' which was repellent to the respectable working classes, for it was precisely their 'independence' that defined their 'respectability.'"[36] The famous homily of that period by Samuel Smiles, which became a world-wide best seller, carried its basic idea in its title: *Self Help.*

Again, a caveat must be entered about taking this as a description of how all Europeans, and especially Anglophones, actually behaved then, or behave now. My argument is designed to elicit the standards in terms of which approval and disapproval were expressed, and these standards are, of course, entirely compatible with servile and dependent conduct on occasion. Nonetheless, Europeans in large numbers often did actually conduct their lives as independently cooperating individualists in creating an immense industrial surge, and in migrating to the New World where a prodigious effort turned nature into productive enterprises.

If, then, individualist moral life may be understood in terms of a game, what conception of a modern society underlies the politico-moral world? The answer is, I think, that politico-moral society is an association of people engaged in the satisfaction of their needs. This formula would certainly describe an economy, which is the most successful of all associations for the reciprocal satisfaction of needs, but in the politico-moral world, the idea is that competition between self-interested agents would be replaced by altruism. This sounds like a much superior form of association, but as economic theorists have known since the eighteenth century, it would make an economy unviable. As Sir James Steuart put it: "Were public spirit, instead of private utility, to become the spring of action in the individuals of a well-governed state, I apprehend it would spoil all." The reason is that "Communities bound by love must be small and isolated. A large group of people cannot be united by love but only by needs."[*]

All societies are, of course, associations for the reciprocal satisfaction of needs, but the altruistic conception of a human association puts a well-distributed satisfaction of individual needs at the center of moral concern, rather than as merely a necessary condition of playing life as a game. The essence of such a society is cooperation rather than competition, and the problem to be solved is that of disparity between satisfied and unsatisfied needs. The members of such a society thus see themselves as sharing in a common enterprise of improving society. The point of a common enterprise is that it needs direction, and it is in specifying what that direction should be that indeterminacy becomes unavoidable. In one sense, the organizer of the satisfaction of needs can only be the state, because only the state disposes both of the authority and the financial power that can direct and sustain this enterprise at a national level. And since we are concerned here with a democratic state, the use of such civil power is assumed to be for the benefit of the people. It will be immediately evident that the rulers presiding over an individualist world would require *a very different kind of authority* from the politico-moral organizer of needs-satisfaction. Individualists have projects of their own to pursue, and are commonly impatient at demands made by an active government. They want to live under the rule of law. The immense accretion of power needed to produce and distribute satisfactions must therefore raise fears for the fate of freedom in the politico-moral world. The individualist is a will authorizing a government to exercise limited powers. How may the freedom of the member of a politico-moral state be understood?

---

[*] Steuart's argument is discussed in Elie Kedourie, Hegel, and Marx: Introductory Lectures, Eds. Sylvia and Helen Kedourie, Blackwell: Oxford, 1995. pp. 115–123.

The assumption will be that the rulers will be facilitators of satisfaction. Here, however, a significant bifurcation opens up between so-called "vulnerable people" (who may appear in a great variety of guises as poor, oppressed, deviant, gang members, excluded, and so on), and those who are not "vulnerable," who are perhaps rich, able bodied, clever, etc. The rulers of a politico-moral association talk directly to the non-vulnerable, but disapprove of them, because as individualists these people basically want to be left alone. The politico-moral position is to construe this individualist sense of independence as being selfish, as indeed actually an expression of greed. It does not accord with ethical concern for a better society.

The distinction in a politico-moral society between the able and the less able also leads to a significant variation in moral discourse. In speaking to the able, the government employs the whole repertoire of moral relations in what has been called its "I-Thou" form. We are here in a world of right and wrong, resentment and indignation, approval and disapproval. The able are understood to be responsible moral agents who may act well or badly, and should be, as it were, held to account if they behave (in some terms) badly.

In understanding the vulnerable, by contrast, the state takes a neo-Stoic attitude, and the delinquencies of the vulnerable are understood to be the necessary consequence of the social (and neurological, psychological, environmental, etc.) conditions of their lives. In a literal sense, the vulnerable have been de-moralized. Their conduct has been "caused" rather than emerging from "reasons."

The basis of legitimacy in a politico-moral world thus becomes the claim to be helping the vulnerable. Individualist states were often thought to be divided into rich and poor, bourgeois and proletarian, and similar groups having distinct and conflicting interests. But these theories, having some rather limited explanatory plausibility, were merely the stock in trade of political parties seeking to mobilize support. Their success until recent times was limited. For centuries, Europeans have agreed on the importance of their freedom and independence. It was indeed this powerful conviction that made rich and poor Europeans agree in rejecting the idea of communism, which only came to power in states that had been ruled despotically. Whether the passion for freedom and independence that saved the West from communism remains as powerful in the politico-moral world is another question altogether.

This tendency to think of contemporary liberal democracies as divided into two sets of people—the included and the excluded, rich and poor, philanthropic and those needing help, etc.—makes it difficult to find an expression to cover the associates in a politico-moral society. "Comrades" has unfortunate connotations, "needy" or "needies" is pejorative, "sharers" does not exactly roll off the tongue. In moral and psychological terms, as we have seen, they have the character of "impulsives." Perhaps we might settle on "optimizers," for it suggests that needs ought to be precisely satisfied, but not, as it were, "over-satisfied," because "consumerism" is to be avoided as the vice of individualism. An important qualification here is to recognize that "needs" has a delusive sense of absoluteness, in which hunger, thirst, warmth, comfort, cultural stimulation, and a schedule of other desirabilities are ideally to be supplied by the rulers of a welfare state. Historically, of course, things recognized as "needs" have become vastly more extended as standards of living have advanced in the Western world, and the satisfaction of needs now means that everyone should live at about the level of a Western bourgeois. A television set, for example, has long been recognized as the kind of necessity that bailiffs cannot be allowed to seize and distrain for debt. In other words, relativities lurk beneath the absolutism of the rhetoric. Should Africans, for example, in being relieved of their poverty, be enabled to live at European levels? Mass migration from the Third World suggests that Africans and others think that this is exactly what they want to happen, but ecologists warn us that any attempt to universalize the Western consumption of meat, for example (not to mention the Western production of carbon), would soon exhaust the reserves of the planet. I have no idea whether this is true or not, but people say it, and they may be right.

The problem of finding a description of the associates in a politico-moral state is revealing. What it brings out is the fact that the subjects of a politico-moral society are understood in terms of contradictory attributes. The contradiction reflects the main paradox of democracy that concerned us in our first chapter. On the one hand, these are people assumed to be the free-standing and independent citizens of a liberal democracy. On the other hand, vulnerable people cannot manage their own lives; that is what makes them "vulnerable." They are a set of people constituted in terms of the social problems they instantiate, such as teenage pregnancy, bullying in schools, obesity, low aspirations, poor parenting, irresponsible drinking, smoking, poor diet, and all the rest of a very long (and expanding) list. And they are not assumed to be responsible moral agents of whom discipline might be demanded and punishment imposed for bad acts. They are inhabitants, or rather victims, of a culture that governments feel must be changed. And it is a further demand of the politico-moral that the rich and able must be ethically directed away from indulging their self-reliant ways toward participating in the project of improving the lives of the vulnerable. The vulnerable must learn how to avoid teenage pregnancy, eat less, exercise more, give up binge drinking, opt at school for more of the harder subjects, and so on and so on.

In the politico-moral world, then, the individualist principle of a coherence-generating order among personally chosen commitments no longer applies. Impulsives don't have much in the way of personally chosen commitment, and are given to fitting in with the peer group and the dominant fashion in their circle. The solution is that they must become responsive to the tutorial operations of the state. Ideally, they should take their bearings from "role models." We have moved, that is to say, back from the moral principle of coherence to the more traditional logic of obedience. Notionally, politico-moral society resembles traditional societies in that the rulers are using their authority to implement the one right way of life, a perfect society, into which each person must fit. The form taken by such a perfect society lacks, of course, the firm religious contours of actual traditional societies, for it is being imposed on a population that for the moment remains accustomed to the individualist ways of the past. The shape it takes can only be dictated by current beliefs about "ethical" or "social" responsibility, and these change from time to time.

There is another important way in which the politico-moral world replicates the usages of a traditional rather than a modern society. The moral conduct required of impulsives results not from a deliberative encounter with rules, sentiments, and circumstances, but rather from a direct understanding of right doctrine, as closely formulated in the dictates of political correctness. The demand is to like and respect everyone. It is an important aspect of the anti-discriminatory force of political correctness that anything else except correct behavior should be as close to *unthinkable* as possible. And where no such right doctrine has as yet been established, subjects are commonly directed toward admiration for a set of "role models" who illustrate the forms of acceptable behavior. The moral experience of the politico-moral is essentially imitative rather than interpretive.

In the individualist world, by contrast, each person is morally responsible for his or her actions. Mitigating circumstances are indeed recognized, often enough in private judgment, and even, indeed, in judicial deliberation, but they have a limited range. In the politico-moral world, the vulnerable begin in a recognized condition we might call "sub-responsibility" and may indeed lose any attribution of responsibility at all. As victims of the miseries of "addiction," or of child abuse, or of broken family life, their conduct may be taken as a direct response to their condition, unmediated by any element of reflection or deliberation. An English judge early in the century decided that the influence of peers on a young thief should be treated as a mitigating circumstance of his offenses, where classic individualism would have regarded any recognition of such influence as a form of feebleness making things worse. The Vatican early in 2007 recognized that being a "Mummy's boy" could count as a ground for annulling a marriage, because some forms of dependence on parents were thought to render a person unfit for the strains of matrimony.

Just as in wartime films even the tough hero was given to confessing his fears, so the ideal state of mind of politico-moral people is a recognition that "we are all vulnerable." It is part of being human, no doubt. In this role, human beings are recognized as creatures of conditions. Some of these conditions are social (such as poverty), others neurological or environmental, and some may be put down to bad luck or misfortune. But it is an absolutely basic distinction between the individualist moral life on the one hand, and the politico-moral world on the other, that individualists, in taking personal responsibility, avoid imposing the burdens of their own lives on other people. The "stiff upper lip" of the individualist comes to be replaced by the idea that talking one's problems through is the way to deal with them. Transactional sharing of experiences is the basic communicative engagement of the politico-moral life. This point becomes increasingly important as one takes into account one further crucial point about the politico-moral: it may in the first instance be taken as a vision of the active and passive halves of a society cooperating in the satisfaction of needs, but its ultimate range is the whole world. The rising populations living in poverty in the Third World are ethically our responsibility, hardly at all theirs. "The world community" is often criticized because it has failed to solve problems of war, poverty, and disease in the rest of the world. Solving them is the collective project of the politico-moral vision.

The individualist stood out against the crowd, but the impulsive understands himself as part of that very crowd, and has in fact assimilated to it by way of a learning process in which he gets accustomed to thinking of himself as a member of an abstract class. This "learning curve" results from media discussions of an endless stream of social-science research about the character and opinions of a vast range of person: men, women, middle-class intellectuals, ethnic groups, autistics, young people neither in employment nor school, pensioners, shop workers, and so on, endlessly. It is hardly surprising that individuals should understand themselves, their situation, their virtues or vices, their expectations, and so on in terms of this inchoate and misleading flow of abstract information about averages, most of it entirely meretricious. Nonetheless, by its sheer bulk and insistence, it creates opinions about the "identity" or "category" to which any person may belong. This is commonly how people come to discover that they are, or are not, some kind of social problem, and a vast amount of almost pointless data presented as "research in social science" reinforces this understanding.

This tendency is conspicuous in the case of "women," who have, as it were, been "trained" to feel pleasure at learning about the first woman to do this or that, as if the achievement had some significance for their own sense of self-worth. No doubt vulnerability to this kind of self-understanding (or self-misunderstanding) depends on the level of intellectual sophistication: the critical are very much less susceptible to it than the gullible. Yet it has its effect on everyone.

Even more herd-like is the fact that young people, on learning that a notable proportion of the population admits in anonymous polling to being engaged in one or other delinquency, sometimes respond by taking this supposed fact as a license for themselves committing it. This is the kind of "other direction" famously illustrated by those Americans who looked up in the Kinsey Report the details of their age and the average sexual performance appropriate to their class—and sought to emulate it.

In other words, identity in the politico-moral world is a more fluid entity than among the individualists. A preoccupation with oneself as belonging to an abstract category hardly goes with those duties to oneself on which individualism is based, and the curious result is sometimes a collapse of integrity. An extremely notable example—notable because so baffling in rational terms—is the ever-rising incidence, according to reports, of student plagiarism. In some exams, and indeed also (rather alarmingly) in tests of competence in driving skill, some people seem to be hiring others to take tests they feel they themselves would fail. Cheating on an exam, or plucking the materials for an assignment from the Internet, would seem to be remarkably self-defeating, because the resulting qualifications would be worth less than they seemed, and the individual would soon find himself at sea in responding to the demands of the world of work. And so, indeed, it actually happens. Employers complain that significant numbers of young people in employment soon reveal themselves as notably underpowered and incompetent in the jobs they are required to do. But then, as we have seen, part of the whole drive of the politico-moral world is to provide a pain-free experience of life, where pain is found in such matters as failing a test, being fired for incompetence, being judged and found wanting, and even, in some cases, being expected to work at all. Advertisers are acutely responsive to the spirit of the age, and much advertising treats real life as occurring when work is over. This cult of the weekend, as we may call it, may be part of the psychological basis of the vast increase in self-diagnosed stress in contemporary life.

Here then is a sketch of the politico-moral as the cast of mind that is emerging out of the individualist moral life, and it is a form of experience difficult to characterize in exact terms. The reason is that semantic stability conceals moral transformation. "Individualism" is a complex idea whose indulgences lie on the surface of its meaning, whereas its associated obligations have to be looked for. In any case, many of those obligations have fallen victim to the liberations of our time: liberations particularly from conventions governing sexuality and situational formality. The old deferences in which one behaved differently with parents, women, teachers, clergymen, and so on have been left behind: everyone is now part of a single human scene and, broadly, one treats everyone the same.

Those conventions from which we have been liberated were widely rejected because they were considered "outmoded," which may merely mean inconvenient. In many ways, the changes are hardly surprising. Today, we have more money, we live longer, and the technologies of contraception and abortion have enhanced individual power. Access to sexual satisfaction used to be the basis on which the stability of marriage, the nurturing of children, the distribution of wealth in families, the reputation of the individual in his circle, and the conditions of companionship into old age all rested. In the politico-moral world, the selling points of marriage, if we may put it that way, have lost most of their point. Sex, companionship, and the benefits of domestic life can all be supplied in our convenience world; all you need is money. Further, living with someone is a difficult business, requiring considerable moral resources of tolerance, humor, and self-control, and those who have been living alone for a decade or more soon come to be ill-equipped for its rigors. Marriage may indeed involve periods of gritted teeth, but it facilitates the deeper understanding of another person, and it can involve emotional ties that deepen with time. Such depth is often lacking in the singleton, and the lack may not be missed until late in life. Neither feminism nor gay liberation have been notable boosts for the institution of marriage, and the attitude of many people toward children is that they are costly and rather demanding—inconvenient, one might say. The classic utility of children—support and companionship in old age—is another of those benefits that can be supplied by money, or indeed to some extent by the social services. Cautious natures—and the politico-moral character is nothing if not cautious when impulse is not in the driving seat—would rather avoid such risky adventures as children. These conditions are part of the explanation of the constant increase in singletons and the declining demography of most Western countries, especially in Europe.

As part of this new arrangement, women have become fully individualized as moral agents, rather than finding a large part of their identity within the family. We certainly find it agreeable that our lives should no longer be dominated by sex, which now seems for the most part like an innocent pleasure available to inclination. Adam Smith thought that there was an awful lot of ruin in a nation, meaning that nations had a considerable capacity to regenerate themselves. We seem to have discovered that there is an awful lot of ruin in a moral system. We have thrown away the conventions of the past, and the world has not fallen in on us. But it is early days yet in this experimental and recreational view of sex, and besides many people have, for the moment, resisted these liberations.

It is also true (to continue briefly summarizing our argument in this direction) that the coming of welfare states has eroded the centrality not only of sexual virtues, but also of prudence and temperance. The state has taken over many of the functions of family life, of unions and friendly societies, and of charities, and in all cases the process has separated the individual from institutions. As we have observed, the operation of rights has had the same effect. It was a famous complaint of socialists that capitalist individualism separated man from man and atomized society. As I have argued, this view misunderstood the character of individualism. Yet as we shall see many of the measures implemented in the welfare state, measures of a socialist kind, have had precisely this atomizing effect on civil society.

In this world, sophistication about how one ought to behave has become little more than a certain kind of knowingness about the world, and as such, is acquired by children at ever-younger ages. The young no longer know their place because most of them no longer have a place to know: they have been assimilated into that single adult world in which everyone behaves in the same way to everyone else. It is a world in which the relationship between action and habit on the one hand, and consequences on the other, is dramatically looser than it used to be. The past was often a scene of woe because various vices of intemperance or imprudence could very quickly catch up with the reckless. Technology and the state have now taken the sting out of many of these consequences, but the march of human folly has kept in step, and a different range of woes (commonly called "social problems") now connects conduct and consequence.

I have so far been summarizing those forms of the politico-moral world that have a kind of continuity with what were often thought, by moralists, to be part of the corruption of a capitalist world. But it is important not to lose sight of the moral continuity with that earlier cast of mind. What I have been calling the moral life, the life of individualists with duties to themselves, has mediated (as we have seen) into what many would regard as much more significant concerns: the problems of poverty and vulnerability, of war and inequality.

At the heart of the politico-moral system will be found the passion of compassion, and the virtue claimed for it is that it has transcended the merely personal and local preoccupations of the moral life and set about addressing the real problems faced by mankind. Whereas the moral life tended to cut people off from each other as a result of distinctions of age, status, authority, and much else, the politico-moral, calling itself "ethical," has swept

away a range of snobberies and superiorities that merely separated man from man or person from person. The vulnerable, the
poor, the deviant are no longer isolated in contemptuous categories and seen as failing standards of respectability, but have been
fully included within communal life and given increasing help
in dealing with their problems. We are tolerant, easygoing, and
we have removed from life many painful judgments about our
inadequacies.

Finally, how might we construe the social and economic structure of a politico-moral society? It may be understood as having
a tripartite character. We may first point to the vulnerable, who
constitute the basic point of orientation in an egalitarian politico-
moral society. They are the poor, the excluded, the genuinely sick
and problematic, the deviant among the youth, those on welfare,
indeed anyone for whom membership in a victim class may be
advanced. Those belonging to ethnic minorities often feature
among their number. These are central as the beneficiaries in a
politico-moral society.

Secondly, the benefactors, who are made up of those
employed or employing others, the self-reliant, the rich, and
the charitable, including anyone involved in philanthropic
endeavors. The economy is, of course, the indispensable material base of the benefactions bestowed by this class, and these
benefactions are largely but not exclusively constituted by taxation. Quite how far this class extends depends on current beliefs
about victimhood. In some feminist theory, all men belonged to
this class, just as all women belonged among the vulnerable. By
some counts, the vulnerable have been found to exceed the entire
population of some Western states, but this can only happen by
fantasies of double-counting. Ethnic females in some creative
statistics count as two. It soon adds up. In the more extreme versions of the politico-moral, the class of benefactors is actuated
basically by greed and fear; their concern is with "profit rather
than people."

Distinct from the beneficiaries in the politico-moral society,
and their benefactors, are the administrators, including politicians, journalists, judges and lawyers, members of tribunals and

commissions, academics, social workers, experts, those who work in international organizations, and other theorists and rulers of the world. Members of this class largely operate in a democratic political environment and thus are above profit and concerned above all with the welfare of people.

Yes, yes, the reader might impatiently say, but where does the power lie? The answer is that, as in any good society, it is diffused. The vulnerable have a certain moral power over others by virtue of being characterized by unsatisfied need. The benefactors are heavily taxed, but since they provide the cash that keeps the whole system going, they have at least the power that comes from the fact that they must have incentives, without which they will not create the required prosperity. Finally, it must be admitted that the real power lies with the administrators who can determine the limits of what is possible. They have the power. It is for the moment a somewhat constrained power, but modern creativity in extending the possibilities of data collection and putting populations under surveillance means that it is growing.

7. IS THERE A THEOLOGY OF THE POLITICO-MORAL?

In one sense, this is a foolish question to ask. Most of those whom we might construe as politico-moral in their mode of conduct and feeling would be secularists, and similar terms such as "materialist," "this-worldly," and even "hedonistic" would apply to them. Religions function as systems orienting the believer in a universe that has been recognized as mysterious. Perhaps it is absurd to think that religion as a phenomenon is in any way relevant to our post-Christian world. But the question is worth at least asking because a civilization that does not rest upon a religion in some sense is rather odd. I have been emphasizing right through the argument that European states are clearly Christian, or post-Christian, in a number of fundamental ways, but this view would be contested by rationalists in terms of the contrast between religion and science. They would see themselves as inheriting not a religious tradition, but its actual rejection.

The secularist argument is that every set of human beings up to our own time has rested upon belief in an invisible and timeless world, usually determined by divine agencies such as the different conceptions of God (and other powers) found among the Christians, Jews, Muslims, and others. The beliefs and rituals associated with these religions have been extremely various, but in no case do they rest upon (what an empiricist or a scientist would count as) evidence. Further, these beliefs have often sustained very nasty practices that we now, rightly, regard as abhorrent. Such practices range from the subordination of women to the persecution of those holding heterodox beliefs. Many of the evils of the world have been justified by religious arguments; it might thus follow that if we got rid of the religions, and therefore of religious justifications for persecution, then various evils would lapse and human beings would be a lot nicer to each other. Indeed, a great deal of religious thought can be attributed to fantasy, and has at times expressed impulses that seem clearly pathological. Our civilization has learned to test its beliefs in terms of evidence, as scientists do, and the result has been that much written in our sacred books has fallen into thoroughly deserved disrepute. We now guide our lives, or many of us do, by evidence-based science rather than by the wishful fantasies of religious believers. Religion in the past was the crutch for societies a good deal more credulous than we are. We no longer need it. We can stand on our own two feet, and we'd better, because they are the only support we have.

The first thing to say about this argument is that it rests upon a tendency almost universal in our time: namely, to understand institutions in terms of the abuses they may give rise to. Families contain child abuse, some teachers cannot be trusted with the cane because they are sadists, some policemen are corrupt and bullying, some businessmen are ruthlessly concerned with nothing but profit, and so on. The result of this tendency, often advanced as the virtue of being critical and facing facts, is to abandon the trust on which decent conduct in the past largely rested, and to replace it with regulation by governments. This attempt to prevent abuse and bring justice into the sphere of personal discretion has created a vicious circle: the more regulation, the less those regulated can be trusted. They become casuists, guarding themselves against trouble. In the twentieth century, communists were entrusted with power in many states on the grounds that capitalists and traditional rulers abused their power and exploited their populations. Fascists came to power on the idea that parliaments were corrupt talking shops. Communists and fascists were a good deal worse than what they replaced. It was certainly true that the institutions they replaced were far from perfect, but the idea that enforcing codes guarantees a reign of justice is strictly for simpletons. It does not. Religions, then, are no less prone to abuses and follies than other institutions, but they also sustain a great range of benevolent and necessary moral solidities.

The second thing to say about this argument is that it misunderstands both religion and science. European thought has for centuries exhibited a dialectical swing between skepticism and a passion for certainty. It has in fact been one of the main selling points of science that it provides certainty in place of baseless fantasy. To think this is to confuse science with technology, in which we can indeed usually produce some reliable consequences, though not infrequently with some unpleasant side effects. Science properly speaking is different. It is a complex of hypotheses (usually about the natural world), which are in a state of fairly constant testing and evaluation. No doubt many scientists today are totally confident about the evidence for a large part of this body of opinion, but they are unwise. Newtonian physics was, and remains, a pretty useful and comprehensive view of the universe we live in, but it gets some things wrong, and we now know better—or think we do. As it happens, Christianity shares in this participation in skepticism because it understands itself not as knowledge, but as faith. The very ground of Christianity begins with a recognition that it is something of a leap in the dark. When beliefs become belief systems, they are likely to lose their founding skepticism and acquire the habits of dogmatism, and this undoubtedly happens with many Christians. It is not unknown in any sphere of belief. Nevertheless, Christianity cannot plausibly be transposed into a set of propositions about God, miracles, prophets, dogmas, and so on, and in this form is thought to be baseless. It is the business of science to be refutable. It is the business of religion, whose functions are various and whose declarations about the world need not be taken as literal description, to be irrefutable. That is precisely why believers can rely on it.

In this area, I take my lead from the German philosopher Eric Voegelin, who took religion to concern itself with beliefs about the beginning and end of human life on the one hand, and with responses to the transcendental on the other. The Book of Genesis exemplifies the first concern, while Moses and the burning bush exemplifies the second. Both these examples, of course, come from the Old Testament, and it was clearly to the Old Testament that the early fathers of Christianity looked in constructing a religion out of what in many ways were the exiguous materials available from the life of Jesus. Exiguous those materials may have been, but they have left indelible marks on our civilization, ranging from the Sermon on the Mount to the distinction between God and Caesar, the basis of our separation between church and state, private and public things. With the church being recognized as the vehicle of Christian truth, the "state" (i.e., any kind of civil authority) became merely a device to permit a fallen world to enjoy a certain minimal peace in this life. Voegelin argues that this amounted to a "de-divinization of the state." And it should be recognized also that the whole idea of a "state" in the European sense is quite distinct from the forms of order found in other civilizations.

Christianity as an orthodox belief was, in historical terms, put together in the centuries after the career of Jesus, and its main elements were in place by the time of St. Augustine at the beginning of the fifth century. With St. Paul, the early Jewish disciples opened their revelation up to the world at large, and they created a church cultivating a faith constituted of shared belief. Such a faith made Christianity a highly intellectual religion, constantly in need of theological and philosophical reflection in order to sustain its unity. It needed schools and universities, though in the unsettled early medieval period it took time before these emerged. A Christian civilization could hardly avoid a philosophical dimension. It was a risky and perilous venture, always in danger of falling apart, and has remained so ever since. It was forever at the mercy of prophets with alternative ideas. It still is.

It would have been a convenient intellectual simplification, for example, if the early fathers had decided (as Arius did) that Jesus was not the son of God, but a supremely good human being; or, alternatively, that he had never been crucified (as monophysites thought) but that this had been merely an illusion necessary for the revelation. Instead, the early fathers opted for the mystery of the incarnation. In doing so, of course, they were also accepting the idea of God having three aspects—a doctrinal element that explains why Muslims regard Christianity with scorn as a form of polytheism. Indeed it was precisely this kind of ground (i.e., the low content of theological mystery in Islam) that led some early modern deists (and also Unitarians and Socinians) to argue that Islam was, in intellectual terms, the most rational of religions. I do not think there is any doubt that these deists got it wrong, and they got it wrong precisely because they did not understand the place of a religion within a civilization. A simple rationalism is no guide to the complexities of any way of life, practice, or religion. The same mistake is currently being made by the secularist opponents of Christianity.

But my design in invoking this sketch is not to go into this particular question, but to follow Voegelin in looking at one among the endless set of heresies that were excluded from orthodoxy by the early fathers. For in this heresy may be seen an interesting pattern or archetype that may suggest a further understanding of our problem. This is the famous Gnosticism, which rejected the conception of religion as a form of faith opening the soul of the believer up to the transcendent, and construed the revelation of Jesus as a form of knowledge supposedly guaranteeing salvation. The key distinction is that between Christianity recognized on the one hand as religion and therefore a matter of faith (i.e., a confidence in a set of beliefs that could not be validated in accepted practical ways) and on the other hand, a claim to knowledge and certainty. Part of the significance of this distinction is that orthodoxy preserved the religious sense of the uncertainty and mystery of the human condition, while Gnosticism presented itself as a key that would unlock the mystery. Plausibly or not, the church fathers saw themselves as saving their followers from superstitiously believing things they could not know, such as mysterious spirits and powers. The Gnostic claim was that Jesus had taught a secret doctrine, known only to initiates. Such knowledge alone guaranteed salvation. Many variations were possible on this theme. It looked highly intellectual but the actual beliefs involved (for example, the passwords needed after death to get past the seven angels guarding heaven, and thus to achieve salvation) were often of remarkable simplicity of mind. Such a structure of belief could clearly accommodate any level of intellectual complexity. Much the same is true of Marxism, which is largely a show of intellectuality for non-intellectual people.

One important Gnostic variation was to turn the Christian revelation upside down. The Genesis story was, according to one influential variation, actually the declaration of an evil Demiurge that had imprisoned men's souls in this fallen world, from which they could only escape through the esoteric knowledge of the Salvationist doctrine. In this story, the serpent supposedly seducing Eve was a liberator and illuminator of mankind, for which reason these heretics were known as Ophites, or snake worshippers. They held the Fall to be a progress from ignorance to knowledge, and elements of this doctrine were domesticated in later Christianity and became current with the Enlightenment. In their general structure, ideologies would seem to correspond with this response to the modern world.

Voegelin takes the view that Gnosticism was relatively recessive for some centuries but was revived because Christianity, as an exploratory faith, could not fully satisfy Europeans. As their civilization developed, it became more confident. An influential version of it can be found in the writings of Joachim of Flora, who "applied the symbol of the Trinity to the course of history."[37]

The first period of the world, according to this speculative idea, was the age of the Father, and lasted until Christ initiated the age of the Son. This would in turn be superseded by the age of the Spirit. Each age would be an "intelligible increase of spiritual fulfillment."

In this schema, human interest understandably focused on the end of history and the coming of the new scheme of things. What for Christians is a vague eschatological culmination of history, so far outside of human experience as to be irrelevant to the faith that sustains this life, becomes in Gnostic speculations the event round which political experience must revolve. It has sometimes been remarked, ironically, that the basic division of the human race is between those who divide things into twos and those who divide them into threes. The modern world is a marvelous efflorescence of tripartists. Hegelians, [Comptists,] and Marxists are all at it, but the instance that particularly interested Voegelin (who had got out of Austria one step ahead of the Gestapo) was the case of the Third Reich. A lot of numerological mysticism seems to have run riot in modern intellectuality. And much of it seems to posit a "re-divinization of the state."

The twentieth century was deeply preoccupied with catastrophes, world-transforming events, and crises of heroic magnitudes, all connected with the end of one order and the coming of another. Men lost their wits, not to mention their lives, in their excitement at a variety of these fancies, and all of them, it seems fair to say, gain their status from their connection with some project of perfection. Voegelin thought that this cast of mind, by which he explained the immense influence of ideologies in the modern world, was the Gnostic transposition of a Christian structure of time into modern politics. The theological term for the last days was "eschaton." The eschaton belonged to the transcendental element of Christianity, the element that stands outside our world of nature. But the divine also works within the world and the term used to describe this is "immanence." In Voegelin's view, the Gnostic doctrine in the modern world had sought to bring heaven down to earth as something that we, with our great knowledge (whatever that knowledge might be imagined to be), might achieve; or, in Voegelin's phrase, which as a masterpiece of jargon is worth the journey through his argument, the Gnostics had "immanentized the eschaton."

It is along these lines, I would suggest, that we might well find structures of thought that seem to replicate those of religious doctrines in the past, and which may on occasion take over some of the functions of those doctrines. Clearly it will not do to interpret as "religious" any passionate enthusiasm people may have, as in the past was often done in casting communism as a kind of religion. The etymology of the word "enthusiasm" (as "full of gods") is not adequate to characterize religion itself. On the other hand, something like the belief in Gaia, nature as a live personified entity against whom we have sinned in our custodianship of the planet, has some of the attributes of a religion—and a religion all the more attractive in that it is a kind of civic cult. In the modern world, many thinkers have deplored the way in which Christianity has set up a dual allegiance for the subjects of national states, and have looked back nostalgically to the civic cults of the classical world. In other words, one significant sign of a religious impulse would be any tendency to regard the state as superior to us: in these terms, any "re-divinization" of the state.

One major change in our conception of the human condition is to be found in our modern conception of sin. A basic element of Christianity was the belief that we live in an irredeemably fallen and sinful world. It may be (as Christians think) that there is an afterlife in which divine power can correct the injustices of our world, but it is certain that any attempt to perfect this particular world will cause more evil than good. Wisdom consists in recognizing the limits of our power, being grateful to God for the blessings we enjoy, and focusing our attention on the much more limited business of making our immediate surroundings a little more tolerable. There remain, of course, many believing Christians in our civilization, but there is certainly one thing most people except some Christians seem to have lost, and that is the belief in our fallen condition, and the humility appropriate to it. As a consequence, it would seem, the constitutive emotion of a Christian civilization, namely gratitude to God for the Christian revelation and for the blessings of a world perfect except for the disorders human beings have brought on themselves, has been turned upside down. In that overturning, we slough off mankind's responsibility for the evils of the world and complain that God was a faulty creator. Instead of the pious belief that God tests man, we have the questioning belief that the sufferings of human beings are tests of God's omnipotence and goodness.

Here then is unmistakably a movement of thought away from the religious toward the determinedly secular. Some commentators think that we have abandoned the idea of original sin in favor of original virtue: all men are basically good. The more precise contrary of the religious view is not that men are basically good, but that they are basically plastic: they are creatures of their conditions, in which case we are ourselves responsible for the way in which they behave. The individualists of the moral life were mixed moral entities, and exhibited both the good and the bad. The dream of the politico-moral world is that modern rationality will overcome this duality.

This is not, then, a religion, but there is something about the politico-moral world that adumbrates the possibility of turning society itself into something divine, something to which we are bound because it is the source from which comes everything we have: our ideas, our power, our releases from existential loneliness. The idea of society as an association of individuals devoted to satisfying their needs posits a society, and ultimately a mankind, to which we are irredeemably in debt, and to which we owe everything we are. It adumbrates a kind of civic cult, but one that can hardly triumph, not only because human beings are in fact radically imperfect, but also because embedded in our societies are the remains of moralities past, and it seems unlikely that they will ever be homogenized as the politico-moral would require.

AMBIVALENCE AND
WESTERN CIVILIZATION

I. MAPPING POLITICS

I have so far been exploring contemporary moral sensibilities in terms of the two ideal types dominating Western civilization, one individualist, one collectivist. Changes in such moral attitudes cannot but also involve changes in political life. The essence of what I am calling the "politico-moral" is that it straddles both moral and political life and is itself partly a political classification. How can we locate it on a map of current political ideas?

In such a mapping, the traditional distinction between left and right cannot be escaped, but certainly needs to be transcended. Dating from the French Revolution, left/right served tolerably well to distinguish aspirations toward revolutionary social transformation (such as those of the *Rights of Man*) on the one hand, and on the other attempts to moderate revolution, or actually go into reverse, as happened in France for a time between 1815 and 1830. "Progress and reaction" became an established cliché for historians of the period. Politics could be presented as a clash between the interests of "estates." But "left" and "right" as mapping dimensions of political ideas spread far beyond these limited circumstances. We still use them today. Given that "right wing" in the twentieth century covered anyone from Milton Friedman to Adolph Hitler, and that "left wing" can take in both Stalin and Clement Attlee, the distinction is clearly a clever formula for getting things wrong. And the reason for this collapse into incoherence resulted from the popularity of communist brand differentiation in the early twentieth century.

Communists bidding for working-class support against the Mussolini's fascists and the National Socialist Workers' Party in Germany needed a rhetorical weapon against enemies fishing for support in the same proletarian pool. One of their devices was to attack as "social fascism" other exponents of collectivism by unmasking them as defenders of capitalism. Fascism itself, of course, was the doctrine of the sometime socialist Mussolini, who (like Lenin) had found a better way to power through a new vanguard movement than by relying on the wayward revolutionary passions of the proletariat. Communists, Nazis, and fascists were all seeking total power, and they all aimed to transform liberal democratic states into collective enterprises by appealing to victims of oppression. They were all collectivist and appealed to socialist slogans.[*]

Recognizing this essential identity of fascism and socialism was, of course, the basis of classification later used to generate the academic concept of totalitarianism[†] in political science, much to

---

[*] This doctrine is, I'm afraid, deeply offensive to anyone on the left, but it is certainly the standard view of anyone who knows anything about Italian fascism. For a restatement of the general doctrine, see Jonah Goldberg, *Liberal Fascism*.

[†] These are, of course, troubled waters, and many academics these days regard "totalitarianism" as a relic of the Cold War. They want to emphasize that along with the fear and repression of communist states was a good deal of idealism internalized from state propaganda. This is no doubt true, but the idea of totalitarianism, like Montesquieu's spirit of despotism, is adequately grasped in terms of the place of fear in the ordering of the state. There is, of course, always more to be said.

the resentment of communists, who insisted that a Nazi racial state was very different from the true community of communism. In some respects, they were right, though it made little difference to the miserable victims of these violent forms of radical social transformation. A further aspect of these taxonomical muddles will be found in the fact that communist gerontocrats such as Brezhnev and Andropov were in the dying days of the Soviet Union regularly described by simple journalists as "conservatives." This too is not quite absurd, but it does illustrate how confused most political rhetoric can be.

Part of the problem with left/right is that it never fitted Anglophone politics. Edmund Burke was no "reactionary." Britain simply lacked the conflict between "estates" that would have made sense of such a distinction, and as a Whig, Burke might well be seen on some terms as "left" rather than "right." Britain never had the kind of *ancien régime* any "reactionary" might want to sustain or go back to, though as we shall see, a few confused people did think that it had. The large issues in British politics were the franchise and later the policy of welfare. Universalizing welfare on a left/right dimension exhibits Otto von Bismarck as left wing, but he was clearly no bleeding-heart socialist. In the vaguely progressive atmosphere of Anglophone welfare states, "right wing" simply ended up either as a term of abuse, covering anything from Iranian Ayatollahs to Southern Baptists in the U.S., or as an abusive label for libertarian believers in the superiority of market solutions for social problems. In more recent times, attempts have been made to salvage the distinction by adding to it a qualifier: "center-left" and "center-right," a device consigning "extremists" to rhetorical perdition. This merely makes the whole vocabulary cumbersome to little purpose.

Mapping political life requires that one must nominate some dimension as separating tendencies from one another. The problem with left/right was that dimensions multiplied so much that almost anything fitted anywhere. The French said *les extremes se touchent*, but in any real dichotomy, they don't. Can we, then, find other dimensions that might be serviceable in the business of mapping the terrain? Let me suggest two that may become increasingly useful.

Burke against the French Revolution clearly cannot be captured in terms of left and right, but it can illuminate if we call him "conservative" without simultaneously consigning him to "rightdom." Conservatism is no safer from rhetorical muddle than any other term, and one of its current meanings refers to whatever happens to be the current beliefs of parties calling themselves "conservative." I want to argue, however, that there is an intellectual meaning to "conservative" that is quite distinct from these simplicities and that makes it both politically and intellectually useful. As a political stance, conservatism clearly enjoins caution in changing the structure of society, especially "from above." It therefore denotes skepticism about the value of proposals for change and reform. The skepticism depends on judging that all changes are likely to have unintended consequences and some will certainly be unpleasant. More profoundly, we cannot know which practices and ideas in our cultural life sustain which desirable or undesirable features of it. My earlier argument that various features of modern welfare states have weakened the virtues of self-control and self-restraint is thus clearly a conservative argument. Intellectually speaking, then, conservatism is a continuous preoccupation with how social conditions and dominant ideas are related to each other, along with a belief that most of the chatter or "noise" in everyday politics is of little value.

The opposite of conservatism in these terms is any kind of radicalism, covering most projects for making changes in the basic structure of state and society. Radicalism in its crudest form is the belief that societies are changeless unless the rulers generate reforms. This is crude because the generic thing called "change" happens all the time, especially in dynamic modern states, and therefore politicians offering "change" are likely to be using some seductive abstract scheme as bait to catch votes. Contemporary democratic politics exhibits a succession of reforms, most of which soon need themselves to be reformed, and all of which need to be "brought up to date" within a generation or so. The essence of contemporary democratic politics, dominated as it

is by radical ideas, is thus a ceaseless churning of policies, regulations, and "visions" demanding constant attention from the electorate. Politicians quite enjoy all this attention.

The basic radical idea, associated by political philosophers
from Plato and Aristotle onward with the danger of democracy,
is that the rich should give up some of their luxuries to meet the
needs of the poor, and we may note on this point that democracy
only came to be viable in European states when the constitutional
formalities were strongly entrenched, and when the level and distribution of wealth had created a middle class large enough to
protect itself against the immediate prospect of being plundered.
In many states in the Third World, these conditions have not been
met, and democracy rapidly mutates into some form of klepto-
cratic authoritarianism.

It might seem that this distinction is merely one more
reworking of the left/right mapping. Conservatives are "right"
while radicals are "left." In such a view, then, Nazis, fascists, communists, and radical socialists all fall into the same camp: they
are all radicals. I have no quarrel with this implication of the classification, but it is certainly not one that everybody would accept.
No radical wants to be associated with such blundering sorcerer's
apprentices as Stalin and Mao, not to mention Hitler and Mussolini. Yet however much radicalism in collectivist forms has left
a trail of appalling failed projects behind it, contemporary politicians find it difficult to face an electorate without advancing some
kind of "vision." They love grand transforming ideas. In conservative terms, it is seldom the business of rulers to be indulging in
such follies, but electoral credulity often forces conservatives into
playing the same game. Occasionally, no doubt, the state must act
radically and decisively, but as Burke put it, medicine ought not to
be the constitution's daily bread. The basic point, however, is that
radicals, who generally want to mobilize citizens for admirable
collective enterprises, are seldom discriminating about the enthusiasms they take up. Not all radicals take up bad projects, but all
the bad projects have been radical.

"Radical" and "conservative" thus seem to me to distinguish
different styles of politics quite usefully, and I am tempted further

to identify radicalism with sentimentality, and conservatism with realism. Conservatives are certainly realists in the sense that they seek to understand politics against a backdrop of what they take to be historical and human realities. And it is further true that, at least within the politico-moral mindset, all radicals are sentimentalists. Their first step in commending any radical proposal for increasing the power of the state is always to invoke compassion by identifying miseries that the state ought to remedy. But this is not a universal connection. A radical racist, for example, need not base himself on the emotion of compassion. In the Nazi case, the appeal was rather to some idea of purity and vitality. So—conservatives are always realists (though they may, of course, get reality wrong), and radicals are in our time almost always sentimentalists.

The term "sentimentality" is, of course, pejorative. "Sentimentality" is by no means the same thing as sentiment. Real feelings are sentiments, but sentimentality generally means emotions that may be triggered by some associated emotion, and are often likely to be superficial. To experience compassion for the suffering of some abstract class may indeed be a serious concern, and can certainly elicit admirable conduct, but it can also be little more than posturing. And since no entire class of people suffering oppression is suffering in the same way to the same degree, the emotion cannot but be directed at an image rather than a reality.

Understood in this way, the politico-moral is an instance of sentimental radicalism. Morally speaking, it takes the form of a standardized challenge to find our essential selves in the enterprise of improving the condition of the vulnerable, and it generally carries the further message that this is a redemptive activity, canceling out earlier moral faults of our civilization. It is that moral dimension of a political program—the finding of our essential selves in an enterprise—that must lead us on to something clearly more complicated. Sentimental radicals in the politico-moral idiom are not merely knights-errant eager to engage with anything they construe as an evil. They commonly have a wider program. And the most plausible identification of that wider program seems to me to be "perfectionism." What is it that perfectionism involves?

2. ON PERFECTIONISMS, PIECEMEAL AND SYSTEMATIC

Perfectionism is an extremely miscellaneous category, but its essential sense is that the business of politics should go beyond "keeping the ship of state afloat"[38] into the more serious project of transforming the human condition. The European tradition of utopian thought is no doubt perfectionist, though not in any way relevant to this argument. Plato is sometimes assigned to this utopian and perfectionist class, but wrongly, because Plato in the *Republic* was (as I understand him) engaged in elaborating a philosophical inquiry. Marx is sometimes dragged kicking and screaming into the ranks of utopian perfectionism, but his account of communism is a prediction generated by an analysis of what he believed to have been the dominant realities of a capitalist culture. Real utopias are merely imaginary, dreams, expressions of the defects of life around us, but they make no claims on reality such as are found in Plato and Marx. These figures ought not, then, to be classed as utopians.

From another point of view, however, Marx is certainly a perfectionist, though of a different kind. Communism, imagined as a form of society emerging from the womb of historical time, was in practice a mobilizing project of revolutionaries who came to power with the aim of creating a new and better world. Intellectually, they had been persuaded that the waywardness and follies of human beings could be explained in terms of social conditions, and having attained total power, first in Soviet Russia and later in China, Cuba, Vietnam, North Korea, and Cambodia, they set about putting the world to rights. In all cases the project was to perfect society. In less sophisticated non-European states, this project could be presented as "modernization," but of a form much superior to the vile ways of capitalists. The road to perfection followed a policy of entrusting all social enterprise to the care of the notionally expert rulers of the states involved. And the test of such intellectual superiority was to have become engaged in the doctrinal adventures of Marxist praxis. To say that this project was not a success would be to state the obvious. In these hands, the very idea of perfectionism became unmistakably associated with death and despotism.

This association is why perfectionism in any explicit form has become an aspiration that cannot speak its name. That it did not disappear altogether testifies to the immense strength of perfectionism as something entirely indigenous to our civilization. It survives, I shall argue, in two forms, and we shall consider each in turn: Firstly, as a piecemeal aspiration to take action that will ensure that at least one identifiable evil in social life will never recur. And secondly, beneath the surface of our Western political life, perfectionist clusters of thought can certainly be found, though they may not announce themselves as such. I shall call this form of the perfectionist aspiration "Systematic Perfectionisms," and the two examples I shall mention are the project of democratizing societies still thought of as *anciens régimes*, and the project of overcoming global ignorance, poverty, and war.

The problem with any kind of perfectionism, as demonstrated conclusively by the ideological adventures of the twentieth century, is that high moral ambitions often go with very low behavior by those in power. The evidence in fact seems pretty clearly to demonstrate the even stronger thesis that low behavior cannot be avoided by rulers making such moral claims. Realists might well contemplate such experiences, and ask: can human beings never learn from experience? Must millions go on dying to recall the world to political realism? There always remains, however, the inspiration of the story of Robert the Bruce and the spider. Time after time, the spider swings across trying to attach his web to the adjoining support, and time and again, fails. But often there comes a time when he succeeds. In the case of totalitarianism, one might observe that the failed attempts left so much death and destruction in their wake that even the trying is hardly worthwhile.

Realists would certainly want to evade the sillier reaches of optimism by emphasizing that no human society can escape human folly, which is a constant in any social theory. Omnipresent in human affairs, it takes many forms. Sheer unmitigated stupidity and incomprehension of what is going on, misunderstanding of rules and commands, and lack of elementary common sense are familiar elements of everyday life, and they ought to play a more central explanatory role in the social sciences than they do. The practical problem is that elementary realism gets lost when intellectuals are bewitched by some fancy new vocabulary—"dialectic," or "racial science," or "national authenticity" are the obvious recent examples, but there can be other varieties: spiritual uplift or military discipline, for example. In our time, the language of science is particularly dangerous, leading hope to trump fear. This time, the fools think, it will be different.

Realism here rests on the one empirical proposition that no perfecting of the world would be possible without entrusting to rulers such a plenitude of power as would addle their wits. Even were they disinterested Platonic guardians, their guidance would have to be mediated through the ideas and sentiments of human beings. Many of those humans are certain to mistake the point of what ought to be happening, and nearly all will sometimes be looking for advantage to themselves. Ideas become subtly changed, passions take over conduct, and no ideal model long survives its encounter with reality. One might regret this as a tragic fact about the human condition, and no doubt it is, but it may also be regarded as one rather engaging element of *la comedie humaine*. The architect of the Final Solution was also Chaplin's Great Dictator. Where would satire and literature be without human absurdity?

But laughter cannot be the only response to human folly; it hurts. The ultimate explanation of the ups and downs of human experience used to be understood by the Greeks as a case of the temptation of *hybris* leading to the *nemesis* that follows. Realism on this score might alternately be taken as replaying Christian warnings about the dangers of pride and the benefits of humility. Human folly is indelibly part of the human condition, and the absurdity of human beings is something we cannot change. Its cost brings misery and pain to people, and such travails endlessly provoke dreams of perfection, but the wisdom of the realist insists that we must painfully learn that many perfections may be worse than the imperfections to which in some degree we have become accustomed.

a. Piecemeal Perfectionism

The remarkable thing, then, is that perfectionism does survive among us, though it takes care to conceal its real character. In its most obvious incarnation, it may hardly be distinguishable from a rational response to the world. Perfectionism here has taken on a piecemeal character in suggesting that imperfection can be removed by stages. Hence we need to return to our definition. Perfectionism is any project or proposal believed to have the power to transform the human condition. The belief is that once a perfectionist proposal has been implemented, things will never be the same again, and the concealed presence of perfectionism may be detected precisely in the currency of that locution about certain bad things never happening again. The key perfectionist idea is transformation,* an illusion that is fed by delight at our immense technological power. Some real great leaps forward have certainly happened in our control over nature. Why can we not have others, some in the sphere of human life? Perfectionism is thus a dream of power. In many forms it rests on what I have elsewhere called "the Bolshevik illusion," which (distinct from Marxist illusions) is the belief that one area of society can be changed while everything elsewhere remains the same. And its implementation depends on the employment of one or other form of technology.

The technologies may be various. Some are bureaucratic, having the form of regulations and procedures designed to control abuses. This is the form taken in discussions conducted in the aftermath of any disaster. Sometimes the hope is that certain

---

* I am concerned largely with *arguments* for a better society, but governments themselves are far from immune to these temptations. The British government, for example, dreams of a comprehensive database supplying all the information it needs about the inhabitants of Britain. And the project has an appropriate name: See Cabinet Office, "Transformational Government: Enabled by Technology," November 2005, Cm. 6683. See the discussion in Jill Kirby, *Who Do They Think We Are?* Centre for Policy Studies, January 2008.

forms of deviance, if diagnosed early enough, can be changed before they have really developed into antisocial practices. The promise is of a world without truants, vandals, and arsonists. The moral defects of these figures have come to be described as "anti-social" and the aim is to move away from old-fashioned punishments toward new techniques that will (as punishment commonly does not) *guarantee* social improvement. Another very popular form of piecemeal perfectionism consists in the attempt to bypass moral problems by controlling the availability of the materials used by bad people. Laws must be introduced to limit the availability of guns, knives, baseball bats, cheap alcohol, pepper, and other instruments of mayhem. Without guns, no gun crime, without knives . . . etc. If children commit these anti-social acts from boredom, the obvious solution is to give them something to occupy their energies. The politico-moral avoids recognizing individual moral responsibility with the same enthusiasm as it embraces collective forms of it.

Even piecemeal perfections cannot, of course, evade the mockery of nature. Hardly had Europeans conquered the problem of hunger in their societies than they found themselves having to face what is currently known as "an epidemic of obesity." Again, we have been able to overcome all manner of frustrating sexual conventions, only to confront the problems of teenage pregnancy and increasing sexually transmitted diseases. And our compassionate indulgence in supplying welfare to teenage mothers has led to the growth of what are euphemistically known as one-parent "families." Families without fathers, however, commonly generate special difficulties of their own, in the form of anti-social delinquency in the next generation. The dream is that by dealing with the initiating circumstance (in this case of teenage pregnancy) we shall cut off its later social consequences. But the imperfections we face are clearly not static; they have a dynamic of their own. The weaknesses of one generation create new problems in the next. What could more pointedly mock our hatred of poverty than obesity? Or what could more dramatically refute politico-moral niceness than its causal role in the emergence of anti-social nastiness in the next generation?

Perfectionism must, then, hide its character, because in our time its evidently millenarian character would invite ridicule. It can only be recognized by its passion for transformation. Even the most credulous democratic electorate will reject genuinely radical plans, so perfectionism in our time has had to have a practical and piecemeal character. But it has other areas in which it can express itself. It can adumbrate the conditions of perfection in the form of rights, and entrench the desired transformations in legal and international structures beyond the easy reach of democratic repeal.

b. Overthrowing *Anciens Régimes*

European thinkers have often indulged in a flirtation with classical republicanism. It was a doctrine particularly vibrant in the so-called Radical Enlightenment.[39] Modern European states are essentially monarchies, and largely remain so even though their kings and queens may not survive in institutional form.[40] The reason these states are monarchical is that they derive from feudal conditions, and feudal monarchies have generated, through complicated chains of development, an individualist version of the rule of law. Being Christian states, they construed human beings as fallen creatures of limited rationality. Recognizing such fallibility, they created tolerant commercial societies based on what Gibbon called "science and taste." And they inherited, of course, the Christian distinction between God and Caesar, public and private life. In this form, though shaken by many kinds of political folly, they have, over many generations, fought off various forms of the totalitarian temptation.

Now this combination of characteristics—monarchy, Christianity, and a certain stubborn conservative resistance to extreme radicalism—constitutes (if abstractly considered) a kind of *ancien régime*, as it featured in the rejections of the revolutionaries in France. Monarchies were understood, in the manner of Roman republicans, as centers of autocracy and tyranny, surrounded by flunkies. They were identified with servility. The Christian religion was obviously a set of outmoded beliefs picked up from a long-vanished Jewish tribal past. And conservatism was clearly a dumb aversion among the ignorant to the changes needed to create a better society. Here was a set of imperfections for which a radical package of perfections lay to hand: republicanism, secularism, and radicalism. They could plausibly be packaged as the formula for freedom. In the imaginative version of it supplied by Rousseau (in one of his moods), it was the discovery that although we think we are free, we are still in chains. Perfection thus became in some degree the overthrow of real or notional *"anciens régimes."*

It is worth pursuing this current form of perfectionism a little further. What does it involve? At one level, an *ancien régime* might be understood as an image of the oppressions of capitalist life, in the United States for example. But in Britain, more obvious targets are easy to find. The abolition of monarchy and the House of Lords are plausible versions of any project of democratization. Getting rid of monarchy today, however, is largely a recessive ambition because the political power of the monarchy is slight, and there are powerful reserves of reverence for an institution that stands above politics and represents the unity of the British. Nevertheless, some classical republicans take a close interest in polling data that may register the popularity of the monarchy going up and down. Every decline provokes republican muttering. And as with all radical aspirations, a successful negative popular vote could destroy an institution, leading it to an oblivion from which no positive vote could restore it. Meanwhile, the House of Lords in Britain has led a strange half-life, as projects of reforming it or transforming it hiss and splutter to little purpose.

Then there is the issue of Christianity regarded in this context as the constitutive superstition of the West. The first decade of the twenty-first century was marked by an evident push for a final triumphant secularization.[41] Evidence-based science should at last be the recognized foundation of our lives, rather than superstition.

And then (along with monarchy and Christianity) there was conservatism, often taken by its enemies as no more than an irrational resistance to improvement, a falsity of consciousness generated by no more significant a source than the interests of the rich. Here in the abolition of these elements of European life is a progressive program for building a democratic and secular radicalism that could at last begin to grapple with the real problems of perfecting our society.

I suppose that the best description of this kind of program would be to describe it as constitutional fundamentalism. The problems of human folly are attributed to bad institutions, especially monarchy. The program might alternatively be regarded as an instance of "the Kantian Fallacy," after the philosopher who thought, in the 1790s, that a Europe of republics could be nothing else but a Europe at peace. How can we be free, asks the progressive, when we are subject to monarchical rulers (even notionally) and dominated by unscientific and outmoded ideas? Monarchy is associated with servility, Christianity with a population on its knees before an imaginary ruler of the universe. And both of these institutions prevent us from taking our destiny into our own hands, standing on our own two feet, and—democratically no doubt—engaging with our real problems, which turn out to be oppressions and inequalities.

As perfectionist aspirations go, this one is not currently distinguished by any great vitality, but the remarkable thing is that it has survived at all. The unavoidable defect of real classical republics is that they spend so much energy being anxious about moral decline. As Montesquieu analyzed them, republics depended on civic virtue, and even the noble Catos of Rome failed to avert such a moral collapse. In European monarchies, by contrast, a certain sort of moral corruption is recognized as inevitable. It is to be found, for example, in commercial incentives to virtue, but its real habitat is the sentiment of honor by which Europeans do the right thing not because it is the right thing, but because they would be dishonored if they did not, This may be, as classical republicans generally think, an "indirect" and inferior form of virtue, but it is certainly a form of virtue, and in a world massively given over to corruptions of every kind, it is not negligible.

Among the unrealities of this version of perfectionism is its historical perversity. Without monarchy, no liberal democracies would have come into being. Monarchies in Europe have long been the notional sources of honor, and as a focus of national unity, they enabled party disputes to develop institutionally into a distinction between government and opposition without degenerating into civil war. Certainly no classical state generated our kind of conversational politics. As for servility and dependence of mind, European monarchies (and America of course belongs to this class) are pretty obviously the least servile of societies in the modern world. North European monarchies are the most free and stable states as well as the least corrupt democracies in Europe, and that means the world. It is significant that the overthrow of monarchy in Russia, Spain, and Germany in the twentieth century led to very bad times indeed.

Monarchy, Christianity, and conservatism are three institutions that virtually define what all forms of Western radicalism find imperfect in human nature, and in the attacks upon them we may sniff the curious sense that those who want to overthrow these supposed elements of *anciens régimes* seek a final solution to the basic source of history as a Voltairean story of crimes and follies. This "final solution"—abolishing monarchy, refuting Christianity, and overcoming conservatism—is no doubt benign and only marginally to be compared to the famous Final Solution of Nazi dreams, but it has the same mad sense of human megalomania about it. That Christianity, taken abstractly as a belief system, has problems may be easily conceded, but it is also the source of the traditions on which Western openness has been created. And intellectually speaking, setting Augustine and Christian theology against Marx and his modern successors is to match giants with dwarfs. Again, if the issue is conservative thought, then Burke, Salisbury, and their successors need hardly fear being unmasked as bearers of false consciousness. But there is a more substantial point.

It concerns freedom. Perfectionism doctrinally can exist in no other context than that of a dialogue about imperfections. The deepest source of the radical drive in Western states is the conviction that we suffer from concealed forms of oppression that destroy our freedom unless they are unmasked. Rousseau's idea that we are enslaved was taken up by many radicals of later generations, and (as we shall see) by all intellectuals who had the mobilizing ambitions of totalitarianism. What, then, is it that makes a slave? Chains and commands, no doubt, but also the slave's own recognition that he or she is a slave. To think oneself oppressed is to think of oneself as a slave. It is a step on the way to releasing in oneself that element of servility that lurks in all human nature. And it was this idea of being oppressed that seduced the Russians into Bolshevism, the Germans into Nazism. They wanted to throw off bourgeois chains in the one case, and the oppressions of the worldwide Jewish conspiracy on the other. Neither Russians nor Germans had been notably servile populations before they succumbed to ideological enthusiasm—but they certainly became so afterward.

The mistake of identifying freedom with liberation is evidently a mark of pretty unsophisticated peoples, and it has been a happy distinction of Anglophones that they have usually managed to avoid its nastier consequences. They did not, however, entirely escape this confusion during the 1960s in universities, which were a textbook example of the destruction of real institutional independence by liberation movements. Suddenly becoming available to unsophisticated and uneducated people, universities succumbed to democratic and liberatory slogans and lost the academic authority that made them distinctive. In succumbing to such servility of mind, they were unprotected against governments bidding to take power over them.

All servility is dangerous. To be even a little servile is to think that whatever is frustrating must be a form of oppression, from which liberation alone will provide release. Often, however, one is frustrated not by "oppression" but by reality, or by an instinct for self-restraint. It is a feature of life to which some kind of "rage" is not an appropriate response. Servility is a personality structure with little protection against the temptations of impulse. The search for liberation is a rejection of the responsibilities of freedom in favor of a release into the irresponsibility of rights. And a right is irresponsible because it is a legally entrenched liberty that does not contain within itself the limitations instinctive in a free society. That is why there is a constant moral fussing in current societies about the necessity to match rights with responsibilities. As a British minister of justice has remarked, human rights are being treated like consumer goods for selfish ends by some people in Britain. "I am really worried about the commoditization of rights, and the sense that people should see their rights as consumer goods," he said.[42]

I cite constitutional fundamentalism merely as one familiar form of contemporary perfectionism, one that lurks a little below the surface of our current politics. While not being particularly sophisticated, it has a certain cachet in universities, because it is likely to give less sophisticated academics the pleasing sense that they are being "socially critical." In this context it is in part a component of the wider doctrine of the intellect as essentially critical, and in part an instance of the politico-moral rejection of our civilization as failing to confront the evils of the world.

c. Ignorance, Poverty, and War

The politico-moral cast of mind is happy to ally itself with other versions of perfectionism, but its own central focus is to destroy ignorance, war, and poverty, both in our own societies, and in the world at large. No small ambition, one might say. These problems have always been with us. Solving them would certainly be a transformation of the human condition. But they clearly raise the most difficult and controversial moral questions. What is to count as ignorance? How is it related to war? The politico-moral transcends the complexities and mobilizes our *political* sentiments for a *moral* crusade. As always, the question becomes: how can this problem-solution nexus be made plausible? Given that moral integrity and political prudence seldom coincide, how can the politico-moral present itself as *both* an imperative moral crusade and as *politically* compelling?

The answer is that the crusade presents itself as both abstract and figurative at the same time, a concept and an image fused together. If we construe these grand problems at the right level of abstraction, then policies become thinkable and imperative in a way that would not survive examination either at the brute level of particular reality, or that of philosophical universality. And it is only by falling into line with a conviction in this form that we can be persuaded to bend all our efforts toward solving these problems as the real expression of our real humanity.

The perfectionist program to conquer poverty is perhaps most plausibly presented in the view that poverty is ipso facto an indicator of injustice.[43] As Thomas Pogge puts it: the "massive persistence of severe poverty is the great scandal of this globalised civilisation and threatens its promised gains in peace, stability and prosperity."[44] Pogge argues that the poor half of humankind consumes less than 2 percent of the global product. Statistically, we are in the world of the poor living on a dollar a day, a proposition hard to make sense of since it depends so much on conditions and currencies, but nothing much rests on this basic feature of the rhetoric of perfection. No one doubts that there are millions of people living in dreadful conditions, doomed to drinking unclean water and eating poor food in small quantities, living on the edge of survival so that a military conflict, a bad harvest, or governmental caprice can kill. Of the facts of the case, there is certainly no doubt.

The moral case for the duties we owe to the poor is analyzed by Pogge in terms of the negative duty of avoiding harm, and the positive duty of creating at least some elements of material adequacy to replace the impoverished conditions of the chronically poor. The negative duty is enough for him to suggest that the causes of such poverty lie in the foreseeable consequences of economic arrangements that have been structured by interlocking national and international arrangements set up by Western states. It thus becomes our duty to modify these arrangements so that "everyone has real opportunities to escape and avoid extreme poverty."

Pogge has little patience with the argument that poverty results from local causes. This is an argument made plausible by the fact that so many states in the Third World have actually learned how to generate wealth. How have Japan, Thailand, Taiwan, and other non-Western areas escaped from being doomed by those "interlocking national and international institutional arrangements"? Social scientists, he tells us,[45] feel "emotionally more comfortable" with tracing persistent world poverty back to "national and local clauses" than to "global institutional arrangements." This kind of remark is just a bit of ad hominem flim flam, and need not be taken seriously.

Marc Fleurbaey, one of Pogge's contributors, also judges the responsibility for global poverty as lying with Western states, because he thinks that poverty results from oppression. Economic constraint and physical violence both reduce real freedom, he argues, taking as "real freedom" a situation of resource-equality between those entering into a transaction—a situation so unusual in the world that it would generate very few transactions at all. People exchange precisely because they are unequal in resources. That is how work, for example, turns into cash. The conclusion Fleurbaey draws is that unequal trade is a form of coercion like physical violence. Poverty, like physical aggression, violates the integrity of the person. Here we have an explosion of analogies designed to reduce all the complexities of economic relationships to versions of the one key concept: oppression.

This sounds like a powerful moral case in terms of rights, and it tempts various writers in this field to suggest some system of global dividends drawn from rich countries and given to poor. Such a global tax would (so the argument runs) begin to deal with global poverty. The thesis is that the poor are poor because they have no money: an irresistible conclusion, indeed. No less irresistible, however, is the judgment that any vast sum of money likely to be accumulated for this purpose would be a magnet for the corrupt, the greedy, bureaucrats on the make, and many other undesirables. Large funds of money for good purposes have a way of producing very disappointing benefits, and that has been precisely the history of much Western aid to the underdeveloped world.

Nor need we take too seriously the idea that poverty results from the way the international economy works, rather than from the culture involved. It would hardly be surprising if some cultures were very much more effective at creating wealth than others. Cultural difference has to do with moral probity, corruption, work ethics, and similar considerations. Some cultures are undoubtedly less successful than others. Africans seem to find it hard to organize themselves in states in which wealth flows to those who work rather than to those with guns or licenses. The Islamic world is another arena of such global poverty; like Africans, Muslims are very keen to migrate to richer Western pastures. Indigenous peoples in the Pacific and in parts of Latin America are also notably dependent on money provided by others. Somehow, Mexicans never seem to manage their economy well enough to discourage thousands of their number from trying the desperate expedient of walking across the border into the U.S.

The idea that severe poverty is caused by structural arrangements that suit the Western states but are disastrous to others is clearly refuted by the success of Asian states. The positive case that bad government is a serious cause of poverty may be illustrated currently from the case of Zimbabwe, where starvation is a direct result of the folly of rulers and not at all from structural conditions of any kind.

The converse evidence supporting the same principle is that the Chinese, who have all the talents and lack nothing of the enthusiasm to grow richer, could over long stretches of the twentieth century succeed only when ruled by the British in Hong Kong and in Singapore, but not in China. The madness of Maoism was a marvelous stimulus to poverty. These elementary considerations are enough to dispose of the simple view that severe poverty is a violation of a human right, and especially one for which we in the West are responsible. Global poverty is certainly terrible, and it would be good to alleviate it, but making its alleviation a right is merely a form of megalomania among normative theorists.

That we may have a duty to suffering individuals is easily granted; that we have a duty to entire peoples who suffer is also pretty plausible. But here again we face the problem of morality versus the national interest. For one thing, any Western responsibility for feeding the world runs into the difficulty that we embrace an open- ended commitment to deal with a problem largely out of our control. One reason for poverty in the Third Word is that the starving populations get bigger generation by generation. A great deal of aid already goes to impoverished countries, but they multiply faster than we can deal with their needs. Some European

THE SERVILE MIND   291

cultures in earlier times used to adapt to changing Malthusian pressures adjustments in the average age of marriage: in good times, people married earlier, in bad times later. Third World countries benefit from medical advantages that have reduced infant mortality, but have no cultural mechanisms to deal responsibly with these problems themselves.

Western difficulties in responding wisely to the problems of ignorance, poverty, and war take on an even darker complexion if we contemplate a future world in which (unlikely as it seems) these problems would have been solved. We may well envisage a future in which impoverished states become prosperous, and hence active players in the already complicated and conflict-ridden world of international politics. The West is demographically shrinking, and there are vastly increasing populations in Africa, Asia, and South America. We would then find ourselves in an international world in which we would be small, weak, and probably still richer than these countries.

You hardly need a crystal ball to predict that such nations would in all likelihood be highly aggressive in their claims and demands on us. Whatever we might have done for them in the past would generate no permanent source of gratitude or even of consideration. International relations have no place for the gratitude one might expect in the world of individuals. The British abolished slavery, but that this notably virtuous act has not qualified the many resentful claims and sentiments advanced by those descended from the slaves.

3.   OPPRESSIONS AND LIBERATIONS

The instinct of perfectionism is to think that all evils are part of an interconnected system, so that there can be no real solution to any particular imperfection without the perfecting of everything else as well. This is the assumption associated with the language of "root causes." Ignorance, war, and poverty are all plausibly understood as interconnected—"plausibly" for the rhetorical reason that the causal connections can each be redescribed in terms of the others. We need not doubt, however, that there are separate imperfections feeding off each other. One piece of radical fundamentalism argues that in the last analysis (as the Marxists used to put it) ignorance is the root cause of them all. The solution, therefore, is "education," though since we are here in a slippery rhetorical world, it is education in an idiosyncratic sense. Education does not, of course, mean education. It means the spread of vocational training combined with an appreciation of liberal and progressive doctrines, especially declarations of rights. The vocational training will help with the poverty, and the liberalism will help to dissipate the prejudices generating human division, and hence also generating war and poverty. The ultimate cause of these evils lies in forms of subordination that must be unmasked as oppression. The program of change is therefore one of liberation. Let us look a little more closely at these ideas.

"Oppression" is a good example of a situational term that became absolutized in political rhetoric. Nearly every relationship in human life—husband and wife, employer and employee, master and slave, ruler and ruled—has been thought by one critic or another to be oppressive, but it makes a large difference whether the oppressed are slaves, serfs, wives, employees, children, or subjects. The particular character and disposition of the notional oppressor also makes a real difference to the experience. In perfectionist thought, the immense variations of actual life are smoothed out in favor of a powerful abstract image of suffering. Oppression is thus a myth, in the strict sense of a story or an idea, covering a vast range of varying situations, but operating as a metaphor that may reconfigure whole areas of human experience. As we have seen, many groups in Western societies themselves are described as oppressed because they have been "excluded." By various counts, the excluded (from one benefit or another, on one ground or another) can turn out (in some British statistics) to be nearly the whole population. A perfected world can only be one in which oppressions (including exclusions) have been abolished, and the basic instrument for beginning this process is to be found in declarations of rights.

Rights facilitate the struggles of the oppressed, and they also raise the question: who will be the agent of change? For while liberation can notionally only result from the struggles of the oppressed themselves, it cannot be complete until it has been institutionally registered and recognized. And, certainly in Western societies, liberation can only come from legal enactment by some institution that disposes of adequate legislative, administrative, and financial resources. Liberation can in the first instance only happen when it is recognized in both the law and in the attitudes of the members of society. States are more or less benign instances of liberatory agency because in politico-moral terms, they are thought to be relatively free from the worst of all motives—profit. Further, many states have signed up to declarations of rights, and are therefore committed to implementing them.

In the immemorial politico-moral struggle against the prejudices of inherited cultures (as the legend tells us), states are on the right side and can be nudged in the right direction by international institutions. The politico-moral project thus involves central direction; it is statist to the core. Perfectionists, however, have high standards, and they recognize that while states are indispensable to some aspects of liberation, they are by no means ideal. They may indeed be free of the profit motive but they remain tethered to the partialities of national interest, which may conflict with rights. They are thus not really partners of choice for the politico-moral movement.

Fortunately, other possibilities can be found. A new collective agent of liberation has emerged in the form of the so-called "Third Sector" in European states. The Third Sector consists of non-governmental organizations explicitly devoted to good causes, and guided not at all by interests but by ideas of justice and the relief of need. In all Western societies, NGOs have flourished, and they dispose of large cash resources, some of which is provided by governments themselves. They constitute a standing pressure group devoted to politico-moral causes. Economies are suspect as being animated by profit and greed, and states by the interests of their peoples. In the world of concerned voluntary bodies, however, perfectionism finds an agent much closer to its own ideals. These are bodies that generally respond to any governmental donative or proposal about (for example) environ-mental self-restraint with the cry: "Not enough! More! More!" They are just perfect, and perfectionists want to entrench them in world bodies as a recognized voice in world affairs.

Some NGOs have already established themselves in the higher terrain of a lucrative internationality. They may be offshoots of the United Nations, or the European Union, or the Organisation for Economic Cooperation and Development, or some similar body. They also have a judicial wing in international courts, and the great thing is that their deliberations are free not only from the profit motive, and from the distortions of national interest, but also from the shifting attitudes of democratic opinion. Here in internationality is evolving the machinery by which the ideal transformation of the world can be advanced, and it is already a focus of loyalty for many people in European states, a focus much more vivid than loyalty to the democratic states to which they actually belong.

The transfer of loyalty away from national states in the West and to international organizations is an element of that self-hatred that is such a remarkable feature of contemporary feeling. It often takes the form of an explicit hostility to patriotism as being a source of armed conflict. National loyalty is a powerful emotion commonly based on a montage of particular images, scenes from literature, fragments of historical anecdote, personal memories, and a discursive sense of belonging to "us" rather than to "them." The "them" are sometimes construed as bad or hostile, but this ele-ment of national feeling is often highly variable, deeply ambivalent, and may hardly exist at all. Alongside these vibrant particularisms will usually be found some universal element in which the *patria* stands for freedom, God, culture, or some other ideal entity. The politico-moral passion for internationalism discards all of these particularities as not merely contingent but often dangerous, since they are the passions that make it possible to mobilize a people for war. The internationalist intellectual seeks to transcend those local affections to which we are largely born, and recognizes as authori-tative only whatever might seem to be authorized by international bodies and whatever is declared in some set of rights, as if global responsibility created a higher form of rationality.

Here then is the general machinery of politico-moral perfectionism, and its aim is to liberate people—from ignorance, poverty, conflict, all forms of oppression indeed.

Liberation sounds like an excellent thing to experience, and we now have at least partial experience of what it actually involves. Take the case of children, who have enjoyed a great deal of liberation in recent generations. They enjoy their own specific rights and, in some countries, a commissioner with an agency whose remit is to implement those rights. And contemporary attitudes, modern technology, and market pressures have had vast and complicated effects on their lives. Hence it is difficult to disentangle entirely the effects of liberation on children from the many other changes in their circumstances.

Difficult, but perhaps not impossible, because it is the introduction of rights that has created a quite new situation. In possessing rights, children are in some degree distanced from the care of the mother and father, the teachers, police, and any others charged with responsibility for their welfare. When the Convention on the Rights of the Child mandates that states shall "protect the child from all forms of physical or mental violence, injury or abuse," it is declaring something no one would wish to contest, but which everyone would want to clarify. Is a parental slap "physical violence," and what constitutes mental violence? When, as demanded, governments legislate to clarify these aspirations, judges and inspectors are not far behind?[46] The child is being moved out of the family ambit of love into the legal framework of justice. As with all codifications, this no doubt saves some children from injustices, but it also invades the coherence of the family unit. Some enthusiasts for perfection want legislation to treat a didactic slap on the legs as an instance of violence and a punishable abuse. Discretion has been removed from the parent and entrusted to remote and abstract institutions. Here then is just one example of that propensity, central to our argument, which leads legislators to treat those they rule as being possibly malevolent incompetents—and by treating them as such, to edge them further toward just that reality.

The same treatment is accorded schoolteachers, whose use of the cane was long an important backdrop to the respect in which they were held. Teachers, no longer trusted to exercise authority with discretion, find themselves faced with a class of barrack-room lawyers, inhabiting a simplified world of permissions and prohibitions, and eager to insist upon their rights. A great deal of schooling among the less disciplined has, as a consequence, become a futile exercise in child minding. The disciplines that used to civilize children—parental, academic, vocational, and so on—have in many cases become unlawful, with bad effects on the capacity of children to apply their minds and control their conduct. In some areas, neighbors complain that the children have become "feral."

This situation supplies the materials with which we may develop a little further our exploration of the oppression-liberation nexus, the basic logic of which agitates the politico-moral version of perfectionism. In doing so, we may have recourse to the old Roman distinction between *auctoritas* and *potestas*. *Auctoritas* was the guidance given by experienced elders, and was the pre-eminent virtue of the senate in republican Rome. It was advice that only the foolish would ignore, but it was not command. Magistrates did not have to do what the senate advised, but generally they did. By contrast, magistrates had the power to enforce decisions. Now the role of parents and teachers (and often, in the past, policemen) was generally an exercise in a kind of authority understood in this Roman sense. It was, one might say, tutorial,[47] and it was a civilized relationship constituted of discretion on the part of the tutor and trust in the child. It is certainly true that some parents, and some teachers, have lacked such discretion—and also true that these cases make excellent material for Dickensian exposures of the brutal misuse of power, but speaking more generally, we may say that the very fact of being trusted itself *constituted* in some degree the discretion required. It is of this subtle and complex relationship that critics are thinking when many of our contemporaries lament the decline of trust in authority[*] today, for it has long been central to the way modern Europeans have lived. To destroy this nexus of trust, to treat authority as if it were no different from oppression, is to diminish one of the major resources of Western life, leaving us unprotected against a more brutish world in which the state claims to save us from the oppressions of social authority.

The mistrust of authority in these and many other cases responds to profound impulses in the politico-moral movement. One of those impulses is its aversion to the use of pain and fear in guiding human conduct, which is in effect the politico-moral rejection of punishment in favor of therapy and rehabilitation. Again, its ideal form of dispute-resolution is by way of talk or negotiation. The key to understanding what is going on is to recognize that authority resembles moral conduct in being one of those "soft" areas of our lives that are hard to protect against promises that more "acceptable" conduct can be *guaranteed* if only people surrender their discretion into the hands of a regulatory state. The destruction of authority in this sense is necessary to the extension of state power. It is, in other words, to facilitate the spread of servility.

Not all of this follows, as we have noted, merely from the liberation process itself. Children now spend vastly more time sitting in front of a television set or a computer screen, and their inactive lives are among the reasons why many are too fat. Families in which two parents are working are sometimes guiltily indulgent of their children in a way that their own parents were not indulgent of them. One result is that children become, at a much earlier age, less dependent on their parents, only to become more dependent on their "peer group." And dependence on the peer group is a servile relationship, whereas dependence on the parents is not. Peer

---

* This idea of authority needs to be distinguished from that of political philosophers such as Hobbes, for whom the authority (or legitimacy) of a state notionally depended on the act of self-obligating subjects. See *Leviathan*, esp. Chs. 13 and 14.

groups, in turn, have become increasingly sophisticated. At an ever-younger age, children come to understand the mechanics of the adult world without understanding its essence. Overconfident about their own maturity, they become detached from the family ethos and absorbed into the limited collective wits of their fellows of the same age. Peers are likely to share, sympathize with, and indeed largely determine what the young think and feel. Parental caution is trumped by the know-all child.

The outcome amounts to a destruction of childhood. The politico-moral liberation of children involves the loss of two barely visible sensibilities that long constituted the way we live. The first is trust in authority, a process in which children learned the elements of caution and prudence. The second has been a childhood that lasted into at least the middle teens. Such a long period of dependence on parental guidance gave children a reflective culture and a distinct individual view of the world, extensively colored (for better or worse, but often for better) by the immensely variable ethos of each family. In replacing this family involvement by the fragile and unreal autonomy exhibited by a new order of prattling manikins who have mastered adult patter without understanding either the pleasures or the problems of adult life, we have condoned a massive "superficialization" of our civilization.

4. THE POLITICO-MORAL FORM OF ASSOCIATION

What is the character of people who have been liberated from the supposed oppressions—some real, some imagined—of past times? What would a politico-moral society look like once achieved? At this point we must plunge into polemic about the relation between individuals (assumed to be distinct units) and the social system that, notionally, forms them. And the exercise will provide us with a remarkable contrast.

In order to bring out this contrast, we must begin from a standard belief about capitalist or commercial societies. They are thought to be guided by the principle of self-interest and concerned with a satisfaction of wants "ceasing only in death," as Hobbes crisply observed. Consumptionism and a mercenary concern with money and status are often added to this rather dire indictment.

In this world, the rich oppress the poor, but each individual is thought to be devoted to nothing more elevated than achieving an advantage over his neighbor.

Such people are conceived of as social atoms, alienated from each other. The bourgeoisie, as it is put in the *Communist Manifesto*, has "pitilessly torn asunder the motley feudal ties that bound man to his 'natural superiors,' and has left remaining no other nexus between man and man than naked self-interest, than callous 'cash payment.'"[48] This view, shorn of some of the melodramatic rhetoric, reappears in a great deal of modern normative political philosophy in which communitarian norms are advanced as an improvement on self-interest and conflicts over status. A sentimental view of feudal life is contrasted with the anxieties of the daily struggle to make ends meet. That this view corresponds to some reality ought, I suppose, to be granted simply because so many people believe it.

Such is the indictment. Will it stick? Two things may immediately be cited as invalidating this caricature of the essential capitalist. The first is that many of these vices—greed, arrogance, jockeying for position, and the rest of it—will be found in the conduct of many people in all societies. The idea that the social condition of capitalism causes them is plausible only to those who are as ignorant of history as they are innocent of anthropology.

The second refuting point is that this caricature gets the idea of self-interest wrong by identifying it with the vice of selfishness, a mistake that merely sets us up as suitable victims for a sermon on the virtue of altruism. Self-interest is in the individual sphere the analogue of national sovereignty in the political. It is the skill of making a rational judgment about the conditions of one's future happiness, and it therefore cannot help but incorporate a concern with the happiness of those whose lives will be affected by any course of action we may take. Self-interest must take seriously the interests of others, because those others in some degree affect the agent no less than he affects them. The spirit in which such a calculation is made no doubt varies from person to person, in some cases being generous and benevolent, in other cases calculating and mean. If one widens the focus of thought beyond this simple fact of experience, one would have to recognize that modern Western societies are marked not only by self-interested concerns but also by massive charitable and cultural endeavors. We would have to be extremely unfortunate not to experience a great deal of altruism and helpfulness. Our lives do not, I think, correspond to the image of human beings as alienated atoms full of mutual antipathy. The indictment clearly fails. That, of course, is the reason why millions of people from states supposedly awash with traditional communal values are so keen to get into our vile cash nexus in which all ties have been so pitilessly torn asunder.

As we shall see, this image of a capitalist society as composed of alienated atoms is untrue, but for reasons we shall come to, it is an interesting idea. In its ideological form, however, it is merely another of those accounts of how miserable and oppressed we are, and the function of these accounts is to mobilize us for submission to some perfectionist enthusiasm. It is a caricature of the world, and its validity ought to be judged by its main fruit—totalitarianism. We must, however, get the grand melodrama* out of the way in order to ask about the real character of modern individualists, who are involved, as I have described them, in a practice of the moral life. What are they in fact like?

The picture is, of course, mixed and ever changing, but far from being helpless social atoms, many of our contemporaries much of the time are complex moral and social entities, generally closely linked with both the families from which they came and to the families they themselves have set up. Every sane functioning human being in a modern society is the center of a network of relations of sympathy and antipathy. These people have ties to friends and colleagues, to employers, churches, and clubs, and they often have causes, political or charitable, to which they devote a great deal of time. Many of them volunteer to make sacrifices in pur-

---

* The grand melodrama does survive, of course, and its current version is epitomized in the aphorism from the film *Wall Street*: "Greed is good." And sometimes, in the politico-moral idiom, "greed" is said to be the animating motive of industrial enterprises. Greed, of course, is a vice, and hence this is the remarkable opinion that our whole economy is founded on just one vice. Mandeville, satirically, at least thought it was based upon quite a number of them.

suit of the enterprises they favor. In formal terms and for some purposes, such as social contract theory or voting, they may be imagined as single wills, but in substance each "individual" in our modern European states is a microcosm of much of society itself. To describe this condition in terms of the single relationship of a "cash nexus" is evidently absurd. The reality is dramatically different: far from being isolated atoms, these individuals can barely be distinguished from the commitments and affections of which they are composed. That is why they have hitherto revealed themselves as a set of people with a remarkable capacity for social creativity and for self-organization.

Consider the speed with which Europeans respond to some unforeseen crisis, and their remarkable capacity to understand very quickly in times of panic which duties they can usefully fulfill and which impulses they must control if the crisis is to be overcome. It is in part as a result of this set of virtues that we have, until recent times at least, been relatively free of corruption, particularly at its lower levels. My contention is, then, that these criticisms of the self-interested character of modern Europeans are precisely the opposite of the truth. "Naked self-interest" will often be found in traditional societies; it will be found everywhere, in fact, but in Europe it has been to some extent domesticated by our remarkable repertoire of "moralities."

Individualism thus lay at the root of the Western institution of civil society, and it is in the highest degree significant that the primary ambition of all ideological movements was to destroy that arena of autonomous self-creation in order to centralize all enterprise in the hands of a masterful state. Only that way could social perfection even be imagined. The man in the Kremlin, the Wilhelmstrasse, Whitehall, and the White House always knew best. With the collapse of the Soviet Union, it was widely recognized that the one thing despotism had fatally injured was the autonomous civil society that individualism has created. No one doubted that reconstituting it would not be easy. Indeed, this problem has become an increasing one for the Western world as a whole, because civil society has everywhere been eroded by governments subsidizing enterprises and trying to take them into something mischievously called "partnership." Enterprise has been "crowded out" by bureaucracy. These developments lead to individuals becoming dependent on the state. To say this is merely to restate, in a familiar form, my central argument. The point, then, is that the idea that modern individualists are merely rat-like competitors seeking to do each other down is precisely the opposite of the truth.

I have argued, then, that the theory of socially atomizing capitalism is false, and that it functions rhetorically as a way of persuading simple people to embrace one or other perfectionist adventure. In the last three paragraphs I have repeated my account of the individualist modern world, and the reason I have done so is to bring out the way in which the politico-moral has sought to undermine the moral life by the simple devices of pejorative re-description. In this way, we may begin to observe the curious "trans-valuation of values" that marks the rise of the politico-moral.

What are we to say, for example, of that family involvement, those "hooks" of responsibility so many of us feel for our nearest and dearest? The answer is that they are deplorable partialities that may lead some of us to become "pushy parents" seeking to send our children to better schools in order to give them a signifi-cant "social advantage" (as it is called) in life. This is bad because, especially if our children are rather bookish, we have a politico-moral duty to send them to the local school so that they may dif-fuse their "social capital" over the less accomplished or perhaps merely less fortunate children. Our duty is to be happy volunteers supporting the state's program of raising standards among the poor and the immigrants.

Again, some people have a deplorable disposition to restrict their spending in later life, so that they may pass on some resources to their children when they die. It is not at all a new opinion that children should be thrown out to make their own way in the world. Today, however, a new version of that judgment has become current: we ought not to bequeath money to our chil-dren because it is our duty to use it to advance the betterment of mankind. It is thought that the ability to dispose of unequal private resources that might put them in an unequal position is itself anti-social.

Consider another odd implication of the politico-moral, and one affirmed by organizations for multicultural equality. In enjoying our freedom, we pursue whatever commitments and responsibilities we have developed as we go through life, but what if our nexus of friendships has the wrong ethnic composition? Our friends might all be white, or brown, or might all belong to the same religion. In that case, our conduct falls under the category of prejudice and needs diversifying. Again, many of us support political causes, but some causes are ruled out of court as "extremist," and thus automatically outside the range of what would qualify us in politico-moral terms as decent human beings. And how do we ourselves live? Our often unhealthy lives may well be devoted to nothing more altruistic than cultivating our enthusiasms, learning new skills or hobbies, sketching, singing in choirs, and exploiting all the remarkable cultural resources Europeans have developed. Worse, many activities would include such selfish pleasures as foreign holidays, smoking, drinking, and much else that is deplorable. It may be that we are selfish enough not to care greatly about the millions of vulnerable people suffering in the world.

My comments might be thought ironic, but they are not. The point is that the simple politico-moral re-description reveals an immensely serious and important fact about the politico-moral: namely, that the current generation of human beings is largely unsuitable material for the basic moral project of our time, which is, of course, making a better world. And our unsuitability for the task lies precisely in our indulging all those prejudices and partialities that are expressions of the fact that we are free. Described one way, we are talking of the vitality of a civil society; described another way, we are talking of a population with so many personal projects, so "self-centered" in its inclinations, as to have relatively little interest in fighting against ignorance, poverty, and war. We have lives of our own to lead. What use are we in the grand business of transforming the world?

In politico-moral terms, this is a very serious question, and the answer lies in the demand that we ought to develop a more suitable consciousness of what the condition of human kind now requires. And we cannot begin to develop the right consciousness without detaching ourselves from those prejudices and partialities that constitute individuals as (in Marxist jargon) "social beings." And this we have seen is precisely what the politico-moral program seeks to do in advancing, as the criterion of virtue, the self-ishness-altruism distinction. This is not altruism, however, of the familiar kind. It must be specifically detached from our own personal affections and directed at abstract classes of need. Altruism is, as it were, "nationalized," so that it can be both morally and politically directed by a public opinion guided toward higher aspirations. We may put the basic point in Swiftian terms: the politico-moral command is that we must adore the abstraction "man" by detaching us from actual involvement with real men and women. Here is the source of one more of those paradoxes and incoherences of the grand ideal project of perfection. We have argued that the account of modern societies as full of atoms separated by the "cash nexus" is false. But the nationalization of altruism, with its attack on the partialities of our own lives, does actually tend to atomize modern societies.

For the odd result of this rationalized altruism is to erode the sociable individuality of the past and turn men and women into what are sometimes these days called "singletons."* This is a useful term whose core meaning is a person living alone rather than as part of some sort of family or other group. I want, however, to extend the term so that it covers not only the increasing number of people who, for one reason or another, do actually live alone, but also those who may indeed live with others but whose inner lives tend to be detached, and who are basically focused on projects for helping strangers. Their basic loyalty is to higher causes rather than to anything local. Their condition might be construed as a kind of isolation, or alternatively as a kind of independence of mind. Quite which of these corresponds to the reality

---

* The term comes, I gather, from Helen Fielding in *The Diary of Bridget Jones*.

is a very important question. The singleton tends to emerge from three important elements of contemporary Western life. I have discussed them all, but let us note them in turn.

Financial and family involvements and responsibilities are less crucial when the state can support individuals in times of need. State welfare provision need not be generous to have an influence on conduct at the margins, and it certainly changes individual terms of prudence in contemplating the future. Income for the individualist was traditionally understood as a resource to be prudently managed in an independent life; much of that management is now being done by the state and income approaches the status of pocket money. Its point is pleasure, indulging impulses. It may well seem odd that state benefits may play a role in developing a kind of alienation by which subjects are distanced from each other. In totalitarian states, of course, the isolation of individuals was achieved by terror: you could not trust strangers who might be working for the secret police. We achieve a milder version of the same thing by welfare. Welfare, by shrinking the risks of need an individual may face, diminishes our involvement with others.

The second isolating development comes from modern technology. Television, the computer, and the mobile telephone are striking instances of the decline of face-to-face social intimacies and contact. The role of convenience in allowing the abstraction of impulses to be quickly and precisely satisfied has already been discussed. Satisfaction in the past required a good deal of cooperation from others; today, money makes available to many immediate satisfactions only possible in earlier times for the most powerful.

The third element contributing to the emergence of the singleton is the rather diffuse influence of the manners and moral doctrines associated with the politico-moral itself. The ideal of equality has as its aim the supersession of all instances in which the situation determined which form of manners was appropriate. In the earlier world, good manners required that our bearing should be different when relating to women, to anyone in authority, to older people, teachers, colleagues, and friends.

These encounters were governed by varying conventions of respect because they accorded a different status to different sets of people. In politico-moral terms, however, these distinctions of status seemed to reveal inferiority/superiority, and thus seemed to be a kind of oppression. The ideal was to replace them with standard issue equality of manners. Anyone wanting to observe the consequences of this evolution of manners need only study the exciting scramble for seats that takes place in crowded public transportation among young and old, male and female alike. It can also be seen in the rights-based self-confidence found among many young people when relating to adults.*

The singleton began, of course, as a parodic sociological category reflecting the fact that in our societies increasing numbers of men and women live alone, sometimes because they had never married, sometimes because they had divorced. Becoming a singleton may be a destiny, or it may be a choice. For women who live alone with their children because the father, or fathers, of those children did not want to live with them, it was probably a destiny, and in many ways not at all an enviable one. But the typical singleton of choice, especially in youth, is often someone in flight from the bracing disciplines of family responsibility. More and more young men and women lead the lives of singletons for longer and longer stretches, and delay undertaking commitments to a later stage of life, if then. Since many at school had failed to master the basics of self-discipline, living entirely at their own convenience means that they end up even more the victims of impulse than they had previously been.

Putting these considerations together leads us to adumbrate a new conception of what it is in politico-moral terms to be a human being. Each person is indeed an individual, in the etymological sense of being a person distinguished from all others, and in social terms each is a kind of unit with two evident roles. The first of these is as a "unit of work," a potential employee, in which dis-

---

* Newspapers early in the twenty-first century were full of reports of the menace of teenage gangs and the dangers of intimidation by "feral" youths, especially in areas of public housing.

tinguishing features such as ethnicity or gender (which for other purposes are constitutive of a social role) must be treated as of no significance. Individuals may be distinguished only in terms of their ability to do some jobs rather than others, and sometimes not even then.

Each person should also be understood as what we might call a "eudaimonic unit," whose essence must be to find happiness and who will be equipped with an appropriate set of rights to do so. This aspect of the new world is sometimes understood by moral philosophers in terms of the conditions of human "flourishing." The happiness of people in experiencing these roles is becoming increasingly an area of governmental attention, often as measured by polling data.

The singleton, then, may be understood as an ideal type, as a kind of social atom in which these two elements, work and happiness, the week and the weekend as it were, are fused together into a way of life. And these units are atoms in the sense that their drive in life is often to avoid having what they take to be their freedom compromised by undertaking powerful commitments. Being human, of course, they often fail, but we may see their ideal development as functional to the perfectionist cause of improving society and the world, for it is obvious that modern creatures locked into the local affections of family, work, society, and a historically determined state are unlikely to be useful instruments of a perfecting cause. The engagements of such individualists are of a quite different kind.

5. CULTURE VERSUS IDEALS OF TRANSFORMATION

Relatively few people would quite fit this ideal type of the singleton, but generation by generation, in recent times, the numbers of singletons have grown, with notable consequences for our society. I am pointing to a trend. The trend results from many things, but one of them is the conflict between what we are actually like and what we would have to be like in order to transform society and the world.

The conflict, in other words, pits culture against abstraction, our ideals against what we actually are. Consider, for example, one influential version of liberation: that of women from the "tutelage" of fathers and husbands. The aim has been to bring women under much more extensive protection by the state, and the program could not have worked without a vast amount of legislation relating to employment, promotion, equity of returns, sexual harassment, maternity rights and leave, domestic violence, and a great deal else. Much improving propaganda has also been needed to persuade men to play their part in this new world of "domestic democracy."

We may suggest that the amount of regulation needed to achieve some specific liberation measures whether it fits our sentiments or not. The more regulation needed, the more perverse the transforming ambition is. The central issue in the case of women was whether domestic life was a form of oppression or not, and the liberation proposed consisted in nothing more imaginative than a demand that women should be allowed into the economy on the same terms as men. Such a change was by the 1960s already in train, but the demand made was that society should undergo the perfecting required if it were to conform to the abstract model of liberation in which no distinction might be made between men and women. As units of work, they were by legislative fiat declared identical with men. In some areas, this was to create a fantasy world. Over a large range of skills, women are no less intelligent than men, but they are weaker, shorter, and generally less aggressive, which makes them good at some things but not at others. As soldiers in the field, they are absurd, and they are not much better in front-line policing. Most of them have little desire to engage in these unlikely professions.

What might this example tell us about the emergence of the singleton? It cannot but be seen as a project to turn women, and therefore men as well, into basically identical and interchangeable units of production whom employers (within certain limits) must value in exactly the same way. In some areas, women were much better than men, in others, rather worse. The test of reality in commercial relationships is a function of employer preference and the price of labor. The radical program of "gender equality" that was imposed by the state on the economy required incessant coercion of employers to make them fit the ideal. There is, however, an important sense in which culture is reality, and the ideal is fantasy.

The liberation of women might be dogmatically advanced simply as elementary justice, and at that point discussion would have to stop. But the more plausible view had to be that it was a response to what all or most women wanted, and to what men too would want if they could be released from the false consciousness of patriarchy, their delusions of oppressive power. Many women, however, did not want to "go out to work." They preferred to manage households. But as the supply of women eager to take jobs increased, so the rewards to labor went down, and many women were forced into jobs so that the family could make ends meet. Another unforeseen consequence was that the discontents of women were now replaced by a problem with men. Some boys rejected school as being "feminine" because educational institutions began to favor steady reliable work rather than a flashy performance in end-of-year examinations, the former system apparently suiting girls better than boys. Some young males took to aggressive machismo because they no longer had the respect of a good woman. We thus found ourselves in a radicalized world in which the distribution of misery and happiness changed greatly, but probably not the relative quantities of each. Whether it was a net advance or not could hardly be judged. It certainly seemed true, however, that the discontents of today could not be solved by returning to the discontents of yesterday. Every time conventions erode, new impulses and demands are released.

Another set of beneficiaries from liberation were homosexuals, now free from the persecution and stigma from which they had suffered in the past. There can be few Europeans (there are vast numbers of non-Europeans) who would wish to reverse this movement. The essence of "gay lib," however, again illustrates the point that a reforming codification of rights merely sacrifices the associated virtues of freedom. Sexuality in European societies is essentially part of the private world. The homosexual in the closet preserved his ambiguity, and his options, one option in particular being that he might for long not actually have, and need not express, a clear sexual preference. The variety of human responses is such that clear binary distinctions destroy the restraints and hesitations that in past times sometimes worked well and sometimes badly. Gay lib, by contrast, became a lobby group and an evangelizing movement eager to lock into gayness at an early age some young people for whom the irresponsibilities of homosexual life might well be less demanding than the disciplines of family life. There is a certain vulgarity about celebrations of gay pride that certainly repelled many fastidious homosexuals (Noel Coward being a notable example) in the past. If one's notion of responsibility includes a concern with the continuance of our civilization, then there is a clear conflict between such responsibility and the advancing of homosexuality as an equally valid sexual option to heterosexuality.

These considerations may be summed up as the recognition that the drive of the politico-moral is to create a world of individuals detached as far as is practical from their inherited loyalties and affections. Children become in important respects wards of the state, women in their capacity of units of production are governed by a legal structure that cuts across the instinctive chivalric relationships on which societies have previously drawn. The state has largely withdrawn its recognition from marriage as an institution to be protected as constituting the very society we inhabit, and thus opened human life further to the ceaseless drumbeat of impulse and its satisfactions. Detached from inherited partialities and prejudices, individuals enjoy as rights a license to indulge in whatever inclinations they might experience.

But what of the moral world? What is the place of right and wrong? I have insisted that human beings are irreducibly moral, and therefore this account of people as focused entirely on maximizing their satisfactions cannot be the whole story. Nor, of course, is it the whole story. For one thing, the politico-moral simplification of the moral world in terms of rights, and of the selfishness/altruism dimension, creates a standardized reference point for moral sensibilities, understood here as behaving generously and altruistically toward abstract classes of people. For another, governments manage attitudes by running campaigns seeking to influence conduct on everything from wearing seat belts to the proper use of condoms. Such campaigns certainly carry the sense of a responsibility that might be thought "moral." One new form of moral approval revolves around the semantics of "acceptability." How effective these campaigns are in sustaining social order must be a central question in understanding the way our states are developing, for there is little doubt that over the longer term, disorder has been increasing.

Some orderly conduct no doubt is a response to official campaigns, but the basic causes of moral and social order in European states undoubtedly still rest on restraints surviving from the individualist moral life. A shadowy recognition of this fact lies in the distinction between the "middle classes" as characterized by a certain amount of social capital, and the underclass implicated in so-called "anti-social" behavior—some of it being unmistakably evil and criminal. Many remnants of moral sensibility have been translated out of moral language into social terminology. Virtuous morals and good manners are often packaged together in an unreflective way as forms of "socially acceptable" and "socially unacceptable" behavior. If that source of order begins to run dry, then the prospects of disorder would be rather menacing.

The language of social responsibility and of social capital, misleading as it is, does fit the conduct of individuals understood as distinct units of human life living under the control of the state. Understood in this way as social creatures, they are assumed to acquire their moral sensibilities from "social conditions" rather than from participating in deliberative moral agency. And this basic point brings us back to the contrast I trailed at the beginning of the previous section. The contrast is between the mistake made by socialist critics of modern capitalist societies in thinking of those societies as "atomizing" their populations on the one hand, and the fact that these very critics of capitalism are now achieving exactly that result in their drive to perfect the human world.

The alienated victim of capitalism was not, in fact, an isolated social atom, because his conduct emerged from the immensely complex involvements he had with others. On the other hand, the communal paragon of the politico-moral world actually is a kind of atom, because he has been persuaded to withdraw his affections from an increasing range of inherited attachments such as patriotism and chivalry. The new doctrine construes this detached condition as a liberation from prejudice that facilitates embracing ideas that have survived the test of argument and evidence. It is, however, simply false that prejudice and rationality can be sharply divided in a world in which judgments about contingent events must inescapably be situational. In this arena, people convinced of the superior rationality of their opinions tend to become tedious and dogmatic. Their opinions are, in any case, over a large area of judgment the standardized responses we have been considering as the politico-moral. Outside those areas, as we have seen, politico-moral people seem prone to indulging impulses toward abstract enjoyments. They think in short-term ways. Contemplating the generality of conduct early in the twenty-first century, and comparing it with that of Anglophone populations (for example) a century before, many will judge that courage, independence of mind, and practical prudence are less commonly found. And this judgment suggests a further contrast between individual and collective realities. A population collectively given over to more ambitious perfections seems to be individually less morally admirable. These people, in their responsiveness to abstract compassion, may be suitable instruments of the project of perfecting the world, but they are hardly themselves paragons of perfection. Is this paradoxical? Indeed it is, but it results from a contradiction within the logic of perfectionism.

The emergence of the singleton is the long-predicted social atomization of Western societies. It has resulted not from capitalism, but from the drive to mobilize human beings as instruments of transforming the human condition. The ideal, no doubt, is that those dedicated to transforming the world should, as it were, instrumentalize themselves, in ways analogous to the self-dedication of those in religious orders. Atomization has always in general been regarded with dismay; it is what socialists mean by "alienation." It signifies a thinness of character. It is necessary, however, if Western societies are to focus their energies on perfecting society and the world. For that project cannot get far if it has to accommodate individuals with their own lives to lead.

We may well doubt, of course, whether the perfectionist project will ever get very far, because human waywardness will never be overcome. But equally, among the many currents of human sentiment now agitating the Western world, the politico-moral crusade is immensely powerful, and will undoubtedly be a voice in our moral dissensions for a long time to come. The didactic programs in which states increasingly indulge may in these terms be recognized as a training in responsiveness to higher callings. For the point of social atoms, in either totalitarian or welfarist versions, is that they are extremely biddable. They can be persuaded with remarkable ease to take up the admirations and rejections rulers may suggest to them.

In at least one crucial respect, however, this whole project has misunderstood the essential conditions of virtue. We may take as our text an off-the-cuff remark of the philosopher Martha Nussbaum discussing "anti-social" behavior as contrasted with what social psychologists sometimes call "pro-social behavior." The issue arose in discussion of the famous Zimbardo experiment at Stanford, in which a random set of young men were arbitrarily distinguished for the period of the experiment into prisoners and guards. The situation was deliberately structured to resemble totalitarian camps rather than Western prisons, and very rapidly the conduct of the "guards" became so oppressive that mental disorder forced an early end to the experiment. The conclusion would seem to be that evil and aggressive conduct is endemic in human nature and is highly responsive to the situations individuals find themselves in. Discussing a new book (*The Lucifer Effect*) by Philip Zimbardo, the social psychologist who set up the experiment, Professor Nussbaum ended on an upbeat note: "Let us hope that *The Lucifer Effect*, which confronts us with the worst in ourselves, stimulates a critical conversation that will lead to more sensible and less arrogant strategies for coping with our shared human weakness."[49]

I don't quite know what "sensible and less arrogant strategies" might be, but I do know that while humility generates some virtues, there is also a vital connection between arrogance and virtue. Why is it that most people behave decently? No doubt in part because of the fact that they are decent and virtuous people. They may well also fear the consequences of bad conduct. "The passion to be reckoned on," as Hobbes remarks, "is fear."[50] But one of the other main bases of virtue lies in the fact that people think, with a certain contempt and derision: "I wouldn't do that evil (base, etc.) kind of thing. I am above such conduct." Some moralists consider such moral arrogance as itself a vice. The ability to understand oneself in such moral terms, however—as a "lady" (rather than merely a woman), or as a "gentleman," or even as an honest person, indeed even as being merely common or garden decent—commonly rests in part on feeling superior to others. In other words, virtue often depends not on humility but on arrogance.[51] Saints may be in a different class, and it may indeed be "the worst treason" for Thomas à Becket "to do the right thing for the wrong reason," but ordinary mortals do the right thing for a whole variety of complex reasons, and one of them is commonly a sense of their superiority to the weak, foolish, or perhaps evil things done by others.

Professor Nussbaum, then, seems to me to get the matter precisely wrong. She makes the elementary mistake of thinking that all goods are coherent, and entirely distinct from evils. Her very remark suggests that she herself feels above what, with some degree of artificial humility, she calls "our shared human weakness." No doubt we ought to feel humility and remorse about the fact that we all on some occasions behave badly, but as a "strategy" for rising above our baser instincts this is a plan for saints. Much of virtue has to do with habit; and some virtue depends on a recognition that vicious conduct is likely in many circumstances to be self-defeating. Victorian moralists were keen that people should avoid occasions of sin, and there can be little doubt that some situations are morally more dangerous than others. No doubt a little humility is necessary to anyone who has power over others. But it is not a plausible foundation for all virtues.

Those Victorian moralists advocating moral alertness to danger were especially concerned about women, on whom the duty rested of avoiding occasions when they might be in danger, and this highlights a further oddity of the politico-moral world. The liberation of women means that women ought to be able to exercise their rights with the same freedom as men, and that freedom in turn means being able (for example) to walk down dark and deserted streets in the middle of the night without being raped or molested, even when having drunk immoderate quantities of alcohol. And indeed this is an entirely reasonable demand to be made on "society." On the other hand, it is extremely difficult to see how such a guaranteed protection of women could be achieved. Walking late at night in isolated situations, women are in fact vulnerable to violent men, as are women half seas over with booze. No society can provide protection in every unlikely situation. In a perfect world, perhaps, this would be no problem. In our own world, however, it leads to highly contestable disputes in sexual relations about whether consent did or did not take place. For women to enjoy this supposed right, either constant vigilance and security must be provided (by men, in general) or the nature of males would have to be transformed. Neither of these conditions is going to be achieved in a hurry. In other words, there is a trade-off between the security of women on the one hand, and the costs to society on the other. The point is merely another illustration of one of our central themes: society and individual wellbeing are at different levels of practice, and that what is good for one need not be good for the other.

We may summarize this argument by saying that the politico-moral individual is a radically simplified creature, stripped of fixed tastes or affections for friends and family in order to be highly responsive to the needs of perfection. Such a person is, as it were, at the beck and call of abstract need; he has no prejudices arising merely from the familiar. He confronts the world with a standard moral component called "ethics," which is in principle equally responsive to all vulnerabilities. Nor does the complexity of his consciousness privilege even the literature of his country. Shakespeare, Racine, Goethe, and their analogues are dead white males concerned with the particular affections of unregenerate individualists whose "affections" are basically the superficial gloss over oppression and the exercise of power. Politico-moral tastes include world music, art, and literature, and there is no place for preferring what is merely our own, and especially for what has emerged from our highly imperfect past.

If this generalized account of the character of an ideal politico-moral person corresponds at all to reality, it reveals a most remarkable fact about perfection. We normally think that those working to improve the world would participate in the ideal improvement they seek to actualize. Each reformer, one might expect, would share in the perfection of the whole. But what we confront is a perfection of aspirations combined with a deficiency of moral engagement.

What is to be admired in human beings is, of course, no less contestable than any other moral issue. Improving the world as a project requires a sensitivity to the guidance of those above us, which we might alternatively view as servility. Just as some virtues depend on a vice such as arrogance, so some vices may well be needed for perfection. Idealists in power have a record of engaging in deception and ruthlessness. In this form, the paradox is that achieving perfection, if it were possible at all, depends on imperfections. To be an instrument of some cause is to sacrifice individuality as the exploration of individually self-chosen commitments. Outside this arena, however, idealists may indulge their inclinations, though even these may have to be guided by the authority of the perfectionist cause. Neither love nor hate should disturb their emotionally placid surface, for their deepest involvement would be the collective project for transforming the world. Indeed, were one looking for a concrete model of such a person, it might be found in the image of the wartime collaborator, always ready to fall in with the demands of power.

As is often the case, we may track some elements of the advance of the politico-moral by following the semantics. One of the interesting developments of modern political discourse has been the multiplication of abstract words that express concepts whose meaning has been entirely divorced from any of the relationships that would give it substance. There is no doubt that the prize specimen of this new linguistic form is "unacceptable." It seems to be a pejorative so indispensable that no one hearing it wants to raise niggling questions about who is refusing to accept what on what grounds. The act is—well, simply—unacceptable! Consider also, "affordable." To whom, we might wonder, at what price, under what conditions? Or "sustainable," in the discussion of climate change. I look forward to the day when police forces advising how to defeat thieves talk about "stealables." And in the politico-moral world, only the right things are "thinkables." This manner of speaking about power is paralleled by the remarkable rise of the idea of "governance" as a set of rules that are simply appropriate, just there, more or less untouched by vulgar politics or by sovereign power.

If the world consists of persons and things, as philosophers often aver, then the simplification of the character of persons might be expected to lead to a compensating new complexity in the things, actions, and especially states of affairs. Perhaps that is just what is happening now.

6.   PERFECTION AND THE AMBIVALENCE WORLD

We might seem to have arrived at a very strange result. The politico-moral crusade to perfect the world makes European individuals better in some terms, but distinctly worse in others. Social perfection seems to demand individual imperfection. Why is it that such a grand program for improving the world should require what we are likely to regard as a dehumanizing atomization? Admittedly, our current judgments will be those of the modern individualist mindset, which admires personal autonomy more than single-minded dedication, but our instinctive sensibilities suggest that the inhabitants of a perfect society ought to be correspondingly more perfect people. Why would our idealists have to be, in terms of our own particular moral admirations, worse rather than better people?

The answer is because they are denying the basic reality on which modern Western civilization is based. The politico-moral, in fusing together moral and political criteria, affirms over a large range of public policies that there is only one right thing to do—or should we say?—one "correct" thing to do. Perfections are monistic. They demand action rather than debate, and the action consists in applying the right principle. Politically, there is only one right way of ordering civil life, and it is *democracy*. Morally, there is only one right relationship between persons, and that is *equality*. Socially, there is only one right way of relating one group to another, and that is *inclusion*. And all of these principles to be applied serve the one overriding perfection, which is in one sense or another, *justice*.

We ought perhaps to add one other overriding principle of the politico-moral version of perfection: there is only one right emotional attitude toward others, which is *compassion*. This follows from the inclusion principle, which diagnoses one of the imperfections in our inherited world as a deficiency in essentially feminine values. Pains and punishments are barbaric, merely outmoded masculine moral devices that fail to improve the character of those who suffer them. The new order of things is based on compassion, and the instincts of mothers rather than fathers are needed. The principle invoked is one of understanding (rather than coercion) but it will be understanding tainted by doctrine: *tout comprendre, c'est tout resoudre*.

It is the monism of perfectionism that makes it clear why the politico-moral is ultimately at war with our individualism. Individualism, and its correlate the moral life, are pluralistic. Indeed, we can only understand this situation if we bring out the fact that our modern Western civilization has developed as a response to one of the basic features of human experience that has, in other civilizations, been almost entirely suppressed throughout human history. In suppressing this reality, virtually all other cultures have sought to live in terms of a concrete system of order in which there is, in given circumstances, only one true value to espouse, and one right thing to do. The customs, and generally the religions, of non-Western cultures have been devoted to making the right way of living the only "thinkability" allowed. This has never, of course, succeeded in avoiding dissension, conflict, and division, but it has always provided the touchstone by which such conflicts would have to be resolved. And in saying this, we are merely observing that *all* ways of life, except our own modern life,

THE SERVILE MIND **319**

tend to be "politico-moral." They are politico-moral in a variety of different ways, but they all share the basic monistic principle, in which evil is deviation from the norm.

The reality on which Western life is based, by contrast, is the recognition of *ambivalence*. At every level of consciousness, contradictory tendencies are, in our institutions, balanced and held in some sort of tension within a structure of laws and conventions. Ambivalent responses to the world are not at all lacking, of course, in all human life, but the general rule, one might almost say the normal human instinct, has been one of conformity to the obligatory thoughts, feelings, and acts sustained by the currently dominant order. Nor is such a rule or instinct lacking in European culture, but the West is no less ambivalent about that than it is about everything else. It is in being able to combine an explicit recognition of ambivalence with a capacity for self-ordering conduct that European life has developed its enormous range and vitality. Ambivalent attitudes are not costless; they can lead to conflicts that are dangerous if they should erupt into hostility and war, and conflict in European life has often done so. Yet suppressing ambivalence in the hope of achieving conformity is no less a gamble. It merely forces the element of struggle and conflict inseparable from human life into other channels.

The Western recognition of ambivalence expressed, for example, in political competition, means that rulers cannot be totally identified with the universal good of the state, for they must also recognize themselves as one particular party or tendency within the politics of the country, accountable and limited in their powers. What any government in power for the time being enacts is, ideally, a kind of synthesis of conflicting tendencies that will not long last unless it also calls up some sympathy in political opponents who are themselves likely to come to power before very long. Again, judges do not declare the universal truth of a divinely ordained system of values, for they are bound by precedent, and by the evidently fallible judgments of the counsel, and sometimes the juries, that appear before them. Priests and clergymen cannot quite be taken seriously as declaring the will of God and the indispensable conditions of salvation, because even the spiritual sphere is an arena of faith, and faith is not to be identified, either in content or form, with the limitations of one particular creed, for we have evolved lots of creeds. Wherever one looks in Western life, competition abounds, and this is not, as Plato thought and other cultures often assume, a regrettable intrusion of the passions into a rational and orderly system; it is part of our very conception of both life itself and the place of reason within it.

It follows that the essence of the moral life, and indeed the social life of Europeans, is limitation. Modern European life is lived in a context of criticism and contestation that clearly marks the limits of power and qualifies the reality of the values any particular person lives by. We often understand persons in terms of their negations. In not being heroic, treacherous, witty, thoughtful, etc., their positive features may appear. Hegel's term for this feature of the European personality—"self-related negativity"—is a wonderful bit of jargon, but the central idea is simple enough. The will contains "an element of pure indeterminacy" but "in positing of itself as something determinate, the ego steps in principle into determinate existence." The moment we are about to speak, or act, belongs (in Hegel's curious terminology) to a universal world in which anything might happen, but the moment we actually speak or act, we have said or done this rather than that. "The will is the unity of both these moments. It is particularity reflected into itself and so brought back to universality, i.e., it is individuality." To act can be nothing else than to particularize ourselves, and it is this junction of the universal and particular that constitutes individualism as Hegel construes it.[52]

Augustine made the point about limitation and reality perhaps more simply: the person, like the poet, can only create by embracing the limitation—in the poet's case, of form, in the person's case, of morality. Just as the power of poetry depends on submission to forms such as rhyme and rhythm, so also personality is the cultivation of the inevitable limitations of each human being. To recognize this limited and fallible character we have is to understand that it is only in cooperating with others, engaging in a range of different activities, that we can successfully cultivate whatever projects we have chosen to espouse. Freedom means, in part, that these projects will be self-chosen. Moralists sometimes talk about the desirability of individuals "realizing their potential," but realizing potential is, strictly speaking, an activity for Aristotle's acorns. The acorns can only grow into oak trees, but human beings are forever meeting forks in the road, and to follow one is to renounce the other. The formula of "potentiality" fashionably— indeed politico-morally—reduces the human to the organic. Individuals may have many "potentialities," but they also suffer from opportunity costs. In pursing one line of development, as they must, they make themselves into a specific, limited something. A certain practical humility becomes our default virtue in recognizing our limitations.

This recognition of personal reality as limitation is a condition of the way in which Western societies have turned the division of labor into a device for creating institutions of immense strength and complexity. The complaint of political-moral critics is that we are competitive rather than cooperative; greed is a vice that pits each of us against others. We have our vices, no doubt, but we have also created modes of cooperation beyond the dreams of other cultures. In many civilizations, each person has a fixed identity as priest, merchant, soldier, scholar, etc., but Europeans may play any of these roles, and in situations of disaster, often do. The manager will help on the factory floor, and the butler may rule his island realm as did the Admirable Crichton. Ernest Gellner compared this flexibility of roles in Western life to the modularity of household furniture that can be arranged and rearranged.[53] Limitation in Europeans thus has the character of *reculer pour mieux sauter*, and the classic image of this mixture of limitation and enterprise is, of course, the story of Robinson Crusoe.

The source of this flexibility of roles in our civilizations is our recognition that we may respond to anything in the world according to very different and often contradictory emotions. *Ambivalence* characterizes the fact that as we go through life, our responses to people, situations, and events are seldom univalent, especially over time. We commonly experience, among other things, oscillation between admiration and contempt, delight and boredom, like and dislike, and any other set of contradictories one likes to mention. No doubt love is sometimes total, for a time, but continued contact is certain to generate hesitations and critical responses. Hate is seldom unaffected by circumstances; the death of an enemy may be a cause for regret. At any given moment, we may wish to preserve forever the feelings we have, but a time will come when we look back and wonder what we were thinking. Marcel Proust is the virtuoso, perhaps one should say the poet, of ambivalence in his recognition that in yearning to turn contingent moments into absolutes, we indulge an illusion. No feeling of the moment can ever be preserved forever unchanged. Modern Europeans are Heracliteans; they live in a world of flux, and they recognize it as such. This is the basis of one of our most powerful vehicles of rationality: the psychological experience we call a "realization," usually a gift of hindsight, and one that usually comes too late to save us, but is an indispensable part of our deliberative resources.

Significantly, ambivalence is virtually inescapable in our understanding not only of individuals, but also of different categories of people. Consider the relations between men and women: they are obviously complementary and ideally characterized by love, delight, and admiration on both sides. Sometimes they actually are. In some moods, the other sex is essential, in others merely tiresome to have around. Men not only love women but also deride them, regard them as silly and emotional, preoccupied with frills and furbelows, and often worryingly unpredictable in their responses. These qualifications are fully reciprocated by women, for whom men are brutish, insensitive, emotionally illiterate, and often very boring in their addiction to spectator sports and toys like motorcars. Individual variations are, of course, immense, but both critics are, of course, right. Men and women are both awful. And the result is that in this area, as in all others, life is the art of surfing or navigating our ambivalences.

Consider, again, our responses to other ethnic groups. They vary greatly, and they range from the positive to the negative. We may admire blacks as authentic and noble, but dislike Asians as commercial and on the make. Jews provoke powerful emotions in some people, and the British have two gears, one of approval and another of disapproval, for all the more prominent nations of the European continent. Continentals take the same ambivalent view of us. And lots of Continentals have a single general response to Yanks, encompassing all the varied inhabitants of North America. A phenomenology of all these antipathies is part of human folly, and no less part of the comedy of life. It provides the materials for an endless stream of jokes. On the other hand, countries can fall apart, and horrible things can happen if these sentiments should become enthusiasms and turn into public policies.

For the most part, these generalized responses are highly provisional, because any sophisticated person will recognize that there are interesting and admirable people to be found in all these categories, along with many people we would strongly prefer to avoid. In surfing or navigating these ambivalences, we in the West generally have recourse to the clear pronouncements of good manners, and those dictate that we should respond to individuals according to the qualities they actually exhibit, and that where our responses are negative, we should conceal them and at least treat such people decently, merely avoiding their company where we can.

Manners, then, are an important part of the skills we develop in surfing the ambivalences we experience, for we respond to those we do not like not according to our feelings but according to our sense of decorum. This is the sense in which a kind of hypocrisy is necessary in Western life, and indeed no doubt in all human life.

It might seem from the argument I am advancing that political correctness, which demands that we should equally respect people of all backgrounds and perhaps even think that all cultures are equally valuable, would merely be an expression of good manners. It is, in fact, very different, indeed virtually the opposite. The basic point is that manners respond to ambivalence, but political correctness is a department of univalence in that it tries to suppress the possibility of conflict altogether. Human beings actually respond to other groups by generalizing particular experiences, whereas political correctness, as a form of the politico-moral, seeks to impose a single *thinkability* on those whose conduct it tries to control. One principle solves all problems: all peoples are equal, and equally valuable. They are not, of course, and no one really believes it. In terms of such things as demands on welfare, criminality, public spirit, and intellectual capacity, some cultures are far ahead of others. Again, for some purposes, men and women, according to their individual talents, are interchangeable units of production in performing some task. For other tasks, this clearly is not the case.

One important problem of this strange psychological technology of correctness is that those who cannot deal with ambivalence also cannot deal with the fact that other people, because they make different judgments, live other lives. Communism, for example, was a version of the politico-moral that could only work if the whole world shared its admirations (not to mention its defects), and it collapsed simply because everybody knew, in the immortal words of Shakespeare's Coriolanus, that "there is a world elsewhere." It was a realization that made populations locked into a rhetoric of "true community" deeply ambivalent, and it was a fatal piece of knowledge that communist rulers could not quite suppress. This feature of all supposedly universal moralities corresponds to the fact that highly despotic societies, in which right conduct is strictly prescribed, can only work if their luckless subjects believe that there is no other way of life. This is part of the reason why traditional societies are so vulnerable to Western contact. The regime of a brutish state like North Korea can only survive in the long term if it can prevent its people from knowing about the world outside.

Manners are a skill, while political correctness is a drill, in some cases actually the result of some bizarre process called "sensitivity training." No doubt good manners themselves may become so much a matter of second nature that they are habitual, as Max Beerbohm dramatized in the story of "The Happy Hypocrite." In that sense, they come to resemble a conviction that there is only one right thing to do. But manners, like the moral life, never cease to be a form of response called forth by unpredictable situations. And it is that skill that is threatened by the politico-moral, in its demand that we should transcend the ambivalent and find salvation in a single correct principle.

7. WHAT KIND OF THING IS THE POLITICO-MORAL?

Finally, let us step back a little, and consider in this section what *kind* of thing the politico-moral is. And in the following section, I shall argue that it constitutes a major crisis in the spirit of Western life, even a kind of civil war.

In one sense, the politico-moral is simply a doctrine about the current condition of the world, along with arguments about what needs to be done to improve it. It has a grand vision, which we discussed at the beginning of Chapter IV. It seeks to banish inequality from society and ignorance, poverty, and war from the world. In one sense, it is the purest expression of the democratic revolution in our lives, standing for the ultimate repudiation of the old hierarchies and forms of conflict. And it is "democratic" in the familiar elitist sense of believing that what the global demos ultimately wants, indeed "must" want, is the same kind of welfarist world we have created in the West. In other words, as with all projects of democracy as perfection, its public relations are far more democratic than its actual practice.

The politico-moral is, however, more than a doctrine: it is a *movement*, which is to say a mixture of argument and sensibility that "takes people up," generates enthusiasms and specific plans and proposals, runs into conflicts with other movements of thought, becomes an important part of the self-understanding of particular individuals, and determines, in barely conscious ways, their views of the world. It can become a vehicle of righteousness and dogmatism, and it can reveal to people aspects of the world they had not previously considered.

As a movement, its practical drive is to convert modern states into enterprise associations, in the Oakeshottian sense.[54] An enterprise association is a state in which a whole society is managed so as to achieve some collective end, such as victory in war.

Enterprise associations are distinguished by Oakeshott from civil associations, in which associates, under law, are free to pursue their own projects. In these roles, the politico-moral is an apparatus of justification and condemnation. From some points of view, it might well be seen as a kind of religion, with affiliations to paganism and vegetarianism, and an outlook particularly sensitive to the vibrations of the idea that the planet is basically organic, a kind of creature, called Gaia. It is particularly attractive to certain types of high-minded clergymen. The idea of a crusade is closer to the essence of the matter than its generally secularist supporters would like. Its ramifications in extending ideas of justice into all corners of life have as yet hardly been fully explored: international and intergenerational justice is merely the beginning of it. It will espouse any conception of justice that might promise to save a divided mankind, riven by conflict and mutual hatred, by turning it into a single harmonious community. Most striking are its sympathies and antipathies: sympathy toward international organizations, and antipathy toward moral individualism, along with a suspicion that objectivity and rationality tend to serve the interests of the powerful.

It is by virtue of this complex character that the politico-moral stands for so much of what we think, feel, and value today. It belongs to our marvelously free and informal world in which we relate to others as uncomplicated equals. Western life early in the twenty-first century remains remarkably pleasant and agreeable. Many qualifications would have to be made to this proposition, but amidst an untroubled material abundance, we commonly live long lives and have the freedom to pursue most projects that interest us. Most of us have no fear of authority, however irritating the increased regulation we must endure sometimes is. It is our very insouciance about the rising levels of surveillance and control, and the decline of integrity, that reveal how little wariness there remains in our understanding of our civilization as free. The arrival of real servility will be something of a surprise to us.

Our very insouciance is partly based on the illusion that the agreeable things we enjoy have emerged from a repressive and unjust past, and we periodically consider how we may further improve our ethical superiority. Our world is alive with high and low culture, and a restless technology is forever producing delightful novelties and gadgets. All these things contribute to an agreeable sense of movement, of progress. We have learned to formulate our condition as one in which we enjoy rights. Most conflicts in our own political life have given way to mediation, and the politico-moral aversion to pain, frustration, and punishment has made life easier for most people, including no doubt for those inclined to delinquency. That our social arrangements present us with things called "problems," and that the thing to do with problems is to solve them, now seems to us the merest common sense. Many of us seldom experience the skeptical cautions that made the conservatives of an earlier generation wary. We are all, that is to say, involved in one aspect or another of the politico-moral view of the human condition.

Yet it is precisely this ease and informality of manners that might trigger a recognition that our contentment is precarious. We live with each other largely on Christian-name terms, which seems to reveal our lack of arrogance, our automatic friendliness. That there is an element of illusion in this practice, however, might be guessed from the fact that we now also refer to our rulers by their Christian names—Maggie, Tony, Bill, Dubya, Gordon, Barack, Dave, etc.—yet *they* are certainly not our intimates. Such an apparently democratic practice in no way qualifies the reality that rulers are remote from us, that their "mateyness" is pretense, and that the considerations they have in mind are very different from ours. The contentment of the better off in Western societies is paralleled by the problems of assimilation experienced by a rapidly rising population of immigrants, and a diminishing moral stability in the less well off. Our lives are increasingly managed by politicians and bureaucrats who at international, national, and local levels are all becoming more intrusive. In other words, the continuing rise in the rate of regulations to which we are subject measures the increasing distance between our culture (which is all the things we are unthinkingly inclined to do) and the abstract rules that power and authority impose on us.

8. THE MORAL LIFE AS THE PURSUIT OF IDEALS

The politico-moral is a grand project for creating a better world. It has raised its sights above matters of vice and virtue, above issues of personal integrity and other such elements of the moral life, and it has focused on the condition of mankind as a whole. It is a form of idealism arguing that most evils in the world, such as war, massacre, and intolerance, result from bad social conditions, such as poverty, ignorance, and oppression. This is a project often formulated as bringing basic human rights to the millions in the world who lack those rights. It is hard, though not impossible, to deny that, were this project to succeed, we should live in a better world. How, indeed, could one deny the desirability of such an improvement of human life unless we admitted that we lacked the elementary decency to sympathize with the sufferings of others? Such is the moral challenge that politico-moral idealism presents to us.

The politico-moral idealist clearly commands the high moral ground in such a discussion. Ordinary human concerns about making ends meet and dealing with difficult associates look insignificant in comparison. Some exponents of the grand project these days go on to criticize foreign holidays, or indulging in an extra bottle of wine over an elaborate dinner, as mere selfishness.[55] A whole new conception of the morally serious and the morally frivolous has come into being. This conception presents problems for those who merely want to live their lives according to their own lights. How can they pass as ethical unless they are told what words they may or may not use in describing fellow citizens,* the way their children ought to be educated, what ethnic

---

* One typical example is the Northern Ireland Human Rights Commission advising staff to replace the phrase "black day" with "miserable day." The term, it was explained, carried a "hierarchical valuation of skin colour." Again, the National Gallery in Britain worried that certain expressions might discriminate against women, and urged that the term "gentleman's agreement" be replaced

distribution of friends they ought to have, and what benevolences are required for them?

The objective that authorities seek to achieve as they increasingly regulate how we think and act is to increase the happiness of the whole of society, indeed, of the world. The aim is to make ours the best of all possible worlds and, like Dr. Pangloss, the idealists are animated by the best of intentions. In this emerging world, the one essential test of being admirable is to share in its benevolent attitudes. And it is at this point that problems begin to emerge. That the feeblest kind of moral excuse consists in claiming, "I meant well" should alert us to the basic weakness of the project. "I meant well" is feeble because it slides into self-flattery, and this is important because one of the main corruptions of the moral life consists in baseless self-satisfaction. The most famous form of this corruption is celebrated in a long literary tradition as hypocrisy, but the politico-moral idealist is not usually a hypocrite. He is merely someone prepared to take good intentions as morally valuable in their own right. Our civilization has long been rather soft on good intentions, even though most of us realize that they pave the road to hell. Many twentieth-century evils (sometimes massacres on a horrific scale) were forgiven by well-meaning activists because terrible events could be attributed to intractable realities rather than to the intentions of the perpetrators. Good intentions alone may be better than bad intentions, but that's about the best of it.

My concern is not with the effectiveness of the grandiose intention to improve the world by "fighting" for peace and "conquering poverty." There is a large literature, much of it skeptical, on the question of the value of massive financial aid to countries in the Third World. Between the conception and the creation, as the poet has it, falls the shadow, and the shadow in this area has generally been the misappropriation of funds to illicit uses, usually corrupt

---

by "agreement based on trust." Again "right hand man" should become "second in command." These happen to have been reported in the *Daily Telegraph* on August 25, 2009, but the endless drip of these versions of correctitude will be familiar to most people.

private benefit. The scale of the problems posed by politico-moral idealism is such that no serious improvement can be expected unless the vast resources of rich Western states can be called upon. The benevolent endeavors of charitable NGOs undoubtedly improve the lives of many individuals, but the condition of whole populations is little affected. Sometimes the cause of poverty is the perversity of malevolent or incompetent rulers, as in North Korea or Zimbabwe under Mugabe, and nothing can be done here, even by what is whimsically called "the international community," unless those states should take on an active police role. The most successful countries in following the Western model of prosperity have in fact depended not on overseas aid, but on cultures capable of harnessing the energies of their populations. And that suggests that we should look more closely at the basic principle of the new benevolence.

That basic principle is that evils result from social conditions. The implication is that little or nothing can be expected from individual responses to those conditions. Cultures, it is admitted, vary, but poverty always leads to violence, conflict, and the other basic evils that history records. In this model, educational success becomes a matter only of how much cash has been invested, longevity is a function of medical availability, communal harmony a result of tolerance being inculcated by higher authority, etc. A further important implication is that *we* are responsible for the conditions in which *they* live. In other words, the world consists of active promoters of good, and passive victims of bad conditions. The heart of the matter, then, is the technological view that implementing ideals is a matter of an active population acting on fundamentally inert materials.

Idealism by its nature invokes a basic contrast between the deplorable condition of the current world, and the aspirations of the idealist. To espouse some ideal solution to the problems of the world—international government transcending national interests, pacifism, generous aid to the malnourished in other countries, and so on—is at the very least to show that one cares about others and wants to help them. Here then are genuine grounds on which idealism is to be recognized as a possible idiom of the moral life. That judgment would find support in the fact that idealists do often act charitably, and some become involved in such activities as educating illiterates abroad, or supplying pure water in less developed countries. It is certainly "doing the right thing," which is one of the formulas by which we recognize the moral realm, and it is part of the reason why idealists are justified in regarding themselves as decent and benevolent.

The problem, however, is that idealism, in its conception of the world (though often not in its actual practice), is at odds with our modern Western way of life. No doubt in some ways we all cherish ideals and seek to promote them, but the actual life we lead generates conflict and competition between groups, ideas, idealisms, moralities, and much else, all held together by the practice of civility. The basic ideal of the politico-moral is harmony. Competition, which is at the heart of European society, is from this point of view on the edge of conflict, and certainly produces as one of its consequences people who lose out. Losing out can be painful. The danger idealism poses to Western modernity is, then, in its tendency to think that in each contested area of human life, some overarching ideal will solve the problems to which the conflicts and tensions of our world respond.

The fact is that the human condition is unavoidably one of great variation in the lives and fortunes of individuals, and those variations result partly from virtue and vice, and partly from luck. Economic enterprises can lead on to fortune but sometimes end up in bankruptcy. If such inequality is taken to be a problem, one solution is central direction of the economy, which might in principle eliminate the role of luck and provide equal benefits to all. It's a great idea, and leads straight to poverty, not to mention despotism and oppression. It might work in a society of angels, but men are not angels, as the founders of the American commonwealth rightly insisted. A less dramatic solution to the problem of poverty consists in authority taking from the rich and giving to the poor.

Again, this is a great idea, except that it often demoralizes the beneficiaries, and makes the rich less enterprising. Beyond a certain point, redistribution diminishes the prosperity, not to mention the vitality, of an economy. Or, continuing this thought, perhaps such equalization is not really possible. We ought perhaps to settle for an open society in which everyone has an equal opportunity to rise if they have the enterprise to do so. This is what happened in the past, in times when governments did not greatly meddle in the way society worked. In the early twenty-first century, however, social mobility seemed to be declining in many countries. In earlier times, rising in the world resulted from the enterprise of individuals, and from the opportunities opened up by the contemporary level of industry and technology. Governments had nothing to do with it. But now governments have become interested in social mobility because it is thought to be popular with voters. And if mobility declines, the government must do something about it. The idealist wants to throw social mobility open to all, and the way to do that is to mechanize it. Today, rising in the world depends largely on access to higher education. Governments have the power to make schools and universities admit those whom the state wishes to encourage. Here the difficulty is that the itch rulers have to interfere with the independence of institutions changes the character of those institutions. Without the necessary virtues—in this case intellectual capacity—students imposed on institutions of excellence merely reduce it to mediocrity. We no longer have real social mobility, but a caricature of it expressed in quotas and numbers. But the intentions were good.

Here then is one sequence in which more or less benevolent rulers, exercising the authority of the state, attempt to impose a system that supplies equality (or "social justice") in some degree. It is an idealist's dream of a managed society in which the point of the management is to save individuals from the pains of failure. An ideal of fairness is to be imposed in order to remove the tensions between success and failure, between the fortunate and the supposedly unfortunate. This kind of social mobility, far from expressing the dynamism of a modern society, is an admission of its feebleness. It is a distribution of supposed "advantages" in society. In the past, rising in the world took courage and enterprise; in the new system, it happens when bureaucrats shuffle lives around.

Again, many people regard the party conflict of contemporary liberal democracies as lacking in wisdom. These states inherit a tradition that, in the Anglophone case, emerged historically from the idea of balance between such elements of society as king, nobles, and commoners. That practice absorbed our more recent democratic ways as the tension between government and opposition. In our century, ingenious experts on elections have played with the idea that electoral success consists in recomposing the issues so that a political party may offer the most popular elements in the program of each of the dominant parties. This is sometimes called "triangulation," and it is no doubt a response to that popular instinct to feel that the best governments would result from a coalition of all the talents rather than from the endless strife between parties. This program leads us to rename political parties "*center*-right" and "*center*-left" in order to exclude a nasty but indeterminate thing called "extremism." Here is the assumption that one right ordering of wisdom ought to guide our politics so that it generates "what the people want," a democratic principle that elites often want to qualify by changing the formula to "what the people ought to want," or would want, in their rational moments.

We have long transcended the old religious impulse to impose on society the one single belief about divine things. Instead, children must be taught at school the basic beliefs of the main religions. It is no doubt admirable that the citizens of a liberal democracy should be familiar with other beliefs, and should learn to respect them, but to create a curriculum for children along these lines has a paradoxical effect. An apparent openness turns into a real closure. The various religions come to be comprehended under the higher rubric of "faiths" and this cannot but distance pupils from taking them entirely seriously. Eclecticism, in other words, becomes not only a belief in itself but an overriding belief, so that anyone who actually believes in Christianity, or Islam, or Sikhism, or any other particular religion, cannot but take on the aspect of a bigot or a fanatic. Comparative religion at this level turns into secularism as the one right ideal attitude. This is particularly true of Christianity, which is today a belief rather less vital than other religions, but remains the constitutive founding of Western civilization. Liberal democracy emerged in Western Christian culture, and nowhere else. And it emerged largely because Christianity distinguished between sacred and secular, and thus private and public, or God and Caesar, in a way permitted in no other religion.

The real character of our civilization is often concealed when our way of life is intellectualized in terms of the "value" of tolerance and openness. The trouble with "values" is that they are thought to be merely chosen, but our tolerance is something different. It is part of our identity, because what we are actually doing is playing a game of a much more sophisticated kind than merely expressing a single virtue. The game is called "civility" and it is the form of life that constitutes our modern identity. It consists in the art of being able to get along easily with other people holding to a large range of beliefs and practices. We respect, in other words, the independence of others, and we expect them to respond to us in the same way. This is the art that allows us to indulge all manner of tensions and disagreements without, usually, falling into open and destructive conflict. It is this feature of the West that lies at the heart of our immense success, and it does not really depend on our sharing any particular beliefs. No doubt there are various attitudes of a moral or patriotic kind that must be pretty widely shared if our civil world is not to become fragmented. Some other practices (such as the Islamic concealment of the female face) are at the outer edge of what, in our free and individualist society, we can tolerate.

The essential point of civility, however, is that while we respect the rights of others, we do not have to admire them or even have much to do with them. In choosing friends, or employees, or any other kind of associate, we have until recently been free to make our own judgments. Many of these judgments have certainly been discriminatory and unfair, but that was a matter for "society," not for the state. To be on the wrong side of discrimination, as Jews sometimes were in earlier generations, was no doubt painful, but there are few pains without some positive implications, and the vitality of Jewish success—in the period before human rights and political correctness flowered—is one of many instances suggesting that disadvantages have many sides to them. Such virtues as endurance, humor, and self-control are called forth. The other aspect of this type of situation is that in a large and vibrant society, no discrimination is universal. There are always other possible friends, employers, and associates. As a solution to this condition, understood as a problem, idealists have foisted on us employment law and anti-discrimination legislation (not to mention political correctness), all devices designed to homogenize the population by removing any significance that might attach to the unequal distribution of virtues.

Here then is a sketch of how the moral world is moving, and the usual qualifications are necessary. Many versions of our inherited moral attitudes remain little less vibrant than before, but politico-moral idealism seems to me the current direction of our moral world. Back in the twentieth century, idealism took dramatic and often horrible forms by turning into ideological projects for the transformation of society. It often issued in totalitarian regimes. In our century, the same drive to replace the unpredictabilities of moral endeavor with a managed set of desired outcomes takes much less dramatic forms, but its scope has expanded, remarkably, to take in the whole of humanity. Politico-moral idealism thus seems to me to be the most influential motif in our civilization. Let me now conclude by considering firstly the respects in which this form of idealism exhibits the servile mind, and secondly the way in which such idealism betrays the genius of our civilization.

The servile aspect of the emerging order consists in a readiness to tolerate the guidance of our thoughts and actions by external bodies. Such a decline in our autonomy results not merely from the passion for making each state an enterprise association, but also our increasing subjection to transnational bodies such as the European Union and international organizations dealing with everything from rights to refugees. The directives and regulations emerging from these bodies are parasitic on our respect for the rule of law, but in fact much of this management of our lives is not only pointless but actively tyrannical. The aspect of servility begins from the fact that these things have been imposed on us, and accepted, remarkably, as if obedience to a variety of often-unaccountable bodies is itself a moral triumph over our selfishness and national partisanship. International declarations of rights, which are the source of some of this guidance, emerge from compromises between parties who are themselves responding to contemporary conditions, but the outcome purports to be a universal wisdom beyond time and locality. It cannot easily be revised, or indeed revised at all. It is true, indeed, that many of these declarations are merely codifying elements of the culture of European states at one time or another, and that they are but fitfully observed by the non-European states that have signed up to them. Our compliance, however, is expected to be exemplary, as an example to the rest.

The consequences of federating power, as with the European Union, are no improvement on universal declarations of rights. The directives of the EU emerge from bodies largely untouched by democratic pressures; they are often bright ideas that appeal to those trying to improve the world by imposing abstract desirabilities on it. Such bodies purport to be nation-transcending forms of wisdom, but they are often financially and morally corrupt, and often produce deplorable results. The European fisheries policy, for example, has virtually destroyed much of the fish in European and particularly in British waters. The effect of the massive transfers of authority away from national governments to international bodies has been to enfeeble the democratic political class of European states. Much of the time national politicians have responsibilities little more elaborate than adapting EU directives to local affairs. They hardly take themselves seriously, and are less and less seriously regarded by the populations whom notionally they represent.

The moral life in its classic form was one in which individualists responded to the demands of life in terms of a coherent self-chosen integrity. There are, of course, many ways of doing the right thing, and many virtues one might exhibit in doing so. Hence the individualist idiom of the moral life on the face of it (and in the eyes of peoples of other cultures) appeared so vulnerably indeterminate and relativistic as to encourage anarchy. We have seen that it was in fact remarkably tough and stable. Far from anarchy, modern Western states were in fact remarkably self-disciplined, and it is the reflexive character of that discipline that makes it *self*-government. A society of self-managed people turned out to be vastly more stable and orderly (as if guided by an invisible hand, to use Adam Smith's formula) than the despotic realms in which some right belief was enforced by power. And in such a world, people accepted the consequences of their actions.

The essence of the servile mind is the readiness to accept external direction in exchange for being relieved of the burden of a set of virtues such as thrift, self-control, prudence, and indeed civility itself. A national health service trades off thrift and the freedom to spend one's own money in exchange for a guarantee that medical help will always be "costlessly" available. Accepting this trade-off, then, comes to be understood as a virtue in itself, to be contrasted with those selfish people prepared to spend their own wealth on better treatment. Obedience here as in other places is wrongly identified with the rule of law. One measure of the moral decline involved in this advance of servility is that corrupt people, ranging from businessmen to legislators, justify a greedy lack of integrity by claiming that they did not break any rules. A casuistical use of the idea that morality is nothing more than abiding by rules comes to be a license for a self-serving misuse of office and responsibility.

One clue to the servility of spirit in contemporary life may be found in the role of abstractions. "The poor," for example, are entrapped in the idea that they are *essentially* poor, because it is an identity that guarantees benefits to them. In the past, those with few resources (and especially the "respectable poor") understood themselves in many ways. They were poor, but also a part of society on whose labor much rested. Many saw themselves in religious terms as immortal souls, others as the backbone of the country superior to the rich, and as people deserving the respect of their neighbors. Above all, they were respectable. In modern public discourse, they feature dominantly as poor and vulnerable, and treasure such a victimhood status because it brings benefits.

The rhetoric of victimhood exploits contradictions. On the one hand, the poor need to be a very large class so that they constitute an indictment of our society, and one whose condition governments need to relieve. On the other hand, poverty must be identified as what in legal terms would be called "a hard case," exceptional in the denial to a section of society of what is rightly enjoyed by the "middle classes." But hard cases, as we know from lawyers, make bad law. Lawyers say this because modifying the law so that a borderline case is entrenched as a principle of justice will soon create precedents that will generate an endless series of hard cases. The viability of law depends on its capacity to generalize human situations, and such generalization cannot possibly provide perfect justice in all cases. Finding a law to cover a hard case leads to the multiplication of hard cases. Similarly, construing poverty as a problem the state must solve generates a whole string of similar problems such as welfare dependency, fraud, the spread of new claims to vulnerability, and so on. This is why taking philosophical understandings of freedom and justice as if they were guides to legislators is a dangerous indulgence in modern states.

It might well seem absurd to diagnose servility beneath the flamboyant conduct of modern European societies. Over the last century, we have been liberated from many of the restrictive conventions inherited from the past. Sexual preferences that attracted legal sanctions in the past no longer do so; indeed, they are a matter for celebrations of "pride." Unhappy marriages no longer constrain individuals to lives of misery. Employees have much greater security from employer caprice. We are certainly not sycophantic with our rulers, with whom in fact we are on pseudo-intimate terms—in casual talk about politics, we refer to them by their Christian names. In many ways, we must be the freest peoples who ever lived, and part of the reason is that we may so easily liberate ourselves from anything inconvenient. It is that very fact that reveals a central element in the way Western life has been changing. We have been liberated from choices that involve commitments into a world in which restraints and frustrations can be costlessly cast off in response to some current impulse. Sociologically, family life has given way to a new condition in which very much larger numbers of people than before live as "singletons." Family life is a discipline demanding self-control; solitary living largely allows the untrammeled indulgence in impulse. Here, as in other areas, convenience trumps responsibility.

My argument is, of course, that the moral vocabulary we inherited from the past now serves to conceal the realities of contemporary life rather than reveal them. We have moved from a morality of respectability to one of benevolence. Respectability depended on many things, and what was respectable in some circles was not at all admired in others. There was an element of pluralism to it. Benevolence begins, and may end, in little more than a vague sense of good intentions toward abstract classes of people. This point has often been made by asserting that the moral and social context of past life was procedural, and that the inequalities of society were largely attributable to the virtues of individuals. Luck no doubt played some part, but generally success resulted from desert. Much contemporary regulation aims at producing substantive outcomes by authoritative fiat rather than as a result of virtuous responses to the challenges of life. Justice, in other words, has given way to "social justice," in which moral responses count for nothing because all situations result from (abstractly specified) social conditions. Again, freedom in European societies in earlier centuries depended on the political and constitutional judgments of rulers. It was in some degree responsive to our judgments. It has now been formularized as a set of rights, and handed over to lawyers and judges. Judges, however, cannot rightly judge the practical consequences of the implications they draw from a system of rights. Similarly, our practice of civility has been handed over to governmental agencies whose accountability is at one remove from Parliament. These bodies (the "quangos") can among other things impose legal penalties for "incorrect speech."

As with any complex development, the picture is mixed. We retain much of the vitality and freedom we have long enjoyed, yet few can mistake the steady drift toward a system in which controlled and homogenized individuals are given advantages on condition that they fit into the place authority suggests for them. The advantages are perfectly real, but so is the dependence they involve. And this diminution of vitality has certainly been sapping British life for a long time. The moral world of the past that constitutes my reference point was in some respects at its height in the period before 1914, and, as many commentators have observed, the First World War was a transforming event. That war, with its terrible losses in the trenches, was set up as a legend of futility, in which the casualties of the new trench warfare were referred to contemptuously by the butcher's metaphor of "slaughter." The soldiers were thus dehumanized. The longer-term result was to weaken British morale. Recognition of the decline of British military prowess was a theme among the top brass of the military in World War II. Writing to General Wavell in 1940, Sir Alan Brooke remarked: "We are not anything like as tough as we were in the last war. There has been far too much luxury, Safety First, etc. in this country. Our one idea is to look after our comforts and avoid being hurt in any way."[56] Churchill worried about the way in which British troops surrendered in large numbers at Tobruk, and in Singapore. The Allies in the course of the Second World War were forced to recognize that German troops were, unit for unit, significantly more effective than British or American troops.[57] That means, of course, that proportionately fewer Germans soldiers were killed or wounded. A servile spirit had already been clearly apparent in the disposition to appease the Nazi government during the 1930s. That safety lies in surrendering one's interests is the basic idea of appeasement, and it raises difficult questions of judgment because compromise is sometimes the rational and proper thing to do. To the servile mind, however, it is always the right thing to do. Standing up for one's interests has costs, but they are as nothing compared with the costs resulting from an abnegation of courage.

The growth of the servile mind certainly weakens Western civilization, and causes a dangerous weakness in a twenty-first-century world containing some powerful and aggressive cultures, many resentful about our recent dominance and eager to appropriate our wealth. Some claim that their cultures are superior to our competitive and often wasteful ways. Others claim to possess divine truth and thus consign the rest of us to the nightmare world of mere error. Such dogmatism is often persuasive to those demoralized by the sophistication of our argumentative and competitive culture. These facts are part of the reason why our civilizational self-confidence is at a low ebb, and many Europeans are eager to appease any resentments of which others complain. Some groups, and occasionally even some governments, feel remorse for the actions of earlier generations that no longer accord with current moral standards. This disposition is at its height in the powerful sense of civilizational self-hatred among some of our elites. Here we have a set of sentiments that lead to a readiness to sink the specific features of European cultures into an internationalism of human rights, an abstract ideal basically designed for export to the oppressive and impoverished despotisms of the world. A kind of strange moral imperialism about our cultural superiorities paradoxically impels many people to appease the demands of others in order to demonstrate our reasonableness.

In this situation, the politico-moral form of idealism threatens us by assimilating our world to that of the cyclical civilizations of the past. Our essential weakness is moral confusion. Servile attitudes have undermined our individualist vitality because they have learned to mimic other virtues such as rationality and compromise. Without a clear understanding of the moral life, benevolence seems to demand appeasing claims made against us. Our very openness about the scandals that afflict us—in matters such as torture, or financial irregularities—are used to reproach us by critics whose own often vastly greater scandals are simply concealed. Many among us feel more remorse for our imperfections than pride in the moral and technological benefits we have opened up to mankind. The grand politico-moral project has ambitions, of course, so large that we can never do enough as agents of bettering the world. The grand drive of the politico-moral for a moral immaculacy resulting from apologies for yesterday's vices and conspicuous virtue in contemporary international relations misapplies individual moral standards to political relations. There is no gratitude in international relations, and very little respect for virtue. Personal moral integrity is one thing, relations between states and peoples is another, and no good can come of confusing these two things.

Politico-morally, our duty of benevolence is to a world of abstract categories, the millions living stunted lives in other cultures. These are people characterized in no other way than the negative terms of deprivation. We know that they suffer, and that is to know enough. But these people also have projects and purposes of their own, and many such projects and purposes are precisely what doom the society itself to poverty. In politico-moral terms, those self-destructive policies are themselves also attributed, in this relentlessly deterministic model, to the social conditions that explain everything else. Even the fatal demographics of population rise among the "bottom billion," which cannot but involve the West in an ever-increasing commitment, are sidelined amid the focus on need and suffering. And the solution to all problems is to implement a set of unitary ideals: democracy, food, rights of women, medical aid, competent government, and so on. The aim is to universalize a world to some extent like ours, and the more like ours, the better. In other words, the project of improving humanity is simply the European program of welfare and social justice writ large.

The aim is thus to replace the unpredictable pluralist tensions of Western life with a set of ideal social conditions whose consequence would be universal harmony. But the great feature of our undoubtedly imperfect civilization is that it can respond creatively to the variations in human responses to the world. It can, in other words, accommodate the ambivalences of human life. A perfect world thus imagined can be nothing else but a set of arrangements that has transcended those ambivalences, and thus one that will have transcended the causes of conflict. Here we have the crux of the challenge of the politico-moral: To achieve harmony, we must suppress human ambivalence, which is to say human variety. To accommodate such human variety is to bid farewell to the dream of harmony and social justice. The dream of perfection assimilates our civilization to all the other cultures in which the one right way of life has risen—and fallen. It is to abandon everything that sustains our vitality.

Even to begin making this program plausible, society must be understood in abstract terms as the source of a single fixed scale of "advantages." Income determines essence. Yet it is impossible to conceive of a society in which many cannot lack one or other of the things currently thought to be advantages. Wealth is generally counted an advantage (but not too much of it!) and poverty a disadvantage. Certainly there seems to be little to be said for the indigence at the bottom, but one does not have to go very far up the scale to find that poverty itself will provoke human responses of many complicated kinds, ranging from the spiritual to the technical, such that these responses constitute distinct ways of life within society, and in that sense can become advantageous. Again, education is commonly an advantage, but it can also disable other talents. There is in fact no advantage that does not have disadvantages, as a little reflection on the economics of opportunity cost will show. As the Greeks used to say, there is no great thing that does not involve a curse. It follows that the freedom that allows individuality to flourish can never be without costs, but it is obviously no less true that the attempt to homogenize the world so that everyone both agrees on what is advantageous and shares in it is (were it conceivable) a situation with costs. Even the most servile of European populations will find itself reluctant to bear them.

The single scale of advantage is no problem in a society of ranks such as the medieval world, because "advantages" are not at issue. A supposedly right ordering of society determines the roles that people play. Nor is it a problem in a society of castes such as the Hindus created. It was not even much of a problem in a genuinely Christian society, because the Christian focus contrasted the poor and the meek with the rich and successful, and both conditions could be understood advantageously. That is why ideologies of revolutionary mobilization had to be hostile to all forms of religion. Alternative scales of value would confuse the activist. Revolution had to be a zero-sum game in terms of the single issue of who enjoys the advantages. The single scale of advantages has not previously been much of a problem in pluralist Anglophone societies, because to a considerable extent people discover pleasures in whatever kind of life that their resources, however small, allow them. Nevertheless, the essence of idealism has been to construe human beings in terms of the demand for, or the need of, more advantages than many of them actually enjoy.

The solution to this problem is, then, the replacement of the unequal advantages that result from individualism by a single system of redistribution. Advantages are nationalized, speech and conduct regulated, variations of practice are tolerated and accepted (giving illusions of freedom) only so long as they fit within an increasingly managed regulatory system, which now emerges from such a variety of authorities, international, national, and local, as to defeat any serious understanding of accountability. Instead of government accountably generating a rule of law, we have the new thing called "governance."

We need be in no doubt about what happens as this process develops. Modern Western states find themselves evolving into societies strangely akin to the most traditional of historical creations. Social justice generates for us the one right way of living, characterized by a kind of justice, a kind of tolerance, a kind of harmony, indeed by a kind of moral system dictated from above. Morality merges with management. Like any system of social life, it has its costs, found in a servile readiness to fit both thought and conduct to that one right scheme of life. But this is imagined to be a scheme in which all the advantages have been so adroitly distributed as to leave no incentive for any individual or group to suffer discontent. All would have been supplied with the satisfaction of their needs, and the canker of envy would at last have been banished from human life. Normative philosophers disagree, of course, about what this structure of advantages will be, but in principle such a thing does exist, and when we achieve it we shall have achieved not only a society lived in terms of the one right scale of values, but a scale so entirely rational as to leave no scope for change or modification. This is, of course, not a perfection available to human beings, but it is the aspiration under which we currently writhe.

The one right scheme of life is rational and universal, but nothing can escape the march of time. Every order that sustains a form of society is subject to subtle modifications, beginning often with the very words it uses to describe itself. We have mentioned the remarkable move from the Republic to the Principate in the history of Rome, and we might pluck from the same history the remarkable way in which an aggressive military regime was in a relatively short time taken over by a religion of humility and withdrawal from the world. There is no predicting the remarkable changes in human sentiments, and one might well be tempted to say that fashion determines all. Further, in all civilizations based on the one right ordering of things, the ordering was a brilliant or a lucky response to circumstances, and the response led on to fortune—for a time. Every mode of life is a formula, and formulas degrade. As with Weberian bureaucracy, routinization can never be avoided. The promise of Western modernity was that a vital and contentious civilization could defeat these ups and downs by its ability to move from one enthusiasm to another without suppressing other tendencies. The very attraction of idealism, of the one right ordering of society, assimilates us to all the many other civilizations that have failed in the past. It throws away the basic dynamism on which our world was founded.

Modern Europe in its dynamism and its competitive practices was never, of course, immune to this process of routinization. It too had dramas of rise and fall, but they usually characterized only some part of it. They were national or dynastic dramas rather than civilization-wide. Europe's intellectual vitality gave it in some degree a self-reviving capacity. It is this vitality that the monistic idealism of the politico-moral is slowly destroying. We may guess that it will not create perfection, but it is dangerous all the same. Few things are more destructive than political dreams of perfection.

ENDNOTES

1. Hilaire Belloc, *The Servile State,* Indianapolis: Liberty Press, 1977 (1913) p. 184.

2. Belloc, p. 178 (italics in text).

3. *Troilus and Cressida,* Act I, Scene iii, pp. 109–111.

4. Sir Thomas Elyot, *The Book Named The Governor,* London: Dent, 1962 (1531) p. 2.

5. Montesquieu, *The Spirit of the Laws,* translated and edited by Anne M. Cohler, Basia Carolyn Miller, and Harold Samuel Stone, Cambridge University Press, 1989, Bk. 8, Ch. 12, pp. 121–2.

6. *Henry IV,* Part II, Act V, Scene ii.

7. Christopher Booker, *The Neophiliacs: A Study of the Revolution in English Life in the Fifties and Sixties,* London: Collins, 1969.

8. Claudio Veliz, *The New World of the Gothic Fox.* Berkley: University of California Press, 1994.

9. Alexis de Tocqueville, *Democracy in America,* Introduction by Alan Ryan, New York: Everyman Library, 1994, Vol. II, p. 199.

10. David G. Green, *We're (Nearly) All Victims Now! How Political Correctness is Undermining Our Liberal Culture*, Civitas: Institute for the Study of Civil Society, 2006.

11. "Olympianism and the Denigration of Nationality," in Claudio Veliz (ed.), *The Worth of Nations*, Boston University: The University Professors, 1993, pp. 71–81.

12. Machiavelli, op. cit., Ch.15.

13. Aristotle, *Politics*, Book III, Section 4.

14. Philippa Foot, "Rationality and Goodness," in Anthony O'Hear (ed.), *Modern Moral Philosophy*, Cambridge University Press, 2004.

15. Max Weber, *The Protestant Ethic and the Spirit of Capitalism*, trans. Talcott Parsons, Routledge: London, 1930/1992, p. 80.

16. Thomas Hobbes, *Leviathan*, Part I, Ch. 8.

17. David Hume, *A Treatise of Human Nature*, Book I, Part IV, Section 6, "Of Personal Identity."

18. Adam Smith, *The Theory of the Moral Sentiments*, Indianapolis: Liberty Classics, 1969, Part III, Ch. 2, pp. 208–9.

19. *The Republic*, Book II, p. 359d.

20. *The Republic*, Book I, p. 351.

21. P.G.Wodehouse, *Thank you, Jeeves*, London: Arrow Books, 1934/1987, Ch. 11, pp. 92–3.

22. For an excellent discussion of Augustine's moral views, see Charles Norris Cochrane, *Christianity and Classical Culture: A Study of Thought and Action from Augustus to Augustine*, Amagi: Liberty Fund Indianapolis, 1940/2003, esp. Ch. 11.

23. Machiavelli, *The History of Florence*, Felix Gilbert (ed.), New York: Harper & Row, Book III, Ch. 2 (". . . *tanto quelli cittadini stimavano allora piu la patria che l'anima.*")

24. R. G. Collingwood, *Autobiography*, Oxford University Press, 1939, pp. 48–9.

25. G. E. M. Anscombe, "Modern Moral Philosophy" in *Ethics, Religion and Politics: The Collected Philosophical Papers of G. E. M. Anscombe*, Oxford: Basil Blackwell, 1981, Vol. 3. p. 32.

26. See the first essay in Oakeshott, *On Human Conduct*, Oxford Univeristy Press, 1975.

27. St. Augustine, *Confessions*, xiii.xi. p. 12, quoted in Cochrane, op. cit.

28. Ernest Gellner, *Conditions of Liberty: Civil Society and its Rivals*, London: Hamish Hamilton, 1994, section 12, p. 97.

29. *Leviathan*, Ch. 3.

30. Isaiah Berlin, "Two Concepts of Liberty," in *Four Essays on Liberty*, Oxford University Press, 1969.

31. Michael Oakeshott, *On Human Conduct*, Oxford University Press, 1975, second essay: "On the Civil Condition," p. 108 ff.

32. Edmund Burke, "On Conciliation with America."

33. John Donne, "Meditation Seventeen," in *Collected Works*

34. See for an extended discussion: F. A. Hayek, *Law, Legislation and Liberty*, Vol. 2: *The Mirage of Social Justice*, London: Routledge and Kegan Paul, 1976, Ch. 9.

35. J. Huizinga, *Homo ludens*, Boston: The Beacon Press, 1950 (1938).

36. Gertrude Himmelfarb, *The De-moralization of Society: From Victorian Virtues to Modern Values*, London: IEA, 1995, p. 35.

37. Eric Voegelin, *The New Science of Politics*, The University of Chicago Press, 1952, p. 111.

38. Michael Oakeshott, "Political Education," in *Rationalism in Politics*, Timothy Fuller (ed.), Indianapolis: Liberty Fund, 1995, p. 60.

39. See for example Jonathan Israel, *The Radical Enlightenment*.

40. See Kenneth Minogue, "Citizenship and Monarchy: A Hidden Fault Line in Our Civilisation," University of London: Institute of United States Studies, 1998.

41. See for example Richard Dawkins, *The God Delusion*; Christopher Hitchens, *God is not Great*,

42. Jack Straw, reported in the *Daily Telegraph*, January 22, 2008.

43. Rebecca Kreide, "Poverty as a Violation of Social Autonomy," in Thomas Pogge (ed.), *Freedom from Poverty as a Human Right: Who Owes What to the Very Poor*, Oxford University Press, 2007, p. 156.

44. Pogge, op cit., Introduction.

45. Ibid, p. 33.

46. United Nations Convention on the Rights of the Child (1989). See Blackstone's *International Human Rights Documents*, P. R. Ghandhi (ed.), Fourth Edition, Oxford University Press, 2004, p. 131 ff.

47. I have explored this theme from another point of view in "Conservatism and the Morality of Impulse," *The New Criterion*, January 2008.

48. *Karl Marx and Friedrich Engels: Collected Works*, London: Lawrence & Wishart, 1976, pp. 486–7.

49. "Under Pressure" by Martha Nussbaum, *Times Literary Supplement*, October 19, 2007, p. 5.

50. *Leviathan*, Ch. 14.

51. David Hume makes an analogous point about vanity in his essay "On the Dignity or Meanness of Human Nature" in *Essays: Moral, Political, and Literary*, Eugene Miller (ed.), Indianapolis: Liberty Fund, 1985, p. 86.

52. *Hegel's Philosophy of Right*, trans. T. M. Knox, Oxford: Clarendon Press, 1952, sections 6-7 pp. 22–23.

53. Ernest Gellner, *Conditions of Liberty: Civil Society and Its Rivals*, London: Hamish Hamilton, 1994, Ch. 13, "Modular Man."

54 Michael Oakeshott, *On Human Conduct*, Oxford: Clarendon, 1975, Part II, p. 108 ff.

55. For example, Peter Singer, *The Life You Can Save: Acting Now to End World Poverty*, New York: Picador Random House, 2009.

56. Quoted in Andrew Roberts, *Masters and Commanders: The Military Geniuses Who Led the West to Victory in WWII*, London: Penguin, 2008, p. 41.

57. Roberts, op.cit., pp. 125, 149.

INDEX

false consciousness, 47

families, 100, 174, 189, 222, 240, 263, 281, 297

family life, 11, 55–56, 127, 214, 227, 259, 310, 339

family names, 245

fascists/fascism, 46, 210, 264, 272, 272n, 275

fatalism, 41

fear

arrogance and, 314

authority and, 98

despotism and, 182

as economic motive, 223

politico-moral aversion to, 297

of punishment, 235

respect and, 99–100

feelings, affronts to, 95–100

females. *See* women

feminist movement, 84–85, 259

feminists, 46, 76–78, 86, 94, 127, 227

feral children, 136, 296, 306n

"final solution," 284

First Reform Act (1832), 17, 23

First World War, 340

Fitzgerald, F. Scott, 113

flattery, 9, 58, 110

Fleurbaey, Marc, 289

flexibility of roles, 321

flourishing, human, 307

folly, human, 278–279

Fonte, John, 112

Foot, Philippa, 120

formality of address, 52–55

fortuna, 40–41

Foucault, Michel, 89

franchise, 23–25, 27–28, 237, 273

fraud, 186–187, 247, 338. *See also* corruption

freedom

of civil life, 138

under common law, 68–69

European Union and, 192

importance of, 252

individualism and, 122, 178–179

in liberal democracies, 121–122

liberation and, 213–214, 286

loopholes in law and, 63

as moral condition, 7–8

perfectionism and, 285

rights and, 70, 213–214

slaves and, 4–5

"freedom of the wall," 140

Freud, Sigmund, 142

functional deference, 58

fundamentalism, 13, 129, 233, 284, 287, 292

Gaia, 269, 326

Galileo, 167

game rules, codification of, 71

Gandhi, Mohandas, 67

gaps, statistical, 39–40

gay liberation, 259, 309–310

gay pride, 88, 310

gays, 102. *See also* homosexuality

Geldof, Bob, 240

Gellner, Ernest, 174, 205, 321

gender discrimination, 80

gender equality, 308–309. *See also* equality

genocide, 80

defects of modern civilization
and, 199–209
defined, 204
from desire to impulse, 240–
248
emergence of, 215–221
ethical claims of, 209–215
fallacies of the "social" and,
221–226
image of modern society,
248–262
political correctness and, 211,
219–220
representativeness and, 226–
231
reward and punishment and,
234–240
stick and carrot problem and,
234–240
theology of, 262–270
the vulnerable in, 251–255,
261–262, 276
politics
abundance of, 2
mapping of, 271–277
morals and, 119–130
the poor. See also poverty; the
excluded; the vulnerable
anti-discrimination and, 78–79,
90–91, 100–102
as beneficiaries of politico-
moral society, 261
duty owed to, 288, 290–291,
302, 342
equalization and, 203–204
government aid to, 36, 109,
190, 302

Labour Party and, 23
redistributive taxation and, 63,
120
resource consumption and, 288
social conditions and, 40–41
takeover of morality by, 101–102
victimhood and, 237–238,
337–338
Poor Law, 250
popular will, 105
popularization of discipline, 98
pornography, 195, 244
positional goods, 91
positive reinforcement, 141
potentiality, 321
potestas, 296
poverty. See also the poor
aid to underdeveloped
countries and, 46, 190, 289–
290, 329–330
alleviation of as right, 289–290
globalization and, 210
as hard case, 338
"make poverty history" concert,
240–241
obesity and, 281
perfectionism and, 287–291
the politico-moral and, 215–
216, 224
redefined, 91–92
Western responsibility for, 256
power positions, 93
pragmatism, 197
preferences, 93
preformatives, 154
prejudice, 46–47, 79, 292–293,
303–304, 310, 312, 315